W9-BBB-923

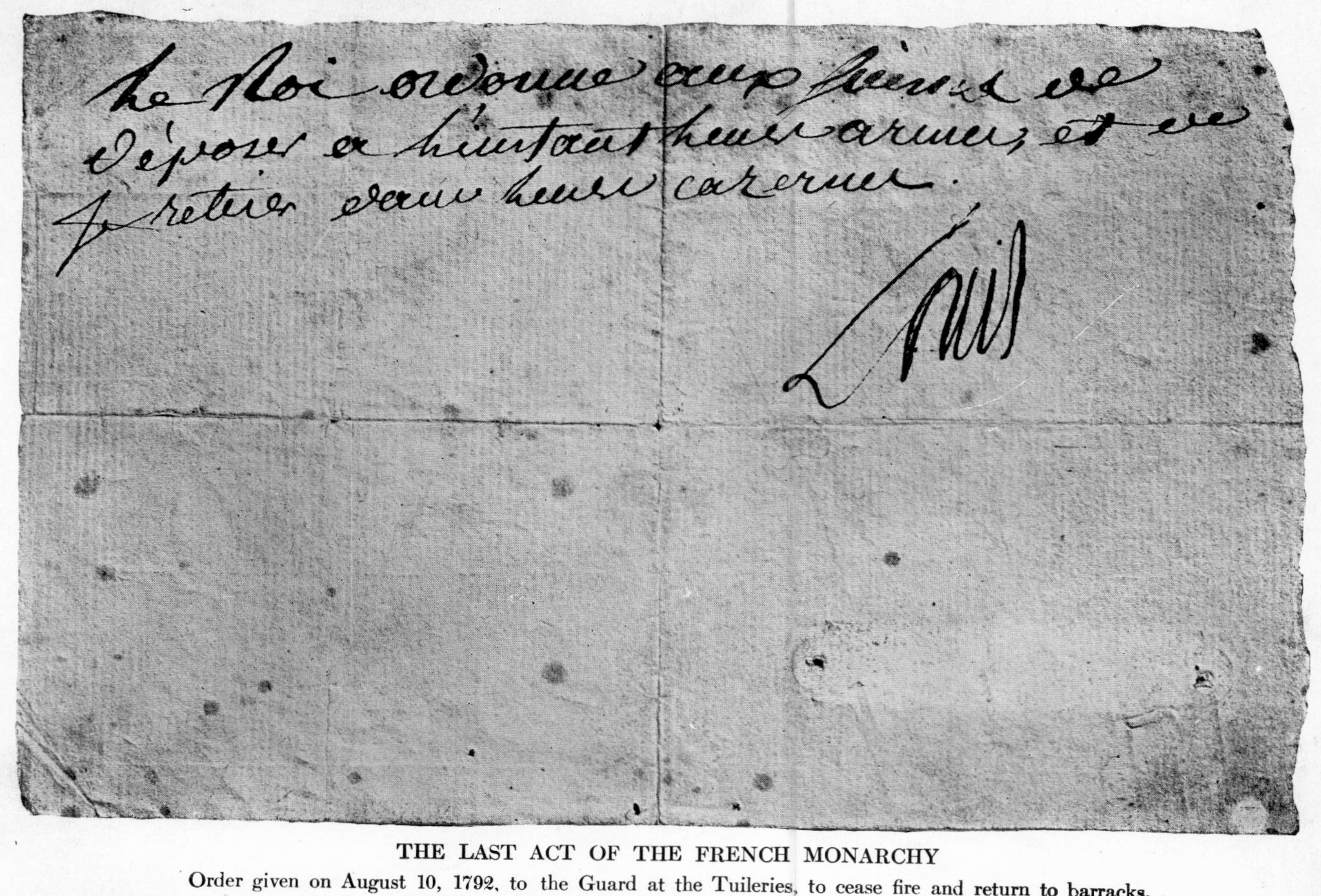
Le Roi ordonne aux Suisses de
déposer à l'instant leurs armes, et de
se retirer dans leurs casernes.
Louis

THE LAST ACT OF THE FRENCH MONARCHY

Order given on August 10, 1792, to the Guard at the Tuileries, to cease fire and **return to barracks.**

(On the authenticity of this document, see Appendix C)

Marie Antoinette

By

Hilaire Belloc

Illustrated

G. P. Putnam's Sons
New York & London
The Knickerbocker Press
1925

Originally published in 1909

Fourth printing, December, 1924
Fifth printing, March, 1925
Sixth printing, August, 1925
Seventh printing, November, 1925

Made in the United States of America

TO

GEORGE WYNDHAM

PREFACE TO THE SECOND AMERICAN EDITION

A NEW American Edition of my Monograph upon the life of Marie Antoinette, appearing so many years after the original publication, merits a few words of introduction to the reader.

In the first place, I see no cause to modify the general judgment which I came to during the full study of my material from twenty to eighteen years ago (the first work was begun rather more than twenty-one years ago). No new material of any importance has come to light in the interval, and the main historical problem, the crux of the whole story (which is the responsibility of the Queen for the invasion of 1792) remains what it was when I went over the ground for the first edition of this book. Indeed I doubt whether the conclusions arrived at will ever be greatly modified by the discovery of new material, for it is a matter rather of judgment than of documentary evidence, or at least rather than of documentary evidence beyond that already in our possession. A sound judgment of the period must determine that Marie Antoinette's action in suggesting the invasion determined the matter more than any other decision, and even if there should come to light a letter, say, directly suggesting another source, I should still conclude that the Queen's appeal was what weighed most.

In minor, but important points, such as the determination of the hour when Choiseul left the main road with his troops and rode back to St. Menehould, I have also recently maintained my original conclusions; for here again is a matter rather of sound judgment upon the main documents than of expecting new evidence. We have to judge the time required for fatigued cavalry to cover the distance across country under particular conditions of soil and weather, and I remain convinced that Choiseul abandoned his post at the earlier hour, and not at the later one which he himself afterwards very naturally named in his own defence.

There has not appeared since the book was written any new evidence upon Wattignies. Some parts of that action, especially upon the left, still remain obscure; but the main lines are clear enough. The decision arrived at by the storming of Wattignies village upon the Austrian flank, was, without question, the manœuvre which relieved Maubeuge; equally without question it was a conception of the great Carnot's. It is a detail worthy of mention that, though the site of the battlefield was in the midst of active fighting during the German advance in 1914 and retreat in 1918, it is still much the same as it was when I studied it twenty years ago. I went over it carefully with a British officer in the winter of '18–'19, immediately after the Armistice, and was surprised to find how little damage it had suffered. It lay, of course, behind the belt of complete destruction which marks such battlefields as the Somme and Verdun, and the line upon which the containment of the German armies lay between the autumn of '14 and the breakdown that began in July, '18. Nevertheless, it is remarkable, considering other sections of the area behind the front line, how much the battlefield of Wattignies has been spared.

I need offer, I think, no new apology for the method of historical presentation which I defended when I first issued this book, which I have discussed in my set of Historical Sketches, *The Eyewitness*, (Messrs. Dent & Co., of London), and which I further use in my book upon *The French Past* that is about to be issued by Messrs. Nelson & Co., of London and Edinburgh.

That method consists in an attempt to reproduce as a living thing the action of the past. It demands a special insistence upon physical details—dress, weather, gestures, facial expression, light, colour, landscape—and a corresponding lack of emphasis upon mere chronicle. It is an attempt, in a word, to tell history as a story, bringing to truth the arts common to fiction in such a fashion that the reader shall see things passing before his eyes.

If that result is to be obtained, two things are necessary with both of which our official historians of the Universities are still inclined to quarrel. The first is a method of literary presentation which shall aim at vividness, and shall not be afraid of violence, coincidence and contrast; for this it is necessary to select details such as would appeal to the eye, to the ear, to the senses, to give every part no more than its due proportion in the effect and in the process to abandon over-weight of innumerable detail, familiar to the author through his reading of his material, yet deliberately left out. But undigested detail is of the very essence of academic or university history, as it is still conceived, because such an accumulation gives the uninstructed reader an impression of prodigious learning in the writer. Now, in my conception of the way history should be written, not the writer but the reader comes first; it is the instruction, and even the pleasure, of the reader which should be the aim of historical writing, not the reputation of the writer for prodigious reading.

In point of fact the method which I have adopted requires, I think, more time, and certainly more activity, than that academic method which I have abandoned. One may spend a week upon the documents of Valmy, and yet not understand the battle. If one adds a single day walking over the battlefield at the same time of year, and under the same conditions of weather as those of the action, one can present it, explain it, understand it, and make it live again. One may spend a month over the details of a political episode, and yet not revive it at all, nor make it even comprehensible, unless one has looked up (in a hundred little allusions, following a thousand chance indications) the costumes, the gestures, the hours, the tints, all the sensual impression of the time.

The second necessary thing with such a method is the elimination of reference. To crowd a page with footnotes is to make it unreadable as a story. Here again your academic history exaggerates reference for two characteristic reasons: it vastly impresses the non-academic reader, and it professes to prove that the writer is inhumanly accurate.

Both motives seem to me ridiculous. I have discovered by experience that the mass of footnotes introduced into our modern academic histories are for the most part mere copies from earlier works, and in a large proportion deceptive. Not one reader in a thousand looks them up; such few as are at pains to do so are amused to discover the large proportion of irrelevance and that a still larger proportion of them refers to works which the historian has not consulted at all. Of course the man who returns, as I have, to the older historical method—the method of the Classics, the mere telling of a true but vivid story—challenges criticism; his details may be denied; he will have to support each affirmation in detail—that is, if he cares so to do—and to give his authorities in articles or letters separate from the book. He must sacrifice a false reputation for learning, and even his reputation for the heavy preliminary work necessary to his achievement. In my judgment the sacrifice is well worth while. For I would make it my business to bring the past to life rather than to establish a reputation for having read much indeed, but tenfold less than I have really read.

H. BELLOC.

Kingsland, Shipley,
Sussex.
April, 1924.

INTRODUCTORY NOTE

The eighteenth century, which had lost the appetite for tragedy and almost the comprehension of it, was granted, before it closed, the most perfect subject of tragedy which history affords.

The Queen of France whose end is but an episode in the story of the Revolution stands apart in this: that while all around her were achieved the principal miracles of the human will, she alone suffered, by an unique exception, a fixed destiny against which the will seemed powerless. In person she was not considerable, in temperament not distinguished; but her fate was enormous.

It is profitable, therefore, to abandon for a moment the contemplation of those great men who re-created in Europe the well-ordered State, and to admire the exact convergence of such accidents as drew around Marie Antoinette an increasing pressure of doom. These accidents united at last: they drove her with a precision that was more than human, right to her predestined end.

In all the extensive record of her actions there is nothing beyond the ordinary kind. She was petulant or gay, impulsive or collected, according to the mood of the moment: acting in everything as a woman of her temper—red-headed, intelligent and arduous—will always do: she was moved by changing circumstance to this or that as many millions of her sort had been moved before her. But her chance friendships failed not in mere disappointments but in ruin; her lapses of judgment betrayed her not to stumbling but to an abyss; her small, neglected actions matured unseen and reappeared prodigious in the catastrophe of her life as torturers to drag her to the scaffold. Behind such causes of misfortune as can at least be traced in some appalling order, there appear, as we read her history, causes more dreadful because they are mysterious and unreasoned: ill-omened dates, fortunes quite unaccountable, and continually a dark coincidence, reawaken in us that native dread of Destiny which the Faith, after centuries of power, has hardly conjured.

The business, then, of this book is not to recount from yet another aspect that decisive battle whereby political justice was recovered for us all, nor to print once more in accurate sequence the life of a queen whose actions have been preserved in the minutest detail, but to show a Lady whose hands — for all the freedom of their gesture — were moved by influences other than her own, and whose feet, though their steps seemed wayward and self-determined, were ordered for her in one path that led inexorably to its certain goal.

CONTENTS

ILLUSTRATIONS

MARIE ANTOINETTE

MARIE ANTOINETTE

I

THE DIPLOMATIC REVOLUTION

EUROPE, which carries the fate of the whole world, lives by a life which is in contrast to that of every other region, because that life, though intense, is inexhaustible. There is present, therefore, in her united history, a dual function of maintenance and of change such as can be discovered neither in any one of her component parts nor in civilisations exterior to her own. Europe alone of all human groups is capable of transforming herself ceaselessly, not by the copying of foreign models, but in some creative way from within. She alone has the gift of moderating all this violent energy, of preserving her ancient life, and by an instinct whose action is now abrupt, now imperceptibly slow, of dissolving whatever products of her own energy may not be normal to her being.

These dual forces are not equally conspicuous: the force that preserves us is general, popular, slow, silent, and beneath us all; the force that makes us diversified and full of life shines out in peaks of action.

The agents and the transactions of the conserving force do not commonly present themselves as the chief personalities and the most remarkable events of our long record. Th agents and the transactions of the force that perpetually transforms us are arresting figures, and catastrophic actions. Those who keep us what we are, for the most part will never be known — they are millions. Those, on the other hand, who have brought upon our race its great novelties of mood or of vesture, the battles they have won, the philosophies they have framed and imposed, the polities they have called into existence, they and their works fill history. That power which has forbidden us to perish uses servants often impersonal or obscure; it is mostly to be discovered at work in the permanent traditions of the populace and its effects are but rarely visible until they appear solid and established by a process which is rather that of growth than of construction. That power which keeps the mass moving glitters upon the surface of it and is seen.

There are, nevertheless, in this perennial and hidden task of maintaining Europe certain exceptional events of which the date is clear, the result immediate, and the authors conspicuous. Of early examples the victory of Constantine in the fourth century, the defeat of Abdul Rhaman in the eighth, may be cited. Chief among those of later times is a decision which was taken in the middle of the eighteenth century by the French and Austrian governments and to which historians have given the name of the *Diplomatic Revolution.*

To comprehend or even to follow the career of Marie Antoinette it is essential to seize the nature and the gravity of that rearrangement of national forces, for it determined all her life. To the great alliance between France and Austria, by which such rearrangement was effected she owed every episode of her drama. Her marriage, her eminence, her sufferings, and her death were each directly the consequence of that compact: its conclusion coincided with her birth; from childhood she was dedicated to it as a pledge, a bond, and, at last, a victim. Though, therefore, that treaty can occupy but little place in pages which deal with her vivid life — a life lived after the signing of the document and after its most noisy consequences had disappeared — yet the instrument must be grasped at the outset and must remain permanently in the mind of all who would understand the Queen of France and her disaster; for it was her mother who made the alliance, the statesman who presided over all her fortunes planned and achieved it. It stands throughout her forty years like a fixed horoscope drawn at birth, or a sentence pronounced and sure to be fulfilled.

The Diplomatic Revolution of the eighteenth century sprang, like every other major thing in modern history, from the religious schism of the sixteenth.

If that vast disturbance of the Reformation which threatened so grievously the culture of Europe, which maimed forever the life of the Renaissance, and which is only now beginning to subside, had broken the national tradition of Gaul as it did that of Briton, it may confidently be asserted that European civilisation would have perished. There was not left on the shores of the Mediterranean a sufficient reserve of energy to re-indoctrinate the West. A welter of small States, hopelessly separated by the violence and self-sufficience of the new philosophy would each have gone down the road an individual goes when he forgets or learns to despise traditional rules of living and the corporate sense of mankind. That interaction which is the life of Europe would have disappeared. A short period of intense local activities would have been followed by general repose. The unity of the Western world would have failed, and the spirit of Rome would have vanished as utterly from her deserted provinces as has that of Assyria from hers.

If, on the other hand, the French had chosen the earliest moment of the Reformation to lead the popular instinct of Europe against the Reformers, and to reëstablish unity, if as early as the reign of Francis I. (who saw the peril) they had imagined a species of crusade, why, then, the schism would have been healed by the sword, the humanity of the Renaissance would have become a permanent influence in our lives rather than an heroic episode whose vigour we regret but cannot hope to restore, and the discovery of antiquity, the thorough awakening of the mind, would have impelled Europe towards new and glorious fortunes the nature of which we cannot even conjecture, so differently did the course of history turn. For it so happened that the French — whose temperament, whose unbroken Roman legend, and whose geographical position made them the decisive centre of the struggle — the French hesitated for two hundred years.

Their religion indeed they preserved. The attempt to force upon the French doctrines convenient, in France as in England, to the wealthy merchants, the intellectuals, and the squires was met by popular risings; those of the French, as they were the more sanguinary so were also the more successful. The first massacre of St. Bartholomew, when the Catholic leaders were killed in the South, was not forgotten by the North; and after the second massacre of St. Bartholomew in Paris had avenged it, the Reformation could never establish in France that oligarchic polity which it ultimately imposed upon England and Holland. In a word, the Catholic reaction in France was sufficiently violent to recover the tradition of the State; but the full consequences of that reaction did not follow, nor did France support the general instinct of Europe, because, allied with the Faith to which the nation was so profoundly attached and had just preserved, was the political power of the *Spanish-Austrian Empire*, which the French nation, and its leaders, detested and feared.

It is difficult for us to-day to comprehend the might of Spain during the century of the Reformation, and still more difficult to grasp that external appearance of overwhelming strength which, as the years proceeded, tended more and more to exceed her actual (and declining) power.

The supremacy of Spain over Europe resided in a dynasty and not in a national idea. It did not take the form of over-riding treaties or of attempting the partition of weaker States, for it was profoundly Christian, and it was military; in twenty ways the position of Spain differed from the hegemony which some modern European State might attempt to exercise over its fellows. But it is possible to arrive at some conception of what that Empire was, if we remember that it reposed upon a vast colonial system which Spain alone seemed capable of conducting with success, that it monopolised the production of gold, and that it depended upon a command of the sea which was secured to it by an invincible fleet. To such advantages there must further be added an armed force not only by far the largest and best trained in Europe, but mainly composed of the best fighters as well, and — a circumstance more important than all the rest — an extent of dominion, due to the union of the Austrian and Spanish houses, which gave to Charles V. and his successors the whole background, as it were, upon which the map of Europe was painted: in the sea of that Emperor's continental possessions, apart from a few insignificant principalities, France alone survived — an intact island with ragged boundaries, menaced upon every side. For the Emperor, then master of the Peninsula, of the Germanies, and of the New World, was everywhere by sea and almost everywhere by land a pressing foe.

However much this Spanish-Austrian power might stand (as it did stand) for the European traditions and for the faith of civilisation which France had elected to preserve, it was impossible for the French crown and nation not to be opposed to its political power if that crown or that nation were to survive. The smaller nations of the North — the English, the low countries, &c. — were in less peril than the French; for these were now the only considerable exception to, and were soon to be the rivals of, the Spanish-Austrian State. Had the Armada found fair weather, Philip might have been crowned at Westminster; but the English — united, isolated, and already organized as a commercial oligarchy — would have fought their way out from foreign domination as thoroughly as did the Dutch. The duty of the French was other; their independence was not threatened: it was rather their dignity and special soul which were in peril and which had to be preserved from digestion into this all-surrounding influence of Spain. To preserve her soul France gave — unconsciously perhaps, as a people, but with acute consciousness as a government — her whole energies during four generations. The defence succeeded. Through a dozen such civil tumults as are native to the French blood, and through a long eclipse of their national power, they treasured and built up their reserves. After a century of peril they emerged, under Louis XIV. — not only the masters, but for a moment the very tyrants of Europe.

The French did not achieve this object of theirs without a compromise odious to their clear spirit. In their secular opposition to the Spanish-Austrian power, it was the business of their diplomatists to spare the little Protestant States and to use them as a pack for the worrying of great Austria, whom they dreaded and would break down. The constant policy of Henri IV., of Richelieu, of Mazarin, was to strengthen the Protestant principalities of North Germany, to meet half way the rising Puritanism of England, and even at home to tolerate an organised, opulent, and numerous body of Huguenots who formed a State within the State. At a time when it was death to say Mass in England, the wealthy Calvinist just beyond the Channel — at Dieppe, for instance — was protected with all the force of the law from the fanaticism or indignation of his fellow-citizens; he could convene his synods openly, could hold office at law or in municipal affairs, and was even granted a special form of representation and a place in the advisory bodies of the State. All this was done, not to secure internal order — which would perhaps have been better affirmed in France as it was in England by the vigorous persecution of the minority — but to create a Protestant makeweight to what appeared till nearly the close of the seventeenth century the overwhelming menace of the Spanish and Austrian Houses.

Such was the policy which the French Court wisely pursued during so long a period that it finally acquired the force of a fixed tradition and threatened to last on into an era of new conditions, when it would prove useless, or, later, harmful to the State. The general framework of that Anti-Austrian diplomacy did indeed survive from the latter seventeenth till the middle of the eighteenth century; but from the time when Louis XIV. in 1661 began to rule alone to that final rearrangement of European forces in the Diplomatic Revolution, which it is my business to describe, the Catholic powers tended more and more to be conscious of a common fate and a common duty. One after another the portions of the old French diplomatic work fell to pieces as the strength of Spain diminished and as the small Protestant States advanced in their cycle of rapid commercial expansion, increasing population and military power; until, a generation after Louis XIV.'s death, Protestant Europe as a whole had formed in line against what was left of Rome.

It would not be germane to my subject were I to enter at any length into the gradual transformation of Europe, between 1668 and 1741. The first date is that of the treaty which closed the last clear struggle between France and Spain; the second date is that of the first great battle, Mollwitz, in which Prussia under Frederick the Great appeared as a triumphant and equal opponent against the Catholic forces of the Empire. It is enough to say that during that period the results of that great struggle were solidified. Europe was now hopelessly, and, as it seemed, finally riven asunder; and those who proposed to continue, those who proposed to disperse the stream of European tradition gravitated into two camps armed for a struggle which is not even yet decided.

The transition may be expressed as the long life of a man — nay, it may be exactly expressed in the life of *one* man, Fleury, for he stood on the threshold of manhood at its commencement and in sight of death at its close: what such a long life witnessed, between its eighteenth and its ninetieth year, was — if the vast confusion of detail be eliminated and the large result be grasped — the confirmation of the great schism and the final schism and the final decision of France to stand wholly against the North. There appeared at last, fixed and consolidated, a Protestant and a Catholic division in Europe whose opposing philosophies, seen or unseen, denied, ridiculed or ignored, even by those most steeped in either atmosphere, were henceforward to affect inwardly every detail of individual life, as outwardly they were to affect every great event in the history of our Race, and every general judgment which has been passed upon its actions.

The Spanish Power, based as it had been, not on internal resources, but on a naval and colonial supremacy, could not but rapidly decline; it had long been separated from the German Empire; it was destined to fall into the orbit of France. On the other hand, the England of the early eighteenth century was no longer a small community absorbed in theological discussion; she had become a nation of the first rank, one that was developing its industries, its wealth and its armed strength. She boasted in Marlborough the chief military genius of the age; she was already the leader in physics; she was about to be the leader in mechanical science (with all the riches such a leadership would bring), and she was upon the eve of acquiring a new colonial empire.

In France the privileges of the Huguenots had been withdrawn, as the situation grew precise and clear, and the breach between them and the nation was made final by their active and zealous treason in whatever foreign fleets or armies were attempting the ruin of their country. In England it had been made plain that the oligarchy, and the nation upon which it reposed, would admit neither a strong central government nor the presence of the Catholic Church near any seat of power: the Stuart dynasty had been exiled; its first attempt at a restoration had been crushed.

Meanwhile there was preparing a final argument which should compel men to recognise the clean and fixed division of Europe: that argument was the astonishing rise of Prussia, for with the appearance upon the field of this new and strange force — an own child of the Reform — it was evident that something had changed in the very morals of war.

When Austria was at her weakest, when the French Court, bewildered but weakly constant to a now meaningless diplomatic habit, was watching the apparent dissolution of the Empire and was ready to urge its armies against Vienna, when England remained, and that only from opposition to the Bourbons, the only support of the Hapsburgs, there was established within five years the permanent strength of Frederick the Great and the new factor of Prussian Power: a complete contempt for the old rules of honour in negotiation and for the old rules of contract in dynastic relations had been crowned by a complete success.

This advent, when every exception and cross-influence is forgotten, will remain the chief moral, and therefore, the chief political fact of the eighteenth century. By the end of the year 1745 Silesia was finally abandoned by Austria; the Prussian soldier and his atheist theory had compassed the first mere conquest of European territory which had been achieved by any European power since first Europe was organised into a family of Christian communities. It had been advanced for the first time that Europe was not one, but that some unit of it might overbear and rule another by arms alone; that there was no common standard nor any unseen avenger upon appeal. That theory had appealed to arms and had conquered.

Within three years the international turmoil, of which this catastrophe was immeasurably the greatest result, was subjected to a sort of settlement. One of those general committees of all Europe with which our own time is so familiar was summoned to Aix-la-Chapelle; representatives of the various Powers confirmed or modified the results of a group of wars, and in the autumn of 1748 affixed their signatures to a complete arrangement which was well known to be unstable, ephemeral, and insincere, but which was yet of tremendous import, for it marked (though in no dramatic manner) the end of an old world.

As the plenipotentiaries left their accomplished work and strolled out of the room which had received them, they were still grouped together by such weak and complex ties as the interests of individual governments might decide. When they met again after the next brief cycle of war, these men were arranged in a true order and sat opposing; for England, Prussia, and experiment of schism on the one side; for the belt of endurance on the other. Since that cleavage these two prime bodies, disguised under a hundred forms and hidden and confused by a welter of incidental and secondary forces, have remained opposing, attempting with fluctuating success each to determine the general fortunes of the world. They will so continue balanced and opposing until perhaps — by the action of some power neither of war nor of diplomacy — unity may be re-established and Europe may again live.

Of the men who so strolled out of the room at Aix one

only, still young, had grasped in silence the necessity of the great change; he saw that Vienna and Paris must in the next struggle stand together and defend together their common civilisation and their resisting Faith. He not only perceived the advent of this great reversal in the traditions of the chanceries; he designed to aid it himself, to mould it, and to determine its character. That he could then perceive of how large a movement his action was to be a part no historian can pretend, for at the time no one could grasp more than the momentary issue, and this man's very profession made it necessary for him, as for every other diplomat, to see clearly immediate things and to abandon distant speculation. But though his work was greater than himself and far greater than his intention, yet he deserves a very particular attention; for this young man of thirty-six was *Kaunitz*, and he, for a whole generation, was Austria.

In so determining to effect an alliance between the Hapsburgs and their secular enemy, Kaunitz equally determined, unknown to himself, the whole fortunes of Marie Antoinette; she, years later, when she came to be born to the Imperial house was, even in childhood, the pledge he needed. It is Kaunitz who stands forever behind the life of Marie Antoinette, like a writer behind the creature in his book. It is he who designs her marriage, who uses her without mercy for the purposes of his policy at Versailles; he is the author of her magnificence and of her intrigue, he is then also indirectly the author of her fall, which, in his obscure and failing old age, he heard of far away, partially comprehended, and just survived.

Kaunitz was the original of our modern diplomatists. In that epoch of governing families not a few nobles were flattered to be called "the Coachmen of Europe": he alone merited the cant term. He served a sovereign whose armies were constantly defeated; he was the adviser of a mere crown — and that crown worn by a woman; in a time when the divergent races of the Danube were first astir, he had at his command or for his support neither a national tradition nor any strong instrument of war, yet, by personal genius, by tenacity, and by a wide lucidity of vision, he discovered and completed a method of "government through foreign relations" which was almost independent of national feeling or of armed strength.

An absence of natural violence, as of all common emotions, was characteristic of Kaunitz. He disdained the vulgar pomp of silence; he talked continually; he knew the strength and secrecy of men who can be at once verbose and deliberate. Nor could his fluency have deceived any careful observer into a suspicion of weakness, for his curved thin nose and prominent peaked chin, his arched eyebrows, his Sclavonic type, ready and courageous, his hard, pale eyes, showed nothing but purpose and execution; and as his tall figure stalked round the billiard tables at evening, his very recreation seemed instinct with plans.

The abounding energy which drove him to success revealed itself in a thousand ways, and chiefly in this, that in the career of diplomacy, where all individuality is regarded with dread, *he* pushed his personal tastes beyond the eccentric. Thus he had a mania against all gesticulation, and he would present at every conference the singular spectacle of a man chattering and disputing unceasingly and eagerly, yet keeping his hands quite motionless all the while. Again, when he entered the great houses of Europe and dined with men to influence whom was to conduct the world, he did not hesitate to bring with him his own dessert, which when he had eaten he would, to the great disgust of embassies, elaborately wash his teeth at table. In the midst of the hardest toil he was so foppish as to wear various wigs — now brown, now white, now auburn. He was a constant traveller, familiar with every capital in Western Europe, yet he so loathed fresh air that he would not pass from his carriage to a palace door unless his mouth were covered. He was a dandy who, in drawing-rooms loaded with scent and flowers, loudly protested against all perfume; a gentleman who, when cards were the only pastime of the rich, expressed a detestation of all hazard; a courtier who, amidst all the extravagances of etiquette of the eighteenth century, barely bowed to the greatest sovereigns, and who, on the stroke of eleven, would abruptly leave the Emperor without a word.

Such marks of an intense initiative, detachment and pride were tolerated in the earlier part of his life with amusement on account of the affection he could inspire; later they were regarded with ill ease, and at last with a sort of awe, when it was known that his intelligence could entrap no matter what combination of antagonist. This intelligence, and the single devotion by which such natures are invariably compelled, were both laid at the feet of Maria Theresa.

He was older than his Empress by some seven years; there lay between them just that space which makes for equality and comprehension between a man and a woman. The year of her marriage had coincided with that of his own; he had come at twenty-five to the court of this young sovereign of eighteen. She had recognised — with a wisdom that never failed her long and active life — how just and general was his view of Europe, and it was from this moment that her interests and her career were entrusted to his genius. He had already studied in three universities, had refused the clerical profession to which his Canonry of Cunster introduced him, and had travelled in the Netherlands, in France, in England, and in Italy, where he was made Aulic Councillor, and enfeoffed, as it were, to the palace.

His abilities had not long to await their opportunity. It was but four years after Maria Theresa's marriage and his own that she succeeded to the throne and possessions of the Hapsburgs: then it was the sudden advent of Prussia, to which I have alluded, began the great change.

Maria Theresa's succession was in doubt, not in point of right, but because her sex and the condition in which her father had left his army and his treasury gave an opportunity to the rivals of Austria, and notably to France.

Europe was thus passing through one of those crises of instability during which every chancery discounts and yet dreads a universal war, when the magazine was fired by one who had nothing to lose but honour. Frederick of Prussia was the warmest in acknowledging the title of Maria Theresa; he accepted her claims, guaranteed the integrity of her possessions, and suddenly invaded them. From the ordering of that march of Frederick's into Silesia — from the close, that is, of the year 1740 — Kaunitz, a man not yet in his thirtieth year, was at work to repair the Empire and to restore the equilibrium of Europe. Upon the whole he succeeded; for though the magnitude of the Revolutionary Wars has dwarfed his period, and though the complete modern transformation of society has made such causes seem remote, yet (as it is the thesis of these pages to maintain) Kaunitz unconsciously preserved the unity of Europe.

In the beginning of the struggle he had already saved the interests of Maria Theresa in the petty Italian courts. At Florence, at Rome, at Turin, at Brussels, his mastery continued to increase. In his thirty-sixth year he was ambassador to London — he concluded, as we have seen, the Peace of Aix-la-Chapelle; by his fortieth he had been appointed to Paris, and that action by which he will chiefly be remembered had begun. He had seen, as I have said, the necessity for an alliance between the two great Catholic Powers. Within the two years of his residence in Paris he had successfully raised the principle of such a revolution in policy and as successfully maintained its secrecy. A task which would have seemed wholly vain had he communicated it to others, one which would have seemed impossible even to those whom he might have convinced, was achieved. To his lucid and tenacious intellect the matter in hand was but the bringing forth of a tendency already in existence; he saw the Austro-French alliance lying potentially in the circumstances of his time; his business was but to define and realize it.

In such a mood did he take up the Austrian embassy in Paris. He was well fitted for the work he had conceived. The magnificence which he displayed in his palace in the French capital was calculated indeed to impress rather than to attract the formal court of Versailles; that magnificence was the product of his personal tastes rather than of his power of intrigue, but the details of his over-ostentatious household were well suited to those whom he had designed to capture. The French language was his own; Italian, though he spoke it well, was foreign to him; the German

MARIA THERESA

From the tapestry portrait woven for Marie Antoinette
and recently restored to Versailles

dialects he knew but ill and hardly used at all. His habits were French, to the end of his long life French literature was his only reading, and his clothes, to their least part, must come from the hands of the French.

He moved, therefore, in that world of Paris and Versailles (as did, later, his pupil, Mercy-d'Argenteau) rather as a native than a foreigner. Even if the alliance had been as artificial as it was natural, he would have carried his point. As it was, he left Paris in 1753 to assume the Prime Ministry at Vienna, with the certitude that, when next Frederick of Prussia had occasion to break his word, the wealth and the arms of the Bourbons would be ranged upon the Austrian side.

Upon that major pivot all the schemes of Vienna must turn at his dictation. Every marriage must be contrived so as to fall in with the projected alliance; every action must be subordinated to the arrangement which would prove, as he trusted, the supreme hope of the dynasty. To this one project he directed every power within him or beneath his hand, and to this he was ready, when the time should come, to devote the fortunes of any member of the Royal House save its sovereign or its heir. To this aspect of Europe, long before the termination of his mission in Paris, he had not so much persuaded as formed the mind of Maria Theresa.

The great and salutary soul of that woman explains in part what were to be the fortunes of her youngest child. Not that Marie Antoinette inherited either the opportunities or the full excellence of her mother, but that there ran through the impatient energy and unfruitful graciousness of the Queen of France a flavour of that which had lent a disciplined power and a conscious dignity to the middle age of Maria Theresa.

The body of the Empress was strong. Its strength enabled her to bear without fatigue the ceaseless work of her office and in the midst of child-bearing to direct with exactitude the affairs of a troubled State. That strength of hers was evident in her equal temper, her rapid judgment, her fixed choice of men; it was evident also in her firm tread and in her carriage, and even as she sat upon a chair at evening she seemed to be governing from a throne.

A growing but uniform capacity informed her life. She had known the value not only of industry but also of enthusiasm, and had saved her throne in its greatest peril by her sudden and passionate appeal to the Hungarians. It was this instinctive science of hers that had disarmed Kaunitz. If he allowed her to suggest what he had already determined, if he permitted her to be the first to write down the scheme of the Diplomatic Revolution he had conceived, and to send it down to history as her creation rather than his own, it was not the desire to flatter her that moved him but a recognition of her due. She it was that sent him to Paris and she that superintended the weaving of the loom he had arranged.

Her dark and pleasing eyes, sparkling and strong, controlled him in so far as he was controlled by any outer influence, for he recognized in them the Cæsarian spirit.

Her largeness pleased him. When she played at cards, she played for fortunes; when she rode, she rode with magnificence; when she sang, her voice, though high, was loud, untramelled, and full; when she drove abroad, it was with splendour and at a noble turn of speed.

All this was greatly to the humour of Kaunitz, and he continued to serve his Empress with a zeal he would never have given to a mere ambition. In deference to her, all that he could control of his idiosyncrasies he controlled. His great bull-dog, which followed him to every other door, was kept from her palace. His abrupt speech, his failure to reply, his sudden and brief commands — all his manner — were mollified in consultation with his Queen. She, on her part, knew what were the limits to which so singular a nature could proceed in the matter of self-denial. She respected half his follies, and her servants often saw her from the courtyard shutting the windows, smiling, as he ran from his carriage, his mouth covered to screen it from the outer air. Her common sense and poise forgave in him alone extravagances she had little inclination to support in others. He respected in her, those depths of emotion, of simplicity, and of faith which in others he would have regarded as imbecilities ready for his high intelligence to use at will.

It was neither incomprehensible to him nor displeasing that her temper should be warmer than his intelligence demanded. The increasing strength of her religion, the personal affections and personal distastes which she conceived, above all, the closeness of her devotion to her husband, completed, in the eyes of Kaunitz, a character whose dominions and dynasty he chose to serve and to confirm; for he perceived that what others imagined to be impediments to her policy were but the reflection of her sex and of her health therein.

Kaunitz saw in Frederick of Prussia a player of worthy skill. It was upon the death of that soldier that he gave vent to the one emotional display of his life; yet he permitted Maria Theresa to hate her rival with a hatred which was not directed against his campaigning so much as against the narrow intrigue and bitterness of his evil mind.

To Kaunitz, again, Catherine of Russia was nothing but a powerful rival or ally; yet he approved that Maria Theresa should speak of her as one speaks of the women of the streets, despising her not for her ambition but for her licence.

To Kaunitz, Francis of Lorraine, the husband of the Empress, was a thing without weight in the international game; yet he saw with a general understanding, and was glad to see in detail, the security of the imperial marriage.

The singular happiness of Maria Theresa's wedded life was due to no greatness in Francis of Lorraine, but to his vivacity and good breeding, to his courtesy, to his refinement, and especially to his devotion. It suited her that he should ride and shoot so well. She loved the restrained intonation of his voice and the frankness of his face. She easily forgave his numerous and passing infidelities. The simplicity of his religion was her own, for her goodness was all German as his sincerity was all Western and French; upon these two facts the opposing races touch when the common faith introduces the one to the other. Their household, therefore, was something familiar and domestic. Its language was French, of a sort, because French was the language of Francis; but while he brought the clarity of Lorraine under that good roof, which covered what Goethe called "the chief bourgeois family of Germany," he brought to it none of the French hardness and precision, nor any of that cold French parade which was later to exasperate his daughter when she reigned at Versailles. He was a man who delighted in visits to his countryside, and who would have his carriage in town wait its turn with others at the opera doors.

Maria Theresa was so wedded, served by such a Minister, in possession of and in authority over such a household during those seven years between the Peace of Aix-la-Chapelle and the French Alliance, between 1748 and 1755. Those seven years were years of patience and of diplomacy, which were used to retrieve the disasters of her first bewildered struggle against Prussia and the new forces of Europe. They were the seven years of profound, if precarious, international peace, when England was preparing her maritime supremacy, Prussia her full military tradition, the French monarchy, in the person of Louis XV., its rapid dissolution through excess and through fatigue. They were the seven years which seemed to the superficial but acute observation of Voltaire to be the happiest of his age: a brief "Antonine" repose in which the arts flourish and ideas might flower and even grow to seeding. They were the seven years in which the voice of Rousseau began to be heard and in which was written the "Essay upon Human Inequality."

For the purposes of this story they were in particular the seven years during which Kaunitz, now widowed, working first as Ambassador in Paris, then as Prime Minister by the side of Maria Theresa at Vienna, achieved that compact with the Bourbons which was to restore the general traditions of the Continent and the fortunes of the House of Hapsburg.

The period drew to a close: the plans for the alliance were laid, the last discussions were about to be engaged, when it was known, in the early summer of 1755, that the Empress was again with child.

II

BIRTH AND CHILDHOOD

2ND NOVEMBER, 1755, TO THE AUTUMN OF 1768

ALL that summer of 1755 the intrigue — and its success — proceeded.

I have said that the design of Kaunitz was not so much to impose upon his time a new plan as to further a climax to which that time was tending. Accidents in Europe, in America, and upon the high seas conspired to mature the alliance.

Fighting broke out between the French and English outposts in the backwoods of the colonies. Two French ships had been engaged in a fog off the banks and captured; later, a sharp panic had led the Cabinet in London to order a general Act of Piracy throughout the Atlantic against French commerce. It was a wild stroke, but it proved the first success of what was to become the most fundamentally successful war in the annals of Great Britain.

In Versailles, an isolated and mournful man, fatigued and silent, who was in the last resort the governing power of France, delayed and delayed the inevitable struggle between his forces and the rising power of England. Louis XV. looked upon the world with an eye too experienced and too careless to consider honour. His clear and informed intelligence would contemplate — though it could not remedy — the effects of his own decline and of his failing will. He felt about him in the society he ruled, and within himself also, something moribund. France at this moment gave the impression of a great palace, old and in part ruined. That impression of France had seized not only upon her own central power, but upon foreign observers as well; the English squires had received it, and the new Prussian soldiers. In Vienna it was proposed to use the declining French monarchy as a great prop, and in using it to strengthen and to revivify the Austrian Empire until the older order of Europe should be restored. Louis XV., sitting apart and watching the dissolution of the national vigour and of his own, put aside the approach of arms with such a gesture as might use a man of breeding whom in some illness violence had disturbed. Thus as late as August, when his sailors had captured an English ship of the line, he ordered its release. The war was well ablaze and yet he would consent to no formal declaration of it; Austria watched his necessities.

It was in September that Maria Theresa sent word to her ambassador in Paris — the old and grumbling but pliant Stahrenberg, that the match might be set to the train: in a little house under the terrace at Bellevue, a house from whose windows all Paris may be seen far away below, the secret work went on.

It has been asserted that the Empress in her anxiety wrote to the Pompadour and attempted, by descending to so direct a flattery of Louis XV.'s mistress, to hasten that King's adhesion to her design. The accusation is false, and the document upon which it is based a forgery; but the Austrian ambassador was Maria Theresa's mouthpiece with that kindly, quiet, and all-powerful woman. It was she who met him day after day in the little house, and when she retired to give place to the Cardinal de Bernis, that Minister found the alliance already fully planned between Stahrenberg and the Pompadour. Louis XV. alone was still reluctant. Great change, great action of any sort, was harsh to him. He would not believe the growing rumour that Frederick of Prussia was about to desert his alliance and to throw his forces on to the side of the English power. Louis XV. attempted, not without a sad and patient skill, to obtain equilibrium rather than defence. He would consider an arrangement with Vienna only if it might include a peaceful understanding with Berlin.

As, during October, these negotiations matured so slowly in France, in Vienna the Empress awaited through that month the birth of her child. She jested upon it with a Catholic freedom, laid wagers upon its sex (and later won them), discussed what sponsors should be bidden, and decided at last upon the King and Queen of Portugal; to these, in the last days of October, her messengers brought the request, and it was gladly accepted in their capital of Lisbon. Under such influences was the child to be born.

The town of Lisbon had risen, in the first colonial efforts of Portugal, to a vast importance. True, the Portuguese did not, as others have done, attach their whole policy to possessions over-sea, nor rely for existence upon the supremacy of their fleet, but the evils necessarily attendant upon a scattered commercial empire decayed their military power and therefore at last their commerce itself. The capital was no longer, in the Arab phrase, "the city of the Christian"; it was long fallen from its place as the chief port of the Atlantic when, in these last days of October, 1755, the messengers of the Empress entered it and were received; but it was still great, overlooking the superb anchorage which brought it into being, and presenting to the traveller

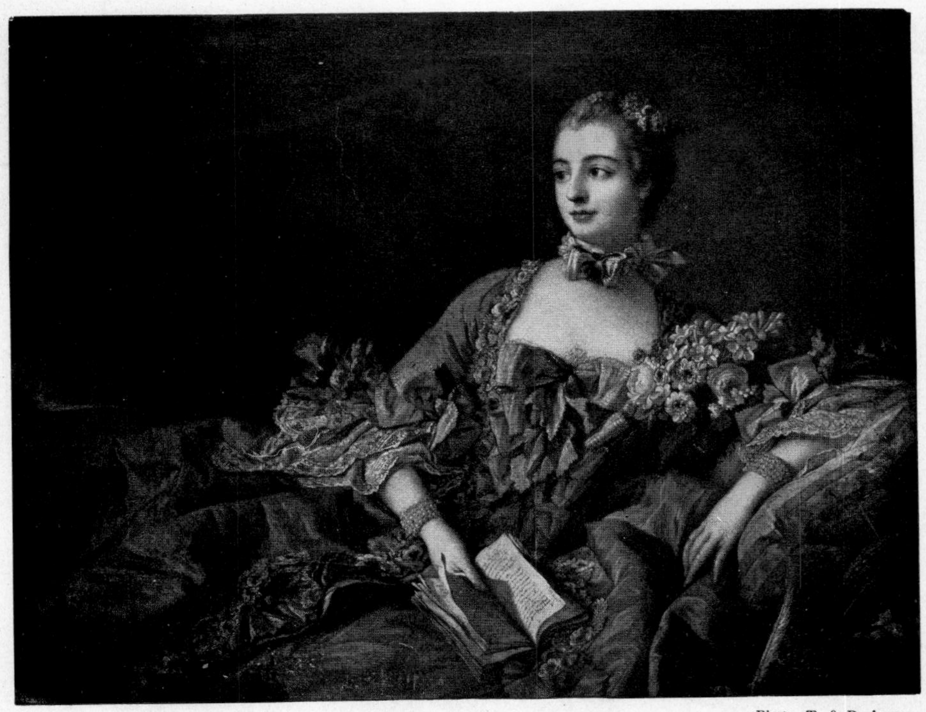

Photo. T. & R. Annan

MADAME DE POMPADOUR

By Boucher. In the National Gallery at Edinburgh

perhaps half the population which it had boasted in the height of its prosperity. It was a site famous for shocks of earthquake, which (by a coincidence) had visited it since the decline of its ancient power; but of these no more affair had been made than is common with natural adventures. Its narrow streets and splendid, if not majestic, churches still stood uninjured.

The valley upon which stood the commercial centre of Lisbon is formed of loose clay; the citadel and the portion which to this day recalls the older city, of limestone; and the line which limits the two systems is a sharp one. But though the diversity of such a soil lent to these tremors an added danger, they had passed without serious attention for three or four generations; they had not affected the architecture of the city nor marred its history. In this year, 1755, they had already been repeated, but in so mild a fashion that no heed was taken of them.

By All-Hallowe'en the heralds had accomplished their mission, the Court had retired to the palace of Belem, which overlooks the harbour, and the suburbs built high beyond that Roman bridge which has bequeathed to its valley the Moorish name of Alcantara. The city, as the ambassadors of Maria Theresa and the heralds of her daughter's birth were leaving it, was awaiting under the warm and easy sun of autumn the feast of the morrow.

In the morning of that All Saints, a little after eight, the altars stood prepared, the populace had thronged into the churches; the streets also were already noisy with the opening of a holiday; the ships' crews were ashore; only the quays were deserted. Everywhere High Mass had begun. But just at nine — at the hour when the pressure of the crowds, both within the open doors of the churches and without them, was at its fullest — the earth shook. The awful business lasted perhaps ten seconds. When its crash was over an immense multitude of the populace and a third of the material city had perished.

The great mass of the survivors ran to the deserted quays, where an open sky and broad spaces seemed to afford safety from the fall of walls. They saw the sea withdrawn from the shore of the wide harbour; they saw next a wave form and rise far out in the landlocked gulf, and immediately it returned in an advancing heap of water straight and high — as high and as straight as the houses of the sea front. It moved with the pace of a gust or of a beam of light toward the shore. The thousands crammed upon the quays had barely begun their confused rush for the heights when this thing was upon them; it swirled into the narrow streets, tearing down the shaken walls and utterly sweeping out the maimed, the dying and the dead whom the earthquake had left in the city. Then, when it had surged up and broken against the higher land, it dragged back again into the bay, carrying with it the wreck of the town and leaving strewn on the mud of its retirement small marbles, carven wood, stuffs, fuel, provisions, and everywhere the drowned corpses of animals and of men. During these moments perhaps twenty, perhaps thirty thousand were destroyed.

Two hours passed. They were occupied in part by pillage, in part by stupefaction, to some extent by repression and organization. But before noon the accompaniment of such disasters appeared. Fire was discovered first in one quarter of the city, then in another, till the whole threatened to be consumed. The disorder increased. Pombal, an atheist of rapid and decided thought, dominated the chaos and controlled it. He held the hesitating court to the ruins of the city; he organized a police; as the early evening fell over the rising conflagration he had gibbets raised at one point after another, and hung upon them scores of those who had begun to loot the ruins and the dead.

The night was filled with the light and the roar of the flames until, at the approach of morning, when the fires had partly spent themselves and the cracked and charred walls yet standing could be seen more clearly in the dawn, some in that exhausted crowd remembered that it was the Day of the Dead, and how throughout Catholic Europe the requiems would be singing and the populace of all the cities but this would be crowding to the graves of those whom they remembered.

That same day, which in Lisbon overlooked the cloud of smoke still pouring from broken shells of houses, saw in Vienna, as the black processions returned from their cemeteries, the birth of the child.

. . . .

Maria Theresa, whose vigour had been constant through so many trials, suffered grievously in this last child-bed of hers. She was in her thirty-seventh year. The anxiety and the plotting of the past months, the fear of an approaching conflict, had worn her. It was six weeks before she could hear Mass in her chapel; and meanwhile, in spite of the official, and especially the popular, rejoicing which followed the birth of the princess, a sort of hesitation hung over the court. Francis of Lorraine was oppressed by premonitions. With that taint of superstition which his faith condemned, but which the rich can never wholly escape, he caused the baby's horoscope to be drawn. The customary banquet was foregone. The dreadful news from Lisbon added to the gloom, and something silent surrounded the palace as the days shortened into winter.

With the New Year a more usual order was re-established. The life of the Court had returned; the first fortnight of January passed in open festivities, beneath the surface of which the steady diplomatic pressure for the French alliance continued. It reached an unexpectedly rapid conclusion. Upon the sixteenth of January the King of Prussia suddenly admitted to the French ambassador at Berlin that he had broken faith with Louis and that the Prussian minister in London had signed a treaty with England. For a month a desperate attempt continued to prevent the enormous consequences which must follow the public knowledge of the betrayal. The aversion of Louis to all new action, his mixture of apathy and of judgment, led him, through his ambassador, to forego the insult and to cling to the illusion of peace, but Frederick himself destroyed that illusion. His calculation had been the calculation of a soldier in whom the clear appreciation of a strategical moment, the resolution and courage necessary to use it, and an impotence of the chivalric functions combined to make such decisions absolute. It was the second manifestation of that moral perversion which has lent for two hundred years such nervous energy to Prussia, and of which the Occupation of Silesia was the first, Bismark's forgery at Ems the latest — and probably the final — example: for Europe can always at last expel a poison.

Frederick, I say, was resolved upon war. He met every proposal for reconciliation with German jests somewhat decadent and expressed in imperfect French, which was his daily language. By the end of February, 1756, the attempt to keep the peace of Europe had failed, and Louis XV., driven by circumstance and necessity, had at last accepted the design of Maria Theresa and of Kaunitz. The treaty would have been signed in March had not the illness of the French Minister, the Cardinal De Bernis intervened; as it was, the signatures were affixed to the document on the first of May. By summer all Europe was in arms. The little Archduchess, who was later to lay down her life in the chain of consequences which proceeded from that signing, was six months old.

The first seven years of Marie Antoinette's life were, therefore, those of the Seven Years' War.

As her mind emerged into consciousness, the rumours she heard around her, magnified by the gossip of the servants to whom she was entrusted, were rumours of sterile victories and of malignant defeats; in the recital of either there mingled perpetually the name of the Empire and the name of Bourbon which she was to bear. She could just walk when the whole of Cumberland's army broke down before the French advance and accepted terms at Kloster-Seven. Her second birthday cake was hardly eaten before Frederick had neutralised this capitulation by destroying the French at Rosbach. The year which saw the fall of Quebec and the French disasters in India, was that with which her earliest memories were associated. She could remember Kunersdorf, the rejoicings and the confident belief that the Protestant agression was repelled. Her fifth, her sixth, her seventh years — the years, that is, during which the first clear experience of life begins — proved the folly of that confidence: her eighth was not far advanced when the whole of this noisy business was concluded by the Peace of Paris and the Treaty of Herbertsburg.

The war appeared indecisive or a failure. The original theft of Silesia was confirmed to Prussia; the conquest of the French colonies to England. In their defensive against the menace to which all European traditions were exposed, the courts of Vienna and Versailles had succeeded; in their aggressive, which had the object of destroying that menace forever, they had failed. In failing in their aggressive, as a by-product of that failure, they had permitted the establishment of an English colonial system which at the time seemed of no great moment, but which was destined ultimately to estrange this country from the politics of Europe and to submit it to fantastic changes; to make its population urban and proletariat, to increase immensely the wealth of its oligarchy, and gravely to obscure its military ideals. In the success of their defensive, as by-products of that success, they had achieved two things equally unexpected: they had preserved for ever the South-German spirit, and had thus checked in a remote future the organization of the whole German race by Prussia and the triumph over it of Prussian materialism; they had preserved to France an intensive domestic energy which was shortly to transform the world.

The period of innocence, then, and of growth, which succeeds a child's first approach to the Sacraments, corresponded in the life of Marie Antoinette with the peace that followed these victories and these defeats. The space between her seventh and her fourteenth years might have been filled, in the leisure of the Austrian Court, with every advantage and every grace. By an accident, not unconnected with her general fate, she was allowed to run wild.

That her early childhood should have been neglected is easier to understand. The war occupied all her mother's energies. She and her elder sister Caroline were the babies whose elder brother was already admitted to affairs of State. It was natural that no great anxiety upon their education should have been felt in such times. The child had been put out to nurse with the wife of a small lawyer of sorts, one Weber, whose son — the foster-brother of the Queen — has left a pious and inaccurate memorial of her to posterity. Here she first learnt the German tongue, which was to be her only idiom during her childhood; here, also, she first heard her name under the form of "Maria Antoinetta," a form which was to be preserved until her marriage was planned.

Such neglect, or rather such domesticity, would have done her character small hurt if it had ceased with her earliest years and with the conclusion of the peace; it was no better and no worse than that which the children of all the wealthy enjoy in the company of inferiors until their education begins. But the little archduchess, even when she had reached the age when character forms, was still undisciplined and at large. There was found for her and Caroline a worthy and easy-going governess in the Countess of Brandweiss, an amiable and careless woman, who perhaps could neither teach nor choose teachers and who certainly did not do so.

All the warmer part of the year the children spent at Schoenbrünn; it was only in the depth of winter that they visited the capital. But whether at Court or in the country they were continually remote from the presence and the strong guidance of Maria Theresa.

The Empress saw them formally once a week; a doctor daily reported upon their health; for the rest, all control was abandoned. The natural German of Marie Antoinette's babyhood continued (perhaps in the very accent of her domestics) to be the medium of her speech in her teens, and — what was of more importance for the future — not only of her speech but of her thought also. In womanhood and after a long residence abroad the mechanical part of this habit was forgotten; its spirit remained. What she read — if she read anything — we cannot tell. Her music alone was watched. Her deportment was naturally graceful as her breeding was good; but the seeds of no culture were sown in her, nor so much as the elements of self-control. Her sprightliness was allowed an indulgence in every whim, especially in a talent for mockery. She acquired, and she desired to acquire, nothing. No healthy child is fitted by nature for application and study; upon all such must continuous habits be enforced — to her they were not so much as suggested. A perpetual instability became part of her mind, and, unhappily, this permanent weakness was so veiled by an inherited poise and by a happy heart, that her mother, in her rare observations, passed it by. Before Marie Antoinette was grown a woman that inner instability had come to colour all her mind; it remained in her till the eve of her disasters.

It is often discovered, when an eager childhood is left too much to its own ruling, that the mind will, of its own energy, turn to the cultivation of some one thing. Thus, in Versailles, the boyhood of the lonely child, who was later to be her husband, had turned for an interest to maps and had made them a passion. With her it was not so. The whole of her active and over-nourished life lacked the ballast of so much as a hobby. She was precisely of that kind to whom a wide, a careful, and a conventional training is most useful; precisely that training was denied her.

The disasters and what was worse, the unfruitfulness of the war had not daunted Maria Theresa, but her plans were in disarray. The two years that succeeded the peace produced no definite policy. No step was taken to confirm the bond with France or to secure the future, when there fell upon her the blow of her husband's death; he had fallen under a sudden stroke at Innsbruck, during the wedding feast of his son, leaving to her and to his children not only the memory of his peculiar charm but also a sort of testament or rule of life which remains a very noble fragment of Christian piety.

Before he had set out he remembered his youngest daughter; he asked repeatedly for the child and she was brought to him. He embraced her closely, with some presentiment of evil, and he touched her hair; then as he rode away among his gentlemen he said, with that clear candour which inhabits both the blood and the wine of Lorraine, "Gentlemen, God knows how much I desired to kiss that child!" She had been his favourite; there was a close affinity between them. She was left to her mother, therefore, as a pledge and an inheritance, and Maria Theresa, whose mourning became passionate and remained so, was ready to procure for this daughter the chief advantages of the world.

The loss of her husband, while it filled her with an enduring sorrow, also did something to rouse and to inspire the Empress with the force that comes to such natures when they find themselves suddenly alone. The little girl upon whom her ambitions were already fixed, the French alliance which had been, as it were, the greatest part of herself, mixed in her mind. Maria Theresa had long connected in some vague manner the confirmation of the alliance with some Bourbon marriage — in what way precisely or by what plan we cannot tell; her ambassador has credited her with many plans. It is probable that none were developed when, a few weeks after the Emperor's death, there happened something to decide her. The son of Louis XV., the Dauphin, was taken ill and died before the end of the year 1765. He left heir to the first throne in Europe his son, a lanky, silent, nervous lad of eleven, and that lad was heir to a man nearer sixty than fifty, worn with pleasure of a fastidious kind, and with the despair that accompanies the satisfaction of the flesh. A great eagerness was apparent at Versailles to plan at once a future marriage for this boy and to secure succession. Maria Theresa determined that this succession should reside in children of her own blood.

Nationality was a conception somewhat foreign to her, and as yet of no great strength in her mixed and varied dominions. How powerful it had ever been in France, what a menace it provided for the future of the French Monarchy, she could not perceive. Of the silent boy himself, the new heir, she knew only what her ambassador told her, and she cared little what he might be; but she saw clearly the Bourbons, a family as the Hapsburgs were a family, a bond in Catholic Europe with this boy the heir to their headship. She saw Versailles as the pinnacle still of whatever was regal (and therefore serious) in Europe. She determined to complete by a marriage the alliance already effected between that Court and her own.

She knew the material with which she had to deal: Louis XV., clear sighted, a great gentleman, sensual, almost lethargic, loyal. She had understood the old nonentity of a Queen keeping her little place apart; the King's spinster-daughters struggling against the influence of mis-

THE FIRST DAUPHIN

The father of Louis XVI.

tresses. She understood the power of Choiseul, with whose active ministry the King had so long allowed his power to be merged; she knew how and why he was Austrian in policy, and she forgave him his attack upon the Church. Though Choiseul had not made the alliance he so used it, and above all so maintained it after the doubtful peace, that he almost seemed its author, as later he seemed — though he took so little action — the author of her daughter's marriage. She did not grudge the French Minister such honours. She weighed the historic grandeur of the royal house, and what she believed to be its certain future. She sketched in her mind, with Kaunitz at her side, the marriage of the two children as, years before, she had sketched the alliance.

It was certain that Versailles would yield, because Versailles was a man who, for all his lucidity and high training, never now stood long to one effort of the will; but just because Louis XV. had grown into a nature of that kind, it needed as active, as tenacious, and as subtle a mind as Maria Theresa's to bring him to write or to speak. Writing or speaking in so grave a matter meant direct action and consequence; he feared such responsibilities as others fear disaster.

It is in the spirit of comedy to see this dignified and ample woman — perhaps the only worthy sovereign of her sex whom modern Europe has known — piloting through so critical a pass the long-determined fortunes of her daughter. There is the mother in all of it. That daughter had imperilled her life. The child was the last of nine which she had borne to a husband whose light infidelities she now the more forgave, whose clear gentility had charmed her life, whose religion was her own, and in respect to whose memory she was rapidly passing from a devotion to an adoration. The day was not far distant when she would brood in the vault beside his grave.

The old man Stahrenberg was yielding his place (with some grumbling) to Mercy. He was still the Austrian ambassador at Paris but his term was ending. Maria Theresa would perhaps in other times have spared his pride and would not have given him a task upon which he must labour, but which his successor would enjoy; but in the matter of her little archduchess she would spare no one. She had hinted her business to Stahrenberg before the Dauphin's death. The spring had hardly broken before she was pressing him to conclude it. Up to his very departure her importunity pursued him. When Mercy was on the point of entering his office (in the May of 1766) Stahrenberg, in the last letter sent to the Empress from Paris before his return, told her that her ship was launched. "She might," he wrote, "accept her project as assured, from the tone in which the King had spoken of it."

Maria Theresa had too firm and too smiling and too luminous an acquaintance with the world to build upon such vague assurance. The dignity of the French throne was too great a thing to be grasped at. It must be achieved. When old Mme. Geoffrin passed through Vienna in that year Maria Antoinetta was kept in the background off the stage — but France was cultivated. The baby, who was Louis XV.'s great-granddaughter, Theresa, Leopold's daughter, was presented to that old and wonderful bourgeoise and made much of. They joked about taking her to France; another baby, after all not much older, only eight years older, was going to that place in her time.

And, meanwhile, the common arts by which women of

birth perfect their plans for their family were practised in the habitual round. The little girl's personality, all gilded and framed, was put in the window of the Hapsburgs. She was wild perhaps, but so good-hearted! In the cold winter you heard of (all winters are cold in Vienna) she came up in the drawing-room where the family sat together and begged her mother to accept of all her savings for the poor — fifty-five ducats!

Little Mozart had come in to play one night. He had slipped upon the unaccustomed polish of the floor. The little archduchess, when all others smiled, had alone pitied and lifted him! Maria Theresa met the French ambassador and told him in the most indifferent way how her youngest, when she was asked whom (among so many nations) she would like to rule, had said, "The French, for they had Henri IV. the good and Louis XIV. the great." Weary though he was of such conventionalities, the ambassador was bound by the honour of his place to repeat them.

There still stood, however, in this summer of 1766, between the Empress's plan and its fruition a power as feminine, as perspicuous, and as exact in calculation as her own. The widow of the Dauphin, the mother of the new heir at Versailles, opposed the match.

She would not retire, as the Queen, her mother-in-law, had done, into dignity and nothingness, nor would she admit — so tenacious of the past are crowns — that the Bourbons and the Hapsburgs had all the negotiations between them. She was of the Saxon House, and though it was but small — a northern bastion as it were, of the Catholic Houses — yet she had inherited the tradition of monarchy, and she might, but for her husband's sudden death, have inherited Versailles itself. She was still young, vigorous and German.

She had determined not only that her son, the new heir, should marry into her house — should marry his own cousin, her niece — but that he should marry as she his mother chose, and not as the Hapsburgs chose. He was at that moment (in 1766) not quite twelve; the bride whom she would disappoint not quite eleven years old! But her plan was active and tenacious, her readiness alive, when in the beginning of the following year, in March, 1767, she, in her turn died, and with her death that obstacle to the fate of the little archduchess also failed.

With every date, as you mark each, it will be the more apparent that the barriers which opposed Marie Antoinette's approach to the French throne, failed each in turn at the climax of its resistance, and that her way to such eminence and such an end was opened by a number of peculiar chances, all adjutants of doom.

The House of Hapsburg was never a crowned nationality; it was and is a crowned family and nothing more. Its States were and are attached to it by no common bond. There is no such thing as Austria: the Hapsburgs are the reality of that Empire. The French Bourbons were, upon the contrary, the chiefs of a nation peculiarly conscious of its unity and jealous of its past. Their greatness lay only in the greatness of the compact quadrilateral they governed and of the finished language of their subjects, and in the achievements of the national temper. Such conditions favoured to the utmost the scheme of Maria Theresa, not only in the detail of this marriage, but in all that successful management of the French alliance which survived her own death and was the chief business of her reign. *She* could be direct in every plan, unhampered, considering only the fortunes of her house; Louis XV., and his Ministers, as later his grandson, were trammelled by the complexity of a national life of which they were themselves a part.

Versailles had not declared itself: Vienna pressed. It was in March that active opposition within the Court had died with the mother of the heir. Within a month the French ambassador at Vienna wrote home that "the marriage was in the air": but the King had not spoken.

In that summer, as though sure of her final success, the Empress threw a sort of prescience of France and of high fortunes over the nursery at Schoenbrünn. The amiable Brandweiss disappeared; the severe and unhealthy Lorchenfeld replaced her.

The French (and baptismal form) of the child's name, "Antoinette," was ordered to be used: still Versailles remained dumb.

In the autumn the parallels of the siege were so far advanced that a direct assault could be made on poor Dufort, the advanced work of the Bourbons, their ambassador at Vienna.

Dufort had been told very strictly to keep silent. He suffered a persecution. Thus he was standing one evening by the card-tables talking to his Spanish colleague, when the Empress came up and said to this last boldly: "You see my daughter, sir? I trust her marriage will go well; we can talk of it the more freely that the French ambassador here does not open his lips."

The child's new governess was next turned on to the embarrassed man to pester him with the recital of her charge's virtues. The approaching marriage of her elder sister, Caroline with the Bourbons of Naples was dangled before Dufort.

The play continued for a year. Louis XV. bade his

minister get the girl's portrait, but "not show himself too eager." He is reprimanded even for his courtesies, and all the while Dufort must stand the fire of the Court of Vienna and its exaggerated deference to him and its occasional reproaches! Choiseul was anxious to see the business ended. Dufort was as ready (and as weary) as could have been the Empress herself, but the slow balance of Louis XV. stood between them all and their goal.

In the summer of the next year, 1768, the Empress's eldest son, Joseph, now associated with her upon the throne, determined to press home and conclude. It was the first time that this man's narrow energy pressed the Bourbons to determine and to act; it was not to be the last. He was destined so to initiate action in the future upon two critical occasions and largely to determine the fortunes of his sister's married life and final tragedy.

He wrote to Louis XV. a rambling letter, chiefly upon the marriage of yet another sister with the Duke of Parma. It wandered to the Bourbon marriage of Caroline; he mentioned his own child, the great-granddaughter of the King. It was a letter demanding and attracting a familiar answer. It drew its quarry. Louis, answering with his own hand and without emphasis, in a manner equally domestic and familiar, threw in a chance phrase: " . . . These marriages, your sister's with the Infante, *that of the Dauphin*. . . ." In these casual four words a document had passed and the last obstacle was removed.

The Empress turned from her major preoccupation to a minor one. This child of hers was to rule in France: she was now assured of the throne; she was near her thirteenth birthday — and she had been taught nothing.

III

THE ESPOUSALS

THE fortnightly despatches from France customarily arrived at Vienna together in one bag and in the charge of one courier. The Empress would receive at once the letters of Mercy, the official correspondence, perhaps the note of a friend, and the very rare communications of royalty. In this same batch which brought that decisive letter of Louis XV. to her son, on the same day, therefore, in which she was first secure in her daughter's future, there also arrived the usual secret report from Mercy. This document contained a phrase too insignificant to detain her attention; it mentioned the rumour of a new intrigue: the King showed attachment to a woman of low origin about him. It was an attachment that might be permanent. This news was immediately forgotten by Maria Theresa; it was a detail that passed from her mind. She perhaps remembered the name, which was "Du Barry."

. . . .

The Court of Vienna, permeated (as was then every wealthy society) with French culture, was yet wholly German in character. The insufficiency which had marked the training of the imperial children — especially of the youngest — was easily accepted by those to whom a happy domestic spirit made up for every other lack in the family. Of those who surrounded the little archduchess two alone, perhaps, understood the grave difference of standard between such education as Maria Antoinetta had as yet received and the conversation of Versailles; but these two were Kaunitz and Maria Theresa, and short as was the time before them, they did determine to fit the child, in superficial things at least, for the world she was to enter and in a few years, to govern. They failed.

Mercy was instructed to find a tutor who should come to Vienna and could accomplish the task. He applied to Choiseul. Choiseul in turn referred the matter to the best critic of such things, an expert in things of the world, the Archbishop of Toulouse. That prelate, Loménie de Brienne, whose unscrupulous strength had judged men rightly upon so many occasions and had exactly chosen them for political tasks had in this case no personal appetite to gratify and was free to choose. A post was offered. His first thought was to obtain it for one who was bound to him, a protégé and a dependant. He at once recommended a priest for whom he had already procured the librarianship of the Mazarin Collection, one Vermond. The choice was not questioned, and Vermond left to assume functions which he could hardly fulfil.

There was needed here a man who should have been appalled by the ignorance he might discover in his charge, who should be little affected by grandeur, who should be self-willed, assertive, and rapid in method. One whom the Empress might have ridiculed or even disliked, but whom she would soon have discovered to be indispensable to her plan. Such a man would have tackled his business with an appreciation of its magnitude, would have insisted upon a full control, would have communicated by his vigour the atmosphere of French thought, careless of the German shrinking from the rigidity of the French mind. He would have worked long hours with little Marie Antoinette, he would have filled the days with his one object, he would have shocked and offended all, his pupil especially, and in a year he would have left her with a good grounding in the literature of his country, with an elementary but a clear scheme of the history and the political forces which she was later to learn in full, with an enlarged vocabulary, a good accent, and at least the ability to write clearly and to work a simple sum. His pupil would have been compelled to application; her impulse would have been permanently harnessed; she would have learnt for life the value of a plan. Such a tutor would hardly have desired and would certainly not have acquired a lasting influence later on at Versailles. His work would have been done in those critical years of childhood once and for all. He would probably have fallen into poverty. In later years he might have appeared among the revolutionaries, but he would have found, face to face with the Revolution, a trained Queen who, thanks to him, could have dealt with circumstance.

In the place of such a man Vermond arrived.

He was a sober, tall, industrious priest of low birth; his father had let blood and perhaps pulled teeth for the needy. His reserve and quiet manners reposed upon a spirit that was incapable of ambition, but careful to secure ample means and to establish his family and himself in the secure favour of his employers. He was of middle age, a state into which he had entered early and was likely long to remain. His mind within was active and disciplined; its exterior effect was small. He thought to accomplish his mission if he was but regular in his reports, laborious in his own study, and, above all, tactful and subtle in handling the problem before him.

To such a character was presented an exuberant child, growing rapidly, vivacious, somewhat proud, and hitherto unaccustomed to effort of any kind, a monkey for mimicry, clever at picking up a tune upon the keys, a tomboy shouting her German phrases down the corridors of Schoenbrünn, a fine little lady at Vienna — acting either part well. The light russet of her hair and her thick eyebrows gave promise of her future energy; she had already acquired the tricks of rank, the carriage of the head and the ready mechanical interest in inferiors — for the rest she was empty. In this critical fourteenth year of hers, during which it was proposed to fashion out of such happy German childhood a strict and delicate French princess, she did not read and she could barely write. The big round letters, as she painfully fashioned them in her occasional lessons, were those of a baby. Her drawing was infantile; and while she rapidly learnt a phrase in a foreign language by ear, a complete revolution in her education would have been needed to make her accurate in the use of words or to make her understand a Latin sentence or parse a French one.

To cultivate such a soil, exactly one hour a day was spared when the Court was at Vienna — somewhat more when it was in the country — and these few minutes were consumed in nothing more methodical than a dialogue, little talks in which Vermond was fatally anxious to bring before his pupil (with her head full of those new French head-dresses of hers, the prospect of Versailles, and every other distraction of mind) only such subjects as might amuse her inattention.

The early months of 1769 were full of this inanity, Vermond regularly reporting progress to the Austrian embassy in France, regularly complaining of the difficulty of his task, regularly insisting upon his rules and as regularly failing in his object. In the autumn the Empress was at the pains of asking her daughter a few questions, notably upon history. The result did not dissatisfy her, but meanwhile Maria Antoinetta could hardly write her name.

Side by side with this continued negligence in set training and in the discipline that accompanies it, went a very rapid development in manner. The child was admitted to the Court; she was even permitted the experiment of presiding at small gatherings of her own. The experiment succeeded. She acquired with an amazing rapidity what little remained to be learned of the externals of rank. The alternate phrases addressed to one's neighbours round a table, the affectation of satiety and of repose, the gait in which the feet are hardly lifted; the few steps forward to meet a magnate, the fewer to greet a lesser man, and that smiling immobility before the ordinary sort, which is still a living tradition in great drawing-rooms; the power of putting on an air in the very moment between privacy and a public appearance — all these came to her so naturally and by so strongly inherited an instinct, that she not only charmed the genial elders of the Austrian capital but satisfied experienced courtiers, even those visitors from France, who examined it all with the eyes of connoisseurs and watched her deportment as a work of art, whose slight errors in technique they could at once discover but whose general excellence they were able to appreciate and willing to proclaim.

She did indeed preserve beneath that conventional surface a fire of vigorous life that was apparent in every hour. Once in the foreign atmosphere of France and subject to exasperation and contrast, that heat would burst forth. She became, as her future showed, capable of violent scenes in public and of the natural gestures of anger — it is to her honour that she was on the whole so often herself. Here at Vienna in this last year her young energy did no more than lend spirit and grace to the conventions she so quickly acquired.

The opening of the year 1770 found her thus, her German half forgotten, her French (though imperfect) habitual, her acquaintance with the air of a Court considerable. Though she was still growing rapidly she was now dressed as a woman and taught to walk on her high heels as did the ladies her seniors. Her hair was brushed off her high forehead in the French manner, the stuff of her frocks and the cut of them was French, her name was now permanently Frenchified for her, and she heard herself called everywhere "Marie Antoinette"; none but old servants were left to give her the names she had first known.

March passed and the moment of her departure approached. The child had never travelled. To her vivacious and eager temper the prospect of so great a journey with so splendid an ending was an absorbing pleasure. It filled her mind even during the retreat which, under Vermond's guidance, she entered during Holy Week, and every sign of her approaching progress excited in her a vivid curiosity and expectation, as it did in her mother a mixture of foreboding and of pride.

The official comedy which the Court played during April heightened the charm: the heralds, the receptions, that quaint but gorgeous ceremony of renunciation, the mock-marriage, the white silver braid and the white satin of her wedding-clothes, the salvoes of artillery and the feasts were all a fine great play for her, with but one interlude of boredom, when her mother dictated, and she wrote (heaven knows with what a careful guidance of the pen) a letter which she was to deliver to the King of France. With that letter Maria Theresa enclosed a note of her own, familiar, almost domestic, imploring Louis XV., her contemporary, to see to the child as "one that had a good heart," . . . but was ardent and a trifle wild.

These words were written upon the twentieth of the month; on the morning of the twenty-first of April, 1770, the line of coaches left the palace, and the archduchess took the western road.

There was no sudden severance. Her eldest brother, Joseph, he who was associated with her mother in the empire, accompanied her during the whole of the first day. Of an active, narrow, and formal intelligence, grossly self-sufficient, arithmetical in temper, and with a sort of native atheism in him such as stagnates in minds whose development is early arrested, a philosopher therefore and a prig, earnest, lean, and an early riser, he was of all companions the one who could most easily help Marie Antoinette to forget Vienna and to desire Versailles. The long hours of the drive were filled with platitudes and admonitions that must easily have extinguished all her regrets for his Court and have bred in her a natural impatience for the new horizons that were before her. He left her at Melk. She continued her way with her household, hearing for the last time upon every side the German tongue, not knowing that she heard also, for the last time, the accents of sincere affection and sincere servility: the French temper with its concealed edges of sharpness was to find her soon enough.

Her journey was not slow for the times. She took but

little more than a week to reach the Rhine from Augsburg — a French army on the march has done no better. It was on the evening of the sixth of May that she could see, far off against the sunset, the astonishing spire of Strasburg and was prepared to enter France; only the Rhine was now between her and her new life.

She bore upon her person during this last night on German soil a last letter of her mother's which had reached her but the day before yesterday. It was the most intimate and the most searching she was to receive in all the long correspondence which was to pass between them for ten years, and it contained a phrase which the child could hardly understand, but which, if texts and single phrases were of the least advantage to conduct, might have deflected her history and that of Europe. "*The one felicity of this world is a happy marriage: I can say so with knowledge; and the whole hangs upon the woman, that she should be willing, gentle, and able to amuse.*"

Next day at noon she crossed in great pomp to an island in mid-river, where a temporary building of wood had been raised upon the exact frontier for the ceremony of her livery.

It is possible that the long ritual of her position — she was to endure it for twenty years! — was already a burden upon her versatility, even after these short weeks. Here, on this island, the true extent of the French parade first met her. It was sufficient to teach her what etiquette was to mean. The poor child had to take off every stitch of her clothes and to dress, to a ribbon or a hair pin, with an order strictly ordained and in things all brought from Versailles for the occasion. Once so dressed she was conducted to a central room where her German household gave her to her

French one, at the head of which the kindly and sometimes foolish Comtesse de Noailles performed the accustomed rites, and the archduchess entered for ever the million formalities of her new world. They had not yet fatigued her. She was taken to Mass at the Cathedral; she received the courtesy of the old bishop, a Rohan, in whose great family Strasburg was almost an appanage.

There was a figure standing by the Bishop's side. She saw, clothed in that mature majesty which a man of thirty may have for a child of fifteen, the bishop's coadjutor, a nephew and a Rohan too. She noted his pomposity and perhaps his good looks, but he meant nothing to her; he was but one of the Rohans to be remembered. He noted her well.

Next day and for six more her journey proceeded amid perpetual deputations, Latin, flowers, bad verses, stage peasantry, fireworks, feasts, and addresses, until, a week after she had crossed the Rhine, she slept at Soissons and knew that on the morrow she would see the King.

The pavement of the long road out from Soissons, the great royal road, had sounded under the wheels of her carriage for now the best part of the day. She had already found Choiseul awaiting her in state and had exchanged with this old friend of her mother's those ceremonial compliments of which the child was now well weary, when, through the left-hand window of her coach, which was open to the warm spring day, she saw before her a thing of greater interest — the league-long line of trees that ends abruptly against the bare plain and that marks the forest of Compiègne.

Into this wood the road plunged, straight and grand, until after a declivity, where a little stream is crossed (near the place where the railway lines join to-day) there appeared awaiting her, as Choiseul had awaited her some miles before, a great and orderly group of people, of carriages, and horses; but this company was far larger and was ranked with more solemnity than others that had met her upon her progress. She knew that it was the King.

The splendour which a history full of trumpets had lent to the French name, the lineage of the kings, the imagined glories of Versailles — all these had penetrated the nursery and the schoolroom of the princess. As she came down from her carriage, with either hand reposing in the hands of her escort, an awe of the Capetian monarchy came upon her, and she knelt upon the roadway in the midst of the Court, of the princesses who now first saw the little heiress of their lives, of the gilded carriages and the men-at-arms.

The King raised her up and kissed her forehead; he motioned forward a heavy, lanky, frowning boy, his grandson, for whom all this pomp existed. The lad shuffled forward, bent a little perhaps, and kissed her in his turn with due ceremony — for he was to be her husband. When this little ritual and its sharp emotions were over she had a moment, before her introductions to the Blood, to the King's mature daughters, to the Orleans and the rest, in which to seize with the bright glance that was always so ready for exterior things, the manner of the King.

Louis XV. was at that moment a man just past his sixtieth year. Long habit had given him, as it gives to all but the greatest of those educated to power, an attitude constrained though erect. His age had told on him, he had grown somewhat fat, he moved without alertness and — a weakness which had appeared but lately — his rare and uncompleted gestures expressed the weight of his body; but his muscles were firm, his command of them perfect, and he still had, especially in repose, so far as age can have it, grace.

The united pallor of his complexion, which had been remarkable in youth, seemed now more consonant to his years. The steady indifference to which he had reduced his features was now more dignified than when its rigidity had seemed unnatural and new. His expression even acquired a certain strength from the immobility and firmness of his mouth whose lines displayed a talent for exact language and a capacity for continued dignity; but his eyes betrayed him.

They were warm in spite of a habit of command, but the sadness in them (which was profound and permanent) was of a sort which sprang from physical appetites always excessive and now surviving abnormally beyond their time. There was also in those eyes the memory of considerable but uprooted affections, and, deeper, of a fixed despair, and deeper far — a veil as it were behind their brightness — the mortal tedium, to escape from which this human soul had sacrificed the national traditions and the ancient honour of the crown.

This great monarch, whom no one since his boyhood had approached without a certain fear, received his grandson's betrothed with an air almost paternal. It was a relaxation upon his part to which he owed, during the remainder of his life, the strongly affectionate respect which Marie Antoinette, vivacious and ungoverned, paid to him alone in the palace.

He presented the rest in turn. She heard names which were to mix so intimately with her own destiny, and when they set out again upon the road she could discreetly watch during the long ten miles to Compiègne, Chartres who would soon be Orleans, the faded faces of the King's spinster-daughters, the old Duke of Ponthièvre; and she watched with a greater care that daughter of his whose foolish, dainty, and sentimental face, insecure upon its long thin neck, was that of a young, unhappy widow: the Princesse de Lamballe.

When they had slept at Compiègne in state, the whole pageant moved on next morning down the Paris road upon the last day's march of that journey, and the child thought that she was now upon the threshold of nothing but an easy glory. She was nearing — amid great mobs and a whole populace come out to greet her, not only Paris and Versailles, but much more — that woman whose name her mother had heard and half forgotten, whose name she herself had never heard. It was a name whose influence was to deflect the first current of her life: the name of Du Barry.

. . . .

There is but one instrument efficacious to the government of men, which is Persuasion, and Persuasion sickens when its agent fails in dignity.

Dignity is the exterior one of the many qualities necessary to commandment; these in some cases touch closely upon virtue, so that, in some situations of authority, a dignified man is presumably a good one. But in the particular case of national government it is not so. The audience is so vast, the actor so distant and removed, that in this matter dignity resides mainly in the observance of whatever ritual the national temper and the national form of the executive demand. Such functions of ritual endanger rather than strengthen the soul of him who is called upon to assume them

To his intimates they appear as mummeries. It is often a sign of personal excellence in a ruler that he is disgusted with them and even casts them aside; but they are necessary to the State. For if such ritual is ill-observed, dignity fails; in its failure persuasion, I say, sickens, and when persuasion sickens, government, upon which depends the cohesion of a nation and the co-ordination of its faculties, breaks down.

The method of government in France at this time was a true personal monarchy.

The institution had increased in consciousness and in executive power down the long avenue of fourteen hundred years. Its roots were in Rome. It stood up in the seventh century as a memory of the Roman Peace, in the eighth as a promise to restore the Roman order. From the ninth onward it was vested in a Gaulish family and already had begun to express the Gaulish unities; by the thirteenth its mission was ardent and victorious. When the religious wars of the sixteenth century were resolved in a national settlement and the Bourbon branch was finally acknowledged, the crown was supreme and the whole people held to and were summed up in the Monarchy. It had made a yeoman of the serf, it had welded the nation together, it had established the frontiers, it had repressed the treason of the wealthy Huguenots: it was France.

The person of the Monarch was public and publicly worshipped. His spoken words were actually law: he could impose a peace; his private decision could suspend a debt, imprison a transgressor, ruin or create an industry. Into such a mould had the French energy forced the executive when the genius of Richelieu and the cunning of Mazarin confirmed the powers of the throne, and left them in legacy to the virile sense of Louis XIV.

This King was very great and cast accurately also to the part he should fill. The conventions and the trappings of the part delighted him; he played it royally, and when he died, though he left the crown to an infant great-grandson, yet its security seemed as permanent as does to-day the security in similar powers of our English rich. But that great-grandson, at first gradually and at last rapidly, undermined the stable seat he had inherited. Louis XV., by his good qualities as well as by his evil, tended more and more to reject the ritual necessary to his kingship. His good breeding and his active physical appetites, his idleness and his sincerity, all combined to weary him of the game, so that at the end of his long reign he had almost ceased in the eyes of the populace to be a King at all.

The Monarchy therefore perished, and mainly through Louis XV.'s incapacity to maintain its essential livery. Its collapse, its replacement (with consequences enormous to the whole of Europe) by that other French formula which we call "The Revolution" or "The Republic" was so exactly contemporaneous with Marie Antoinette's marriage and with her presence at Versailles, that far too great a part in the catastrophe is assigned to her own misjudgments and misfortunes. No error or disaster of hers gave the death shock to the institution with which her life was mingled; that stroke had been delivered before the child crossed the Rhine, and the moment when the blow was struck was that in which Mercy had penned the name "Du Barry," which Maria Theresa had read so carelessly in Vienna on the same day that brought the letter sealing her daughter's marriage.

The public appearance of Madame Du Barry was the turning point in the history of Versailles, and the little archduchess, when she came upon French earth, did not bring a curse to her new country, for the destiny of that country was already determined; rather this France which she had entered had prepared a tragedy for her and a fate expected by her own unhappy stars.

Those who have watched the destruction of an old and strong wall will remember that it seemed at first to resist with ease every battery of the assault. At last there came one effort, more violent than the rest, which broke long, zig-zag lines throughout the fabric. The work was done. A few succeeding impacts visibly disintegrated the now loosened stones until the whole fell rapidly into ruin. So it was with the French Monarchy. The Regency, the floating theories of public criticism, the indeterminate foreign policy, the military reverses of the Seven Years' War, the careless lethargy of Louis XV. in State affairs, had impaired the fabric of tradition, but that fabric still stood. It might yet have been restored and made whole had not the King in his last years chosen a particular mistress and presented her in a particular manner, which threw chaos into the scheme which every Frenchman took for granted when he considered his sovereign. This last thud, coming after so many accumulated tremours, loosened all the wall. The trials and distractions of the next reign did but pull apart, and that easily, the loosened stones. The imposing posture which the French demand of their symbols had been dropped by the old King; the new one could not restore it. Choose at random any man or woman of your acquaintance in history, put them upon the throne after the death of Louis XV., and though the succeeding quarter of a century would have varied somewhat with various individualities in power, the doom of the Monarchy would by none have been averted.

Let us see what happened when that fatal news of Madame Du Barry's advent spread through the Court and the capital of France and reached, like the ripple of a wave, the shores of Vienna.

The King (as has almost every other king in history) had indulged his body; he had also indulged his desire for intimate companionship, his man's whim for an expression, a tone of voice, or a gesture. This licence, which to their bane is granted to privileged and symbolic men, had led him into every distraction. His amours were many, but middle age had fixed his routine, if not his constancy, upon one woman of remarkable character.

Madame de Pompadour, as she came later to be called, was not of the nobility. To have taken a mistress publicly from the rank of business people was a serious reproach to the King; but though the mass condemned such an alliance, and though the wealthy, both of the middle class and of the courtiers, found an added blame in the financial reputation of her father and the notorious lightness of her mother, yet there was about this young, vigorous, and commanding hostess something that could prevent too violent a reaction of opinion.

She was extremely rich; her drawing-room had held all the famous men of her day; her education was wide and liberal, her judgment excellent. She played and sang with exceptional charm. She had good manner; she rode, spoke, read, and entertained as might the principal of her contemporaries.

The acknowledged position of such a woman at Court, though a new degradation, was a tolerable one. It was easy for the most reserved to understand how, in those years between thirty and forty when the strongest affections take root, the King had found in her company a sort of home. Her character was, moreover, comprehensible and secretly sympathetic to that vast proprietary body, the Bourgeoisie, which then were and are now the stuff of the nation.

She was prudent, she could choose a friend or a servant; her vivacity did not lack restraint. She was decent, fond of quiet silk, of good taste in decoration and of management. Her position at Versailles was a sort of conquest effected by the middle classes over the Court. Such a mistress, ruling for many years, the nation received at last with far more calm than could the buzzing nobles of the palace. As she (and the King) grew older, as her power became absolute and his individual presence grew remote, the situation was acceptable to Paris even more than to those who immediately surrounded the throne.

She died. There was an interval of puzzled silence about the person of the King. No one dreamt of a new power at Court. A nullity of action in the King himself, a few more stories, obscure and scandalous, the end of the reign and the accession of the heir who should bring with him such reforms as all the intellect of the country demanded: these were the expectations which followed her death, and especially were they the hope or the certitude of that group of men, mostly not noble, who had long managed both law and finance.

This prospect had, however, omitted one capital factor in the calculation. Louis XV., during these long years of regular habit, had grown old, and age in such a character, thus isolated, thus re-entrant, and yet hungry for whatever might tempt the senses, could only lead to some appalling error. In years he was, when Madame de Pompadour died, but little past fifty, but that blindness to exterior opinion and that carelessness for the future which properly belong to an age much more advanced, had already spread like a veil over his mind. After an interval of less than four years from the Pompadour's death, the nation and the capital and those leaders of opinion who awaited a mere negative decline full of petty rumours but controlled as to great affairs by that Choiseul whom the Pompadour herself had chosen for Minister, were presented with the Du Barry: the scandal and its effect were overwhelming.

This woman was a prostitute.

IV

THE DU BARRY

THE presence of the Du Barry at the Court of Versailles, the fact that this presence preceded the Austrian child's arrival, that it was first publicly admitted at the first public appearance of the Dauphiness, and that the four years of her tutelage were overshadowed by the new Royal Mistress was the initial and irretrievable disaster of Marie Antoinette's life. It moulded her view of the nation and of the family with whom she had now to mingle; it deeply affected the populace she was to attempt to rule; it cloistered, warped and distracted her vision of France at a moment in adolescence when vision is most acute and the judgment formed upon it most permanent. All the Queen's tragedy is furnished by the early spell of this insignificant and licentious woman.

With her advent was introduced for the first time into the Court that insolent and calculated disregard for rule in gesture and vocabulary in which the rich will often secretly relax their ordered lives, but which, when it appears publicly amidst their daily furniture, is as shocking as nakedness or as blood.

Judged in the pure light of human morals the position of the Du Barry was surely less offensive to God than that of any mistress any King has ever chosen. Louis wronged no one by this whim. He wrecked no remains of chastity — the woman had never known the meaning of the word.

He wronged no subject (as has and does almost every royal lover in every amour) — her marriage had been but a hurried form run through to satisfy etiquette, "that she might be presented at Court." He provided himself with a companion too inferior to make political intrigue her main ambition, and with one that could and did surround him with an abject but constant, familiar, and comfortable affection. It was such a vagary of old age as those in which have terminated countless lives, when old gentlemen of breeding but of enfeebled will surround their last years with youth and with the vigour, tainted vigour, that is inseparable from vulgarity. There is not one of us but has come upon a dozen such unions: they are often confirmed by a tardy marriage.

But in the case of Louis and this scandal of his a necessary element to such disgrace, the element of retirement, was lacking. Those symbols which, if they are insisted upon, are mere hypocrisies but which, taken normally, are the guardians of a tolerable life, were outraged. The eyes of the noblewomen at Versailles were full, some of a real or affected timidity, others of a real or affected dignity. Such ladies as chose to be sprightly or even to advertise their loose habit with over-brilliant and vivacious looks, retained, considered, and could always assume, refinement; but the beautiful eyes of the Du Barry were brazen. The *mignardises* which are always ill-suited to a woman might be deliberately affected by the less subtle of the more elderly beauties: with the Du Barry, despite her evident youth, they had already become native and ineradicable. She lisped alarmingly; she lolled, or, when it was necessary for her to sit erect, was awkward. Her entry into a room was conscious; her assertions loud, her amiability oiled, her animosities superficially violent. It is upon solemn occasions that such deficiencies are most glaring, and solemn occasions were of continual recurrence at Versailles. In a word, she was most desperately out of place, and therefore produced an effect as of dirt, jarring against whatever was palatine and splendid in the evil of the Court by her parade of the loose good-nature and the looser spites of the Parisian brothels.

Yet it is not difficult to see what had brought the King in to so fixed a relation with her. Whoever will compare any of the portraits of her by Drouais with any by Boucher of the Pompadour will see, not the same character indeed, but the same brows and forehead.

Louis could not continue in those early and familiar relations with her which had become a necessity to him, unless in some way her place were publicly acknowledged; but to force such a personality upon the Court, to give it precedence and to see that its position should be permanent, was an effort he had avoided for months. A scene was intolerable to him. He suffered from the most common defect attaching to men of lineage and wealth in that he feared, or rather could not endure, the prospect of violence. Orders even, and debate, if they were of a personal and verbal kind, he shrank from as do some men from loud noises. The more important and decisive of his actions were effected in short notes, every line of which, as we read them to-day, manifest his urgent need of isolation: of getting the business done without the friction of another presence, and once done, put aside for ever.

For the public presentation of the Du Barry the marriage of his grandson, and especially the presence of the little archduchess, offered a fatal opportunity. It would be impossible for the malicious to allude to the office of the Mistress in the presence of the child; the occasion would compel the princes and princesses of the blood to attend, and would equally forbid any general revolt. He determined to give the archduchess a formal banquet on the journey before the Court and its company had reached Versailles, to summon to it the chief members of the Court, and to let them find at table, without warning, the woman whose existence had hitherto not been spoken of in his presence.

The official limit of Paris upon the west — in those days — a line drawn far beyond the houses and enclosing many fields, gardens, and suburbs, ran from what is now the Trocadero to what is now the Arc de Triomphe. Outside the gate or barrier was an empty space of land but partially cultivated, and with no more than a scattered house or two upon it, save where, along the waterside and on the hill above it, clustered the village of Passy. This empty space merged gradually into what were then the wild and unfrequented Boulogne woods. Just on the edge of these, in a situation which was close to the town and yet upon one side accessible to the forest, stood a royal hunting-box called "La Muette," which had gradually developed into a little palace. Here, on the evening of the day after Compiègne, the long and splendid train of the Court arrived, bearing in the chief coach the King, the Dauphin, and this new Austrian girl for whom Louis had already shown so much respect and tenderness, and whose entry into her rank he was yet to distort.

The day had been long for the child, but her curiosity and the vitality of her years had forbidden her to feel fatigue.

Dense mobs of people, cheering and running by the side of the carriages, had indeed been familiar to her since her babyhood, but the vivacity and the shrillness and the surprising contrasts of this active civilisation, its solemn roads, its simple architecture, broken by an occasional and unexpected magnificence, the long lines of ordered trees which here seemed as native as in her own country they had seemed artificial and foreign; the half-hour's glimpse of an austere French convent which she had had when she visited at St. Denis (in passing); the King's daughter, veiled among the Carmelites; the outskirts of a gigantic city such as she had never known — all these sufficed to distract her until the fall of the cold spring evening, when the line of carriages clattered into the paved courtyard of La Muette.

As though such experiences were not sufficient to bewilder her with the new world, the girl found when she came to her room, attended by Madame de Noailles and the ladies of her suite, such a parade of diamonds upon her table as to-day one will see only in the vulgar surroundings of a public show.

The instinct for gems which was latent in her, but which the extreme simplicity of the Austrian Court had not permitted to arise, awoke at once. They were the diamonds of the woman who would have been her mother-in-law, had she lived, or rather who, had she lived, would never have permitted this marriage. They had reverted to the Crown upon her death, and Louis XV. had had them placed there upon Marie Antoinette's table in readiness for her appearance; he had so sent them partly from a sort of paternal kindness, partly from a desire typical in him to exceed even in giving pleasure; but also, perhaps, partly to atone for the harm he was about to do her. For when the child came down, some two hours later, and was led in the strict etiquette of the Court procession into the dining-hall of the little palace, she could not but notice throughout the meal that followed a constraint less natural than that regular constraint of the French court life which, in twenty-four hours of experience, had already struck her quick apprehension. It was not that men and women waited for the King to speak, but that their answers were given without vivacity, and with that curious mixture of restraint and purpose which she had already perhaps noticed, in her brief acquaintance with the French, to be the mark of their conversation in anger. She saw also that the old King looked straight before him with something of sullenness in his dignity, and she saw sitting next to him a woman whose presence there must have perpetually intrigued her imagination. That woman was the Du Barry.

To whatever adventures and novelties the children of gentlefolk are exposed, there is always one note of vulgarity which they can make nothing of, and which, while it offends them, disturbs and astonishes them much more than it offends. In the midst of that curiously silent, erect, and very splendid table, where forty of her sex and of her rank were present, the presence of this one woman was in its nervous effect like the intolerable reiteration of a mechanical sound interrupting a tragic strain of music. The Du Barry had not the art, so common to the poorest members of the nobility or of the middle class, when they would slip in among the wealthy, of remaining silent and of affecting a reverence for her new surroundings. She held herself with a loose ease before them all, was perhaps the only one to laugh, and permitted herself an authority that was the more effective because it hardly concealed her very great hesitation in this first public recognition of her place.

What the child Marie Antoinette made of such an apparition will never be known. Her first letters to her mother upon the matter come later, when she had fully understood the insult or at least the indignity which had been done her. The only record we possess of her emotion is this: that when just after supper some courtier was at the pains to ask her with infinite respect and a peculiar irony, what she had thought of Madame Du Barry, she said, "Charming," and nothing more.

Next day in the early morning the coaches took on again the last steps of the journey to Versailles. Twelve miles which were a repetition of those scenes, those crowds, and those cheers of which the little archduchess was now sufficiently weary, but which were leading up to that event towards which her childhood had been directed, and which could not but drive out of her mind the doubts of the evening before.

By ten o'clock the procession had passed the great gates of Versailles; three hours were spent in the long, distressing, and rigid ceremonies of the Court in whose centre she was now placed and whose magnificence now first enveloped her. It was one before the procession formed for the marriage ceremony, and had placed at the head of it the girl, and the boy whom, in this long trial of two days, she had but little regarded.

She came under the high vault of the new, gilded chapel as full of life as the music that greeted her entry. On her left the boy, to whom so much publicity was a torture, went awkwardly and with the nervous sadness of his eyes intensified; his gold braid and his diamonds heightened his ill-ease. He managed to give her the ring and the coins proper to the ceremony, to kneel and stand when he was told; but she went royally, playing, as girl-children so easily play, at womanhood, and smiling upon all around.

The contrast was gravely apparent when they passed together down the aisle with the Quête, and when they sat — he effaced, she triumphant — during the little sermon which the Grand Almoner was bound to deliver. The Heir was not relieved till the Mass was over and the book was brought wherein the signatures of the witnesses and principals to a marriage are inscribed.

It is natural to the extreme of privilege that it should affect occasional and absurd simplicities. The last generation of Versailles was eager for such things, and it had become the custom that a royal marriage should be registered not in any grand and parchment manner, but in the common book of a parish church, the church to whose parish the palace was nominally attached. Father Allart, the rector of this, in whose hard and unimportant life such days were set, came in to give the book. The Grand Almoner set it before them and they signed — the King first, with his large and practised name; the Dauphin next in a writing that was thin, accurate and null. He passed the pen to this little new wife of his who was to sign third. At so practical a test her womanhood dropped off her, her exceedingly ignorant childhood returned. She got through the "Marie" with no mistake of spelling, but the letters were a trifle uncertain and the word askew. Why had not someone ruled a line as lines are ruled in copy-books? "Antoinette," the second word, was larger and gave more trouble; the last letters fell away deplorably, and when it came to the third name, "Josepha," it was too much for her altogether. She did her best with the "J"—it ended in a huge blot, and she became so flurried that she spelt her last name anyhow, without the "e," and let it go to pieces. She was relieved to give the pen to Provence, who, though he was yet so young, wrote his name strongly like a man. Artois, Mesdames, the Orleans followed. Each as they signed could see at the head of the page that deplorable and dirty scrawl which the child, whose advent each of them feared, had left as a record of her fifteenth year.

The Court left the chapel. As they passed into the outer galleries of the palace before the enormous and increasing crowd which thronged the stairways and the landing-floors, the air seemed much darker than when they had passed in an hour before. Through the great windows the sky could be seen lowering for a storm. As she entered the private apartments to receive homage the darkness increased; the ceremony was not over before a first loud clap of thunder startled them; the rain fell with violence upon the populace that had crowded the gardens, the fireworks set out for that evening were drenched, the fine dresses of the Paris shop-women were spoiled; all the grandeur in front of the palace was lost in umbrellas. It cleared, and they crushed in, with their muddy boots well scraped, to file in thousands, a long procession urged on by the Guards, and passing, behind a barrier, down the immense hall, where the tables were set for cards. The King and his Court played solemnly like actors who must pretend to see no audience, sitting thus as a public symbol of the nation.

The crowd passed thus, company after company, staring at Monarchy and at the dresses and the gems till the West grew dark, and the myriads of candles reflected on a wall that was all mirrors, lent that evening its true colours. When the last reluctant sight-seer had looked his last over his shoulder, and had felt the tapestry drop behind him, the ceremony ceased, the tables were cleared, the King rose and conducted the bride to her room. A full ceremonial of etiquette was wearily and thoroughly performed, the Grand Almoner (once again) blessed the children's bed, and that was the end of the marriage.

Outside, the crowd went back through the May night to their lodgings or to Paris, full of feasting, damp, surrounded by the fresh air that follows rain. They carried with them a confused memory of a great outing — music, grandeur, diamonds, innumerable lights, no fireworks, and a storm.

V

THE DAUPHINE

WEDNESDAY, 16TH OF MAY, 1770, TO TUESDAY, 10TH OF MAY, 1774

WHEN the mock-marriage was over and the night passed, and when, with the Thursday morning, the long routine that was to be her life opened upon her, the child could watch with less excitement and with less illusion the nature of that new world. Her vivacity was not diminished, but her spirit immediately adopted a permanent attitude of astonished observation towards emotions and conventions whose general scheme she could not grasp at all. Daily the incidents which passed before her while they violently moved, also repelled her senses; she was reconciled to them only by their repetition.

Versailles was the more bewildering to her because, in all its externals, it was the world she had known from her birth. The French cooking, architecture, dress, and social manner had for a century imposed themselves upon the palaces of Europe; but the French mind, now first in contact with her own, remained to her a marvellous and unpleasing revelation, which, even after years of regarding its energy, still shocked her.

There was a ball that night. She danced with her bright-eyed and tall young brother-in-law; at what he was sneering she could not understand, nor even if the boy's expression was a sneer: she knew that it was strange. She did not notice the absence of half the Court; she did not know that her mother's request for Precedence to be given to the Princesses of Lorraine had raised this silent French storm; had she been told she would not have comprehended. The extreme and individual French jealousies, the furious discussions that underlie the united formality of French etiquette, were alien and inhuman to her German breeding; for active and living, almost Southern, as was this Viennese girl, she enjoyed to the end the good simplicity of her mother's race. She danced with young Chartres. If something in him chilled her, she could not divine what it was in that character which even then seemed closed, and which later was to make him vote her husband's death, and sit at wine in his palace while she sat a prisoner and widowed in her prison at hand.

For days the feasts continued and for days her unexpected experiences of persons and of a strange nationality were relieved by pageants and popular clamours which, at her age, could distract her from weary questions. It was at one of these that there sounded once more that note of disaster which came at rhythmic intervals across her life and continued to come until a climax closed it. She had leave to go with her aunts, the King's daughters, by night with a small escort to see the public holiday in Paris which celebrated her marriage. She was to go without ceremony, not to be recognized, merely to satisfy a child's curiosity for a spectacle in her own honour. As the coach came up the river road towards what is now the Trocadero hill she could already see far off the flash of the rockets, and she heard with increasing pleasure the roar of a great crowd met to do her honour. As she neared the great square which is called to-day the Place de la Concorde she was disappointed, as children are, to see that the coach was late; the great scaffolding and final set-piece in which her initials were interlaced with those of the Dauphin was sputtering out in the inglorious end of fireworks — but something more intimate to her (had she known herself) and worse than her childish disappointment had marked the moment of her arrival. The coach was stopped abruptly, the guards closed round it, and it was turned back at once towards Versailles. As it rumbled through the darkness more quickly than it had come, she seemed to hear in the distant clamour both fierceness and terror. It was a sound of panic. She heard the news whispered respectfully and fearfully to her aunts during a halt upon the way. Perhaps they thought her too young to be told. She complained as she went that the truth was concealed from her, and when they reached the palace late that night she was crying. Next day the news was public, and she learned that after this first rejoicing in what was to be her capital city, there had been crushed and maimed and killed many hundreds of her people; it proved one of those misfortunes which, as much from their circumstance as from their magnitude, remain fixed for years in the memory of a nation, and the day on which she learned it was the last of the month of her wedding.

During the summer that followed this presage she learnt the whole lesson of Versailles. She was still a child. Mercy still wrote of her to her mother in a tone which, for all its conventional respect, was a tone now of irritation against, now of amused admiration for, a child. She had her daily childish lessons with the Abbé Vermond and daily exasperated him by her distractions. She still wrote painfully her childish letters to Maria Theresa, took her little childish donkey-rides, and was strongly impressed, as a child would be, by those of her elders who alone could show some authority over her—Mesdames, her husband's aunts. She was growing fast; and there is nothing more touching in the minute record of her life than the notes of her increasing stature during this year, so oddly does the nursery detail contrast with the splendour of her place in Europe and the titles of her rôle.

She was still a child, but as her fifteenth birthday approached and was passed she had learnt (while it wearied her) the full etiquette of her part, and she had begun, though imperfectly, to recognise what were the politics of a Court and in what manner intrigue would approach her; how to avoid or master it she discovered neither then nor at any later time throughout her adolescence and maturity.

With the advent of winter and its long and brilliant festivals, another thing which she had begun to comprehend in the Palace became for her a fixed object of hatred; the position and influence of the Du Barry.

She knew now what this official place was which the Favourite held. Her disgust for such regulation and pomp in such an office would in any case have been strong, for Marie Antoinette came from a Court where the sovereign was herself a woman and where all this side of men's lives was left to the suburbs; that disgust would in any case have been sharp, for she was too young and too utterly inexperienced to be indulgent: it would in any case have been increased by a sense of isolation, for all around this German child were the French gentry taking for granted that everything touching a King of France, from his vices to his foibles, must be dressed up in a national and symbolic magnificence. Her disgust would, I say, in any case have risen against so much complexity allied to so much strength, but that disgust turned into an active and violent repulsion when she saw the Du Barry not only, as it were, official but also exercising power. This to her very young and passionate instinct, whether of sex, of rank or of policy, was intolerable; it was the more intolerable in that the Du Barry's first exercise of power happened to go counter to interests which the Dauphine regarded rather too emphatically as those of Austria and of her family.

The chief Minister of the Crown, the Duc de Choiseul, kindly, sceptical, well bred and rather hollow, had been, if not the mere creation or discovery, at any rate the ally of Madame de Pompadour. Madame de Pompadour had been a statesman herself: Choiseul had perpetually supported her and she him, more especially when he ran in the rut of the time, showed himself conventionally anti-Christian, and (having been educated by the Jesuits) was drawn into the intrigue by which that order was suppressed. He had been Ambassador at Vienna, though that in a year when Marie Antoinette was a baby, so that she had no early memories of his snub-nose and happy, round face; but she had known his name all her life from the talk of the palace in Vienna, and she had known it under the title which he had assumed just after her birth. The Duc de Choiseul was for her, as for every foreigner, a name now permanently associated with French policy and a Minister who was identical with Versailles. Maria Theresa was grateful to him for having permitted the marriage of her daughter: that daughter after some months of the French Court very probably imagined that he had not only permitted but helped to design the alliance. It was against this man that the Du Barry stumbled.

It would not be just to accuse the young woman Du Barry

of design. The State was a very vague thing to her. She held good fellowship with many, owed her advancement to Choiseul's enemies, and was, in general, the creature of the clique opposed to him, while for D'Aiguillon, who already posed as the rival of the elder man, she felt perhaps a personal affection. She was very vain and full of that domestic ambition which comes in floods upon women of her sort when they attain a position of some regularity. She loved to feel herself possessed of what she had learned in the old days to call (in the jargon of her lovers) "office," "power"; to feel that she could "make" people. As for the pleasure of an applauded judgment, or the satisfaction of that appetite for choice which inspires women of Madame de Pompadour's sort in history, Du Barry would not have understood the existence of such an emotion. The most inept and the most base received the advantage of her patronage, not because she believed them capable of administration, but simply because they had shown least scruple in receiving her, or later, amid the general coldness of the Court, had been the first to pay her an exaggerated respect. As for those with whom she could recall familiarities in the past, she was willing to make the fortunes of them all.

Though such an attitude could easily have been played upon by the courtiers of her set, it could never have supplied a motive force for her demands nor have nourished the tenacity with which she pressed them; that force and that tenacity were supplied to her by her own acute sensitiveness upon her new position. The angry pique to which all her kind can be moved in the day of their highly imperfect success was aflame at every incident which recalled to her the truth of her origin and the incongruity of her situation: in her convulsive desire to revenge against every slight, real or imagined, she found an ally in the old King, her lover. He also knew that he was in a posture of humiliation, and under his calm and tired bearing he suffered a continual irritation from that knowledge. As he pottered about his frying-pans, cooking some late dish to his liking, or went alone and almost furtively down the hidden stair between her little, low, luxurious rooms and his own rooms of state, his silent mind was even less at ease than in the days, now so long past, when an utter weariness with the things of the flesh and a despair of discovering other emotions had first put into his eyes the tragedy that still shines from them upon the walls of Versailles.

All, therefore, that the Du Barry did, through Louis XV. as her power increased was not for this or that person whom she feared or loved; it was rather against this or that person whose presence she found intolerable. All that she suggested, so far as persons were concerned, the King was ready to achieve.

Had some married woman of force and subtlety formed the centre of opposition to the favourite, the reign would have ended easily. Mary of Saxony, the Dauphin's mother, had been such a woman and would, had she lived, have conducted affairs to a decent close. Fate put in the place of such a woman first, three old maids — the King's daughters — and next this little girl, the Dauphine.

The origins were slight, but in its course the quarrel gathered impetus. At first came that silent great supper-party at La Muette and the instinctive repulsion which the child felt and which this woman from the streets as instinctively resented. Next, in the summer, one of the Dauphine's women had a sharp quarrel with the favourite in the stalls of the Court theatre. The favourite had her exiled from

Court, and the Dauphine, crying secretly with anger in her rooms, could obtain no redress. During the summer absences of the Court in the country palaces a perpetual travel and larger room to move prevented an open battle; in the following winter that very grave event, the exile of Choiseul, sealed the difference.

It was the error of Choiseul not that he had opposed the favourite's entry — on the contrary, he had thought it a useful whim that would amuse and occupy his sovereign — but that he could not take her seriously. His "world," his relatives, his intimates, those whom he had placed and salaried during twelve years of power, were outspoken in their contempt for the Du Barry. Her own simple spite lumped all together and made the Minister the cause of her difficulties and their victim. For months she had half amused, half frightened Louis by an increasing insolence to De Choiseul at cards and at table. He had met this insolence at first with the ironic courtesy that he must have shown in his life to a hundred such women; later by a careful and veiled defence; last of all by a resigned and somewhat dignified expectation of what he saw would be the end.

When a society approaches some convulsion the pace of change increases enormously with every step towards the catastrophe. "*This* at least no one dreams of. *That* at least cannot happen!" But this and that do happen, and at last all feel themselves to be impotent spectators of a process so forcible and swift that no wisdom can arrest it. Political literature in such moments turns to mere criticism and speculation; it no longer pleads, still less directs. So it is to-day with more than one society of Western Europe; so it was with the close of Louis XV.'s reign.

In May, 1770, when the Austrian Alliance was con

summated by the arrival of Marie Antoinette, and by the wedding at Versailles, the revocation of the one conspicuous statesman in France would have seemed impossible. He had no more capacity than have the most of politicians, but he did at least reach that rough standard demanded in that trade, and his name was rooted in the mind of his own public and of Europe. If the dismissal of Choiseul had been proposed in the summer, there still remained enough active force opposed to this new Du Barry woman to have prevented the folly; but at the rate things were going every month weakened that force; by the end of the year it was too late to act in his defence.

On Christmas Eve fat Hilliers came lurching out of the Favourite's room and brought Choiseul a note in Louis' hand. It was a short note exiling him to his place at Chauteloup and relieving him of office.

There was no one to replace the Minister: the action was that of a common woman who exercised a private vengeance and who could conceive no reasons of State. Yet no one was astonished — save perhaps the child to whom so vast a change was the climax of all that had bewildered her since she had first spoken to the French Court.

Maria Theresa and Mercy, her ambassador to Versailles, had that knowledge of the world which permitted each to find footing, even in such a welter. Each from a long experience knew well that the depth of political life moves slowly for all the violent changes of machinery or of names. Each felt the Alliance — the object of all their solitude — to be still standing in spite of Choiseul's fall; and each divined that their little Princess, who was the pledge of that alliance at the French Court, and whom they destined, when she was Queen, to be its perpetuator, might at this moment weaken and ruin it: her probable indiscretion and her simplicity were the points of danger. Her plain spoken anger might ruin their plans for a recovery of Austrian influence. Each, therefore, concentrated upon a special effort — Mercy, by repeated visits from the Austrian Embassy in Paris to the court at Versailles and by repeated admonitions; Maria Theresa (in whom the fear for her daughter's future and position was even greater than her solicitude for the Austrian policy) by repeated letters, too insistent perhaps and too personal wholly to effect their object.

Marie Antoinette was persuaded to a certain restraint, but she was neither convinced nor instructed. She saw the whole situation as a girl would see it, in black and white: Madame du Barry was of the gutter, and had yet been able to destroy a name which she had always heard associated with the fortunes of her own family and the dignity of the French Crown. The complexity of the situation, the short years it was likely to last, the necessity during those years of weighing the intricate and changing attachments of the great families in their interlacing groups — all this escaped her.

So little did she see the intricate pattern of politics that, when Louis XV., less than two months later, exiled the higher courts of law and all but roused a rebellion, she did not connect with the reign of her enemy this act of violence which isolated and imperilled the Crown; she thought it royal, immediate, and just, still seeing mere kingship as children see it in a fairy tale, beneficent and paternal.

The six months of administrative anarchy that followed meant nothing to her. When, in July, D'Aiguillon — inept, a mere servitor of the Favourite's — was at last appointed to the vacant post of Prime Minister, this act — in its way more astounding than the dismissal of Choiseul — was only remarkable to her because it was the Du Barry's doing. And during the whole of her sixteenth year she represented at Court a fixed indignation which, in her alone, steadily increased as the powers of the Favourite became absolute; for as Marie Antoinette approached womanhood she developed a quality of resistance which was the one element of strength of her early character, but from which was fatally absent any power to design. That obstinate power of resistance was to raise around her multiplying and enduring enmities; it was to mature her in her first severe trials, but it was also to bring her to the tragedy which has lent her name enduring and exaggerated nobility.

This opposition which the Dauphine offered to Madame du Barry, an opposition which did but rise as that woman (during 1771) opened, one after the other, all the avenues of power to her lowest or least capable courtiers, took on no form of violence.

Marie Antoinette, as the pale auburn of her hair and her thick eyebrows darkened, as her frame strengthened and her voice took on a fuller tone, added to the vivacity of her childhood a new note of passionate emphasis which was ill-suited to her part, and which in any circumstances but those of luxury would have approached vulgarity. In many minor matters she forebore to put the least restraint upon a momentary annoyance; she would have some design she disapproved destroyed; a bookcase, though it was Gabriel's, she had broken before her eyes, to appease her discontent. But in the major matter of this quarrel she put on a sort of solemnity, and her resistance took the simple but unconquerable form of silence. She would not recognise the Favourite, though she were to meet her five times a day, and she would not address one word to her.

That silence, which kept open at Court a sharp wound and which stood a permanent and a most powerful menace to all that had power at Versailles, became for Mesdames, the King's daughters (who had first given this example), and for all the defeated parties a welcome symbol—though for the Princess herself it was a most perilous one. To break that silence was the effort of every converging force about her. Her mother in repeated warnings; Mercy, the King, and most of all the Favourite herself, came to think it a first point of policy that what might have been pardoned in the child should not remain a cause of acute offence in the woman. She was now nearly eighteen months at Versailles; she had entered her seventeenth year. But whenever the Du Barry crossed her in the receptions or met her eyes at table, whatever beginnings of a salute may have escaped the loose manner of the Favourite, she suffered the mortification of a complete refusal. The feminine comedy was admirably played, and for the Dauphine the King's mistress remained a picture or an empty chair — sometimes to be blankly gazed at — never to be recognised or addressed.

There was indeed a moment in August when the Dauphine's resolution wavered. Mercy had visited the Du Barry; he had spoken to her intimately and with gallantry. He had probably promised her the graces of the Dauphine; he returned to Marie Antoinette to press his advice. So pressed she promised her mother's ambassador that she would speak, but when the moment came and the meeting had been carefully arranged, after cards at evening, she remembered too much: she remembered perhaps most keenly a recent thing, the choice of one of this woman's friends, in spite of her protests, for one of her ladies in waiting. She strolled to the table where Mercy and the

Favourite were talking together. As she came up Madame du Barry put on an air of expectation which invited her approach. The girl hesitated and turned back. A scene not consonant to that society was avoided only by Madame Adelaide, who had the presence of mind to summon her niece at the critical moment of the insult; but the fiasco led to further and more peremptory orders from her mother, to a long and troubled interview between Mercy and the King, and at last to the conclusion at which they all desired. The Dauphine recognised the Du Barry; but the recognition came in a manner so characteristic of Marie Antoinette that it would have been better for her and for them if they had not won their battle.

Upon the New Year's Day of 1772 at Versailles, on which day it was agreed (and this time most solemnly vowed) that a greeting should be given, and during the formal reception held at Court that day, there came a moment when in an uneasy silence, the moving crowd of the Court saw the Dauphine approach the Favourite, pass before her, and say as she passed — not so directly nor so loudly as might be wished, but still so that the Du Barry might have taken the words as addressed to herself: "*There are very many people at Versailles to-day.*" Before a reply could be given her she had passed on. Next day she said to Mercy: "I shall not let that woman hear the sound of my voice again."

The moment of time during which this quarrel reached its height was one of extreme anxiety to Maria Theresa, and indeed to all. It was that during which the first public renunciation of the international morality which had hitherto ruled in Christendom was in negotiation at the instance of Prussia. It was secretly proposed that an European government should be disregarded without treaty and subjected to mere force without the sanction of our general civilisation. Frederick had suggested to Russia long before with deference, recently to Catholic Austria with a sneer, the partition of Poland.

It is characteristic of the more deplorable forms of insurgence against civilised morals that they originate either in a race permanently alien to (though present in) the unity of the Roman Empire, or in those barbaric provinces which were admitted to the European scheme after the fall of Rome, and which for the most part enjoyed but a brief and precarious vision of the Faith between their tardy conversion and the schism of the sixteenth century. Prussia was of this latter kind, and with Prussia, Frederick. To-day his successors and their advisers, when they attempt to justify the man, are compelled still to ignore the European tradition of honour. But this crime of his, the partition of Poland, the germ of all that international distrust which has ended in the intolerable armed strain of our time, has another character attached to it: a character which attaches invariably to ill-doing when that ill-doing is also uncivilised. It was a folly. The same folly attached to it as has attached to every revolt against the historic conscience of Europe: such blindnesses can only destroy; they possess no permanent creative spirit, and the partition of Poland has remained a peculiar and increasing curse to its promoters in Prussia; to their mere accomplices in St. Petersburg it has caused and is causing less weakness and peril; while it has left but a slight inheritance of suffering to the Hapsburgs, whose chief was at the moment of the crimes but a most reluctant party to it.

There is not in Christian history, though it abounds in

coincidence or design, a more striking example of sin suitably rewarded than the menace which is presented to the Hohenzollerns to-day by the Polish race. Not even their hereditary disease, which has reached its climax in the present generation, has proved so sure a chastisement to the lineage of Frederick as have proved the descendants of those whose country he destroyed. An economic accident has scattered them throughout the dominions of the Prussian dynasty; they are a source everywhere of increasing danger and ill-will. They grow largely in representative power. They compel the government to abominable barbarities which are already arousing the mind of Europe. They will in the near future prove the ruin of that family to which was originally due the partition of Poland.

Enormous as was the event, however, both in its quality of evil and in its consequences to mankind, it must not detain the reader of these pages. Its interest here lies only in the first and principal example which it affords of Marie Antoinette's direct and therefore unpolitical temper. She was indeed only upon the verge of womanhood — she had but completed her sixteenth year, but her failure to understand the critical, and, above all, the complex necessities of the Hapsburgs at that moment was characteristic of all the further miscalculations that were to mark her continual interference with diplomacy for twenty years. It was imperative that Austria should find support in the grave issue to which Maria Theresa had been compelled against her conscience and her reason. Berlin and St. Petersburg suddenly having agreed to a material aggrandisement, help was imperative, and help could only come from her ally at Versailles. Upon this one occasion, if upon no other, the young daughter of the Empress was justified in working for her family, and that could only be done through the woman whose influence was now the one avenue of approach to Louis XV. A recognition of the Du Barry was essential to Vienna in that new year of 1772. The Dauphine made it, but she made it in such a way that it was a worse insult even than had been her former silence. Had war broken out that spring, at the melting of the snow, it is possible or probable that Versailles would not have supported Vienna against Prussia and Russia in arms.

There was almost a quarrel between the growing girl and the Empress, her mother. To that mother she still remained the child who had left Vienna two years before; but then, in Versailles and to those who saw her, this year made her a woman.

That she had passed the boundary of adolescence was apparent in many ways. She was more and more enfranchised from the influence of elder women — notably of her husband's aunts, her intimacy with whom faded throughout 1772 and disappeared in 1773. Her step had acquired that firm and rather conscious poise which was to distinguish her throughout her life. The growth of her stature was now accomplished, and she was tall, and though her shoulders had not the grace and amplitude which they later assumed, her figure had, in general, achieved maturity. Her hair, now a trifle darker and browner in its red, her eyebrows, always pronounced but now thicker and more prominent, announced the same change. Her motives also, though insufficient in judgment, were deeper in origin. Her resistance to her mother's and to Mercy's most pressing insistence in the matter of the Favourite was a resistance no longer even partially suggested to her by others; it was due now to a full comprehension of the old King's degradation, and to a formed abhorrence of the Du Barry. Moreover, when she yielded for a moment — as she did perhaps three times in the course of two years — it was with some measure of thought: she consented to approach the King's mistress at moments when the ambassador or her mother had convinced her by speech or letter of an acute necessity; but already, in her excuses when she refused, she began to use the argument of a woman, not of a child — she pleaded "the authority of her husband": it was a phrase in which she, least of all, put faith.

With this advent of womanhood there came, of necessity to a character so ardent, fixed enmities. She was no longer despised as a child; she was hated as an adult. Mesdames, the King's daughters, whose influence over her had disappeared, joined, in their disappointment, the over-large group of her detractors. The fatal name of "Autrichienne," the foreign label that clung to her at the scaffold, originated in the drawing-rooms of the three old maids, and all around her, as her power to order or to fascinate increased, there increased also new hatreds which attained to permanence, because her German memories, her eager action, her crude and single aspect of the multitudinous and subtle French character, her rapid turning from this pleasure to that, her ignorance of books and of things, lent her no power to wear those courtiers down or to play a skilful game against them.

Forgetfulness was easy to her. To help her to forget she had the intoxication of that moment which comes once in life and in the powerful blossoming of our humanity. Her eighteenth year, the last year before she ascended the throne, was the great moment of her youth.

She had not been beautiful as a child, she was not destined

to real beauty in her womanhood; but at this moment, with the spring of 1773 and on to that of 1774, there radiated from her the irresistible appeal of youth.

Paris, which had learnt to despise and half to hate the Crown, which had felt itself widowed and abandoned by the emigration of the Bourbons to Versailles, caught her charm for a day. When she made with the Dauphin her first official entry into the city, great crowds acclaimed her perpetually; she had that emotion, so dear to women that it will drive them on to the stage itself, of a public applause directed toward their persons: the general applause of Paris was almost an applause of lovers. For just these passing hours on a sweet day in early June she saw and loved the city wherein her doom was written upon every stone, and for these hours the Tuilleries which she inhabited were faëry and so full of delight that she could not tell whether the air was magical or owed its fragrance only to the early flowers.

In such a mood, daily drinking in happiness and a certain sense of power, admired almost openly by distant men and — very likely — by Artois, her young brother-in-law, who had known her all these years, she passed the high tide of the summer and autumn, and found in the ensuing winter for the first time that lively and absorbing interest in social pleasure which very largely determined her life.

Of the balls in which she danced, of the masked balls that were her special delight, one stands out in history — and stood out in her own memories, even to her last hour, a night unlike all others.

. . . .

The reader has divined that the marriage of May 1770 had been no marriage. It was contracted between children;

and years must pass — years which were those of the school-room for both of them — before Maria Theresa could expect an heir with Hapsburg blood for the French throne. But the years passed; the child was now a woman, and still the marriage remained a form.

From an accident to which I will return in its proper place, the Dauphin and herself were not wife and husband; and to this grave historical fact must largely be attributed the disasters that were to follow. For the moment, however, this misfortune did little but accentuate her isolation and perhaps her pride. In her childish advent to the Court it could mean nothing to her. Lately she had understood a little more clearly; but she was pure; her training was in admirable conformity to her faith. She was not yet troubled — until the opening of that last year, '74, with its gaiety and pride. This season of vigour, radiance and youth lacked the emotion which has been so wisely and so justly fitted by God to that one moment through which we make our entry into a full life. She was married to the heir of France: her virtue and her pride forbade her to be loved. Yet she was also not married to that heir, and her life now lacked, and continued to lack, not only love but the ardent regard that was her due.

No Frenchman could have turned her gaze. Between her temperament and that of her husband's nation the gulf was far too deep. But one night, late, as she moved, masked in her domino, through the crowd of a Paris ballroom, she saw among so many faces whose surface only was revealed to her another face of another kind, a boy's. It arrested her. The simple and sincere expression which Versailles had never shown her, the quiet manliness which, in Northerners, is so often allied to courage and which stands in such contrast to the active virility of Gaul — all that which, in the secret places of her German heart, unknown to herself, she thought proper to a man, all that whose lack (though she could not analyze it) had disturbed and wounded her in the French palace, was apparent in the face before her. She asked his name and heard that it was Fersen. He was a Swede, the son of a considerable political noble, sent here on his travels with a tutor. She went up and spoke to him.

She could look into his eyes and see their chivalry. His low, handsome forehead, his dark brows, his refined, firm lips, his large and gentle eyes, completed in detail the profound impression with which that first glance had struck her. Once she had begun to speak to him, so masked, she continued to speak continually. A boy of eighteen is far younger than a girl of his age — they were born within six weeks of each other, and he was a child compared with her; he desired her, she consenting, and he became hers in that moment. When they had separated and he reached his rooms at morning there was ready in his heart what later he wrote down, that the Dauphine was delightful, and that she was the most charming princess he ever had known. She upon her side had followed him with her eyes to the door of the great assembly. She was not to see him again for four years, but during all those years she remembered him.

. . . .

This was the way in which Marie Antoinette entered life, and almost simultaneously with that entry came her ascent of the throne: the old King was changing.

He suffered. His digestion failed; from time to time

he would abandon his hunting. It was in the January of 1774 that the Dauphine had met Axel de Fersen. Before the spring of that year Louis XV.'s increasing infirmities were to reach their end.

Gusts of strong faith swept over him in these failing years, as strong winds filled with a memory of autumn, will sweep the dead reeds of December. His fear of death, and that hunger for the Sacraments which accompanies the fear, came to him in dreadful moments. For thirty-eight years he had neither communicated nor confessed. All his life he had avoided the terrace of St. Germain's, because a little lump far off against the eastern sky was St. Denis, the mausoleum of the kings, and he had not dared to look on it. But, with no such memorial before him, death now appeared and reappeared.

Once in his little private room — it was late at night and November — he played at cards with the Du Barry. They were alone, save for an old crony of his pleasures, Chauvelin, which well-bred and aged fellow stood behind the woman's chair, leaning upon it and watching the woman's cards in silence, his rapacious features strongly marked in the mellow light of the candles. Something impelled the woman to glance up at him over her shoulder. "Oh, Lord! M. de Chauvelin, what a face!" It was the face of a dead man. She leapt and started from it, and the body fell to the floor.

The King, his age and apathy all shaken from him, shouted down the empty corridors: "A priest! a priest!" They came, and in the presence of the King absolved what lay immovable upon the shining floor, in a hope or wish that some life lingered there. But Chauvelin was quite dead.

Now, in his last Easter, the dread came back for ever and inhabited the King. Upon the Maundy Thursday of '74 (it was the last day of March) the Court were all at Mass, and the sermon was ending. The priest, strong in that tradition of Bossuet which had not perished, turned to the royal chair and related for his peroration the legend of an ancient curse: "Forty days, and Nineveh shall be no more." All the Court heard it and forgot it before the chanting of the creed was done — but the King was troubled. He reckoned in his mind; he counted dates and was troubled.

The liturgical times went by; he abandoned his mistress; he lived apart and gloomy: but his Easter duties were not accomplished, nor did he communicate or confess, nor was he absolved. Then the cloud lifted and he began to forget, and the tie which held him to the Du Barry and which had in it now something of maturity and routine, was very strong upon him. He yielded and returned to her where she waited for him down the park at the little Trianon. His domesticity returned — but not for long.

It was upon Tuesday the twenty-sixth of April that he came in from hunting changed. He would not eat. He wondered a little and was cherished by his companion, but his fever grew. Next day he woke to suffering. He attempted to hunt, but his knees were weakened and he could not ride his horse; and coming back to Trianon, he groaned with his head in torment. His dread increased; but his doctors, who had been long familiar with his moody interludes, thought little of the thing. They carried him back through the trees to the palace, to his own room in the Northern wing, and that day and the next, as the fever grew, rumours went louder and louder in the palace. On the Friday, at eventide, as a candle chanced near the face of the sick man, the doctor looked closer; and in the next hour, before midnight, the Princess Clothilde, talking in Madame de Marin's room in whispers to the Duke of Crois, opened a note from the Dauphine. She cried aloud: "They say it is the small-pox!"

They dared not tell him. He had the assurance to demand the truth, and when he heard it he said: "At my age a man does not recover." He maintained from that moment, through the increasing torment and disfigurement of his disease, a complete mastery over himself and even to some extent the power of ordering the Court. He saw to it that his grandson, the Dauphin, should not come near his room, for of all the royal families in Europe the French Bourbons alone had not been vaccinated. He accepted the services of his daughters.

One thing alone he hesitated on, and that was to relinquish the society of his Favourite.

He was too proud and too silent a man for his contemporaries or for ourselves to know the full cause of his hesitation. Passion at that moment it could not have been. The possibility of his survival he had himself denied, and his every phrase and act showed how clearly he felt the approach of death. He himself had drawn the secret of his malady from the reluctant Cardinal whose duty it was, as Grand Almoner, first to inform him of his danger, but whose worldly fear of consequence had kept him from speaking — though he was urged to his duty by every prelate at Court. The King was in no doubt as to the nature of the soul, nor as to the scandal which, under the special conditions of his throne, his one great frailty had given. He knew the Church; he could not, as might a philosopher, take refuge in the memory of good deeds to outweigh the evil, or (as might a monarch of a different civilisation) in the deep hypocrisies which there shield birth and wealth from self-knowledge. His Christian faith was strong and clean. Yet he hesitated. If he still clung to the Du Barry, it was perhaps, because nothing was left him in the visible world but the gaiety and the assiduous care which had endeared this woman to him.

She kept near him throughout the first hours of his malady, and every evening, when the princesses had left their father's room, she would come in by a private further door and sit beside the little camp bed on which he lay. She overcame all repugnance; she soothed his pustuled forehead with her hand. He felt, perhaps, as though to abandon her was a first breaking with life.

The aged Archbishop of Paris, himself suffering grievously from the stone, bore, not without groaning, the jolting journey to Versailles; he came to undertake himself what the Grand Almoner dared not do — to demand the dismissal of the Favourite. He was not allowed into the King's room. The group of courtiers continually present in the outer chamber, the Œil de Bœuf, could watch with much amusement the gestures of command and of refusal that passed between the Archbishop and the Duke of Richelieu in the antechamber beyond. At last he was admitted, but it was arranged that others should be present, and nothing passed between him and the King save a word of condolence from each for the other's suffering.

It was by no stimulation from without but by his own act that the King took the last step in his penance. Upon Tuesday the third of May, towards midnight, Madame du Barry being with him, as was her custom, to tend him through the night, he said to her, in those brief sentences of his which had for years forbidden discussion or reply, that he must prepare for his end and that she must leave him; he told her that a refuge was prepared, and that she should want for nothing. She stumbled half fainting from the room to the Minister whose career she had made, the Duke of Aiguillon, believing with justice that he was not ungrateful, and in his rooms she cried and lamented through what remained of darkness.

With the morning the King gave D'Aiguillon his orders, and that afternoon the Duke, worthily loyal although his career was ended, sent his own wife to take her in a hired carriage, without circumstance and therefore without disgrace, to their country house some miles away. It was the thirty-fourth of the forty days.

That evening the King asked Laborde, his valet, for Madame du Barry. The servant answered that she was gone. "Already?" he sighed, and her name was not heard again.

Thursday and Friday passed: the first with a rally which the more foolish hoped would save the life of the King; the second with the disappointment of all that corrupt and intriguing clique which depended upon his recovery.

Meanwhile the Dauphine kept her rooms. She knew what desperate court would be pressed upon her husband and herself were the doors to be opened; nor did the Dauphin give a single order of the hundred that were already solicited of him, save that all should be ready for the whole Court to leave for Choisy. Early upon the morning of Saturday this seclusion was broken: long before the common hour of the palace, at half-past five, a roll of drums awakened its people, and the princess came down with all her ladies to see the Sacrament carried through Versailles.

Between a double row of the guard, under the great canopy that was reserved for such solemnities, the priests carried the Viaticum, and about It in a long procession as It passed, were the torches and the candles. She stood with her sister-in-law at the head of the crowd in the great hall outside the bedroom door; she endured the stench of corruption that filled the air, though every window was open to the morning; she caught, by her tall stature and straight carriage, the scene that was acting within.

Between the purple robes and the surplices, in the ring of waxen lights, she saw the old man, whom alone she had respected and indeed loved in her new home, attempt to raise himself, calling: "*My great God has come to me. . . . My great God!*" She saw him with what strength he had plucking the cotton cap from his head and failing in his effort to kneel. His face was no longer the face she had known, but crusted dark and hideous, swollen, horrible. She heard the Grand Almoner repeat the King's strong phrase of repentance, passionately solemn, and she knew the voice so well that perhaps she also heard the mumble in which he urged its repetition. Then the doors closed; the Court dispersed. She regained her apartments and the isolation and the strain returned. They told her of his increasing delirium, of the crowds that came from Paris daily, of the certain approach of death. So Sunday and Monday went by — the thirty-eighth, the thirty-ninth day.

The dawn of Tuesday broke upon a clear sky. It was the fortieth day.

The spring on that fine morning turned to summer, and before noon the park was full of a crowd which moved as though on holiday. The Parisians had come increasingly

LOUIS XVI.

The principal bust at Versailles

since Sunday into Versailles. The inns were full and at all the tables outside the eating-houses of the town the people eat their midday meal with merriment in the open air. Between the Park and the town, huge and isolated, already old, the palace alone was silent. There, each group shut close in its own rooms, awaited the one dismissal, another the fruit of long intrigue, another, in a mixture of eagerness and dread, the new weight of royalty. It was the tenth of May, and still the agony endured. A candle burnt in a window above the courtyard. Passing groups looked up at it furtively; grooms, with bridles ready in their hands, glanced at it from beneath the distant doors of the guard-room and saw it twice renewed, as one o'clock and two struck through the afternoon from the chimes of St. Louis. Three struck. They looked again and it was still shining.

Within, his head supported by Laborde the valet, his mind still clear, the old King still attempted with his distorted lips the answers to the prayers for the dying. He heard them faintly and more faintly in that increasing darkness which each of us must face. When the priest at last came to those loud words, "Go forth, thou Christian soul," his murmuring ceased. The candle at the window was extinguished. The clatter of horse-hoofs rose from the marble court and the jangling of stirrups against mounting spurs. The Duke of Bouillon came to the door of the room, stood before the silent crowd in the Œil de Bœuf, and said with ritual solemnity: "*Gentlemen, the King is dead!*"

At that same hour on that same day, a British man-of-war sailed into Boston harbour. She bore orders to impose the tax on tea which ultimately raised America.

VI

THE THREE YEARS

TUESDAY, THE 10TH OF MAY, 1774, TO EASTER SUNDAY, APRIL 19, 1778

FROM the death of Louis XV. to the close of the summer of 1777 is a period of somewhat over three years. In those three years the fates of the French monarchy and of the Queen were decided. For though no great catastrophe marked them nor even any considerable fruit of policy, and though an onlooker would have said no more than that something a little disappointing had, in the process of these years, chilled the first enthusiasm for the new reign, yet we can to-day discover within their limits most of those origins from which the ruin of the future was to come.

For the Queen especially, whom hitherto her minority, her seclusion and the deliberate silence of her childhood had guarded, the opportunities for action which her husband's accession suddenly offered were opportunities of fate, and the three years with which this chapter has to deal were for her young and exalted innocence of eighteen like that short week of spring when seeds are sown in a garden: they were a brief season of warmth, of vigour, and of clarity during which circumstance sowed for her in every variety the seeds of misfortune and of death. All is there: the advent of an uneasy gaiety; the solace of gems, of cards, of excessive friendships; the vivid but wholly personal, erratic and capricious intervention in matters of State; the simple confidence in the policy of her mother's Austrian government and the continual support of it; the enmities which all active natures provoke, but which hers had a talent for confirming; the friction of such an activity against the hard and, to her, the alien qualities of the French mind — all these, which the princess could try to ignore when her husband was but heir and she in her retirement, appear with the first months of her liberty as Queen, strike root, and are seen above ground before she has completed her twenty-second year. And with these positive irritants their negative reactions also come: the Court assumes its divisions; the stories and the songs and the nicknames begin against her; the popular legend concerning her is conceived; the trend of the Orleans faction in antagonism to her is established, and a new generation contemporary with, or but slightly senior to, her own has become fixed within the same three years in a direction which — though none then saw it — could not but destroy her in the progress of years.

To understand in what way the common accidents of that brief three years' term moved to their great effects it is necessary to know two things: first, the physical infirmity under which Louis XV. suffered, and, secondly, the nature of the Bourbon Crown he wore; for it is the conjunction of such an infirmity with such an office that lends to the first years of his reign and to the first errors of his wife their capital importance in the history of that one woman and of the world.

. . . .

Louis, it had first been whispered, and was now upon his accession commonly asserted, could have no heir.

When first the mere form of marriage between him in

his boyhood and Marie Antoinette (a child) had been solemnised, no public and no familiar regard was paid to the relations between them. The great ceremony was necessarily esteemed a solemn and irrevocable betrothal rather than a wedlock, and (as I have already said) it was taken for granted that in some two or three years the process of nature would continue the royal line.

But as the princess advanced to her sixteenth, to her seventeenth year; as her upstanding and vigorous youth achieved first a full growth, then ripeness, then maturity, and yet provoked no issue, the common explanation of such an accident could not but be generally given and the impotence of the Dauphin was universally accepted. At eighteen, in the last autumn of the old King's reign, the young wife had stood apparent and triumphant, clothed with a charm which, if it was not that of beauty, was certainly that of exuberant life; a whole ball-room had been arrested at her entrance; the crowds of Paris had quickened at her approach; the lively look, the deep brows, and the full hair, tender and vaguely red, which Fersen had seen suddenly revealed, were those of a woman informed with an accumulated and expectant vitality. It was not in her that the defect could lie. Louis, so it plainly seemed, was deficient and was in title only her husband.

A conjunction of this kind is not uncommon even in an active, healthy, and laborious lineage of the middle rank; among the wealthy it is frequent, in the genealogy of families which carry a public function, such as those of monarchs or of an oligarchy, for all the careful choice which their marriages involve, it is often present. Such accidents are provided for. In many cases probably, in some certainly, a suppositious child is introduced; when that course is difficult or repugnant the situation is acknowledged, the consort chooses between her devotions and a lover; all the planning and all the necessary preparation which attach to the succession regard the brother or cousin, who is henceforward accepted as the heir, and *his* position is the more highly established from the contrast his vigour may afford to the paucity of the reigning incumbent.

I say such a conjunction is of a known type in history; there were precedents for action and a certain course to be pursued. Monsieur, the King's brother, would have attracted the service and respect to which his then vigorous intellect was fitted. The Queen's vagaries would have been contemptuously excused, for she would have stood apart from the line of succession, and her character would have been indifferent to her husband's subjects. The Crown as an institution would have suffered little, though its immediate holder would have lost personal prestige, had the conjecture of Louis' impotence, which was, upon the King's accession, common to the Court and the populace, been confirmed.

Now that conjecture was, as the future showed, erroneous. A very careful, sceptical, and universal observer might have discovered, even as early as this year of Louis' accession that it was erroneous.

In the first place the gestures, habits, and character of the King were not such as should be associated with this kind of imbecility. His body was indeed unhealthy and diseased; it was the body of a nervous, overgrown, loose-limbered child, inherited from a nervous father and from an exhausted race; a body which nature would have removed as it removed his son's, had not the doctors built up upon its doomed frame an artificial bulk of flesh. I say he was diseased, but not in the manner then believed. The febrile attachment to violence, the lack of humour, the weary eye, which betray an insufficiency of sex and which we so frequently suffer in political life and at the university, were quite absent in Louis. Contrariwise he was good-humoured and kindly (saving to cats), very fond of hard riding and capable in that exercise; he was further of an even though astonishingly slow judgment and possessed that desire to *make* (to file, saw, fit, design, ply a trade of hand and eye) which is an invariable accompaniment of virility. He loved and practised mechanical arts, such as the locksmith's or the watchmaker's. There was nothing in him of what is nowadays called (by a French euphemism) "The Intellectual."

Were positive evidence lacking such general contrasts between what he was supposed to be and what he was would still have great weight; but evidence more exact can be discovered. The letters written by Marie Antoinette to her mother afford it.

Maria Theresa was in an increasing torment, as each passing month excited her bewilderment, lest her daughter should furnish no heir to the French throne and the object at once of her strong motherly affection and of her political scheme should fail. Her questions were frequent, urgent and clear: her daughter replied to them in terms which a very little reading will suffice to illumine. Marie Antoinette was young and, as I have said, essentially pure; she did not fully comprehend the nature of a situation which was undermining her serenity and gravely marring her entry into life, but she was able both to express her dissatisfaction and yet to assure the Empress upon more than one occasion that she had at last a reasonable hope of maternity. These hopes were in each case disappointed. That such hopes, on the one hand, certainly existed, and that the whole atmosphere of her married life was, upon the other, false and almost intolerable, depended upon the fact that Louis suffered from a partial — and only a partial — mechanical impediment. This impediment a painful operation would suffice to remove; but the knowledge that it was but partial, the divergent advice of doctors and the lethargy which invariably deferred his decisions, all impelled the young man towards procrastination, with the result that in a few months — the brief period immediately and before his accession — his wife had learned that fever of the mind which accompanies alternations of nervous incertitude; she had weighing upon her a perpetual and acute anxiety which was the more corroding in that it contained so considerable an element of physical ill-ease.

The detail is highly intimate and would merit no place in any biography but this. It must be fixed, and has been fixed here, first because to neglect it is to ignore the misfortune from which (if from one origin) flowed the destruction certainly of the Queen, and very probably of the French Monarchy itself — a matter of moment to every European; secondly, because history has never yet given it its true place nor fully set forth its nature and importance.

In such a situation Marie Antoinette's quick nature took refuge in every stimulant; wine she disliked — it was among her few but marked eccentricities that throughout her life she would taste nothing but water — but gaming, jewels, doubtful books, many and new voices about her, violent contrasts, caprice upon caprice, unexpected visits, sudden passions for this or that new friend, excessive laughter (and excessive pique), emotions seized wherever they could be found — watching in merry vigils for summer dawns, masked balls that took up all the winter nights, escapades: in a word, a swirl of the fantastic and the new became for her a necessity that — had it taken some one form — would have been called a vice. Her dissipation was driven, as vice is driven, with a spur; it was compatible, as vice is compatible with her original virtues; it produced, as vice produces, a progressive interior ill-ease. She was a tortured woman in those years.

Children became a craving to her.

One day as she went, with the lady who was supposed to control the etiquette of her life, as she went sadly in her coach along the western road, she turned off it along a by-lane for her pleasure, and reached that village of St. Michel which lies upon the slope of the hill above Bougival. As she passed through the village in her grandeur and took the Louveciennes road, she saw a peasant child and, by a sudden but most intense and profound impulse, caught it up and said she would make it hers. It was a little tiny boy, still a baby, toddling upon the road; it had been christened James; the name of its parents was Amand. The freak was good news for them; they blessed her, and she went away. And the child was to be adopted and brought up at her expense, and she was to watch it in Versailles.

Very many years later his name came up again, obscure, but fixed, in the roll-call of a battle, and we shall read it once more, stamped across the strange sequence of her life.

. . . .

If anyone desires to see, in a very modern and tawdry mirror, what evil had possessed the mind of this well-born lady, let him watch (from some distance) a certain financial world in London and that cosmopolitan gang in Paris to which that world is allied by blood and in whose support — whenever it is endangered — they are to be found, for in Paris and London they are one. With far more refinement and with infinitely greater variety, she (like those modern money-dealers) sought in a rush of fantastic and novel experience to assuage a thirst. *They* have no plea save the coarseness of their lineage. *She* had for excuse the gnawing of a position which none about her comprehended and which she herself, though her body resented it, saw but dimly with her young mind, and which disturbed her as a confused, intolerable thing.

From within, therefore, she is amply to be excused; but consider the effect of her fever upon those who saw her. Consider the effect of this new manner of hers upon the public function of the French Monarchy.

The French have, with their own hands, destroyed the conception of "a king": in Europe to-day we look around and find nothing of monarchy remaining. A few impoverished symbols, a few indebted, a few insufficiently salaried men, of whose true character the public knows nothing, afford or do not afford unifying titles for a bureaucracy there, an oligarchy here: in Italy a national name, in Spain a moribund tradition. But that monarchy which the Gaulish energy had drawn out of the stuff of old Rome was another matter; it was a sacramental alliance between an *idea* and a *thing*.

The *Idea* was that of the Gallic formula "without authority there is no life" — for authority is authorship: this Gallic formula also sustains the faith.

The *Thing* was one lineage of actual living men: devoted

from father to son — sacrificed almost as in a public sacrifice — condemned to the perpetual burden of being mixed into this Idea and of supporting the burden of its intensity and power.

There had descended from the Merovingian and the Carolingian families to the Capetian, bearing a power that increased with every century, the conception of a creative executive made flesh; an executive that should reside in the living matter of a family of men who should be seen, known, touched, loved or hated; who should rapidly pronounce new and necessary laws, actively preserve the yet more necessary body of ancient and fundamental custom, observe in public the religion of the community, and, above all, lead in battle. That was the rôle; that was the mould. the bond of heredity forced many an incongruity into that mould (a child sometimes and sometimes a madman), yet — so short is one human life in the general story of a nation — the gap thus formed was rapidly filled by a successor, and the permament impression remained of a soldier incarnating a community of soldiers.

This institution had now endured for much more than a thousand years. This Gallic institution had impressed itself (here, as in Germany, by imitation; there, as in Britain, by direct importation) upon all the civilisation of the West. It had grown old, as must all human institutions that have no direct sustenance from forces outside time; but even so it maintained a mysterious vitality. Its kings were anointed. It held a sort of compact with the Divine, and in this its old age was still alive with a salutary if a grotesque publicity.

The King and Queen of France were the least protected of any in the realm from insult, satire, and gibe; even where their own law protected them a general conspiracy, as it were, the instinct of all society, defended the pamphleteer.

The King and Queen were publicly owned: all they had was public money; all they did they did before a crowd. Every week they dined at a table in a vast hall. Their nobles stood by but did not eat — before them a thousand or (according to the weather) ten thousand of the populace defiled curiously and unceasingly. They prayed in public. They were expected to receive in public the applause or the condemnation of all. They were public for the destruction of secret things, conspiracies, masonries, Templars, trusts, rings. They were publicly approached by any at random and publicly claimed as the public redressers of wrong — always in theory and often in actual fact. Nay, their physical acts were public. They dressed and undressed before an audience — or rather *were* dressed and undressed by these. The birth of every royal child was witnessed by a mob crowding the Queen's chamber.

The vast inconvenience of such a part was but one aspect of its sanctity, and the Crown united, as in the heart of a mystery, the functions of Victim and of Lord.

Amid the great new wealth of the eighteenth century, and in the glare of its brilliant new intelligence, it may be imagined with what a fence of tradition and precedent public opinion and its own nature insisted on defending this national centre. The anecdotes of that rigid, minute, and often inhuman etiquette are too well known to need repetition here. Two instances may suffice.

The Queen could drink nothing by night or by day but from the hand of the highest in rank of the women present, nor could this last accept the glass and the water save from the hand of a page. The King must not eat at all until he had performed an ablution like a priest: the vessels of this and the napkin were sacred; rather than put them to a profane use, when they had once done their service they were destroyed by fire.

Such extravagances in the old age of an institution lend themselves to ridicule as do (for instance) the fantastic ceremonies of our House of Commons or the comic-opera costumes of our court officials and of peers. But though, isolated, they present this weakness, collectively, and seen in relation to the function they serve, such survivals have a meaning, and a consideration of such ceremonial helps men to a comprehension of the institution it surrounds.

Conceive, then — for it is the note of all this chapter — the impact of such a mood as that of the distracted Queen upon such a Court, stiff with such traditions and living under such a bright beam of publicity, the mark of a million eyes all keen to discern whatever trifle was done between midday and dawn! Marie Antoinette chafed impatiently against this central national institution. The fever now upon her caused her always to despise and sometimes to neglect the rules that were of the essence of her position. The moral and internal constraint which tortured her inflamed her to "live her life"; but for those of great wealth and opportunity such a mood is and must be dissipation; dissipation in its fullest sense: the dispersion not only of character and of self-discipline, but of responsibility, of externals even, and at last of power. It meant, and necessarily meant, the patronage of those far below her and their consequent estrangement; the contempt of those immediately beneath her and their consequent enmity.

Just after the old King's death the Court was at La Muette. She must needs, to prove her liberty, go up and talk familiarly to an old gardener like any Lady Bountiful. The old gardener's annoyance is not recorded; that of her ladies is. They complained to the King, who was troubled, but who, knowing the truth, answered, "Let her be."

That same day, when a deputation of the Burgesses' wives paid her their court, coming from the city at her gate and full of ceremony, she could do nothing more dignified than giggle at their awkwardness and at their dress. In the intervals of, according to each, a pompous greeting, she must whisper to one or other of her ladies most unpompously; the very servants were rendered uneasy by her manner.

In how many ways and how rapidly this mood (this physical, fatal, necessary mood) was to wear down her position immediately after her accession to the throne many examples will show. The best and the most general aspect from which one may first regard it is her attempted immixture in public affairs, for that also was a fretful and personal thing, part of her mood.

. . . .

The first six or seven months of the new reign cover the period which was officially that of mourning for Louis XV. and are for the general historian of this importance: that in them was fixed the new ministerial tradition which culminated in the summoning of the States-General.

This new tradition owed nothing to the Queen. She was hardly aware of its presence. For her the choice of new Ministers was a personal and almost a domestic business in which she somehow had a right (and could find it entertaining) to play a part — she knew not what or how. That part of hers turned out, as a fact, a small part and indecisive, utterly without plan; but such as it was it marks her necessity for action and change, and exhibits her place beside the King. In the intervals of choosing a new hairdresser and a new dressmaker, she paused now half an hour, now an hour, in the cabinet, hearing names which she hardly knew, and giving random advice which must have strained her audience to the very limits of toleration.

It was not mere Austrian action. Her brother the Emperor would often beg her not to meddle; the Austrian ambassador, Mercy, deplored her innocence of affairs and her inability to follow any one interest for one hour. Her mother wrote affectionately and worriedly, giving her the stale old advice of supporting Vienna — but fearing her capacity to do so. Meanwhile, the Queen herself acted from the simple motive of being seen about, and added to this the equally simple motives of private tastes. Thus she would have restored Choiseul to some office. He came up a month after the accession, and she greeted him very kindly. He had helped to make her Queen, he was the traditional ally of Vienna, and though Vienna certainly did not want him now, Marie Antoinette went by the name and its associations alone: she judged as a child would judge. The King, who had no intention of accepting Choiseul, made a little awkward conversation with him, the opening of which turned pleasantly upon the old man's baldness, and next day Choiseul went back home, "to see to the tedding of his hay."

Again, the choice of Maurepas for chief Minister, four weeks before, was not — as has been represented — hers.

The King chose his father's old friend rather for permanent adviser and companion than as a first Minister — which title indeed he never received, and that Maurepas entered at all was the work not even of the King himself, but of his aunt, Mme. Adelaide. In the confusion of the first two days when Sartines, Choiseul, Machault were all possible as prime ministers and all discussed, Madame Adelaide repeatedly suggested Maurepas' name. To her and her sisters he was a tradition, part of a time which these old maids looked back to with regret as the last time of dignity, before mistresses had destroyed their father's Court and half exiled them to their apartments.

Maurepas was seventy-three; he had left office between forty and fifty, and had done so from a quarrel with the Pompadour. This alone recommended him to Louis XV.'s daughter; that he should have been untouched by the vile interregnum of the Du Barry recommended him still more. Madame Adelaide had known him in power when, as a girl of seventeen, the eldest of the sisters, she was certain of life, in tune with her great position, and pleased with all she saw. Now after twenty-five years, which had been increasingly marred by a distant and bitter isolation from the Court, his name recurred to her as that of a fellow-sufferer and a memory of her youth. Madame Adelaide's devoted service in her father's last illness (she had caught the small-pox herself in attending him) gravely increased the weight of her advice. It was through her that Louis XVI. received the old man, and, once received, he remained. True, MarieAntoinette had carried the message to the King from his aunt, but she had done no more than this.

If it is asked why, with so little influence, the Queen's perpetual interference was none the less permitted, and why this girl of eighteen, vivacious as she was ignorant, might ceaselessly bustle in and out of the council chamber, the answer is not that she was Queen — for no Queen had yet acted thus at Versailles, nor would any woman conscious of power have done so — but first that her whole self was now restless beyond bearing, and next that the King was ashamed to withstand her whom, afflicted as he was, he could hardly propose to command or regulate. With every fresh opening of the council door she made an enemy, with none a friend; but Louis all the while could only answer, "Let her be."

In one thing only during these months had she a clear object, and that was not a policy: she was determined to be rid of the Du Barry's name. That woman was far away, exiled to Burgundy from the moment of the accession, to return afterwards to Louveciennes, but some of her clique remained, hated by all the populace and half the Court as much as by the Queen. With so much support Marie Antoinette succeeded. Three weeks after the death of Louis XV., D'Aiguillon was relieved of the department of Foreign Affairs: the grant of public money which he received on his resignation — it was but £20,000 — would seem to us in modern England pitifully small, for we take it for granted that public officials should have a share in the public funds. But it is significant of the time and of the French temper that the grant was vigorously opposed and was obtained only on the personal demand of old Maurepas, who (by one of those coincidences so frequent in aristocracies) happened to be the uncle of this his chief political opponent.

Here was Marie Antoinette's one success. The Austrian Court and Embassy had desired to keep D'Aiguillon — he could be played upon. Marie Antoinette had rejected their advice, she had gone, day after day, to the King, until he had consented to deprive D'Aiguillon of his post — and immediately her deficiency was apparent. To deprive D'Aiguillon was, in politics, not necessary, and, if accomplished, not final. To find someone for the Foreign Office who should at once be able and yet work contentedly under old Maurepas was of both immediate and of weighty importance. She refused to interest herself in the matter!

Luckily for France, Vergennes, then the representative of Louis at the Court of Stockholm, was chosen by the good judgment of the King, in spite of an impossible oriental wife.

Vergennes, approaching his sixtieth year, tenacious, silent, industrious, highly experienced, and microscopic, as it were, in the detail of diplomacy, was just such an one as the French needed to conserve the forces of their nation, to balance the smaller states against the rivals of Versailles and to choose the very moment for the attack on England which, later, was to establish the United States. It is probable that, but for him, in the embarrassment of French finance and the consequent weakness of French arms, the nation would have fallen into some German conflict or have been abused before some German contention. As it was, the French owe in great part to Vergennes that peaceful accumulation of energy which permitted the revolution to triumph.

In the nomination of this considerable diplomatic force the Queen had no part at all.

She had no part in the nomination of Turgot.

It is difficult to write the name of "Turgot" without admitting a digression, though such a digression adapts itself but ill to any account of the Queen.

Turgot is the name that dominates the first two years of the reign for every historian. The time has hardly come to criticise him. Criticism of his faults is easy; a full appreciation is difficult, so near are we still to his time, and so exactly did he represent the spirit which was at that moment germinating in every intellect, so active was he in its expression. The over-simple economies, the plain egalitarian political theory, the positive scepticism (the Faith was then at its lowest throughout the world), the glorious self-possession, the rectitude, yes, and the interior glow of the "Philosophers," all the Genius of the Republic was incarnate in this man. When upon that singular date (it was the 14th of July) he entered the Ministry, there entered with him the figure, winged for victory yet austere, whose mission it was to create the great and perilous Europe we now know. I mean the Republic. Already Napoleon was born.

Marie Antoinette had no knowledge of this spirit. It had not approached her. She knew vaguely that it was indifferent to her religion (to which the very young woman was already sensibly though slightly attached). She knew much more clearly from current talk that it (and Turgot) stood at that moment especially for *Retrenchment;* and that word *Retrenchment* she approved, for she had no conception of the sensations that might ensue upon it to her own life if from a word it should become a policy. And Turgot himself had spared her sensibilities by doubling her pin-money.

I say she had no part in the nominating of Turgot — in his fall she was to have too great a part.

By the end of August the new Ministry and its policy were complete. All the Du Barry gang and all the memories of Louis XV.'s end were gone — burnt and hanged in effigy by the populace as well. In their place sat a council whose actual head and principal figure was the young King, slow, large, assiduous, freckled, pale, in a perpetual obese anxiety, ardently seeking an issue to the entanglement of his realm; whose senior was the chiselled old Maurepas, intensely national, witty, experienced in men, but neither instructed nor of a recent practice in affairs; whose foreign affairs were dealt with by the methodical gravity of Vergennes; whose navy was in the honest hands of Sartines, and whose finance — the pivot of every policy, but in France of '74 life and death — lay under the complete control of Turgot.

I have said that finance had become for the French in 1774 a matter of life and death; and the point is of such capital importance to the Queen's story that I must beg the reader to consider it here, at the outset of her reign.

What was the economic entanglement of the French Crown at this moment? The reply to that question is not part of Marie Antoinette's character and conduct, but it so persistently and gravely affected her life and it is so dominating a feature of revolutionary history that a clear conception of it must be entertained before any general understanding of the period can be achieved. Not that the financial difficulty was a main cause of the Revolution — to assert as much would be to fall into the puerile inversion which makes of history an economic phenomenon — but that the financial difficulty was a limiting condition which perpetually checked and perverted the thought of the time whenever that thought attempted to express itself in action.

The clearest background against which to appreciate the

finance of old monarchical France is that of the England which was its triumphant rival.

The United Kingdom had at that time less than half the population of France. The territory of England was in much the same proportion — at least, her arable and industrial territory. Her white colonial population was larger then, in proportion to her home population, than it is now, but she had not then the full wealth of India to tax nor the vast revenues now drawn, both in usury and in true profit[1] — from Australasia, Southern America, and Africa. In other words, the prosperity of England at that time was domestic and real; it contained no parasitic or perilous element which a war could interrupt and a defeat destroy. This England bore with ease a national debt of over 130 million pounds. She was about to engage in a struggle which would nearly double that debt, and yet to feel no weakness. She raised a revenue of ten to eleven millions, which in a few years rose without effort to fifteen — then at the end of it all she was free to triple her debt during the great European war against Napoleon, and yet triumphantly to increase, and, when the war was over, to survive, the only nation with a credit, and at once the bank and the workshop of Europe.

France, so much larger in area and population and inheriting so superior a tradition of magnitude, had all but failed. With citizens double the English in number, and with an arable soil in proportion, the French Crown could only with the utmost difficulty attract to the exchequer a sum of barely twelve — at the most and counting every expedient, thirteen — million pounds from the national

[1] I mean by usury interest levied upon unproductive loans; I mean by true profit the share of produce legitimately claimed by the lender of funds which have been put to productive use.

income. Briefly, England could support with ease a larger debt than could this neighbouring nation, twice her size; England could spend with prodigality as much as that nation was compelled to spend with parsimony; and England could raise without effort a revenue already equal, soon to be superior, to that which the rival government could but barely extract from its subjects.

Nor does this comparison exhaust the contrast between financial health and disease upon either side of the Channel. England thus prosperous was increasingly at ease; France thus exhausted was increasingly embarrassed. Deficit followed deficit; that expenditure should exceed revenue had become a normal annual incident publicly discounted, nay, a sort of fixed ratio appeared between what *should* be and what *was* the income of the government, and the expenditure exceeded revenue with a solemn regularity much in the proportion of 44 to 37. In the American War, which either nation was approaching, England, defeated, was to incur 170 million of debts, and yet to emerge, a few years after the defeat, financially stronger than ever in the Wars of the Revolution. France, victorious, was to incur but a third of that liability, and yet in the Revolution France was compelled to declare herself insolvent.

Why did so startling a contrast appear? To us to-day it is almost inconceivable. The French are now somewhat less in population than the English, they pretend to no serious empire beyond the Mediterranean, yet they raise for national purposes a larger revenue, and they raise it with far greater facility; they support a debt double our own, without troubling the least gullible and most thrifty investing public in Europe. Considerable additions to their total liability hardly affect their credit, while England's falls by a quarter of its index upon the issues of a hundred and fifty millions. The value of their agricultural land rises rapidly, as does that of their urban; they find public money for enterprises which we scout or neglect. Their universities, though dependent on public funds, abound; their national church, deprived of official assistance, flourishes on but a fraction of their surplus wealth; their historical buildings are kept up in magnificence upon public funds. It is difficult, I say, for an Englishman to try to appreciate the overwhelming economic advantage which, under George III., England enjoyed over the Bourbons, who were her rivals; because in the course of a century, and especially of the present generation, the tables have been turned. It is England now that is in doubt as to her financial position and her fiscal methods. It is in England that money is lacking for necessary social reforms. It is English credit which fluctuates with violence, and English direct taxation which is strained to breaking point.

In the time of which I write all these perils and disadvantages attached to France and to France alone. The France which England faced in the great struggle was a France labouring in anxiety for money, and the cause of that increasing pressure is apparent to History: the *method* of public economics had failed in France then as perhaps it is now failing here in England.

Men inherit, and of necessity every generation is shut in with custom. Who would in England to-day dream of taxing the mass of Englishmen — or rather, of taxing them directly and to their own knowledge? The very idea is laughable! There may be coming into a coal-miner's cottage in Durham twice the income of a clerk, but who would dare send in an assessment or talk of a shilling in the pound? The clerk must pay; the miner go free — for such is the tradition of the Six. Who would rate the houses of the wealthiest class as the houses of the middle class are rated? It would seem madness. So, but in a more acute fashion, did the financial system of France suffer at the end of the eighteenth century. Its data, its conventions were those of an older state of society long departed. It pre-supposed the manor, and the manor was dead; it pre-supposed the self-contained countryside at a moment when the various provinces of the whole State had long been intimately bound together by commerce and when strong international links of exchange had already begun to arise. The evil was a fiscal system out of touch with the realities of the time. The remedy was a violent and rapid remodelling of that system. All could perceive the evil, many the remedy; but custom and the collective force of private avarice in the individual minds, checked, and checked sharply, with the blind control of a natural force, all reform that attempted to act and to do. The attempt at reform was baulked, as a natural force baulks human purpose, by a million atomic actions. The million separate interests refused it.

For such an attempt, for such audacity, Turgot with his austere, convinced, and isolated mind, was better suited than any other man; yet even he in a very few months had refused to level the hard-grained social knots which blunted every tool of the reformer who would level the inequalities of the State. Within two years his attempt had failed and he had resigned — but while the resistance of the tax-payer counted for much in his resignation, the increasing ill-balance of his young Queen counted for more.

During the first part of his administration of finance

her ill-balance was not so marked as to give promise of what was to come. No folly, no conspicuous extravagance marred the first weeks of her reign — her inchoate and girlish interruptions into the Council were of ill-omen; but as the new Court settled down into its stride, accumulated its first traditions and began to take on a character of its own, her aspect in the public eye was daily fixed with greater clearness, and the impression so conveyed to a nation already in rapid transition was a further element of irritation and confusion.

For the permanently present threat of poverty and embarrassment, which with every year corroded more and more deeply the public service and rendered less and less stable the general equilibrium of the State, lent to the habits the Queen was about to form, and still more to the public exaggeration of those habits, a gravity they could never otherwise have assumed. It was part of her lot that she could not, from the very nature of her position, understand the relationship between her petty extravagances and the popular ill-ease.

She was right. Her extravagance, such as it was, came slowly — nay, though showing excess in her character, it was never really excessive in amount; the sums we mention when we speak of it are trifling when we compare them with the financial debauchery of our own age. Why, that whole annual increase in her allowance which Turgot has been blamed for making would not have paid for one night's riot in the house of some one of our London Jews, nor even when her expenses did exceed the limit she should have set upon them; even when, as month followed month, the love of jewellery and the distraction of cards involved her in private debt, the sums so wasted in a whole year were not what some of our moderns have scattered in a few days. Her total debts after two years were less than £20,000! Moreover, careless and wasteful as the girl was for those well-ordered times, her excesses never bore an appreciable proportion to the scale of the public embarrassment. Her difficulties were never so great but that the sale of a farm or two could meet them. Had the Bourbon Crown enjoyed a private as well as public revenue, her lack of economy and of order would perhaps never have been heard of.

But it is the characteristic of any morbid condition that the slightest irritant produces an effect vastly beyond its due consequence. The financial embarrassment from which the Kingdom suffered may or may not have been relievable by the plain and harsh methods of Turgot — it is a question to which I will return — but even if they were so relievable, their immediate application could not but be an aggravation of popular suffering; and just in the years when increasing economic difficulty and sharp economic remedies for it were catching the public between two millstones of poverty below and retrenchment above, the populace had presented to them, upon a pinnacle whence she could be observed on every side, a young woman who in some sense summed up the State, and yet who, in mere externals at least, showed a growing disregard for method and a pursuit of every emotion that might distract her from what the French thought her duty, but what she knew to be the tragedy of her marriage.

The mourning of the Court forbade display until the autumn of 1774, and though with the autumn and the winter there was some relaxation of ancient rules and some revolt already observable upon Marie Antoinette's part yet there against the fixed and inherited rules of her station was nothing which had yet seized the popular imagination nor even gravely affected her position within the narrow circle of her equals. It was not until the next year, 1775, that the error and the misfortune began.

It had long been intended that her brother, the Emperor Joseph, should visit France, and by his more active character persuade Louis XVI. to an operation which he perpetually postponed. The repeated adjournment of this visit (which was to resolve so many doubts) was among the fatal elements of the Queen's early life. In the place of that sovereign, the youngest child of the Hapsburgs, Maximilian, little more than a boy, fat, and what would have been called in a lower rank of society deficient, waddled into the astonished court at La Muette in the opening of February.

The accident of his arrival did neither the Queen nor the Court any great hurt among the crowds of the capital. His startling ignorance and heavy lack of breeding amused the crowd; they were glad to repeat the amusing anecdotes of his awkwardness as later, in their Republican armies, they were glad to caricature his obesity when he had achieved the ecclesiastical dignity of a princely archbishopric. But among her intimate equals the visit was disastrous. The Princes of the Blood insisted upon receiving his call before they paid their court to him, since he was travelling incognito. It was a point (to them) of grave moment. The Queen rubbed it in with spirit. She would not let him pay such a call. She told them that her brother "had other sights to see in Paris and could put off seeing the Princes of the Blood." The King stood by during the quarrel, irresolute, upon the whole supporting his wife. The King's brothers for the moment supported her also;

but the kernel of the affair lay in her disregard of inherited tradition, in her contempt for those fine shades of mutual influence and deference which to the French are all-important indications of authority, but which to her were meaningless extravagances of parade. Chartres, during the progress of what he thought an insult, she a piece of common sense, deliberately left the Court, publicly showed himself in Paris, and was applauded for his spirit.

This wilfulness, this picked quarrel, sprang from the same root as, and was similar to, whatever other fevers disturbed her entry into her twentieth year.

The Queen conceived a violent affection for the Princesse de Lamballe, a young woman of the Blood, but Piedmontese, the widow of a debauchee — a simpering, faithful, stupid, sentimental and most unfortunate young woman, often gushing in her joy, next in grief wringing her enormous hands. It was an attachment almost hysterical and subject to extreme fluctuations. The Queen conceived a second attachment, with the opening of this year 1775 for another woman, as good-natured indeed, but more solid and more capable of intrigue, than Madame de Lamballe, the Comtesse de Polignac. In the empty society of the one, in the full and babbling coterie of the other, Marie Antoinette expended the greater part of her energy. Finding to hand, as it were, the De Guémenées (and Madame de Guémenée constitutionally fixed as "Governess to the children of France" — children that did not exist), she plunged also into the Guémenée set, and there she discovered, for the first time in her young life, a powerful drug for the stimulation of whatever in adventurous youth has been wounded by disappointment and youth's hot despair — gambling. The gambling took root quickly in this girl who hated wine and had desired so much of life. It was large in '75; in '76 it was to be ruinous to her watched and doled allowance.

Meanwhile the tailors and the milliners and all the ruck of parasites were taking advantage of the new reign to play extravagant experiments in fashion, to build fantastic head-dresses, and to load humanity with comic feathers. She did not create such novelties, but she was willing to follow them.

The young bloods, in one of those recurrent fits of Anglomania to which the wealthy among the French are subject, must introduce horse-racing. She passionately approved. It gave her gambling the familiarity or lack of restraint which she was determined to breathe for the solution of her ills; it gave her the feeling of crowds about her, of pulse and of the flesh.

Young Artois, the youngest of the King's brothers, because he was the most vivacious of those nearest her, must be her constant companion. Mercy noted his "shocking familiarity"; he feared that scandals would arise. They did.

Again, as the new reign advanced, her unpolitical and most unwise concern for personalities showed more vividly than ever. Because the ambassador in London was in her set she must take up his cause with a sort of fury, when he was accused of abusing his position for the purpose of commerce. He was acquitted, but, much more than the trial or any of its incidents, the open and passionate attitude of the Queen struck the society of the time. So in the very moment of the coronation she again openly received Choiseul, though she knew that he could never return to Court, that her mother and all Austria disapproved.

Much worse than all of these, the constant jar upon her nerves broke down a certain decent reticence, the barrier of silence which should, always in a woman of her age, and doubly in a woman of her position, be absolutely immovable. She publicly ridiculed the painful infirmity of the King. Her sneers at his incapacity were repeated; they crept into malicious, unprinted songs; she permitted herself similar confidences, or rather publicities, in her correspondence; she wrote them with her own hand, and there is little doubt that others besides those to whom they were addressed saw that writing. He, poor man, went on painfully with his duty, hour by hour in his councils, considering the realm, distantly fond of her, but necessarily feeling in her presence that mixture of timidity, generosity, and shame, the secret of which was no longer private to his wife and him, but, through her lack of elementary discipline, spreading grotesquely abroad in exaggerated and false rumour to the world.

So much had been accomplished by her own character and destiny when a full year had passed after the old King's death. She had made the Crown a subject of jest, her character suspect, her husband, that is, the foundation of her own title, ridiculous, when the date had arrived in the summer of '75 for the solemn coronation of Louis at Rheims.

Mercy, with an inspiration sharper than that which diplomats commonly enjoy, had suggested her coronation side by side with that of the King. Such a ceremony might have retrieved much. Precedent was against it, but after so very long an interval precedent was weak; at best it could but have afforded a spiteful and small handle for the enmities which Marie Antoinette had already aroused. She had but to insist, or rather only to understand, and her fate would have halted. She was indifferent. The miraculous moment when high ceremonial and the subtle effect of historic time combined to impress and to transform the French nation, the moment of the unction of the King, found her nothing more than the chief spectator in the gallery of the Cathedral transept looking down upon all that crowd of peers and officers whose position in the ceremony was exactly fixed.

She had come in to Rheims the night before under a brilliant moon, driving in her carriage as might any private lady. The "chic" of such an entry pleased her. She had allowed the King to precede her by some days — and whatever magic attached to the ritual descended upon him alone, and left her unsupported for the future. Her letter to her mother, written upon the morrow of the occasion, shows how little she knew what she had missed. The Court returned to Versailles, the careless vigour of her life was renewed, the thread of her exaggerated friendships and her exaggerated repulsions was caught up again.

When her young sister-in-law was married a few weeks later to the heir of Piedmont and Savoy, she did not conceal her relief at the departure from court of this child with whom, for some reason or another, she could not hit it off. When Madame de Dillon, with her Irish beauty, passed through the Court, that lady moved Marie Antoinette to yet another violent friendship — luckily of short duration. As for the Princesse de Lamballe, she had already revived for her the post of Superintendante of the Queen's Household (a post that had not existed for thirty years), and later she insisted upon there being attached to it the salary (which France imagined enormous) of £6,000 a year.

It is of great interest to note that public dissipation or abandon of this kind, glowing familiarities, long-lit and brilliant nights, an ardent pursuit of what had become to her a very necessity of change — all, in a word, that was beginning to fix her subjects' eyes upon her doubtfully and not a little to offend the mass of the nobility around her, all that was found in her insufficient to the niceties and balance of the French temper, was easily excused by foreign opinion. Just that something which separates the French from their neighbours was lacking to the foreign observance of this foreign woman. Her carriage, which to the French was a trifle theatrical, seemed to foreigners queenly; her lively temper, which the French had begun to find forward, was for the foreigner an added charm.

There is no need to recall the rhetoric of Burke, for Burke was not by birth or training competent to judge; but Horace Walpole, who was present that very summer at the Court of Versailles, and saw the Queen in all her young active presence at her sister-in-law's wedding-feast, writes with something of sincerity, and, what is more, with something for once of heart in his words. He thinks there never was so gracious or so lovely a being.

One judgment I, at least, would rather have recovered than any of theirs. It has not been communicated. I mean that of Doctor Johnson. For Doctor Johnson some months later stood by the side of his young girl friend, behind the balustrade at Fontainebleau, watching curiously with his aged and imperfect eyes this young Queen at the public ceremony of the Sunday Feast. The old, fat, wheezy man, who now seems to us England incarnate, stood there in the midst of the public crowd behind the railing, blocking its shuffling way as it defiled before royalty dining, and took in all the scene. The impression upon a man of such philosophy must have been very deep. I believe we have no record of that impression remaining.[1]

Though Marie Antoinette's carriage and her manner had founded of her so beneficent a legend abroad and had begun in her new home so much of her future disaster, with those who knew her most intimately and who were of her own blood, with the Hapsburgs of Vienna, her conduct, certainly not queenly, seemed not even tragic. They scolded sharply, and the Emperor, her brother, crowned a series of violent notes by one so violent that Maria Theresa kept it back. To her childlessness (which was for them a fault in her), to her conduct (which her own family who had known her as a child exaggerated at such a distance) was added the exasperation of remembering that with some elementary caution she might have acted as the agent of the allied Austrian Court whose daughter she was; they were angered in Vienna to see that, instead of so acting, she wasted her position in private spites and private choices.

In fine, when the Day of the Dead came round and the leaves of '75 were falling, she could look back from her twentieth birthday to her accession, and the view was one of eighteen months of mental chaos wherein one emotion rapidly succeeded another, each sought for the purpose of distraction and oblivion, and of feeding in some sort of fire-work way that appetite for life which Louis could not nourish with a steady flame. With the next year further elements were to be added to those existing elements of dissipation. The foundations of the future, which she had already levelled out, were to be strengthened. The public

[1] The life of Doctor Johnson has become an object of such widespread national study that more than one reader may be acquainted with his judgment of the scene. If it exists, it should be published to the advantage of history.

judgment of her was to become more apparent, and the legend which at last destroyed her was to take a firmer root.

The year 1776, for ever famous in the general history of the world, was the climax and the turning-point of this early exuberance and excess. In its first days, during the hard winter which marked the turn of the year, she had begun amusements which for the first time permitted her to cross the barrier which divides the reproach of one's intimates from public scandal. Her play had grown from mere extravagant gambling to dangerous indebtedness, and she had been bitten by the love of jewels, especially of diamonds. In this year, too, the simple and somewhat empty friendship which she still slightly bore to Madame de Lamballe was finally replaced by more violent caprices; she began to associate with the powerful Guémenées, with the gentle but subtle and intriguing Countess of Polignac.

Her indiscretion rose continually. In February she was seen with the Princesse de Lamballe whirling over the snow into Paris, without an escort, as a private woman might, to the disgust and the hatred of the crowd.

The exhilaration of the cold — for her who was from Vienna — the exhilaration of her twentieth year, her love of merry domination over the timid little tall companion, whom she so soon was to abandon, drove her from audacity to audacity. Her sledges, which had been but a domestic scandal at Versailles, dared to reach Sèvres, St. Cloud; they crossed the river, because the hunting wood of Boulogne invited them. Upon one fatal morning she traversed that last screen and shot through Paris on her shining toy.

The sledge was daringly, impudently alone. There was no guard, no decent covering for royalty, no dignity of pace or even of ornament; its pace was a flash, and its high gilding a theatrical *décor;* mixing with that flash and that gilding was the jangling of a hundred little bells.

The streets were all aghast at such a sight. Sèvres and the villages round Versailles had stared, bewildered, to see a Queen go by in such a fashion; but Paris was too great to be merely bewildered, and Paris grew angry, as might an individual at a personal insult offered.

The next month saw her first reckless purchase of gems; she pledged her name for £16,000, and acquired in exchange of that debt diamonds not only expensive beyond the means of her purse, but unworthy of her rank and of the traditions of her office.

To such follies she added her personal interference in the matter of Turgot. That bright-eyed, narrow, intelligent, and most un-Christian man, had missed the problem ready to his hands. In time of war, with a good army and a soldier behind him, he might have solved it; in a time of luxury, misery, and peace he could not. In the very days when he was propounding his theories of unfettered exchange and of direct taxation for the salvation of the Monarchy, the harvest of '75 had failed. In the one exceptional moment of famine when interference with trade was certainly necessary to French markets, his free trade doctrine was imposed. A popular hatred rose against him, and he was hated not only by the populace, who felt the practical effects of his economic idealism, but by the rich handful who were still devout and who could not tolerate his contempt for the Faith, by the corrupt who could not tolerate his economy, and by the vivacious who could not tolerate his sobriety. His rapid and fundamental reforms, moreover, were opposed by the Parlement of Paris[1] as by a wall. They refused to register the edicts. He had still great influence with the King, though hardly with any other effective power in the State, and in the month of March the King in a Bed of Justice compelled the Parlement to register Turgot's decrees and give them the force of law. It registered, them; but none the less Turgot was doomed.

Mercy, who saw very clearly that the man must go, but who also saw clearly the extreme danger that the Queen ran in taking upon herself any part in his going, did all that his influence could command to prevent her interference. He spent his energy and his considerable persuasion in vain. The one motive force and the only one that could persuade her to public action had already stirred the Queen; she believed herself to have received a personal affront; the Cabinet had recalled a favourite from the Embassy of St. James's. The girl was determined upon revenge, and because Turgot, as Comptroller-General, showed most prominently in the Cabinet, it was upon Turgot that her wrath fell, or rather it was Turgot falling from power whom she precipitated by her final influence. Upon the 10th of May, Guines, whom the Cabinet had recalled from London, was raised to a Duchy in a public note; by the 12th, Maurepas had told the Comptroller-General that his office was vacant, and Marie Antoinette talked wildly of sending him to the Bastille.

There was at this time in Paris a man called Necker with whom history would have little concern had not the accident of the Revolution later thrown his undetermined features into the limelight. He was a product of Geneva,

[1] It should be made clear, though it is elementary, that the Parlement of Paris, by nature a supreme court of law, exercised also the anomalous but traditional function of registrar of royal decrees. Nor was a law a law until this body had consented to enroll it or had been overcome by a grave, rare and solemn public ritual of the King's called "a Bed of Justice."

a money-dealer, therefore, and a Calvinist by birth and trade — in no way by individual conviction, for his energies had long been directed to the accumulation into his own hands of the wealth of others. His reputation as a solid business man was therefore high, and he was very rich; of moral reputation, as the Catholic French understand the term, he had none.[1] His dealings with the treasury had brought his name forward, and in a few months, under a different title, he replaced Turgot at the head of the embarrassed finances of the country! . . . Societies in dissolution do such things.

His conception of reform was what one might expect from such a lineage. He cooked the public accounts, flattered all to remain in power, was hopelessly void of any plan, and, to meet the crisis, just borrowed: the first of modern stock-jobbers to conduct a state, and the model to all others. He was destined to become a sort of symbol of liberty . . . and therein he is an example to democracy as well as to money-changers.

To the signal folly of precipitating Turgot's fall the Queen was content to add further marks of excess. As though her purchases earlier in the year had not been sufficient, she must buy bracelets now worth three years of her income — bracelets, the news of which reached Vienna — and she must give rein to every conceivable indulgence in the passion of gambling. All the world talked of it, and all that summer, as the influence of her new friends rose and as her careless excitement reached its limit, the fever grew.

---

[1] His vivacious and ugly daughter was to be a catch famous throughout Europe. Years later Fersen—of all men!—was suggested to her. Pitt in '85 had a bite at her ill-gotten dowry. Luckily for the girl, she escaped him, but she married De Staël, became famous, wrote her lively and didactic comments on the Revolution, grew uglier still, showed a small black moustache, at last wore a turban and drove Napoleon to despair.

At Marly, during the summer visit of the Court, later in the year at Fontainebleau, she carried on the scandal. One autumn night in this last place bankers from Paris kept the faro tables open for thirty-six hours; they were the hours before her birthday, and the Mass of All Saints was held before a Court, pale and crumpled with the lack of sleep. The morrow, her twenty-first birthday, was sour with the memory of the reproach against that debauch. The Court returned for the winter to Versailles, and Maria Theresa determined that it was time for the Queen's brother, the Emperor Joseph, to make the journey he had long promised, and to stem these rapids which threatened to become a cataract in which everything might be swept away. Her scolding letters to her daughter were accompanied by active plans for the journey of her son. She expected, and not without reason, that that son's advent would change all, for she knew that he would have the direct mission to persuade Louis to an operation, to relieve the imperfect marriage of the burden that pressed upon it, and to remove from the life of that young wife the intolerable nervous oppression whence all this increasing violence proceeded.

It is to the Emperor's journey, therefore, that all one's attention should be directed as one reads her life from the closing days of 1776 to his appearance in Paris, after repeated delays, in the spring of the following year.

Meanwhile that other spirit whose action was to come in upon her life, America, was born. The week that had seen Turgot's dismissal had seen passed in Philadelphia the Pennsylvania Resolution of Separation from the English Crown, and in the keener intellectual life of Virginia it had seen produced upon the same day the first statement of those general principles which the Colonies had drawn from Rousseau, and upon which were to be based, for whatever good or evil fortunes still attended it, the democracy of our time. The revolt grew from those skirmishes of '75 that had begun the civil war, to the Separatist decisions of '76, the strain upon England's tenure of her empire increased, and Vergennes all the while watched closely, hoping from that embarrassment to find at one moment or another the opportunity for relieving his country from the permanent threat of an English war.

It was a difficult and a perilous game. A British success might be, or rather would be, followed by swift vengeance against the embarrassed and fettered Crown of France. The Cabinet of Versailles would need allies against what was believed to be an all-powerful navy and for eighteen months Vergennes was working to obtain these allies, in spite of the terror which the British fleet inspired. This policy, whose ultimate results were to be so considerable and so unexpected, took a new shape upon a certain day which should perhaps be more memorable in the history of the United States than any other. I mean the 28th of November of this year 1776.

Early that morning, the weather being clear and the wind southerly, a pilot from the rocks of Belle Isle had made out three ships in the offing, but they were hull down; later, he saw one bearing a strange, quite unknown flag. He sailed towards it. The colours were those of the new Republic, and the stars and stripes flew above a sloop of war that carried Franklin; she had with her two English prizes for companions. Franklin landed. Within three weeks he was in Paris, and by the first week of the New Year he was at Passy in the suburbs, the guest of Chaumont, from whose great house and wide park proceeded the careful intrigue by which the Thirteen States were finally established in their Independence.

All who can pretend to history have respect for Vergennes, but that respect is far heightened by the close reading of what followed.

Alone of the European States Great Britain could not be balanced but could balance. Great Britain was secure among them and their insecurity. Great Britain alone in her growing monopoly of industry and in her impregnable self-sufficiency, economic and military, could not be pinned down into a diplomatic system; she alone could afford to scorn alliance, and could in a moment change from friend to foe and strike at any exposed and vulnerable part of the European group — especially at a maritime neighbour. The British army maintained a proved excellence of a hundred years; it was particularly famous for its endurance; its records of capitulation were rarer than those of any other; it could afford to be small; its infantry stood fire brutally and could charge after losses that would have been fatal to its rivals; it had for framework the squires and the yeomen of solid countrysides, for material the still manly remains of a peasantry in the English shires, the Highlands, whose native language, diet, and race were at that time corrupted by nothing more alien than a little garrison. Finally, there was then available to the full for purposes of war the vigour of an as yet unruined and not yet wholly alienated Irish.

A navy, adequate in numbers, but no drain upon the productive power of the nation, gave mobility to this force, the soil of these Islands fed the people upon it, and meanwhile an industry, textile and metallic, such as no other country dreamed of, supplied an increasing and overflowing resource for war. It is but a hundred and thirty years since things were thus. A vast change has passed, and it is difficult for the modern student, perplexed and anxious for the future of his country, to enter into the international policy of his fathers; yet must he grasp it if he is to understand what a revolution was effected by the issue of the American War; for it is probable that when the first complete survey of modern Europe is taken, the separation of the American colonies will establish a fixed date which marks not only the division between the monarchical and the beaurocratic, the old and the new Europe, but also, in our province, the division between what had been England and what later came to be called "the Empire" — with the destinies befitting such a title, and the colonies to which it is attached.

Vergennes saw that this England, free upon the flank of his embarrassed country, was now suddenly engaged in the most entangling of nets, an unpopular and distant civil war. He knew that with a Protestant population of her own blood (at that time the States were in philosophy wholly Protestant, in tradition entirely English) would only be attacked by the governing families with the utmost reluctance. There was no fear of extreme rigours, or of sharp, cruel, and decisive depression; there was sympathy and relationship on both sides. Therefore the war would drag.

Vergennes had seen, two years before, the little English garrison permitting the inhabitants to arm and drill without interference; he knew that opinion in England was divided upon the rebellion. His whole attention was concentrated upon the prolongation of that struggle and upon postponing, to the last, the intervention of France. His attention, so given, was successful, and he secured his object.

At first and for as long as might be he would support, unseen, the weaker of the combatants. He received Franklin, though privately; he refused ships or a declaration of war. Arms and ammunition he liberally supplied — but he did so through a private and civilian person, whom he vigorously denounced in public, who had to go through the form of payment from the United States, as might any other dealer, and who was very nearly compelled to go through the form of receiving heavy punishment as well. The private firm so chosen was "*Roderigo Hortalez et Cie*"; the modern cheat of anonymity in commerce had begun, and *Roderigo Hortalez* was, in reality, that same shifty, witty, courageous, and unsatisfied man who had already played upon Versailles and Vienna and whose pen was later to deliver so deep a thrust at the Monarchy. Caron, or, to call him by the title of nobility he had purchased, "De Beaumarchais."

. . . .

While Vergennes was acting thus, every effort was being made at Vienna to advance the journey of the Emperor: postponed from January to February, from February to March, that journey was at last undertaken, and with the first days of April, 1777, Joseph was present upon French soil, and driving down the Brussels road towards Paris.

But all that while, in spite of his advent, the rush of the Court had increased, and to the twenty other fashions and excitements of the moment one more had been added — enlistment for America. The youngster, who was typical of all that wealthy youth, not yet sobered or falsified by fame, La Fayette, was determined to go; and almost as a pastime, though it was a generous and an enthusiastic one, the American Revolution was the theme of the Court in general. It became the theme of the Polignac clique in particular, a theme sometimes rivalling the high interest of the cards or lending an added splendour to fantastic head-dress and to incongruous jewels.

And the Queen meanwhile, quite lost, pushed the pace of all the throng about her, despairing of any remedy to that evil which her brother was posting to reform.

If Fersen had been there!

. . . .

Upon Friday evening, the 18th of April, the Emperor Joseph drove past the barrier of St. Denis and entered Paris. It was already dark, but the stoic was in time for dinner. He was in strict incognito, that he might be the more admired, and had given out the arrival of "Count Falkenstein" to all the world. He slept in the humblest way at his Embassy; he had hired two plain rooms in Versailles by letter — at a hotel called "the Hotel of the Just," presumably Huguenot; next day he paraded as The Early Riser and was off to Versailles before the gentry were out of bed: the whole thing was as theatrical as could be. He wished to meet his sister alone — but he let everybody know it. He came up to her room by a private stair — and spoke of it as an act of simplicity and virtue. The man was of the kind to whom — most unhappily for them and their founder — Marcus Aurelius provides a model. His certitudes were in words or negations; his pride in things facile and dry; his judgments vapid, determined, superficial and false — in a manner Prussian without the

THE EMPEROR JOSEPH II.

From the tapestry portrait woven for Marie Antoinette and recently restored to Versailles

Prussian minuteness. In a manner French, but with none of the French clear depth and breadth. Of hearty Germany he had nothing; and among all the instruments of action designed in Gaul he could choose out only one, the trick of sharp command, which the accident of despotic power permitted him to use over a hodge-podge of cities and tongues.

The task before him, which was the re-establishment at Versailles of the interests of Austria, comprised two parts: first, he must counsel or compel the Queen — who stood for Austria at Versailles — to such conduct and dignity as would permit her to exercise permanent political power; secondly, and much more important, he must force the King to that operation from which he so shrank and yet by which alone the succession of the Crown through Marie Antoinette could be assured.

For the first of these tasks, the reform of his sister's conduct, Joseph's empty character, without humour and without religion, was wholly insufficient — nay, it provoked the opposite of its intention. The obvious truth of his harsh criticism moved the Queen, but his bad manners, his public rebuke, offended her more. His precise (and written!) instructions forced upon her one irksome and priggish month of affected rigidity; she did but react with the more violence from the absurd restraint. With the second and more positive task he was more fortunate. His brutal questions, his direct affirmation and counsel, his precise instructions, all conveyed in the sergeant-major manner which is of such effect upon the doubtful or the lethargic, accomplished their end. Louis inclined to the side which had for now three years urged medical interference; he submitted to an operation, and the principal question at issue for two great States was in this secret manner accomplished: it was the one success, the only one, of Joseph's tactless and unwise career. It was of the highest consequence to him and his house, and all Europe; for, his counsels once obeyed, the maternity of Marie Antoinette was ultimately sure. When the Queen should have borne a child there could but follow the rage of disappointed successors, a secure and increasing influence upon her part over her husband, through this the antagonism of the monarchy of the nation, and at last the Revolution and all its wars.

The reader may inquire the precise date of so momentous a detail. It is impossible to fix it until (if it still exist) the document once in the hands of Lassone be published; but we can fix limits within which the operation must have taken place. It must have been within that summer of 1777, in one of three months, June, July, or August; probably in late August or the beginning of September It was certainly later than the 14th of May, when, according to Mercy, the private interviews upon the matter between Joseph and Louis were still unfinished. Marie Antoinette's letter of June 16th makes it probably later than that date. A phrase of Maria Theresa's on the 31st of July, referring to news of the 15th (the last news from Mercy), makes it possible that she thought all accomplished by the 15th of July. A phrase of Mercy's on the 15th of August makes it more probable still. By the 10th of September a phrase used by Marie Antoinette in her correspondence with Maria Theresa makes it certain.[1]

Compared with this capital consequence of his journey the rest of Joseph's actions, opinions, and posings in France

[1] See Appendix A.

are indeed of slight importance. His affectation of retirement and simplicity, his common cabs, his perpetual appearance in public and as perpetual pretence of complaint at his popularity are the tedious trappings of such men. In some things he was real enough; in his acute annoyance with the Queen's set, for instance — especially with Madame de Guémenée, and her late hours, high play and familiar, disrespectful tones. He was sincere, too, in his astounding superficiality of judgment; he was keen on science, eager for the Academies, and in that scientific world of Paris which boasted Lavoisier and the immortal Lamark, discovered that "when one looks close, nothing profound or useful is being done."

At the end of May he left for a tour in the French provinces. His ineptitudes continue. He has left notes of his opinions for us to enjoy. He judges the army, and condemns it — all except the pipe-clay and white facings of the Artois Regiment. That pleased him. He saw nothing of the cannon which were to break Austria and capture a woman of his house for Napoleon. He judges the navy after a minute attention, and finds it — on the eve of the American War!—thoroughly bad. One thing he does note clearly, that Provence, the King's brother, has been going through France in state, as though sure of the succession. After what had passed at Versailles, such expectations on the part of Louis XVI.'s brother must have bred in Joseph a mixture of anxiety and amusement.

He returned to Vienna, and began to address himself to his next failure in policy and judgment — he coveted Bavaria. The death of the Elector of Bavaria would raise the issue of his succession. That death was approaching, and Joseph began to intrigue through Mercy, through his mother, and as best he could through his sister, for the succession to the Duchy and for the support of France against Prussia in his outworn, out-dated ambition. While he still played with such toys, much larger forces were ready to enter the scene, and changes that would make the little balances of German States forgotten; for as that summer of 1777 heightened, dry, intensely hot, and as all the air of the life around Versailles was cleared by the new intimate relations of the Queen and her husband; as the chief domestic problem of the reign was resolved, as it became increasingly certain that the royal marriage would soon be a true marriage and the way to the succession secure, there had come also the certitude of war with England in the matter of the American colonies.

It is upon this latter certitude that attention must now be fixed, before one can turn to the tardy accomplishment of the Queen's hopes for an heir. The foreign policy of that moment is essential to a comprehension of her fate, for upon the unexpected turn of that unexpected conflict with Great Britain was to depend the fatal respite which destiny granted to the French Monarchy: a respite of years, during whose short progress the financial tangle became hopeless, the Queen's ill-repute fixed, and the Crown's last cover of ceremony destroyed.

I say there had come a certitude of war with England. Of three things one: either England would reduce the rebels; or, having failed so to reduce them, she would compromise with them for the maintenance of at least a nominal sovereignty; or, she would wholly fail and would be compelled wholly to retire. In the first case it must be her immediate business to attack the French Government whose secret aid had alone made the prolongation of rebellion possible; in the second case, with still more security, and a still more confident power, she could attack an enemy which, because it had not dared openly to help her foes, had earned their contempt and lost its own self-confidence. In the third case she would find herself free from all embarrassment and at liberty to destroy a rival marine, whose inferiority was incontestable but whose presence had been sufficient to embarrass her complete control of the North Atlantic, and to sustain — however disingenuously — her rebellious subjects.

In any one of these three issues a war with England must come. But these three issues had not an equal chance of achievement. A complete victory of the British troops, probable as it was, could hardly result in a permanent military occupation of a vast district, English in blood and speaking the English tongue. A complete defeat of British regulars at the hands of the varied and uncertain minority of colonists, and the acknowledgment of American independence by a Britain unembarrassed in Europe, was an absurdity conceivable only to such enthusiastic boys as was then the young La Fayette, to such wholly unpractical minds as that of Turgot, or to popular journalists of the type which then, as to-day, are uninstructed whether in historical or in military affairs.

The middle issue was so much the more probable as to appear a calculable thing: the troops of George III. would determine the campaign, but the settlement following the expensive success of the British army would be a compromise whereby the colonies should be free to administer their own affairs, should be bound in some loose way to Great Britain, and should stand benevolently neutral towards, if not in part supporters of, her position in Europe.

The formula which guides a commercial State such as Britain in its colonial wars has long been familiar to its rivals; it is as simple as it is wise. Though we give it the epithet of "generous" and speak of the "granting of self-government," while enemies will call it, with equal inaccuracy, "a capitulation" followed by "an alliance," the nature and purpose of such compromises are those of a fixed policy and one upon whose unalterable data the British Empire has been built up.

It was in the nature of things that the British Government in this summer of '77 should first seek to master the Americans in the field, next compromise with the defeated colonials, set them up as a nation nominally dependent, really allied, and so find itself free in Europe for the great duel with France. At Versailles Vergennes prepared not attack but resistance, and pulled with an accurate proportion of effort all the strings that should delay Great Britain, on the one hand, and, on the other, unite into one body of resistance against her the Atlantic seaboard of Europe and the principal navies of the continent — that is, the Powers of France and the Peninsula; the admiralties of Versailles, Lisbon and Madrid.

As the Emperor Joseph's carriage rolled westward along the main road of Brittany, approaching the gates of Brest, Vergennes was signing for despatch to the Spanish Court that note of his which inaugurated the active part of his plan of defence against England. Precisely a week later, Burgoyne and his forces started southward from Canada upon what should have been the decisive march of the British campaign in America.

A consideration of the map will at once convince the reader, first that Great Britain was in a position suitable to immediate victory, and, secondly, that the military advisers of her government had formed the best possible plan for its rapid accomplishment.

What was the military object of the war? The control of a seaboard: a seaboard stretching indeed through fifteen degrees of latitude, and extending in its contour over far more than fifteen hundred miles, but a seaboard only. Behind it lay districts which for military purposes did not exist — untouched, trackless, resourceless. The life of the colonies, especially their life during the strain of a war, flowed through the ports.

Again, this band of territory ran from a long southern extremity, whose climate was unsuited to active work by Europeans, through a middle temperate interval to another extremity of winter fogs and rigorous winter cold. A continental climate rendered the contrast of North and South less noticeable, for the warm continental summer embraced it all, and the cold continental winter penetrated far south; but that contrast between the two halves of that seaboard was sufficient to afford a line of social and political cleavage already apparent in the eighteenth century and destined in the nineteenth to occasion a great domestic war.

Again, there lay behind this seaboard, at a distance nowhere greater than three hundred miles nor anywhere much less than two, that valley of the St. Lawrence which Great Britain firmly held; her tenure was secure in the diversity of its race, religion and language from those of the rebels and in the unity which the admirable communications of its great waterway confirmed.

Here then was a line already wholly held, the St. Lawrence, and parallel to it a line already partially held, and always at the mercy of the British fleet — the ports of the seacoast. Up and down the belt of land between those parallel lines went the scattered bands of the rebels. Even their organised armies were loosely co-ordinated in action and expanded or diminished with a season.

The obvious strategy for the British was to cut that intervening belt in a permanent fashion by establishing a line from the St. Lawrence to the sea, and so to separate for good the forces of their opponents and then to deal with them in detail and at leisure.

An accident of topography afforded to this simple problem an obvious key: just down that dividing line, which separates the nothern climate and the Puritan type of colony from the rest, a sheaf of natural ways leads from the coast to the valley of the St. Lawrence, and of these the plainest and by far the best is the continuous and direct depression afforded by the long, straight valley of the Hudson and continued in one easy line along the depression marked by Lakes George and Champlain. There is not upon all that march one transverse crest of land to be defended nor one position capable of natural defence, and in its whole extent water carriage is available to an army save upon the very narrow watershed where (according to the amount and weight of supplies) two — or at most three — days must be devoted to a land portage. But even here, between the foot of Lake George and the Upper Hudson, existed then what is rare even to-day in the New World, a road passable to guns.

Under such conditions, even had the rebellion been universal and homogeneous, the strategy imposed was evident. The sea was England's; the English forces had but to land in force, to occupy one or more of the ports at the outlet of these ways leading to the valley of the St. Lawrence, and simultaneously to march down from that valley to the sea. They would thus cut the rebellion in half; the cut so made could easily be permanently held, and the English henceforth could operate at their choice and in increasing numbers from any point of the coast against either section of a divided enemy.

I say this was the obvious plan even had the rebellion been homogeneous or universal; but it was neither — and nowhere was it weaker or more divided against itself than on this very line of cleavage. It was precisely in the valley of the Hudson and at its mouth that the British could count upon the greatest hesitation on the part of their opponents and of most support, sometimes ardent support, on the part of their friends. New York was thoroughly in the Royal power and the plan of marching from the St. Lawrence down to that harbour seemed certain to conclude the campaign. Leaving such garrison as New York required, Howe sailed with 20,000 men in this opening of the summer of 1777 to attack some one of the harbours; after a cruise of some hesitation he sailed up the Delaware and landed to march on the source of supply, Philadelphia. At the same moment Burgoyne set out upon his march from the St. Lawrence valley to the sea.

Each was easily successful. Washington, covering Philadelphia from a position along the Brandywine, was completely defeated. Philadelphia was in British hands before the close of September; an attempt at relief was crushed in the suburbs within a week. As for Burgoyne, his force, though it amounted to less than a division, was equally at ease. He swept easily down Lake Champlain: the American irregulars abandoned the isthmus and their positions near Ticonderoga, which were militarily identical with that pass. He pursued the enemy to the extremity of the water, and on southward up the valley, towards the watershed; defeating every rally and confident of immediate success.

It was but early in July, and he had already accomplished half his route, and could boast the capture of over a hundred cannon — mainly of French casting.

All had gone well. The news reaching London, reached Paris and Madrid by the mouths of English Ministers and Envoys, whose tone was now of an increasing firmness, and who, in the immediate prospect of success, began to ask in plain terms how matters stood between France and Spain, and whether these two Bourbon crowns were prepared for open war.

Vergennes was in an agony of writing, of secrecy and of defence, urging Spain to draw secretly close to France that both might stand ready for the inevitable blow which England would deliver when the colonies were once subdued.

What followed was Burgoyne's woodland march of a few miles across the portage from the lakes to the Hudson.

The cause of that march's amazing delay, and of the disaster consequent upon such delay, will never be fully explained; because, although not a few acquainted with European roads and European discipline and arms are also acquainted (as is the present writer) with the unmade country traversed by that force, yet there was no contemporary who, by a full double experience of American and European conditions, could present in his account the American advantage in such a country at that time, and the corresponding difficulties of European troops. From Fort Anne, where the last American force had been scattered, to Fort Edward, where the Hudson is reached, is one day's easy walking. It took Burgoyne's army twenty-one. I have neither space nor knowledge to say why: German slowness (half the army was German), the painful construction of causeways, officers (one may suppose) drinking in their tents, a vast train, an excess of guns, a fancied leisure — all combined to protract the delay. The month of July was at an end when the British reached the river, and, having reached it, the men were on fatigue day after day bringing in the guns and supplies that had come by water to the extremity of Lake George.

In this way August was wasted, and an attempt to raid draught cattle a few miles to the south-east at Bennington in Vermont was, in spite of the active loyalty or treason of many colonists, defeated and destroyed — a disaster due to the foreign character, the small number employed, and the dilatory marching of the troops so detached. It was mid-September before the army crossed the Hudson to its western bank, where a small auxiliary force approaching from the Mohawk valley was to have joined it. That force failed to effect a junction. All were bewildered, and now a heavy rain began to soften the green ways and to swallow the wheels of the guns. Burgoyne reached no further south than the site of a drawn struggle before the mouth of the Mohawk. And already the American irregulars, on hearing of the British difficulties, had gathered and grown in number; they were at last near double the invading force, and September was ending. The woods were full of colour as Burgoyne's little army fell back — but a few miles, yet back; an irresolution was upon it, because advance was no longer possible, and yet a full retreat would mean the failure of all the large plan of England. There was a rally, a success, a failure, and the loss of guns. With October they were beneath the heights of Saratoga. Certain supplies attempted to reach them by crossing the river; the far bank was found to be held by the increasing forces of rebellion.

It was determined to abandon the effort and to retire — at last, but too late. The road to the lakes was blocked; more guns were lost; the enemy were gathering and still gathering, a random farmer militia whom such an entanglement tempted: they were soon four to one. An attempt at relief by the little force down river from New York had failed. On the 12th of October, a Sabbath, the harassed army reposed. On the 13th a Monday, Burgoyne ordered an exact return of forces, forage, and supply; some five thousand were to be found, but not four thousand men could stand to roll-call armed; not two thousand of these were British; perhaps a week's supply remained; of all his park thirty-five pieces alone were left to him. He called a council, to which every officer above the rank of lieutenant was summoned, and that afternoon the proposals to treat were drawn-up and despatched; by ten, Gates, in command of the American force, had sent in his reply. Tuesday and Wednesday were taken up in the terms of an honourable surrender — not exactly observed. On Thursday, the 16th, these terms were signed, and on that day, that repeated day the 16th of October, the keystone of the British plan in North America had crumbled, and the strong arch of a wise strategy was ruined.

It was but a small force that surrendered in those lonely hills to a herd of irregulars. The causes of the failure were many, tedious, gradual, and therefore obscure; but the effect was solemn and of swelling volume. It roused the colonies; it slowly echoed across the Atlantic; it changed the face of Europe.

The French Court, at the moment of that surrender in the woods three thousand miles away, sat at Fontainebleau, decided for pleasure.

Goltz, watching all things there for the King of Prussia, his master, wrote (on that very day) that the French had let their moment slip: England was now secure, he thought —for one of the great weaknesses of Prussia is that, like self-made men, she has no instinct for fate.

Florida Blanco (upon the very day that Burgoyne's troops piled arms) was writing from Madrid to Vergennes that "the two courts" (of France and Spain) "should do all to avoid cause of complaint on the part of Great Britain at such a time."

Vergennes himself, gloomily alone amid the foolish noise of Fontainebleau, in the sweat of late hours and gaming, thus abandoned by Spain and seeing his hopes of the Spanish alliance going down, wrote (on that same 16th of October, the day that Burgoyne's troops piled arms!): "The Ministers of England think her the mistress of the world. . . . My patience has been hard tried . . . true, the two (Bourbon) crowns must go warily. . . . I hope the constraint may end, but I have no wish for war. . . . I only ask that England shall not compel us to do what she dares not do herself, that is, to treat these Americans as pirates and outlaws."

In such a mood of despondence and of anxiety the French Foreign Office awaited the first blow England might choose to deliver; in such a mood of reluctance and fear Spain refused to declare herself on the side of the French should

England choose to strike; and in such a tension Western Europe stood for one week, another, and a third, when, early in November, came the first rumours of the truth. How they came it is impossible to determine. They came before known or common methods could have brought them; they came before true news, like a shadow or a presage. On the 7th of November Vergennes had written to Noailles of a hint of some English defeat, "not too much to be trusted." On the 15th he was wondering at the insistence of the English ministers upon their Pennsylvanian successes, at the English silence upon the Hudson march. As the month wore on, as the English insistence grew gentler, the English silence more profound, Vergennes determined his final policy; but even as he was drawing up his memorandum in favour of recognition to be granted to, and of alliance to be concluded with, the United States, on the 4th of December, and before this document was signed, full news came and all was known. The 4th of December is a day propitious for arms; it is the gunners' festival.

The issue was not long in doubt. Upon the 5th, the story and consequence of Saratoga were drawn up and despatched on every side. Upon the 6th, the fateful document calling the American delegates to an audience with Louis was submitted to that King, and he wrote in his little sloping hand at the foot of it that word "*approuvé*," which you may still read.

Upon the 8th, Franklin at Passy drafted, Deane, Lee, and he also *signed*, their memorable acceptance. The days that followed, to the end of '77 and beyond it, were occupied in nothing more than the confirmation of this revolution in policy, and it was certain that by the

New Year the French Crown would support the Rebellion in arms.

. . . .

Such were the three years in which the seeds of the Queen's tragedy were sown: they were sown deep. The stock of her disaster was established in a vigorous soil; but during the silent period of its growth, before the plant had come to its evil maturity, a few deceitful years were still to hide from her the sequence of her fate. For the two glories of life were upon her, victory and the birth of children.

In common with all her Court the Queen could now, in the hale winter of '77–'78, imagine herself upon the threshold of a new and fruitful life. Her chief anxiety was now dispelled, for she might await securely the advent of an heir. Her vivacity and her distractions seemed now as harmless as her habit of changing pleasures was now fixed; her casual but active excursions into public affairs had now in her husband's eyes an excuse or motive they formerly had lacked, and her political interference, though utterly without plan, was even destined to achieve for a moment a peculiar, if deceptive, success.

This period of her life ends with a scene which the reader may well retain, for it sums up the change; a scene which forms the happy conclusion of so much unrest and the introduction to a brief, a most uncertain, but — while it lasted — an enlarged and a conquering time.

The new year had come. The winter festivities of early '78 were at their height awaiting their end at the approaching carnival. It was the 21st of January — a date thrice of great moment to the French people — and the Queen was holding a ball (characteristically hers) in the palace. There was a fuller life that evening, in the glare of a thousand candles, than had yet been known; a more continuous and a more vivacious noise of laughter and of music. Paris had come more largely than usual; there were many strangers, and the air seemed full of an exultant conciliation. Upon this joy and movement there fell a sudden silence; it was a silence the Queen well comprehended and had expected too, for Provence, coming straight from the Council, had entered the room and had given her the message she awaited. The message was repeated, whispered first, then louder and more eager questions and replies were everywhere heard; voices rose louder: young Artois openly cheered.

The English ambassador had turned at the unusual scene and knew its meaning; he despatched to his Government that night the news that the Independence of the United States had been recognised and orders to the French navy signed.

What followed may be briefly told. In somewhat over a fortnight the treaty of recognition and of alliance with the new Republic was concluded. The approaching affair with England began to equal, very soon it wholly surpassed, in interest and peril the petty Bavarian quarrel, and though war was not formally declared, French ships were in February already attacked by English. In mid-March the treaty was notified by the French Ambassador in London to the Prime Minister of England; forty-eight hours later Lord Stormont at Versailles, had demanded and received his papers. A month of preparation passed.

At last, upon Easter Sunday (the 19th of April in that year) two couriers riding crossed each other at the royal gate of

Versailles — the one reaching, the other leaving, the palace. He that drew rein and was ending his journey bore great news: D'Estaing had sailed from Toulon with twenty ships of the line, and the campaign was opened. He that set spurs and was but just beginning his post bore great news also, for he had upon him that letter (it is still preserved) in which Marie Antoinette told her mother that now she was certainly with child.

VII

THE CHILDREN

EASTER SUNDAY, APRIL 19, 1778, TO MONDAY, OCTOBER 22, 1781

THE expectation of an heir, the Queen's ascendancy over her husband, the promise of adventurous war, proceeded with the year. Meanwhile the little business of Bavaria somewhat marred the hopes of the now renewed and invigorated monarchy. It is a business history should make little of; hardly a combat — rather a diplomatic rupture soon arranged. It covered the year exactly — it was settled with the close of it; but it had its significance in the Queen's life, *for her political action in it confirmed and extended the popular idea that Marie Antoinette was treasonable to French interests in the department of foreign affairs.*

The most apparent thing of that moment was the new certitude and strength of the Queen now that she was to be a mother. Her love of change became less frivolous, more mixed with character; her old passionate friendships, her appetite for colour of every kind — in jewels, in fantasies, in voices — took on some depth and permanence. Even her interference with public affairs was no longer the mere whim that had been the bane of Turgot: it had objects; those objects were pursued, though they were personal and unwise. Unfortunately her mother and Mercy persuaded her, just as her strength appeared, not to the aggrandisement of her husband's throne, but to the mere fending off Prussia from Maria Theresa's land in the Bavarian quarrel. There arose concerning her action a swarm of whispers, voices not yet of moment, though numerous in the taverns and clear at Court.

The Elector of Bavaria had died while Versailles and all the Court were in the height of their absorption in the American Rebellion; just in that last December which was full of the first active approach of Vergennes towards the American envoys. The passing of the Electorate to another branch of the family, and that branch childless, or rather lacking direct legitimate issue, threw the musty anarchy of German archives open to the lawyers; they were rummaged and a dust arose. The various fragments out of which the old Duchy and the newer Electorate were pieced together found claimants everywhere, and the two heads of antagonism were necessarily Vienna and Berlin: Berlin, which would support the heir to the old Duchy — at a price; Vienna, which would protect the reigning Elector for the reversion — on doubtful pleas of inheritance — to some half of the mosaic over which he ruled.

There was here no plain conscience of civilised right against a northern and blundering atheism such as had earlier supported the defence of Maria Theresa against the too successful cynicism of Frederick the Great. The ambitions of Joseph were the ambitions of a philosopher; they were at least as empty and by no means as thorough as the soldierly ambitions of his opponent, the King of Prussia: the injury was mutual, the contempt of justice equal, for Joseph was a pupil of Frederick's in wrong-doing. To each, however, the complex little territorial quarrel seemed of secular magnitude. Maria Theresa was maddened with anxiety and wrote, so maddened, despairing appeals to her daughter at Versailles. Mercy moved all his persuasion to persuade the intervention of France. Vergennes as resolutely refused to be involved. England was approaching Austria, to the detriment, it was hoped, of the Bourbons, the whole weight of diplomatic thought was at work, and Europe was warned and threatened with incredible futures as one or the other of the two enemies armed for the acquisition of a titular sovereignty over the tortuous and overlapping boundaries of a feudal ruin. Such were the petty concerns of statesmen and even of demagogues in a year when the young men who were to fight at Valmy were already boys. The politicians wrangled over the Bavarian succession as we to-day wrangle over colonial things, imagining them to contain the future fate of Europe.

The Queen at first did little. Mercy complained of her detachment. She was occupied in the greater matter of her maternity, passing all the time of the first leaves and the early summer rains in quietude at Marly; she would have no Court about her, and when she wrote to Maria Theresa it was perpetually of the child. That seclusion and that hope so much attached to her the new affection and the new pride of Louis that when at last she spoke to him, and spoke with increasing violence, for her family and for Vienna, she largely accomplished her aim. She did not intend to involve the Foreign Office — Vergennes was apparently immovable — but so great was now her influence with Louis that by autumn she did obtain a tardy intervention, and until she obtained it she showed in every way her determination to be heard. The first acts of war in July moved her to countermand a feast at Trianon; during August she frequently disturbed the Council by her

MARIE ANTOINETTE
From the principal bust at Versailles

presence. In September she put forward an uncertain proposal for mediation. It was refused, and her anger added to the difficulties of the French Crown. But she did obtain — the forgotten act was to re-arise, enormous, at her scaffold — she did obtain a subsidy. Treaty demanded it: it had been refused: the whole duty of the Bourbon Crown was to watch finance — yet fifteen million went to Austria. The taverns made it a whole convoy of gold; there were songs against the Queen, accusing her of "paying out French gold." Older and worse stories about her were revived. The printed obscenities from London and Amsterdam began to flow. The set at Court which had called her openly "the Austrian" before her accession, and since her accession had in secret still so called her, passed on the term to the street, and the nickname was common in Paris before the end of the year.

All these things she had forgotten before the winter closed upon her, and her hour approached. They were indeed little things; seedlings. Much greater was the coming of an heir and Fersen's return.

. . . .

He had come back late in August. The moment she had seen him, with his tall, upstanding gait and serious eyes, she came forward and reminded him (and those about her) of his old acquaintance — he was a friend. The lad was still quite young; here was she now a woman, and the effect of four years, changing her so greatly in body had less changed him in body; it had less changed her in heart. For as the days fell shorter and autumn lapsed into winter, his rare and brief notes betray the growing charm of the woman who perpetually remembered him. All through the months of the cold, through the time of her approaching childbirth, and through the gaieties of the new year that succeeded, he remained. Many noted her visage and her tone, once especially when she sang and looked at him during her singing. At last he also — when in April he left the Court, bitten with the gallant adventure of America, like so many of his rank — he also had understood. She followed him perpetually with her eyes; she followed him as he left her rooms again for the last time, and it was noted that there were tears in her eyes. A wealthy woman rallied Fersen as he left upon his conquest; he was now old enough to deny gravely that any woman of that Court had deigned to consider him: having so denied it he was gone.

As for the Queen, she wrote or spoke of him in public as a young nobleman only, now known and worthy of advancement, and since she kept the rest strictly in her heart no emphasis here of that which lay at the root of her life would give it dignity or value in these pages. Yet throughout these pages the name of Fersen should be the chief name.

He was gone for five more years after so brief a sight of new things.

. . . .

Meanwhile the Court awaited the birth of an heir.

There was a murmur all around. Monsieur had written frankly enough to the King of Sweden that his hope of the succession was gone. The Court was transformed, and Marie Antoinette especially was a new power: the light calumnies were grown heavy now; the revenge for personal touches was becoming a State affair; a weight of office was upon her, for she was now to be half the Crown and the true wife of a King who governed, and the mother of a King after him.

It was on the 19th of December, in the very early hours long before dawn, that her husband was warned: in the forenoon her travail began.

I have said that the French Monarchy was a sacramental and therefore a public thing. The last act of its public ritual was about to be accomplished; for the last time it rose to the mystical duties of its office and dared to mix with the nation, not as a person, but as an Institution for whom, being immortal, peril was nothing, and, being impersonal, decency and comfort nothing. Could it have so dared again it would have been saved, but it did not dare.

The populace demanded admittance to the birth, and were admitted in the ancient way. The square room in which the Queen lay, upon a low little camp-bed before the fire, was crowded in a moment; upon the carved marble of the chimney-piece two street arabs were seen climbing. The market-women were there, mixed with the ladies of the Court, and a great press of the poor from the streets had found an entry and were packed also upon the great stairs outside. Everything was a-buzz and a-tiptoe, questioning, craning for the news; the market-women commiserated and complained; the ladies-in-waiting stood silent, each estimating the event — the change there would be at Court, the strong place the King would now hold, and above all, the new power of the mother — the little heir, the boy who should dispossess Monsieur, exile Artois perhaps, and recapture the heart of the crowds to the Bourbon name.

For some critical moments there was a silence.

Vermond (the tutor's brother), who was her doctor, or her midwife, had ordered every crevice to be closed. Even the chinks of the window had paper gummed to them. In such an air and under such an ordeal the Queen fainted. Louis in a passion of sense thrust his arm through a pane of glass and let in the winter cold; Vermond lanced a vein, and with the bleeding and the fresh draught of air the Queen returned to life. They told her that the child was a girl.

. . . .

There were great crowds at her churching and some eagerness. The Latin Quarter was impassable with folk as her coach crawled up the hill towards the shrine of Ste. Genevieve. The square in front of the Cathedral was very full — but they lacked a Dauphin. The King was glad enough. When, upon Christmas Eve, the child had grasped his finger, he had told his pleasure to all. Her name and godparents, her household and her future were discussed as solemn things. But in Versailles the air was dull with anti-climax; they had depended upon, or braced themselves for, or begun their intrigue against, a son of France — and none was there.

The little girl who thus was born alone survived. Her brothers perished — the heir in prison; her father and her mother both were publicly destroyed. She lived. The country house of her old age I well remember, a solemn and lonely place, small and grey and deep in the woods — long empty. It fell into ruins, was sold for stone, and a road driven over it; but after nightfall horses refused to pass the place, and legends of darkness clung to the last blood of the Bourbons.

It was but the close of January when the Queen returned from La Muette and her churching to Versailles and the disappointment of Versailles. It was just a year from the ball-room scene that had meant war with the English. That year had done nothing but maintain the struggle to the surprise and encouragement of the French Ministry; it had done no more, but even that was much. The naval actions had been at the worst indecisive, the English communications along the rebel coast were now in perpetual jeopardy, and would so remain until a French fleet was destroyed: none was destroyed. Even an attempt to blockade the French in Boston harbour had failed, and in November D'Estaing had slipped away from Byron under the advantage of a storm. Of all the operations of that year perhaps the most momentous to history was the chance and inconclusive fight of July in the Atlantic, for it gave the Queen occasion to doubt the courage of Chartres and to ridicule it: and Chartres, soon to be Orleans, found his growing hatred of her fixed forever.

As for her, she kept her carnival, the carnival of 1779. Her less light purpose now earned her reproaches far more deep than those which had pursued her first childless years; but in her new hopes she could forget them, and her much rarer omissions did not remain in her mind. She did not see how solidly the foundations of her fate were being laid in the dark, and how every trivial folly was her foe; no act of hers proved great enough to destroy the last effect of these trivial follies.

She went to the Opera-ball on Shrove Tuesday with the King — it was a folly (they said) to leave Versailles so soon. She went without him a week later — it was a folly to go alone. That night, her coach breaking down, she must take a public fly — a piece of common sense. She spoke of the adventure, and it pleased her hugely, but the populace twisted it into I know not what adventures, repeated and enlarged in a thousand ways.

When in April the measles incommoded her, she must retire to Trianon for a month — it was common sense; but it was "breaking roof" with the King and therefore a lesion in the constant etiquette of the Crown. She took with her her young sister-in-law, Madame Elizabeth, whom she had once petulantly avoided, and now, saner, loved; and Madame de Lamballe was there too. It was common sense; but her absence from the Court was hateful, was an insult to the courtiers, and the presence at the Trianon during the day of four gentlemen, her friends, was more hateful still. The lies poured out in a printed stream from London; and the Paris coffee-shops, and the drawing-rooms too, had now woven round her an enduring legend of debauchery more real than things witnessed or heard. The calumny was fixed.

If a moment must be chosen of which one can say that it was the decisive moment in her public ill-repute, the moment before which that repute was yet fluid, the moment after which it was set, then that moment must be found in this summer of her twenty-fourth year, 1779. It was an effect coming well after its cause: the high tide of a wave that the first reckless three years had raised.

It may be asked whether, had some shock or some necessity wholly changed her, had she given up every lightness as she had already given up most excesses, she might not yet have warded off the approaches of a distant judgment. No, she could not. The character of the attack upon her she could have modified; but she could only have diminished its volume by increasing its intensity, or its rapidity by extending its already almost universal vogue: she could not have escaped it. The most sober actions of that enthusiastic nature would now for ever be criticised. Had no money gone on slight pleasures, the money spent in every error of foreign policy would have been put down to her; every unpopular dismissal she was to be guilty of, innocent or no, and her name was to be, in every story of intrigue, however incredible, pre-judged. She was destined, henceforward, to be forgotten in victory and remembered in defeat, nor could anything have saved her save a sudden comprehension of France. No God revealed it to her, and to the general protest that was rising beneath her came accident after accident, some hardly of her doing, some not at all, but every one pointing towards the single issue of her fate, not one in aid of her.

The nights of August were hot and the early autumn also. The customary tours of the Court had been countermanded to save money. The princesses walked at evening and mingled with the crowd on the terrace of the palace, where was the band. It gave scandal. It gave scandal that she should walk later with Artois. It gave most scandal that Madame de Polignac, with her refined and silent face, her gentle deep-blue eyes under that dark hair — a type not national — should so entirely possess the Queen.

The Polignac clique demanded and obtained on every side. It was a double evil: a proof to the Court that the aristocracy as a whole were excluded from favour and that a faction ruled; a proof to the nation that, at a time when finance was the known burden, and when, in the midst of prosperity, a permanent crisis weighed on the impatient poor and the public forces alike, the executive, the King, could blindly spend money and endow every Polignac claim. The sums involved in this patronage of the Polignacs, as in every other public extravagance of the French, were small. The debts of a Pitt or a Fox were far larger, the luxury of our modern money-dealers are mountainous compared to them; but they fell on a nation wholly egalitarian, unused to and intolerant of government by the wealthy, and a nation which regarded (and regards) its government as the principal engine to use *against* the rich, not in their aid.

Trianon, not enormous in its cost, grew to be yet another legend, and that legend was not diminished when, in the summer of 1780, a little theatre was opened there, a little stage for the Queen.

All the world did such things! None could blame her — yet all did. After all, one great house after another had put up its show — most of them more costly than hers: but there was in her gradual extension of the amusement something that aggrandised it and made it a public talk; her invitation to the great Paris companies of actors, her very seclusion at first, with its opportunity for rumour, later her open doors, swelled the comment and the offence of Paris. Paris detested the private theatre from the first. There was in it a mixture of carelessness for the State and of personal abasement which it could not tolerate in a French Queen; yet how simple was the distraction to her, and how could the subtleties of these Paris critics, themselves the best actors in the world, deriding acting and despising it, be comprehensible to her? She played on

The King came often. He applauded. She permitted — in this year 1780 at least — no one but the royal family to witness her from the audience . . . but the parts were many and needed many players. She made dull Campan, her librarian, manage for her; she gave no place in the distraction to those who thought their presence about her to be a most solemn right and duty. In the autumn to the acting she must add singing, though her voice was not always in tune and was often displeasing in its lack of volume. Stage parts demanded stage lovers, and hearing this, Mercy in his turn opposed. He came at her invitation (but he insisted on being hidden behind the lattice of a box), he applauded her acting somewhat, was courtier-like to her singing — but he disapproved.

Silent, a little bent, low-voiced, a man of but fifty-three — though seemingly older — Mercy was now at the height of that long career during which for twenty-two years he was Austria itself permanently present before Marie Antoinnette, a spy over her for her mother's sake and for her own, a devoted servant of the Hapsburgs and Lorraine.

His nobility was of the Empire: a Belgian from Liège, a man without nationality, and with no comprehension of the rising religion of patriotism, he had from his childhood formed part of that cosmopolitan soldiery which was the shield of Maria Theresa; he lived for that Great Lady who maintained him in his embassy, and in his manner and tradition he maintained the character it had had under his master, Kaunitz.

He had passed all his early manhood in that splendid riverside house in Paris which the dandyism of the great diplomatist his teacher had demanded. His youth — reserved, awkward and probably laborious — had left him very observant. He had adopted for life all the externals of the Parisians, but — with the narrowness of his profession — he had failed to see that inmost part of them which was so soon to launch the tempest of wars against all that bunch of private interests on which he depended, and to destroy it. The French Crown was nothing to him, and whether in Paris, at Versailles, or down river in his great country house at Conflans, the French nation left him careless. He was lord of a French manor in Lorraine, of another near his *château* on the river. His wines were French, and marvellous, and cellared in 15,000 bottles, which the peasants of the Oise drank for him joyfully in '92 — nothing more saddened the old man in his exile when the Revolution was on.

His horses were superb. Even of coachmen he boasted two — each beautiful and large; each equal in domestic rank.

Unmarried, he maintained with dignity an opera-singer of some fame and of the refinement customary in that trade; at the close of his life he left upon record their "close and rooted friendship."

Such was the man who for nine years had watched his princess as she grew to womanhood and at last to motherhood at the French Court, and for nine years had sent those long, regular, and careful letters to Maria Theresa which are now our source for quite half the history of the place and time. His life also was at a crisis and a change in this year of 1780, for in the autumn of it his great sovereign died.

Maria Theresa was sixty-three. She was still vigorous in body, powerful in voice, alert in brain, but for many years a great melancholy had not abandoned her. She had continually contemplated her husband's tomb; her letters to her children, and especially to the Queen of France, were full at the last of an approaching silence. The Bavarian trouble had broken her; in the long expectation of a grandson to the French throne she had been disappointed; the future of her daughter had terrified her — for she saw the gulf. It was upon the 24th of November that she felt her fatal illness; until the 29th she wrote and dictated her affairs of State, and on that very date wrote at length to the Queen. Then she saw Death coming visibly; she staggered into a chair, and with words of rational charity upon her lips she died.

It was a week — Wednesday, the 6th of December — before the news could reach Versailles. It came at evening. Marie Antoinette saw suddenly receding, as the sea had receded from Lisbon at her birth, the principal aspect of her life. The memory of her mother, and the constant letters — scolding, anxious, loving, or imperious — had been her only homely thing where everything around her had been alien and increasingly alien. Her mother for nine years, her mother and Mercy's voice, had been tangible: all the rest was strange. That deep inner part which she did not or could not show, which she herself perhaps did not know, and which appeared but three times upon the surface of her life, rose through its eager and not profound levels of sense. Her whole frame was broken; she spat blood. She put herself that hour in black of every kind disordered, and she met the coming year charged with a sorrow that could now never wholly leave her. But that year was to give her the two chief things of that phase in her life — the news of a successful battle and the birth of a son; and a third — the woman *La Motte*, through whom the chief of her evils were to come upon her.

Far off in Virginia, La Fayette lay at Richmond with a handful of men. Cornwallis made a dash for him and failed, marched back, burning and plundering, to the coast, received a confused tangle of orders, entered Yorktown and awaited the English fleet. Washington had heard how Grasse in the West Indies would sail with the French fleet; he marched southward to join the French commanders. With him was young Fersen, who for so long had not seen France and who was there volunteered for America: with him also was Rochambeau and all his men, and they hurried to victory together through the wet, heavy summer of 1781 along the Atlantic plain.

Meanwhile in Versailles nothing was toward. The Court had lost its old gaiety in the stress of the war and of the "economies." The Queen awaited and implored a son. The Emperor, coming in July 1781, for the second time to a country he despised, "found much improvement," was entertained at Trianon, and went away. It was August, hot, drowsy, and silent; it was September, and an intense anxiety for the birth — now at last, if it might be — of an heir.

And as that September passed, two things came into this strange life upon which so many varied things arose and joined darkly in their dates; each accident was quite unknown to the Queen.

The first was this, that the British fleet coming up to save Cornwallis found Grasse already within the bay, was beaten off, and with it the chance of succour; so that La Fayette and Washington meeting could and did, just as the month ended, lay siege.

The second was this: that up in the mountains of Alsace, a lady, a friend, introduced a younger lady and a poor one to the notice of the Bishop of Strasburg. He was that coadjutor to the see, now succeeded to it, whom Marie Antoinette had seen as a child — the first to meet her in France after her crossing of the Rhine. He was now the Grand Almoner, and was spending the end of the hot season in his palace of Saverne. It was thus that the woman *La Motte* first touched her victim, the Cardinal de Rohan. And it so happened that the Cardinal de Rohan, who had been the first to greet the Queen on her passage of the Rhine as a child, now aspired to be her lover, or — as his fatuous misconception of her would have put it —"one of her lovers." She for her part had resolutely avoided him. He was odious to her. Upon his ambition and credulity this woman La Motte was to play.

. . . .

It had been upon April 25 that Cornwallis in the Carolinas had broken camp and started northward, to conquer and to hold the central seaports of the rebels, as he had conquered and held Charlestown. On the 20th of May his two hundred miles were marched, and he had joined the troops in Virginia.

That march was not followed in Versailles — and even had it been followed, nothing would have been thought of its progress. The war had lingered so long, the issue had so dragged that no chance could be foreseen, and the tangle of those wildernesses without roads, hardly with towns, was beyond European imagining. They knew that young La Fayette was still desolate somewhere there — they knew no more. Fersen — if more than his bright image came to her, if rumours of his letters home could come to her— must have given the woman who remembered him something of his own lassitude: cooped up as was that Swede in New England, without supplies, without money, cursing the Americans, telling the French Cabinet they were masters of folly, saying the Southern States were conquered by the British, and complaining with a Northern complaint of the indiscipline of the French. But there was greater business to engage attention at Versailles; the Queen was again with child; and Necker, failing at the vast financial tangle, had fallen.

Just as Cornwallis and the army in Virginia met to complete the war, Necker had been sent back from his command of the exchequer to those private and less reputable dealings with which the Puritan was more familiar and at which he was more successful than in the financing of a military nation. The Queen, who had not driven him forth at all, who would have had him remain, was blamed because she did not save him. The rising Democratic opinion of Paris had already vaguely begun to favour Necker's ineptitude: he was a foreigner; he had no faith (save the Genevese mask); he was novel, he was a change — he was therefore demanded, and his dishonesty was not comprehended; yet that dishonesty was even then about to cost some price to the French State, for by his counsel and after his dismissal appeared that first sham Exchequer Statement to deceive the nation, to cajole it into a loan, to embitter it for the future; and the blame of the trick was to fall on the Crown and not on him, its author.

. . . .

It was October, 1781: Cornwallis was surrounded in Yorktown: the British fleet had failed to relieve him and

THE COUNTESS OF PROVENCE
From the bust at Versailles

the siege advanced; the parallels were opened; they were firing at six hundred yards, and Cornwallis still held on. The third week, and they were firing at three hundred: two redoubts still forbade a nearer approach. On the 14th, the two redoubts were carried by the French, and next day came the storming.

The river lay near a mile broad behind Yorktown: he might yet cross to Gloucester; his guns were dismantled and his force shattered, more by sickness than by fire, but he made the attempt, and the wind defeated him. Upon that ominous Friday, the 19th, he laid down his arms, and England had lost the war. By an accident native to lingering campaigns, a series of chances and one coincidence at the end — the entry of the French fleet — had suddenly determined the issue: the young boys of the French Court, heretofore grumbling and themselves disliked, were suddenly become heroes; the colonists, "half savages," "mostly traitors to the English," were suddenly become "the athletes of Liberty"; many in England and all the Rivals of England made up their minds that the business of England was at an end.

. . . .

It was Fersen, with his command of French and English, who had negotiated that surrender. Soon he would return.

. . . .

At Versailles that October Friday and the week-end following it were still. For the few days the Court was silent. The issue of the expected childbirth had been debated or feared; it was now not mentioned in an intensity of expectation. The morning of the Monday that silence continued. The King had ordered his Hunt;

four of the carriages were already started; when he bethought him before he left to see the Queen again. He thought her to be in pain, and though she denied the pain, he ordered the Hunt to return, and an unusual rumour and press at once filled the great galleries. It was a little after eleven o'clock when the passages and halls were full of a gathering crowd, and the cold and splendid staircase which made the royal life at Versailles a public thing, a thing of the open air, were already crammed before noon by a mob of the populace; but this time custom was disdained and the doors were shut fast. Within the Queen lay groaning on her pallet-bed before the fireplace, but there was air around her: no such press as had all but killed her three years before. Yet that exclusion of the populace helped to kill the Monarchy.

At one o'clock a Swedish noble, chancing to be at the Queen's door, was told the news. He was caught and electrified by it as though he had been of the French blood. He turned to the first woman he met and said: "We have an heir!" Now that woman happened to be Provence's wife, and the scene—her red anger and her disdain, his bewilderment—were taken up at once into the laughter of the moment. All the world laughed or cried; it was like the excitement of a great victory turning the tide of a disastrous war.

The Queen, when she could speak, noting the silence round her pallet, and hearing the noise without, said faintly and smiling: "I have been a good patient. . . . Tell me the truth." They were still silent, and she was sure that another daughter had been born, till the King came in and said to her:—

"The Dauphin begs leave to come in."

VIII

FIGARO

MONDAY, OCTOBER 22, 1781, TO APRIL 27, 1784

THE birth of an heir struck, as it seemed, an epoch in the evident transformation of the Monarchy, and in the increasing position which Marie Antoinette occupied upon that scene; not that such a birth was either unexpected or unlikely. The Court and the nation had known for now three years that the royal family was established; it was certain that children would now support and surround the throne, and even in the preceding year nothing but a natural accident had postponed the hope of a prince. But the living presence of the child, the founding of a secure succession within so short a period from the earlier disappointment, had, as have all symbols, an effect greater than that which calculable changes could expect.

A wide popular enthusiasm, though later it was extinguished, did for the moment rise spontaneously to the encouragement of Government, and that initiative which the French had for centuries demanded and still demanded from the custodians of their State was, as it were, thrust into the hand of Louis.

Of all qualities in ruling that which this people will least forgive is ease: in their delight at the news of a Dauphin, France, and particularly Paris, implicitly urged to energy if not the good-humoured and slow-thoughted man who was in theory the whole executive, at least the machinery of which he was the centre. A new phase of one sort or another had certainly begun.

Sudden causes of change are never unaccompanied by coincidence; allied forces invariably converge upon the main cause of change and unite for a common effort. Three such advancing supports synchronised in these last months of 1781 — the new aspect of the Austrian Alliance, the success in America, and the death of old Maurepas, who since the accession of Louis XVI., had presided at the Council. Each of these accidents was singly powerful; in their combination they were irresistible; and a moment of opportunity to which a man of rapid decision might have given the greatest effect, was apparent even to Louis in the close of that year.

The result of Maria Theresa's death, and of Joseph II.'s uncontrolled power in Austria had now matured. The naïf but persistent enmity of the Emperor towards the Faith — whose doctrines were in his little vision as barbaric as the Gothic architecture, and whose rapid elimination from European culture he took for granted — was, if not the mainspring, at least the chief expression of that general action whereby he imperilled his house and profoundly modified the situation of Austria. His preparation to rob and destroy the religious orders, his unconcealed contempt for the ideal they represented, his similar pretension that patriotism was a superstition, his petty but sincere conviction that none save material benefits guided by moral abstractions were of use to mankind — in a word, his despotic atheism — culminated in an "Edict of Toleration," which, when allowance is made for a century's development, may be compared for its affront against the customs of his subjects to that which had cost James II. of England his throne. In itself it had no bearing upon France and was hardly heard of in that country, but it was a recantation of all that Maria Theresa had stood for; it meant an open admiration for Frederick of Prussia, his method and his principle; it argued a philosophy which would, not reluctantly and of necessity, but eagerly and of set purpose, overset old traditions and sacred landmarks that had attempted the suppression of a national language in Hungary, and was to suggest time and again as a simple solution of political problems, the denial of all that for which men have always been prepared to die.

This act, the precursor and the type of so many others of his, was signed in Vienna during that same month of October, 1781, which saw the happy delivery of his sister at Versailles, and the culmination of the American War upon the Chesapeake. Nay, these capital events fell within one week. It was upon a Monday that the Edict was promulgated, upon the following Monday that the Dauphin was born, upon the Friday between that the English and German garrison in Yorktown laid down its arms.

The success of the war in America, especially the dramatic finale of Cornwallis's surrender, had an effect upon opinion in Paris which, though it was sudden and short, was yet very powerful. The French, having of all nations by far the most general experience of war, are slow to adventures of such a kind as their intervention in America: the Court had been especially slow; the King perhaps the most reluctant of all — in the last peril of death he exclaimed against the memory of that campaign. Once engaged, therefore, if matters had gone ill (as the French troops in America most characteristically swore they would go ill!), or even if a long and indefinite campaign had dragged on through succeeding years, so that the full financial effect of the struggle could have been felt before its close, then the whole weight of blame would have fallen upon Versailles. As it was, Yorktown came like the thrust of a spur, and the Monarchy, doubtful as was its course, leapt forward.

The death of Maurepas was the last coincidence of these three; it was as exactly synchronous and as full of effect as either of its fellow accidents. The capitulation of Lord Cornwallis was known in Paris precisely thirty-one days after it had taken place. It was upon the 19th of November, a Monday, that Louis had the news. The Queen had not yet risen from child-bed. Louis was sitting with her in her room when the Duc de Lauzun was announced, and gave the message that Yorktown had surrendered. Upon the Wednesday following, De Maurepas was dead. The importance of that passing lay in this, that Louis, at such a juncture, now first attempted to be free.

All men are chafed, and that perpetually, by what they know of their own defects, and Louis could not forget, from his accession onwards, that it was always in him to yield to a quicker brain. He thought it shameful in a King. He never yielded from weakness, but often from bewilderment. His own decision would come to him after he had acted on the decision of another. He understood, he desired to act, later than did his advisers: often so late that, by the time his will was formed, occasion had passed. If, when his slow judgment had matured, he found it different from that upon which immediate action had been taken, he was angered. If that immediate action had proved disastrous, he was secretly indignant that his slower wit had not prevailed. But, stronger than all these reasons, the mere instinct of the imperfect warned him to a distaste of guidance.

He had, however, come to the throne a boy; in years but twenty, in experience (save in the excellent art of horsemanship) null. He had found ready to hand his old minister, Maurepas, courteous, active, with a good though a too facile judgment; a patriot whose career had been ruined by the mistress of Louis XV. (in itself this was a recommendation to the young King), and a courtier whom his father, the Dauphin, had, upon his deathbed, pointed out to be the true counterweight to the irreligion of Choiseul: Louis XVI. had accepted such a guide and had upon the whole not repented of his choice. For seven years the young King had received the counsel of this old man; a habit had been formed, and a strong affection with it. But as Maurepas approached his end, as the gout forbade him his former clearness of thought, and a continual confinement interfered with his attendance at the Council, the maturer judgment of Louis began, though secretly, to assert itself. He showed for the depositary of so lengthy a Court tradition a filial devotion; he would come in person, and familiarly, to bring news to the old man's room — notably the news of the Dauphin's birth was so given, domestically and alone. There subsisted between them one of those intimate relations which so often arise between the permanent official upon the one side, and the responsible authority upon the other: it became a personal tie, and when Maurepas died Louis would renew it with no one. After some hesitation the King lit for a first minister upon Vergennes, but he would not give to this new officer the official title; he was jealous of a fuller power which he now proposed to exercise continuously and with a more direct affirmation than in the past. Louis was incapable of the task he so attempted, but if ever there was a time in the reign when such a task could be attempted, this autumn and winter of 1781 was that time.

Here then was the field: a treasury embarrassed, but relieved, in appearance at least, by a frank audit — for the cooked accounts Necker had prepared before his dismissal bore that aspect and title of a public audit; great and unexpected success in a doubtful foreign war; a monarch possessed of a power approaching that of a modern Cabinet, and now ready to experiment with that power; abroad, Joseph II., who was the chief element of international politics and the national ally of France, had entered upon a new direction of the Austrian House. Upon such a field was to work the increasing influence of the Queen.

It is true that a certain part of her repute was now fixed in public opinion: that she was extravagant, that she was bound to favourites, that she was foreign. The legend had arisen in Paris, and no detail of her action, no appreciation of complexity could easily alter the simple conclusions of the Parisian populace. But, on the other hand, she was the mother of the heir, her position was stable while the opinion of the capital was not so, and it did not seem impossible that in the long course of years the great and dumb national mass should be so indoctrinated in her favour, as the growth of her children, an older judgment in her, and perhaps a continued peace and a return to prosperity, should restore the tradition of the monarchy or rather confirm it in its new characters.

If the King was now ready to act and to reform the State, Marie Antoinette was of far more influence with him than ever she had been before. It was hers, if she chose, to regulate the new phase of Government. She did in part so choose, and she might have succeeded. Her habits would, indeed, have continued — her cards, her theatre, her gems, her familiarity — but all, as it were, tinctured, accepted, taken with the life of the Court and little affecting a new-found order. Had the problems presented to her been of those that fitted her intuition or experience, she might even then have lifted her fate. For a year and for more than a year — all 1782 and on into 1783 — the solidity of her position was assured; the future was apparently prepared. A group of trifling incidents passed her quite, or almost, unperceived in the midst of an established leadership in Europe, of royal visits that cemented a general alliance, and of accomplished hopes; another year passed, she was presented — her influence being then at its height — with the affair of the Scheldt, a problem in which the interests of her Austrian House clashed with that new patriotism which, least of all things French, could she understand. She blundered, she necessarily blundered; but as she looked around to see what forces were left her, she found not only the results of that blunder confronting her, but an appalling menace proceeding from a direction wholly unconnected with her life — from the business of the diamond necklace — and beside it, grown suddenly quite loud like an offensive chorus of disdain, the voice of a writer whom she had half patronized and wholly despised, the neglected voice of Caron — Beaumarchais: by the beginning of '84, one of those accidents — the pen of

Beaumarchais — had shaken her influence and that of all the Monarchy; by the end of '85 the other — the affair of the necklace — had destroyed it.

. . . .

The year 1782 opened upon the new gladness of the Queen; her churching at Notre Dame (now customary) was marked, if not by a vivid popular greeting yet by no coldness. At the Hôtel de Ville in the evening she met an official and commercial world that was warmly hers; she shared as warmly in the glories of the American news; she would have driven home in her own carriage the wife of La Fayette to show her enthusiasm for his triumph and his return. Her ampler manner, her more contained and settled bearing, was consonant with the position she had gained; it promised her, in those who saw and approved it among the magistracy of the city, a continuance and an increase of influence. Back at Versailles she continued without scandal, and yet at a fast-rising expenditure, the habits which had now become permanently hers: new fashions in dress perpetually changing and in head-dress, cards to the small hours, and her private theatre at Trianon still receiving her upon its stage to the applause now, not of a half-dozen or so of the royal family, but of a full audience; many courtiers, many friends of friends, and even the officers of the Guard were permitted to see her painted behind the foot-lights, to note her true rendering of vivacious parts, and to accept when she sang her imperfectly-trained, insufficient and somewhat violent voice. Of these regular dissipations the last was the most criticised, though even that seemed by this time so normal that of itself it did not lessen her growing power; but in distant connection with her taste for such things there arose, and precisely at this critical moment, a discussion which was largely to affect her life: it was the discussion upon the "Mariage de Figaro."

The "Mariage de Figaro" was no great thing; it was a well-written play from the pen of a man, now advanced in middle age, whose diction and care for letters were typical of his own time, but whose vices were entirely modern. Born in a low position, his darting mind had carried him to a sort of fluctuating eminence, especially in wit. He had taught music to princesses, married an infatuated widow, adopted her name of Beaumarchais, purchased some insignificant post and with it a nominal right to the "de" of nobility, preserved his health, speculated, probably robbed, certainly made and lost considerable sums, traversed and thoroughly understood English society, repaid its hospitality by advancing the American cause in France, speculated upon the commissariat of that campaign, rendered jealous years ago the equally cynical Voltaire, and now, at fifty, was getting talked of again in the matter of his new play.

He and it were little things to Marie Antoinette, but the rumour of them was considerable, for, a few months before, at the end of the past year, the King had heard that this "Mariage de Figaro" was not tolerable. It was a satire upon all established things. The play was already ordered for the Théâtre Français. Louis had it read to him privately, and for once made a rapid decision. As literature he could not judge its considerable merits; as politics he put his foot down: such laughter at such an expense to government and all tradition were not to be borne — and the licence was withdrawn. The public rumour rose and grew.

Every witty lady about the Court and in the capital, many

more who desired a reputation for wit, insisted upon reading the play; upon hearing it read aloud; upon having Beaumarchais come and read it aloud. All the Polignac world was mad on it. Loménie de Brienne boasted that he had heard it oftenest. The Princesse de Lamballe moved heaven and earth to have it read by the author in her very rooms.

The "Mariage de Figaro" was, therefore, to the Queen a perpetual phrase on the lips of the smart, literary and unliterary: it is doubtful if she read a line of it, but she heard of it and heard of it again. She forgot it for the moment; later she remembered it again — not to her good.

Meanwhile a much larger matter vexed her. In the midst of her active and interested life, of promotions, personal successes and habitual pleasures, the insistence of her brother Joseph continually pursued her, and a mixed anxiety, an anxiety to be political, an anxiety to escape responsibility, came to her almost daily — from Mercy immediately, ultimately from Vienna: she felt upon her the uneasy burden of the Hapsburgs.

While her mother still lived there had at least been between her and Marie Antoinette an unbroken habit of command upon the one side, obedience and protest upon the other. The pressure of Vienna had been a natural one then. Maria Theresa possessed, moreover, the tact not only of a woman, and of a religious woman, but the large vision of a careful and perilous diplomacy brought to success. Joseph lacked all these: religion, honour, tact, acquaintance, experience. His commands to Mercy were as crude as any of his judgments upon the world: "Had Mercy seen the Queen?" "Was she doing her duty by the

House of Austria?" "Would Mercy suggest this, that?" "Since the Queen was so powerful with the King, why had this, that detail of French policy not *exactly* suited the demands of the Empire?" Broken by the buffer of Mercy's long experience these arid and unfruitful hastes came less brutally to the ears of Marie Antoinette. She never felt herself the servant of her family, nor in direct antagonism to the Crown of her husband; she felt only that she was perpetually required to be doing — she hardly knew what — much as in her mother's time, but without the aid of her mother's handwriting and remembered voice; certainly without her mother's wisdom to control.

The pressure from Joseph II. continued; it was to be two years before it took effect in a great matter, but when that matter arose the Queen's plain service to Vienna — something far in excess of what she had shown in the Bavarian affair — showed how much that irksome and long pressure had effected. She came to act as an Austrian army would have acted, and quite understanding all she did, she came very near to betraying her allegiance to the French throne.

For the rest these early months of '82 were filled, among her pleasures and her rising power, with other annoyances; notably that from time to time her friends in that excessive society of hers spoke to her of their debts, and she knew well that in the matter of money grants at that moment of increasing embarrassment in public finance the King himself was slow to listen to her.

There were many such friends. The greatest and the nearest perhaps of those whom Marie Antoinette knew to be embarrassed were the Guémenées, and the Duchesse de Guémenée, the titular governess of the Dauphin, a woman whom she met most constantly and cherished, closely concerned her.

She further suffered the ceaseless and recurrent advances of the Cardinal de Rohan. It had become enough for her to see his handwriting upon a note to make her burn the thing unread. Her dislikes were now often reasoned, always steady; it was enough that she had to meet the Grand Almoner upon State occasions of religion or ceremonial; her society she forbade him. Had the Cardinal wanted proof of that stupidity which he was later to plead in Court as the excuse of his follies, he could have given none better, nor any of more weight with posterity, than his complete ignorance of such a woman as was this daughter of Maria Theresa, and his absurd advances to gain her intimacy, her support, and possibly her heart. Had he known women even vaguely, by types, this florid and handsome man would have abandoned at fifty the attempt to interest a vital, impetuous woman of twenty-seven, loving swift pleasure, but superior to him in rank, chaste, a mother, and carrying against him in particular a traditional grudge for the loose jests which, during a brief embassy at Vienna, he was wont to pass at the expense of her own people. But the Cardinal de Rohan did not know women even in the mass, and it was necessary, as he thought, that he should play cards with her and be from time to time one of the fifty or so who eat supper with her at Trianon. He had the weakness of stupid men when they are well born and have attained office — I mean the ambition for political titles.

A thousand lesser incidents of this time she could not herself, had you asked her daily, have recorded. One among such petty details it is worth the reader's while to recall, though it had made upon her even less impression than the babble about Beaumarchais' play; though it passed completely from her memory. It was the presence now and then upon the stairways of Versailles, and for moments only, of a short woman, very fair, with a small, well-arched foot, and delicate hands, quick and even furtive of glance, not beautiful but attractive and provoking in face, dressed in a manner that combined excess with the evidences of poverty, but in her gestures of a passable breeding. This figure was often seen; now leaving the room of some lady of the Court, now crossing the courtyard on foot towards the town.

The Queen may or may not have heard that this woman, though an adventuress, was (from over the left) a Valois; of some birth, therefore, but very poor, and given to borrowing small sums: Marie Antoinette's sister-in-law of Provence, Madame, may or may not have told the Queen that she had got this woman a tiny advance of thirty pounds upon her tiny pension of twenty-four. Whether her name of "De la Motte," or so much as the presence of this chance passer, was noted by Marie Antoinette is not known, but certainly if either were it took no more place in her mind than any other of the hundred insignificant names she heard and forgot every day. Moreover, after the early spring of 1782, this woman was no longer seen at Versailles; she had borrowed a few pounds, and was gone.

With May the true life of the Court and the active interests of the Queen awoke to receive the first of those great political visits which form the historical pageant of Versailles: the heir of Catherine of Russia came with his wife, and the whole year might almost have been named from so conspicuous an event.

The inordinate pomp of royalty in its old age had led to

a fashion of incognito which did not have, and was not intended to have, its occasional modern effect of privacy, but which, by cutting short interminable and necessary ritual, left a crowned traveller the freer for luxury and dissipation. It saved them the judges, the orators, the Governors, the Universities — in general the middle classes, and left them free for actors, wine, and their own company, and the frenzied plaudits of the innumerable poor. The Emperor of Austria had set the fashion five years before; it was followed now by the Russian Court, and Catherine's son chose to present himself in France under the somewhat theatrical alias of the "Comte du Nord."

The Grand-Duke Paul had the face of a Tartar, and — what was piquant—the manners, and, above all, the ready epigrams of a Parisian. His wife was a huge German woman, rather absolute and — what was curious — learned. For exactly a month they dominated the Court of France; from the end of May to the end of June they filled it with their presence, and not a little of the hankering after French things and French alliances, which, much later, distinguished Paul III. during the revolutionary wars, may have sprung from this short and vivid episode of his twenty-eighth year.

It is characteristic of Marie Antoinette that the prospect of a great encounter and of the society of equals confused her; it is equally characteristic of her that once she had got over that nervousness she drew the young man and his wife at once into that rather isolated and over-familiar circle of intimates with which Mercy, her brother, and the French reproached her, but without which, as it seemed, she could not live. Behind the solemn and rare functions, the regal hospitality of the Condés at Chantilly and the Court ball at Versailles, was a whole atmosphere of gambling and private theatricals; of plays at Trianon, intimate suppers, costly presents given at a moment's thought, and, very late at night, in the rooms of Madame de Polignac or in the Queen's, when the King had left them, a complete ease full of little improvised dances and familiar jests. In such an atmosphere the German Grand-Duchess maintained, perhaps a little stiffly, her formal compliments, but the Russian Grand-Duke went headlong; he suffered the spell; there was even a moment when he confided to the Queen his humiliation at home and the tyranny of his mother Catherine.

Upon one matter the husband and the wife most certainly agreed, for to the second it was belles-lettres, to the first Parisiana: they must have things read to them "by the authors." All the little tricks with which the wealthy and leisured inveigle the masters of the pen to visit their palaces, to amuse them for an hour, were set at work.

Of the many so caught one was especially demanded, and the Queen heard again, not without boredom, the perpetual name of Beaumarchais. "Oh, yes, you must hear Beaumarchais!" Madame de Lamballe had got him to her rooms. It was difficult, but she had got him. The Archbishop of Toulouse knew him well. He was splendid. "You must hear him read this play of his; it has been forbidden, you know. It is seditious. It is so witty, and he does read it so well!" The Comte du Nord and his wife asked no better than to be in the swim. Beaumarchais was willing enough; he came and read to them, and they heard from his thin ironic lips, saw illustrated by his exact gesture and brilliant, ambitious little eyes, the edge and sharpness of a drama that worked — once it was public —

like an acid, to the destruction of all their world. How they applauded!

That warm month of long evenings that fade into early dawns shining with lamps in the park, with candles and mirrors in the vast length of the palace, was approaching its end, when, for the last time, Marie Antoinette devised her last considerable fête — once more at Trianon.

It was to be a garden fête at night: by this time certainly wearisome to the Grand-Duchess, but to the Grand-Duke attractive — with this one flaw, that on the morrow he would be gone. The fête was held; it was brilliant and full. At its close when, as custom demanded, the royal party passed out, down a lane of guests on either side, the Queen saw — for a moment — a pair of red stockings; the legs were neither meagre nor young. All the rest of the figure was a large dark cloak, but she caught beneath the hat of it the somewhat flushed and large face of the Grand Almoner.

This little incident disturbed her. Here was a private gala of her own, given only to those of her private circle privately invited by her, and this odious man must creep in. Next day when her guests were gone she spent some portion of her considerable energy in ferreting out the culprit. The incident was traced to the lodge-keeper of Trianon, who had taken a bribe from the cardinal under a promise that if he were let in he would keep a strict disguise and would not penetrate into the gardens. The lodge-keeper was sent his way to starve, and later — since he really did begin to starve — was given back his place by this impulsive woman.

It was a very little though a very exasperating incident that a great officer of the Crown, whom etiquette compelled her to meet in chapel, but whom she had carefully excluded from her intimacy and her privileges, should have appeared by a trick at a party so especially her own. Perhaps she remembered it as one remembers for a long while petty accidents that have sharply moved us for an hour. He certainly remembered it, for he had been found out in no very dignified manœuvres. He was certainly sore; but in men of his stupidity, of his privileges, and of his habits of luxury, hatred is no enduring passion. His ambition, however, such as it was, remained; he was the more determined to succeed in that high object of recognition and of friendship with the Queen, from the results of this disastrous attempt and from the failure of his appearance on that June night at Trianon. . . . . It was but a week later that Madame de la Motte came into Paris, called at his palace in the Marais, and reminded him of his earlier charities.

The uneventful summer came and passed, full of the customary glories, of the customary distractions. No date marked evil or good. The American War, though it languished, was now decided, and England had given up the struggle. The reform of the French finances, though ceaselessly a topic of council, was as ceaselessly neglected. The Emperor continues to badger Mercy, and Mercy to badger the Queen upon matters of no importance save to Joseph II.'s ill-considered plans of aggrandisement.

. . . .

Fersen, pottering between Philadelphia and Baltimore, wrote home — wearily — but not to her.

. . . .

It was a long summer of nothingness, during which Marie Antoinette's position was confirmed, her public view a trifle, if but a trifle, enlarged. With her habits permitted. her popularity sufficient, her influence established, she had a foretaste of that security such as should accompany middle life, and such as is native to women for whom such satisfaction is allied with maternity; she turned for an added interest to her children.

The little Princess Royal could talk and run; the baby Dauphin knew his sister already and moved his arms at her approach. The two children between them filled daily a larger and more natural place in the Queen's thoughts. They could not indeed weaken the habits which those first feverish three years had rooted and the next had done nothing to destroy, but their innocence and the nameless bond of flesh enlarged her; their growth, their surprising discovery of new days. It was not wholly without reason that the King their father grew at this moment to listen in smaller things to her advice beyond that of others.

Ceremonial, or rather lucrative, as were the functions of the Princesse de Guémenée, she was yet constantly in attendance upon the children, of which she was titular governess, and the Queen was constantly in her society. The charge was a great one; if it had first been granted as a favour to one of the set of favourites, it had now ripened into something more, for the common interest in such a couple as Madame Royale and the heir gave rise, in this middle of '82, to an occasional communion between the Queen and the gouvernante, which neither found in the general and much more continual amusement of their set. Their intimacy was the greater that the children had been sent through the park to Trianon during the hot weather, that the Princesse de Guémenée was with them secluded there, and that there she and the Queen were necessarily often alone together. In her favourite retreat and under her domestic trees, the approaching vaccination of the little girl — a matter of moment at that time — and a dozen details of the sort concerned them. By a petty accident of a sort common to aristocracies, the Cardinal de Rohan, the Queen's aversion, happened to be own brother to Madame de Guémenée, the Queen's chief friend. Not a word was said in favour of that brother, for these were matters upon which even the Queen's favourites were compelled to keep silence; but the populace, who do not understand such complexities, remembered the relationship.

The complaints of the lesser woman upon the debts of herself and her husband — though such complaints are wearing to the closest friendships — did no more than slightly weary the Queen. They were soon forgotten, for Marie Antoinette held in a profound manner that faith in chance good fortunes and in ultimate relief without which those who never labour could not live; and when the complaints were done with, she turned to speak of the children.

So August went by and most of September, when, one morning at the close of that month, Monsieur de Guémenée very suddenly declared that he could not so much as attempt to pay his debts, and threw himself upon his creditors.

It was a shock. I have repeatedly insisted in this book upon the insignificance of French extravagance in the close of the eighteenth century, in comparison with the modern figures of our Plutocracy, and on the modesty of the sums the historian has to deal with—£5,000 a year was a princely fortune; the Cardinal de Rohan's £30,000 a year seemed almost the revenue of a State, an income beyond computation. Well, in such a world, accustomed to such a scale of wealth, the Guémenées went bankrupt for a solid million of our English pounds. It opened a whirlpool in the finances of the time, and the creditors, to make matters worse, were of every rank and spread throughout the kingdom; there were peasants among them, prelates, farmers-general, and — most clamorous of all — a few large and many small shopkeepers of Paris. To these last — especially to the smaller ones — delay would be fatal. Delay was precisely the expedient chosen.

There exists a little, ill-written scrawl addressed to the princess; it is ill-spelt, with words omitted in its haste. It runs: "You have heard that my daughter's vaccination has gone off well — I breathe again! . . . The King will see you get those letters all right." That scrawl was written by Marie Antoinette and the "letters" mentioned were the *Moratorium* which a French King could of his own free will impose as might the caprice of a judge upon the process of law. It was a royal decree forbidding during the King's pleasure the recovery of a debt. The creditors must wait till it was lifted.

That little scrap of paper was not known to the populace — it was not discovered till a few years ago — but the populace, with an instinct that rarely failed them during the pre-revolutionary and revolutionary time, guessed by what influence had been granted this privilege of delay; with all its fatal consequences to the smaller folk, who spread their anger until Paris was humming with it, and even the remoter provinces (notably Brittany), wherever there was a wretched unpaid creditor to be found, whispered the name of the Queen.

She, upon her part, felt she had done next to nothing — an obvious and small act of courtesy for a dear friend. She had chosen that very moment to be at La Muette with the Court — not at Versailles, to which such things were native, but right at the gates of Paris, and there thought fit to do something more for her friend than the trifle already effected. She went to the Chancellor of the Exchequer, Fleury — at a time when the Treasury in its deep embarrassment was expecting the counter-shock of the American War, at a time when the last additional taxes could hardly be paid — to ask him if (irony of ignorance!) "something could not be done" for the Guémenées. Fleury could do nothing, and it was as well.

. . . .

All this while and all that summer and autumn the little, active, furtive woman, De La Motte, the Valois with the well-arched foot and the shifty but provocative eye, was pecking at De Rohan: now knocking discreetly at his palace doors in Paris, now travelling, as cheaply as could be, to his great château in the Vosges — borrowing a few pounds, and again a few pounds. It was a very little thing, like a drifting rag in a great city — but a rag infected with the plague.

. . . .

In such a commotion as the crash of the Guémenées made, no one noticed that the Queen procured for her chief friend, for one who hardly desired it and who was ill fitted for it, for Madame de Polignac, the high post which Madame de Guémenée had been compelled to resign. The new charges such an appointment involved were forgotten in the torrent of feeling that followed the great bankruptcy. It came just as the excitement upon America had thoroughly died down, just as the bills for that war had to be met, and just as winter was upon the populace. The new taxes were collecting, the whole financial system was at a breaking point, when early in '83, Fleury resigned the finances. His fall was furthered by the Queen, who remembered his refusal.

If, a year before, the satire of Beaumarchais had been wisely suppressed by the King, and if nine months before, even the reading by heirs apparent of so fierce a piece of wit was thought hazardous, now it was plainly a peril. To extend the fame of that solvent of society, even by discreet recitations within the palace was unwise; to act it, to add to its native force of aggression gesture, life, and publicity of the stage, would be a piece of madness. Most ardently was that amusing piece of madness desired by the lassitude of the Court and by those amateurs in changing pastime who surrounded the Queen. It is said that she pleaded again for her friends, and begged, as she had before, for the piece to be licensed. If she did so, she failed; for leave to act the "Mariage de Figaro," even upon the private stage of a courtier, was again refused.

Side by side with such details went the growth of yet another great European conflict, and with it once again the pressure of Austria upon Marie Antoinette.

For over a century the Scheldt had been closed to commerce by international treaty, and the trade that should naturally flow along that magnificent estuary of which Antwerp is the port had been artificially deflected to Holland. The Austrian Netherlands were therefore mechanically starved of a trade that had once been pre-eminent in Europe. It was as though Lancashire should be forbidden by a parchment to use Liverpool to-day, and should be dependent upon Preston or — as would more probably follow — upon Bristol and Glasgow. That part of the Low Countries which is, roughly speaking, the Catholic part and most of which is now included in Belgium formed, by an accident of history, an isolated fragment of the Hapsburg domain, and the closing of the Scheldt acutely affected a monarch whose mind, being narrow, was especially alive to anomalies that interfered with the rotundity of his rights. There was to Joseph II. something monstrous in the decay of Antwerp and the silence of that vast waterway—something out of nature, like the diversity of tongues, within his empire; it was a sentiment he felt less keenly in matters less disadvantageous to himself.

The chief beneficiary by this quaint artifice was, of course, Holland, but, among the greater powers, England. If anyone would know why, he has but to travel to-day from the Pool of London to Antwerp, and wonder next morning at the orderly and teeming crescent of the quays. Antwerp is London's chief and most dangerous rival.

It was, therefore, during the failure of England in America that Joseph proposed the destruction of so ancient an instrument as the Peace of Westphalia and determined upon the opening of the river. To such a project the assent of France was essential, but the Cabinet of Versailles, in one of those acts of wisdom which were not unknown to the decaying Monarchy, postponed the discussion to the close of the war. The war had been over since the autumn of '82; the peace had been signed at Paris in the new year. It was in 1783, therefore, that there began the growing pressure of Joseph II. upon Mercy, of Mercy upon Marie Antoinette, to see that the interests of Austria in this matter, as in others of the past, should predominate at Versailles. This purely Austrian move, though it took months to mature, was the political motive of the whole year, and side by side with it, like a tiny instrument accompanying a loud orchestra, went the rising popular demand for Beaumarchais' play: also, just once or twice and for a moment only, one can hear in the background the occasional note of Madame de La Motte. Thus on Candlemas Day (a feast of the 2d of February) she was seen at Versailles. It was a brief episode; she stood patiently in the rank of petitioners waiting for the Queen to pass upon her way to High Mass, and presented some modest demand — directly or indirectly — for money. It was refused, with a crowd of others, by the secretaries appointed to examine such things; and, if the Queen's eyes had rested upon her face at all, no sort of impression of her remained. The Queen entered the chapel, and the Cardinal de Rohan pontificated there.

"Figaro" was more amusing and deserves a greater mention. All the jokes of the spring and all the society question was of "Figaro." By June, somehow or other, by some intrigue, very possibly by a word from the Queen, the scandalous, the delightfully tickling attack upon all their privileges, their scandals — their very life; the comedy that half of them already knew by heart, and from which the younger could recite whole passages in Beaumarchais' very manner, was to be acted at last — but only for the Court. Of course, such a scandal could not be allowed in Paris, or in the town. The Hall of the Menus Plaisirs was got ready, the parts were learnt, the actors of the Comédie Française were come, the courtiers and their wives had their tickets in hand, the carriages were at the door, the theatre half full, when a messenger came from the King bearing a *lettre de cachet*, a peremptory, secret and immediate order: the "Mariage de Figaro" was not to be played.

All who have seen a jostle of the wealthy suddenly

deprived of some pleasure — especially of a satire upon themselves — may imagine the anger that arose. Meanwhile the King, who had bethought him so late of this vigorous act, murmured thoughtfully in his room that probably in the long run Beaumarchais would have the best of it.

He had. By September M. de Vandreuil had the play ready for "the ladies" and young Artois — he had put up a private stage. The smart and the literary were assured there would be no disappointment — nor was there. Beaumarchais had been recalled by a special secret messenger from England, whither he had retired in a pretended pique; secret permission was given, the "Mariage" was secretly played (before two hundred people), and the thing was done. Play-acting and a sort of passionate frivolity had conquered the State. I must ask pardon for wasting so many lines upon so light a matter.

Two greater things were at hand: Calonne was about to be put at the head of the finances; Joseph II. was beginning to be decisive about the Scheldt.

The business of the Scheldt had dragged all through 1783. The active hostility of France and England had ceased a year before — to the grave disadvantage of England. Peace had been actually signed for nine months, yet nothing had been done, and the Cabinet of Versailles still temporised. To Joseph this recalcitrance upon the part of his ally was not only irritating, as had been years ago the French hesitation to support him in the Bavarian chance of war, it was incomprehensible; he could lay it to nothing but folly. To what depths of folly Versailles might descend he would admit even his clear brain incapable of judging. The French lay, as he conceived, open to every attack.

Theirs was a power visibly in decay which had made indeed a chance lucky move beyond the Atlantic, but which could not long continue great. It was surely their duty, as it was obviously their policy, to be guided by Vienna. It was not till now — after so many years! — that he had come across the sharp French "jib" which has since his time disconcerted so many diplomatists.

For the statesmen of that people, under every régime, at least, every modern régime (wherein I count the later ministers of Louis XV. and the anti-clericals of the present Republic) — have much in them, whatever their rank, of their own peasantry. It is as though the Frenchman, when he acts as a Minister for the collectivity of France, were collectively inspired and thought like the mass of ploughmen that build up his nation. As the peasants perpetually bewail the weather, so he the times. As the peasants curse authority (which they are so zealous to maintain as a guarantee of property), so the statesman the régime of his epoch. As they will speculate rashly once in a generation, so he in the Seven Years' War or in 1870. As they for years after such an error build up a fortune in the stodgiest securities, so he will build up alliances and an army in the long periods of national repose. As they with protestations of ruin and yet with courtesy will relinquish as make-weight to a bargain some article wholly worthless to them, so he will reluctantly throw into the diplomatic scale some barren or untenable possession overseas. As they in a bargain ask with the most natural air a most fantastic price, so he in a diplomatic proposition. But, above all, as the French Peasantry, when their apparent stupidity tempts the city man to ask for something that really concerns them, become first dumb, then nasty, so the

French Statesman, quite unexpectedly and in one clouds over and reveals an astonishing obstinacy to yi any point of material value to his nation.

The opening of the Scheldt was of no advantage to France. The existence of a strong Austrian State to the north of her was a thing to avoid; the diplomatic tradition of a hundred years was in support of Holland, and, though the Austrian Alliance had changed much, it had been made to exercise pressure towards the Elbe, not towards the North Sea. Hence for all the courtesy, the postponements, the protestations of a continued warmth in the alliance and the rest of it, France steadily refused to move. The Emperor Joseph did something he had been slow to do of recent years: he wrote directly to his sister.

. . . .

Far off in the Vosges Madame de La Motte, the little, proud, active woman with the furtive eyes, was closeted with the Cardinal de Rohan in his château of Saverne. She had, she told him, *all but* recovered her true place as a Valois; she needed aid for a *very* little time longer. Here was a bill upon a Jew, down on the plain in Nancy; quite a small bill — not a hundred and fifty pounds. The Cardinal backed her bill.

. . . .

Marie Antoinette could not for the life of her have shown you the Scheldt on the map; she knew her own incompetence, the advice she proffered was null or uncertain, and, in any case, whatever slight suggestion she may have made, was quite passed by in the counsels of her husband. From that moment Joseph was turned, if somewhat slowly, towards action. He would clear the Scheldt by force, and compel the Cabinet of Versailles to follow; he took his time and made his plan — but he did not succeed.

The advent of Calonne was not the least of the accidents that impeded him, and Calonne's appointment with its large consequences was partly — as were now so many things — the work of the Queen. A man of fifty, provincial, a gentleman, a good lawyer; Calonne was a friend of the Polignacs; and Marie Antoinette, on that account alone, supported his candidature to the Direction of Finance: when she knew him she grew to dislike him. He was intensely national, vigorous, gay, a trifle too rapid in thought, ambitious, virile with a Latin virility; he was of a type she could never affect, and it is certain that he despised her intellect and resented her interference with affairs — he probably showed it.

But once he was appointed to the Treasury her distaste came too late. That department, as the entanglement of the public fortune increased in complexity, grew to absorb in importance every other. The complete autonomy of each minister within his department (which was a necessary consequence of Autocracy and the mark of government at Versailles) left him independent of his colleagues. The vast consequence of any Exchequer Act at that moment and thenceforward made the Exchequer supreme over War, over Home, and even over Foreign affairs.

It is difficult to describe the man: his acts must describe him. It is enough to say that he was not corrupt, that he carried through his attempt with courage, that he spent the public money largely and gaily to forward his plan of procuring a large increase of revenue rather than a large reduction of expenditure; that he was saddled with the remains of the American War debt; was heir in office to dishonest and incompetent Necker, and that, so far as mere administration could, it was he in particular who later opened the Revolution by one act of courage, and not without deliberation, when he clearly saw that an active nation needed action to live: for it was he who summoned the Notables and so convened the first of the Assemblies.

. . . .

The winter of '83-'84 was very hard. The new taxes — imposed in the desperate attempt to fill the Treasury during the preceding year, before Calonne came, were just beginning to tell. The new loans — which were Calonne's own — hung over the prosperity of the State. . . . The Queen was at ease; the letters of Rohan no longer came for her to burn; he no longer crept by tricks into her presence. . . . Then there was "Figaro." "Figaro" was being talked of more than ever. . . . The King must give his consent . . . he had given it to a private stage. . . . Come, would he not give it for the public? The play lay there, in the minds of the leisured and the wealthy; it was potentially a destroyer of the State, on which they battened; but boredom is stronger than appetite with the smart, and the smart urged "Figaro" on towards its full and final publicity.

The winter drew on towards spring. It still froze hard. Calonne continued loans and largesse. "To be free of tangle you must borrow; to borrow you must be at ease; to be at ease, you must spend." He spent largely upon the poor of Paris; he consented to fêtes; he took the thing at a charge. As a nation in the grasp of a dreadful foe might win through by loan upon loan and pouring out fresh millions, bribing colonial soldiers recklessly — five six, seven, ten shillings a day, and to hell with the commissariat — so he in the grasp of an embarrassed fiscal system that was dying in an agony and that nothing could recover. Such procedure invited force of itself; it paved the way for a vast physical, armed change to effect renewal. With the old régime no man could have done anything, not the gayest or the most daring; and what régime has ever changed itself? Colonne was killing the old régime.

He even attempted to feed the people of Paris by free gifts. But still the people of Paris were not contented, and above them, in the ranks that make "Opinion," there was an increasing demand, an insistence for the "Mariage de Figaro." It was already March, and the play was still disallowed.

. . . .

In his bishop's palace that March, the woman La Motte was telling the Cardinal de Rohan one of those truly considerable lies upon which history turns; a lie comparable to the lie of Bismarck at Ems — or to any other that any of my readers may cherish. The Cardinal sat listening, his florid, proud, prominent, unintelligent face all ears. "*She had reached the result of so much patient waiting. Her dignity of Valois* (and she was a Valois) *was to be recognised; her lands* (she had no lands) *were to be restored to her. It was the* QUEEN *whom she had conquered: the* QUEEN *was now her friend, her intimate friend. The* QUEEN *would do anything in the world for her. Through her was Rohan's avenue to the* QUEEN. *Her poverty was at an end. She could soon repay so many years of his kindness.*"

. . . .

Marie Antoinette was concerned with little in those weeks; it is just possible she again spoke a word for that eternal "Figaro." If she did she was but one of a hundred — and the King gave way. The censorship should be removed, but on condition that certain passages most offensive to the established order of the State should be deleted. On that point Louis would not budge . . . it made all the difference. They were deleted, and the King — misjudging now — said (not without foreboding): "I hope it will be a frost." On the first night the Public answered him.

A vast crowd broke for hours against the railings of the Comédie Française, a crowd in which every kind of man was crushed against every kind. The doors opened to a mob that stormed the theatre like a citadel, and that, when it entered, could see, in reserved places, and entered in earlier than the public, every head in Paris that counted. Even Monsieur, deep in his private box, was there, and there behind their bars were the Parliament, the Ministry — even, discreetly, the Church.

The play began. . . . To-day, in a society which it has helped to create, its jests seem obvious, its epigrams platitudes. To that eager people, starved of reform in the midst of a huge transformation of society, they were brilliant exactitudes of wit, struck off like bright coins — precisely the thing desired. This man found satisfied as the play proceeded his revenge against bought law, that man his brooding against an old insult of privilege, that other his disgust at an apparent national decline, yet another his mere hunger: and all these Frenchmen found in the play an echo of their national contempt for a government that cannot excuse itself, even by logic; all found and each found his necessity for passion against existing things assuaged by the sparkle and the venom of the play. They roared at it with delight as men do at the close of successful assault. They laughed as do men satisfied to repletion. They felt a common enemy gone under. There was not one so privileged but had heartily supped of ridicule against some aspect of the society he had learnt to despise.

The curtain fell to a storm of triumphant noise. The Parisians went out into the darkness full and fed with the idea of change, and a great crack had opened in the walls of the palace. It was the 27th of April, 1784.

IX

THE DIAMOND NECKLACE

FROM APRIL 27, 1784, TO AUGUST 15, 1785

AS the summer of 1784 broadened through May and June, it led on the Queen to every grace of life, and at last, as it might have been imagined, to security. The season itself was fruitful and serene: the establishment of prestige abroad — so often a forerunner of evil to European nations — was now triumphantly achieved. There was now about the Court an air of solidity and permanence, which the visits of foreign princes continued to confirm, and this air (thanks to Calonne's largesse) seemed less poisoned by that financial ill-ease which had turned even the last victories of the American War into doubtful and anxious things.

Marie Antoinette had entered into that content and calm which often introduces middle age after a youth tormented by an inward insecurity. Her inheritance was sure. Her children had not yet betrayed the doom of their blood. The legend of her follies meant daily a little less, because daily it became more and more of a legend worn by time, dangerous only if its set formula should be filled with life and reality by some new scandal. The violence of her youth now seemed exorcised; her fulness of feature, which had shocked the taste of Louis XV.'s Court, accorded with these her later functions of authority. She was indeed in that full flower of womanhood which later so perturbed the memories of Burke and lent one famous passage of sincerity to his false political rhetoric.

As Marie Antoinette so entered at last into maturity, and, it would seem, into peace, the comedy which was to bring upon her every humiliation entered upon the Stage of this World. In the waters below her, Jeanne de La Motte de Valois, fishing for goldfish, struck and landed her Cardinal.

Gustavus of Sweden, Northerner and Flibbertigibert, the same that had slung diamond necklaces round the Du Barry's little dog and the same that had despised the Dauphine, was at Court in the early days of that June, and saw the Queen now a woman; his affections were immediately moved. There was a touch of flirtation between them; on her side also a real friendship which for years continued in correspondence — for the softness of the North never failed to soothe and to relieve this Austrian woman caught in the hardness of French rules and the pressure of French vitality. He had come as the "Comte de Haga," and she feasted him well. That new toy, a balloon, was sent up to amuse him — she had it called by her name — and he was shown all that Trianon could show by day or by night. She was the more gracious from the awkwardness of Louis, who came ill-dressed to meet Gustavus and who was slow with him. She gave him deference. She consented, at one great supper of hers, to stand with her women and supervise all, while he was seated. Only she would not dance with him; she said she danced no more. . . .

Meanwhile, accompanying the King of Sweden and ever at his side, Fersen was come again to Versailles.

He was now a man. War had made him. Marie Antoinette could silently watch in him a very different car-

MARIE ANTOINETTE

By Madame Vigée Le Brun

riage and a new alertness of the visage, but his eyes still bore the tender respect that she had known and remembered.

He was now for some years to come and go between Versailles and the world. He was a Colonel of French Horse, and his place was made. . . .

The King of Sweden went down well; the Court was full of him. The Queen surpassed herself in well-receiving him.

The month of June was filled with this sincere and pleasing gaiety; but all that June, far off, the La Motte was going and coming in her secret ways, talking to the Cardinal of letters to her "from the Queen," assuring him that these letters gave proof of his growing favour. She did more and boldly; she affected to *show* him those royal letters!

There was a soldier of sorts, cynical, ramshackle, hard up, like all her gang, Retaux de Villette by name; he it was who wrote these letters whenever the La Motte might ask him—so much a time. They must have amused him as he wrote them! He was at no pains to disguise his hand; he wrote straight out to his "dear heart," the Comtesse de La Motte Valois, anything she asked him to write — especially praise of Rohan — and when he had written it (at so much a time) he would boldy sign "Marie Antoinette" with a flourish; and the La Motte would show the letter to Rohan, and Rohan (that is the amazing and simple truth) would believe them to be the Queen's!

If the Cardinal had any doubts at all they were easily dispersed. Cagliostro, who enjoyed the Illumination of the Seventh House, and had powers from the other world, most strongly reassured him — for a fee; the seen and unseen powers all combined to reassure the fatuous Rohan, and he was ready, as June ended, to believe not only that he was in favour with the Queen, but in very peculiar favour indeed, and that all this show of avoidance and silence upon her part was a mask necessary to conceal a deeply-rooted tenderness. She might turn her head away when the Grand Almoner passed on his rare and pompous occasions of ecclesiastical office in the galleries of Versailles. She might refuse to speak to him a single word. She might, whenever she deigned to speak of him to others, speak with complete contempt and disgust. She might (as she had and did) successfully prevent the smallest honour or moneys coming to him. But, oh! he saw it all! It was but a mask to hide her great love — and, sooner or later, he would have his reward for such long and patient waiting!

He in his turn wrote—constantly. To the letters the La Motte showed him — dainty scented notes on little dainty sheets of gilded blue (but written, alas! by such rough hands) — he would answer, with imploring, respectful, adoring lines, handed to the La Motte that she might give them to her great and high friend. Now he could understand why Cagliostro had promised him in oracular enigmas that "glory would come to him from a correspondence," and that "full power with the Government" was immediately awaiting him. He was ready to assume it.

July was empty enough for the Queen. Her guest was gone; there was little doing at Versailles. Her amusements, especially her theatre, she had deliberately given up, determined to let the legend against her die. She waited through the dull month a little worried. Her brother the Emperor was still fussing about his diplomatic quarrel, the opening of the Scheldt, and the rest of it; she was anxious for him and for peace. Henry of Prussia would soon be visiting Versailles, there intriguing (as she dreaded) against her Austrian House. But, on the whole, the month of July, 1784, was a dull month for her. It was not dull for the La Motte.

The male La Motte in early July sauntered, on those fine, sunny days, in the Palais Royal. He was looking for something; he was looking for a face and a figure not too unlike those of the Queen of France. It was not a difficult thing to find; the type was common enough, and in the first days of his search he found it. The woman was a woman of the town, young, with a swelled heart, as it were, and no brains; she was timid, she was ready to swallow anything offered her. He followed her with gallantry, and found that her professional name was D'Oliva; her true name the more humble one of Le Quay. For a week or so this new lover of hers went on like any other, he appeared and reappeared most naturally; but when the week was over and he had grown most familiar to her — and perhaps with his birth and high accent most revered — La Motte confided to her great and flattering news. *There was a great Lady at Court who sought her aid in a matter of vast importance*, and that great Lady spoke perhaps for a Lady greater still. The grandeur of the position was left to brew, and on the 22d of July, when it was already dusk, the great Lady (who was the female La Motte) swept into the poor girl's humble lodgings — a vision of the Court and the high world; she told the wide-eyed hussy things that seemed too lofty for human ears. *The Queen had need of her.*

For herself (said the La Motte) she was the Queen's one great, near friend (she showed a letter — one of the famous letters), and if the D'Oliva would do as she was begged to do, the gratitude of the Queen would far excel in effect the paltry 400 *pounds* that *she*, La Motte, would give. Come, would she help the Queen?

Oh, yes! the D'Oliva would help the Queen! She would come next day to Versailles!

Why, then, all was well. . . . And that very night, post-haste, the interview over, Madame de La Motte galloped off to Versailles to take a room with her maid.

For the Queen the dreary month was ending — there was no trouble upon her horizon. She had written again to Sweden; she asked for, and obtained, the reversion of the See of Albi for a friend of the King of Sweden's. There was no other news.

History does not show perhaps one situation more wonderfully unlike the common half-happenings, complexities and reactions of real life, nor one more wonderfully fulfilling the violent and exact, simple, and prearranged ironies of drama, than the contrast of that night: the Queen in the palace, ignorant of any ill save the old and dwindling tales against her, listless after a summer month of idleness and of restraint — and coming right up at her, down the Paris road, the woman who was to destroy her altogether.

The La Motte and her maid got into Versailles very late. They took rooms at the Belle Image. Next day La Motte and Rétaux, the soldier, came, bringing the poor girl D'Oliva, with them; and after a short walk in the town, during which she was left in the hotel with that "great Lady," before whom she trembled, they told D'Oliva that they had seen the Queen and that all was well. They waited till the morrow. On the evening of that morrow, the 24th of July, Madame de La Motte warned the D'Oliva that the time was come. She dressed her all in white, magnificently; she gave her a letter and a rose, and said: "To-night we go into the Park together, and there you will see for a moment a great Lord. Give him this letter and that rose, and say these words: 'You know my meaning!' You will have no more to do." It was about eleven, a dark night and no moon, when the two women went together into the vast gardens of the palace.

As you stand in the centre of the great façade of Versailles, and look westward down a mile of formal lawn and water, there lie to your left in the palace what were the Queen's rooms, and to your left in the gardens a large grove called "the Queen's Grove," in which are the trees that can be seen nearest to her windows or to be reached most quickly from what were her private doors.

Near and within this grove, by an appointment which the La Motte had sworn him to observe, paced and repaced the Cardinal. The La Motte had told him he would see the Queen.

In an enormous cloak of dark mysterious blue that covered his purple to the heels, in a broad soft hat that flapped down and hid his face, this fool of magnitude paced the gardens of Versailles and waited for the delicious hour. Behind him as he paced followed respectfully a man of his—one Planta, a sort of insignificant noble. The hour came. The La Motte found the Cardinal. She led him along a path among the high trees — and there for a moment near a hornbeam hedge that grew there, he saw dimly a woman in white, showing tall and vague in the darkness. This figure held forward to him in some confusion a rose, and said very low, "You know my meaning!" Rohan seized the hem of the white dress and kissed it passionately but before another word could pass a man came forward at speed and whispered as in an agony: "Madame! D'Artois is near — Madame!" The La Motte said "Quick! . . ." The thing in white slipped back into the shadow of a bush, the Cardinal was hurried away — but his life had reached its summit! He had heard dear words from the lips of the Queen! . . .

Marie Antoinette was asleep perhaps, or perhaps chatting, muffled, with Polignac's wife, or perhaps, more likely, by her children's nursery beds, watching their repose and questioning their nurse in the wing of the great palace hard by. A hundred yards away, in the darkness of the grove outside, that scene had passed which set the train of her destiny alight; and the explosion caused by it ruined all that creviced society of Versailles and cast it down, casting down with it the Queen.

There existed at that time a necklace. Fantastic stories have been told of its value; of those sovereigns to whom it was offered, and who, with a sigh, had been compelled to refuse it. It may very likely have been offered to Marie Antoinette (with her old passion for jewels) some years before, in '79, after the birth of her first child. It may be that the King would have given her the expensive thing — £64,000 was the price of it — it may be he had never seen it. At any rate, all the world knew that the unrivalled necklace existed, and had for some years existed as the property of two Court jewellers who worked in partnership, Bœhmer and Bassange, and that they could not find a purchaser. The reader should remember this necklace, for though it will not be before him till six months after this July of '84, yet, but for the scene in the "Queen's Grove," Rohan would never have handled it, and had Rohan never handled it, there would not have arisen that enormous scandal that came so opportune to new rumours and new angers, and in the end dragged down the Queen.

. . . .

With August came Prince Henry of Prussia and all the bother of him. The Emperor was pressing the Dutch more and more. France was half inclined to prevent that pressure, in spite of the Austrian Alliance. France was determined, at any rate, to prevent Austria, allied or not, from strengthening herself upon the North and East. England, to keep the Scheldt shut, was more than half inclined to prevent that pressure, in spite of Holland's attitude during the American War. Prussia stood by to gain — and part of Prussia's chance was the opportunity of feeling and influencing Louis XVI.'s Cabinet.

Prince Henry came, as Frederick's brother, to feel and to influence; to see how much could be done by way of separating Vienna from Versailles. It was a strain on the Queen. What could she know of these intrigues and counter-intrigues? She saw things, now as ever, few and plain; she saw a Prussian separate her House and the House into which she had married. Therefore Prince Henry's visit was a difficulty to her. She solved it as one might expect of her character, by avoiding him. She wrote to the King of Sweden a little too familiarly, and assured him that she had hardly seen the visitor: she "was at Trianon continually, with intimates only." Paris thought much of him (for Prussia was then, as now, efficient); she was very properly fatigued, but, improperly, she did not conquer her fatigue. During all his stay he saw her perhaps not half a dozen times, though he (as might be expected of his character or of any of his descendants, ancestors, or collaterals) stayed on and on and on. . . . He stayed steadily on in France till November!—and before November enough had happened!

The little Dauphin was really ill. His mother was anxious. St. Cloud was bought for him, in some vague hope that the "air" was better there—as though the "air" of one suburb more than another could cure the rickets of the Bourbons.

Next, it was known that the Queen was again with child. She wrote of it (familiarly enough) to the King of Sweden.

More than this, war was apparent. The Emperor's smouldering quarrel with the Dutch had broken into flame; upon the 4th of October, 1784, an Imperial ship had sailed up the Scheldt to see if the Dutch would oppose an entry. The Dutch did oppose it; they shot at the Imperial ship and took it, and every ruler in Europe put his hand to the hilt of his sword.

So far Marie Antoinette had done little at Versailles, but be worried by all this complex quarrel; a fortnight before the incident she had told her brother that "really she was not so important at Versailles"; she hoped it was a thing to shirk. Now that the guns had begun, she was in a panic and made a call upon her old and natural violence. She effected little: Vergennes and the tradition of French diplomacy were too much for such tantrums, but the superficial aspect of her action was striking. It was known that she continually saw the King, that she made scenes, that she stormed. It was known that she was "Austrian" in all this, if it was not understood by the people that she had failed. On the contrary, when in the upshot a compromise was arranged, she appeared once more in that most odious light — a woman sending French tribute to Vienna.

For when the Emperor consented to the closing of the Scheldt (it was not till February of the next year that he gave way), the French Cabinet, which had firmly supported Holland, was gradually influenced to guarantee the indemnity which the dignity of the Imperial Crown demanded: it was close on ten million florins.[1] The Dutch refused so large a sum. The Queen wrote, cajoled, insisted in favour of her brother, her House, and Austria. The French Foreign Office, true to its tradition of taking material interests seriously, stood firm and backed Holland steadily. At last the French agreed to take over and to pay as sponsors for Holland one-half the sum demanded of the Dutch Government, if thereby they might avoid war in Europe. The payment was due to the Queen's vigour or interference, and meanwhile there had arisen one of those large and sudden affairs which give everything around them a new meaning, which emphasise every coincident evil, and draw together into their atmosphere every ill-will and every calumny. Just before Marie Antoinette appeared before the populace as one who was sending millions of French treasure to her foreign brother, came the explosion — in the interval of all this diplomacy and negotiation — of what is called in history "The Affair of the Diamond Necklace." The truth with regard to that famous business is as follows:—

When the Cardinal de Rohan left the Park that midnight of July after the rapture of a word from the ridiculous D'Oliva, he was fallen wholly in the hands of the

[1] The fiction of the indemnity is entertaining. The Dutch were to yield Maestricht as the equivalent to the Emperor's granting the closing of the Scheldt. The indemnity was to "redeem" Maestricht.

La Motte. *She* it was, as he thought, who had done this great thing for him. *She* had given him the Queen; and he was now entirely sure of his right to act for Marie Antoinette and to serve her. The La Motte began by begging money of him for the Queen's pet charities. She obtained it: first, two or three thousand pounds at the end of August. Rétaux wrote the letter: "It was for people whom she wanted to help." Rétaux signed it with his "Marie Antoinette": and Rohan paid. A few pounds of it went to the unhappy woman whom La Motte had used, the rest to creditors or show. Much of the time when the Scheldt business was at its height, just as Prince Henry was leaving and all were talking of the Queen, in the autumn of 1784 a new letter came (again from Rétaux' hand) asking for *four thousand.* There was the signature "Marie Antoinette," there the beloved terms, and Rohan blindly paid: his man took the money to the La Motte, "to give the Queen." The Cardinal was sure of his way now; he was a master; the Queen was under obligation to him. The money was spent in a very lavish display by the male and the female La Motte. They travelled with grandeur; they visited in a patronising manner the earlier home of their poverty; they lived high. With the end of the year 1784 more money was needed — and here enters into history that diamond necklace which had so long been waiting its cue to come upon the stage.

The name of La Motte was now current — in the mouth alone and among the populace, not at Court — for one who could do much. Bassange heard, from a friend, of the La Mottes: of Madame de La Motte. He sent the friend to see whether his white elephant of a necklace could be moved towards that quarter. Madame de La Motte said wisely that she must see the jewels, a day or two after Christmas. She saw them; for three weeks they were kept on the hook. Upon the 21st of January, 1785, a date that has appeared before and will appear again in this history, she sent and told them that the Queen would buy, but (in her usual manner) a "great lord" would be the intermediary; and on the 24th, by the time it was full daylight, the great lord came in the winter morning to do that little thing that led to so much at last. It was the Cardinal de Rohan who came, handled the jewels, bargained, promised four payments (at six-monthly intervals) of £16,000 each, the first for the first of *August* (the date should be noted), and demanded delivery on the 1st of February. The jewellers brought the gems on that day to his great palace in the Marais, and he then told them frankly that the buyer behind him was the Queen.

They saw her signature, "Marie Antoinette de France"; they saw a part at least of her letter, to the effect that she the Queen was not accustomed to accommodation and therefore begged him to negotiate. They were satisfied, left the necklace, and were gone. That night the Cardinal gave it to Madame de La Motte at Versailles, or rather, hiding himself in an alcove, saw it given to a man who acted the part of the Queen's messenger and who was, of course, Rétaux.

All this, I say, passed on the 1st of February, 1785.

Next day, Candlemas — just two years after Madame de La Motte had made her desperate effort to approach the Queen with a petition — Rohan and the jeweller, one as Grand Almoner in the high religious function of the day, the other as a man in the crowd, each watched the royal party go by and noted the Queen; each missed the jewel that surely she should be wearing on the morrow of its purchase, and each saw that it was not yet worn. Each for different reasons wondered, but each for different reasons was silent, and each determined, for different reasons, to wait. Meanwhile the necklace was in the custody of the male La Motte ready for its journey to London, the refuge of the oppressed.

Lent passed. On Easter Sunday the Queen's third child — he who became the Dauphin of the Imprisonment — was born. If, thought Rohan, the Queen had purposely waited before putting on the necklace, in order to avoid a coincidence of date between *his* visit to the jewellers and *her* first wearing of the gem, surely a long enough space would have passed by the time of the Relevailles, the ceremonial churching in Notre Dame which followed the birth of every member of the Blood Royal. The Relevailles approached. It was more than eight months since the Cardinal had been given that rose at midnight, and he began to grow anxious. The necklace haunted him. . . . Far off in London, the male La Motte was selling, stone by stone, the better part of it; the rest Rétaux was carefully disposing of in Paris itself.

It was on May 24 that the Queen proceeded to Paris for the ceremony of the Relevailles. All the antique grandeur was there and the crowds, but over all of it and over the crowds a new and dreadful element of popular silence. The guns saluted her through a silent air. In the streets of the University the very wheels of her carriage could be heard, so hushed was the crowd. The rich in the opera that evening cheered her, but going in and coming out through popular thousands she heard no cheers. She supped in the Temple with Artois, whose appanage the

PORTRAIT BUST OF THE DUKE OF NORMANDY

The second Dauphin, sometimes called Louis XVII., who died in the Temple. This bust was broken in the fall of the palace, and has recently been recovered and restored to Versailles

liberties of the Temple were, and she could see through the night in his garden, as she had seen so often before in his feasts and his receptions, the dimmer and more huge from the blaze of light near by, that ominous great Tower which, it is said, she had always dreaded and dreaded more acutely now with an access of superstitious fear. "Oh! Artois, pull it down!" The Grand Almoner was present at this high function; he watched her and marvelled that the necklace should still be hidden away.

The next morning she could be certain how Paris had changed. There was throughout its air a mixture of indifference and of dislike that poisoned her society with it. Paris now thought of her fixedly as the living extravagance of the Court. St. Cloud was at their gates to reproach her, with its title of the "Queen's Palace," its printed "Queen's" orders on the gate. The Deficit was there to reproach her. Her very economies, the lesser festivities, the abandoned journeys of the Court, her rarer and more rare appearances in the capital, the lack of noise in Trianon, were, in the public mouth, a consequence of past excesses. The judgment was false, but it stood firm.

Her undue influence over the King and the councils of the King was another legend, less false than that of gross extravagance. There was no proof, but a crowd has more judgment than an isolated man, and the crowd divined what we now know. They had divined it in this critical year which saw France balancing on the verge of war with Austria, and which, before its close, saw the payment of the Dutch indemnity by the French to the Queen's brother at Vienna. All her action for twelve months was wholly Austrian in their eyes, and they were wholly right. It was in such a popular atmosphere, so sullen and so prepared, full for a year past of "Figaro's" ironic laughter against a régime already hurrying to its end, that the explosion of that summer was to come; for the 1st of August was near, and with it the time for the first instalment upon the necklace.

In June the Comte de La Motte was back from London paying part of the money he had received for the diamonds to a Paris banker — one Perregaux.

In July — on the mid-Tuesday of the month — Bœhmer, in his capacity of Court Jeweller, brought to Versailles certain jewels. He brought with him also a letter which he gave to the Queen at midday as she came out of Mass; he gave her the letter with mystery and with profound respect, and was gone. The Queen read that note; it was incomprehensible to her. It assured her of her jewellers' unalterable devotion; it begged her to believe that Bœhmer and Bassange were willing to accept her "latest proposals," and it ended with their satisfaction that "*the finest set of diamonds in the world should adorn the greatest and the best of its Queens.*" Whether Marie Antoinette had even heard of the necklace in the past we cannot tell, though probably, like all the rest of the world, she had. Whether she had or not, the note was equally mysterious to her. The Comptroller of the Household, the Baron de Breteuil, was told of the little bother; he sent for Bœhmer, asked him what on earth the note meant, but he only received mysterious replies leading nowhere.

If it be asked by the reader why, seeing a complication of some sort before her, Marie Antoinette did not at once order an investigation to be pursued by the police, the answer is simple enough to anyone acquainted with her character: the annoyance bored her. Her instinct was simply to avoid it. She may (some say so) have spared herself trouble upon some theory that the jeweller was mad: anyhow, she spared herself the trouble.

If it be asked how the complication ever arose, why that enigmatical letter was written, and why, once written and delivered, Bœhmer should have hesitated and equivocated meaninglessly in his answers to Breteuil, the answer is simple when one hears what had just passed in that lower world of duped Cardinal and intriguing, most impudent of adventurers, rapscallions, and spiritualists.

Madame de La Motte had been driving Rétaux of late to write more frequently than ever his "Marie Antoinette" letters to the Cardinal. The poor soldier was not a woman, he was not even a writer of fiction, and he had been kept hard at it to force the note of love so often and in such various ways; until at last, one letter had been ordered of him saying, as the date of the first instalment approached, that "really the price was too high." Couldn't the Cardinal, for her sake, get some £8,000 off the price? If he could, the Queen would pay on the 1st of August, not the £16,000 then due, but a full £28,000. The Cardinal read and obeyed. The jewellers were agreeable. Hence Bœhmer's note of July 12th, and hence (since he was convinced that the Queen, by the very method of her purchase, desired secrecy above all things) his evasive replies to De Breteuil.

Thus, in that world beneath of which she knew nothing, things were coming to an issue against Marie Antoinette: one last event did all. Upon the Saturday before the payment was due, the Cardinal (acting upon a further letter) gave Bœhmer something over £1,000 and said to him that it was free money — over and above the fixed price — to console him for the unwelcome news that the first instalment could not be met quite punctually. Come, the Queen would certainly pay on the 1st of October; it was but two months to wait. He had seen it in a note of the Queen's which the Comtesse de La Motte had just shown him.

It is probable that even the Cardinal had become suspicious now — he says as much himself — but his pride and his fear of exposure held him. As for the jeweller, the interview of that Saturday broke his back; he was distracted. On the Tuesday (or the Wednesday) the climax of the comedy was reached. The Comtesse de La Motte met the two partners Bœhmer and Bassange together and told them boldly that the signature "Marie Antoinette de France" was a forgery — so there! In the stupefaction that followed she added the quiet advice that for their money they must bleed the Cardinal — "He had plenty" — and so left them.

Then followed that general scurry which is the note of embroglios as they flare up towards their end. Bassange runs here, Bœhmer runs there; the one to Rohan in his Episcopal Palace, the other to those who can help him with the Queen — notably to Madame de Campan, who has left an exaggerated and distorted account of the interview. To Bassange the Cardinal (anything to gain time in the hurly-burly) swears the signature is true; to Bœhmer Madame de Campan, with her solid, upper-servant face, announces the redundant truth that he seems to have been let in. As for the La Motte, she flies to Rohan, and he (anything to keep things dark and to protect a witness to his incalculable stupidity of a coxcomb) consents to hide her; he gives her asylum in his great house.

Next Bœhmer goes to Versailles — at once — and implores the Queen to see him. The Queen has really had her fill of this kind of thing; she refuses. But next week she consents, and the revelations begin.

It was at such a moment, with such storms about her, in the full and growing unpopularity of her Austrian influence in the affair of the Dutch indemnity, in the full and growing renascence of the legend of her extravagance, that Marie Antoinette had determined not only to play once more in her theatre at Trianon — the chief reproach of the past, a legend with the populace for unqueenly exposure, for lack of dignity, for expense — not only to break her wise resolve, which had been kept for more than a year, that her plays should cease, but actually to play another piece by that same Beaumarchais whose wit was the spearhead of the attack upon the old régime. The decision came neither of cynicism nor of folly upon her part; it came of tragic ignorance.

It was while she was rehearsing her part of "Rosine" that she was persuaded — probably by Madame de Campan herself — to send for Bœhmer and to hear his tale. He came upon the 9th of August, Tuesday, by the Queen's command, to Trianon. At first he simply asked for the money he believed his due. When he saw that Marie Antoinette neither understood why it should be paid, nor for what, nor by whom, he told the whole story as he had heard it. He was sent off to write down coherently and at length in a clear memorandum the details of this amazing thing, and when he had gone the Queen raved.

Each consequence and aspect of the abomination, as each successively appeared to her, struck her with separate and aggravated blows. Her name linked with a libertine whom, of all libertines, she most loathed — a man who was the object of her dead mother's especial contempt! The half-truths that would come in; her love of jewellery — now long conquered, but now widely remembered! Her secret debts — now long paid, but already a fixed idea in the public mind! At the best that such a man had thought it conceivable that she should be such a woman; at the worst that the world might believe it!

Upon Friday the report of Boehmer came in. She mastered it that day and the next, and on Sunday the 14th, the eve of the Assumption, she begged her husband to spend all the day with her at Trianon. He willingly came. They together — but surely at her initiative — determined on a public trial. Mercy would have done what we do now in England when there is danger of public scandal and the weakening of government; he would have paid the La Motte woman something to be off. Vergennes was strongly in favour of silence — as strongly as Downing Street would be to-day — for he was of the trained diplomatic kind. The King's honour, the Queen's intense and burning indignation against calumny persuaded them to risk publicity.

The course taken was, I repeat, not a course easy for my modern readers to understand; we take it for granted in the modern world, and especially in England, that a matter of this sort, involving, as it were, all the social fabric, is best snuffed out. Thus the French Foreign Office were willing to destroy the Pannizardi telegram, and rather to give a traitor the advantage of concealing damning evidence against him than to risk a rupture with Italy. Thus the English Home Office allows criminals of a certain standing to go free rather than endanger social influences whose secrecy is thought necessary to the State; nor do we allow any to know what sums or how large are paid for public honours, nor always to what objects secret subscriptions of questionable origin — in Egypt, for instance — are devoted. Louis XVI. and his wife at this critical moment decided otherwise and upon another theory of morals. They decided to clear by public trial the honour of the Crown. That decision, more than any other act, cost them their thrones. It has preserved the truth for history.

. . . .

The Feast of the Assumption has for centuries attracted the French by its peculiar sanctity. Even during that phase of infidelity which, before the Revolution, covered all their intellect and still clings to the bulk of their lower middle classes, the French maintained it. Even to-day, when a fierce anti-Christian Masonry has moulded groups of artisans and intellectuals into ardent champions against the Faith, the Assumption is universally observed. In the Court of Versailles, though now but a ceremony, it was the noblest ceremony of the year.

It was warm noon upon that 15th of August. The Court in all its colours stood ranked outside the Chapel Royal. The Grand Almoner, the Cardinal de Rohan, taller than the prelates and the priests around him, stood ready in procession to enter and to celebrate the Pontifical High Mass as soon as the King and Queen might appear; but the King and Queen, and a minister or two in attendance, were waiting behind closed doors in Louis' private room. The procession still halted: the Court was already impatient: the doors still stood closed. They opened; a servant came out and told the Cardinal that the King wished to see him a moment. The servant and he went in together, and the doors shut behind the purple of Rohan's robes and the lace upon his wrists and shoulders.

The Court outside grew weary of waiting. A quarter of an hour, twenty minutes passed; it was near the half-hour when those doors opened again and the Head of the King's Household, the Baron de Breteuil, appeared with the Cardinal at his side. A lieutenant of the Guard happened to be by. Breteuil summoned him and said aloud: "The King orders you not to leave the Cardinal as you take him to his palace: you are answerable for his person."

So Rohan was arrested, and there is no record who sang Mass that day.

X

THE NOTABLES

AUGUST 15, 1785, TO AUGUST 8, 1788

FOR the Queen the decision to send the Cardinal to trial was a final action. The thing was done — and, for that matter, nearly done with.

When she could find time in an interval of her occupations to write to her brother Joseph — it was not till a fortnight later — the whole letter, though it dealt in detail with the affair as one deserving a full explanation, was written upon a tone of relief. It was tuned, all of it, to one key-phrase: "I am delighted to think that we shall never hear of this filthy business again."

Hardly was that decisive act accomplished than there suddenly appeared upon twenty points of the horizon, not only in frontal advance but upon either flank and in either rear of the perilous position she occupied, as many separate forces unconnected or but vaguely in touch with one another; some directly antagonistic to others, but all having it in common that the Queen was their objective, and that the trial of the Cardinal had been their signal for mobilisation and the march.

It is in the character of unwisdom to analyse and to proceed upon the results of analysis: in the character of wisdom to integrate the whole point. The analysis of the situation just before the Cardinal's arrest showed clearly one great factor of opposition, the Rohan clan. They were everywhere in France contemporary and in France historical; they filled Marie Antoinette's generation and a hundred years. The sisters, cousins, brothers-in-law were ubiquitous. Paris was conspicuous with their palaces, the Court with their functions, the provinces with their loyal dependants or necessary adherents. They were the nucleus of the strongest group that remained to the wealthy nobility. The Guémenées, the Soubises, even the Condés, were one with all the Rohans. A Rohan put to open trial would have in that day the effect which a chief of our modern financial gang put to open trial might have to-day. Imagine one of our judges forced to try a Rothschild!

The Queen saw clearly — it is always easy to see one simple thing clearly — that one Rohan force opposed to her; she determined to brave it; but latent, unconscious of themselves until her own action called them into being, how many other forces were there not!

There was no member of the higher nobility but to a greater or less degree felt vaguely a right to immunity from such publicity — and this man was of the highest of the nobility, a type. There was no member of the clergy but could formulate a clear historical and legal right to the exemption of a cleric from the judgment of a lay tribunal — and this man was of the highest of the clergy.

Had he been Archbishop of Toulouse or Sens, or any wholly Gallic see even, his case would have been simpler; he was Bishop of Strasburg and his metropolitan was of Mainz: the Archbishop of Mainz was a conceivable opponent.

He was a prince of the Church: Rome had a right to speak — and almost did.

He was a prince of the Empire: Vienna had a right to speak — and almost did.

Austria and France had for now two years been at a strain: it was just two years since Joseph had written his first serious letter upon the Scheldt to his sister: the government of Austria was embittered, and had for sovereign a man who would not refuse to trade upon the embarrassment of Versailles. The last negotiations for indemnity against the opening of the Scheldt were still pending. The moment was opportune.

The Cardinal could be judged by but one tribunal of the King's, and that a quasi-governmental body which had for a generation stood in increasing opposition to the Crown — the Parlement. For them also the moment was opportune.

He could be tried in but one town, and that town the capital, which had now taken up such a definite position of hatred against the Queen; in but one part of that town, in the Palais, right in the heart of Paris upon which all the crowds of that unity so easily converge, and whose towers were a perpetual symbol of the Monarchy which had deserted its ancient seat for the isolated splendour of Versailles.

But of much more weight than even these considerable and separate bases of resistance was that indefinitely large body of smaller and more fluctuating dangers whose integration the Queen should have seized if she was to save herself from destruction.

There are in politics, as in physics, conditions of unstable equilibrium in which a mass of fragments, seemingly in repose, may at a shock be exploded. Their energy lies ready to be released by the least disturbance. It is the business of statesmanship to remove or to dissolve such as these before large things are undertaken, lest a violent motion explode them. A thousand such lay about the palace of Versailles, threatening the Queen. Whatever particular grudges (even in friends) had had time to grow, the memories of hatred in enemies, the last of the Du Barry's faction, the last of D'Aiguillon's. The suspicions of the devout against her frivolity, the contempt of the philosophical for her religion, the irritation of the politician against her presence at the Council, the necessary enmity of Calonne — all the imperfect and capricious pleasures she had failed to pursue, all the losses, dismissals, and humiliations rightly or wrongly laid to her charge, were there, not consciously prepared, but fatally bound to spring to life if once a body of action against her took visible form. That form the trial of the Cardinal was to present. When such a body of opposition was in motion all would attach themselves to it, each from an aspect of its own. All the old dangers, as each appeared, made alliance with the new and immediate perils.

Madame de La Motte was arrested three days after the Cardinal, in the early hours of the 18th of August, just back at dawn in pomp from a great provincial party in Champagne. Her husband fled to London, there to meet a sympathy readily extended to such exiles, and to keep in touch with those centres of enmity against the French Crown and religion with which he was familiar. It was on the very day when Paris was in the first busy rumour upon the whole matter — when it was learned that the Cardinal had been allowed to burn half his papers, that La Motte had got away, that suspicion was permitted to attach to the Queen — it was upon such a day, the 19th of August — that the Queen chose to re-open the theatre at Trianon and to re-open it with a play of Beaumarchais'.

Many tragedies in history contain some such coincidences but none so many or so exact as those which accompany and determine the tragedy of Marie Antoinette.

Consider the position: the legend of her extravagance has rearisen — unjustly. Trianon is — unjustly — the chief popular symbol of that extravagance. The theatre of Trianon, the most in view, the most obvious of its expenses, she had wisely suppressed during many months. The park at St. Cloud, at the gates of Paris, is a further count in the indictment against her. Her visit to Paris for her churching in May has proved her grievously unpopular: the hated financial agreement with Austria in regard to the Scheldt is developing, as it is believed (and rightly believed), under her guidance. Upon all this comes the thunder-clap of Rohan's arrest — and just as men are beginning to comprehend and to explain it, just as the public and foreign enmity necessarily suggest her complicity, say that "there is more than meets the eye," that "you will see, the Queen will make victims of them all; but she *is* responsible for the purchase of the gems!" Just as the obvious lies were establishing themselves through the embryonic press of those days and the café gossip — in that very Assumption week she chooses to appear upon her stage at Trianon, dressed and painted for a part written by whom? By the man Caron — Beaumarchais by purchase — whom all the vulgar now associated with the most successful attack upon the existing régime, whom the older and the higher world remember as the associate and perhaps the partner of the Jewish clique in London that had published the first dirty lie against Marie Antoinette's chastity when she was as yet but a child of eighteen.

Why was such a folly committed? The answer to that question is all around the reader to-day. That society did not know its doom. It was "chic," it was "the thing" for the ruling powers to read and to see acted criticism upon themselves. The little spice of danger — they could think it no more — was a piquant addition to jaded and well-known pastimes. But the Queen! How terribly more great and more real the living consequences were to be to *her* than to any such abstraction as "a régime": *she* was to see and to feel continued physical violence, to be menaced with muskets, to be forced from her husband before his death, to have her child dragged from her; she was to be wholly abandoned, tortured silently by a subterranean silence and at last publicly killed.

To the coincidence of that piece of folly another was soon added. All the succeeding month was full of the last negotiations with Austria: on the 19th of September public discussion of the necklace had gone far enough to move her to a long letter; she wrote and explained disdainfully to her brother — on the 20th was definitely signed the obligation on the part of France for half the Dutch indemnity. Austria received — for no reason save the Queen's pressure and an imaginary relief from war — about a million pounds. With the public debt already a matter for debate and about to become the critical matter for action, it was a monstrous thing.

Budget for budget — stating the proportions in terms of modern revenue — it corresponded to what a payment of between ten millions or twelve would be to-day. Stated in terms of ease of payment, of ability to pay, it represented far more than such a sum would represent in a modern budget — and not a penny of that humiliating obligation need have been incurred but for the Queen.

Those historians who regard as beneath discussion the

great popular cry of the Revolution that Marie Antoinette "sent money to Austria" are too ready to neglect whatever is rhetorical. Tumbrils of gold did not pass — as the populace believed — but this enormous obligation was incurred, and incurred through her and in favour of her brother.

That autumn, winter, and spring the necklace was the theme. The confused currents of opinion had this in common that all accused the Queen, just as, in the great modern parallel of the Dreyfus case, the confused currents of opinion, differing widely and sometimes in direct opposition on vital points, had it all in common that the Catholic Church was the real defendant throughout and the real villain of the piece. According to some Rohan was the Queen's lover, afraid to accuse her or perhaps too fond — but at any rate he had purchased the necklace by her orders. According to others the La Motte had been the Queen's cat's-paw in tricking Rohan. According to others again, more extreme, the Queen had been herself the actual agent throughout, and would now, by an official pressure, procure a verdict against her lover and her friend in order to whitewash her own character. In general the absurdity which took most hold was nearer to the latter theory than to any other: it became a test point simply whether Rohan would be acquitted or condemned. Rohan acquitted, the Queen (by some wildly illogical process of general opinion!) was supposed to be proved guilty of authorship in the whole affair. If Rohan was condemned, she was equally guilty of authorship — only, in that case the mob and the foreigner would say that wicked judges had proved pliant to Court influence.

As in the modern trial which I have already quoted as the great historic parallel to the trial of Rohan, no evidence could affect the minds of those who had already concluded: to make their fixed conclusion fit in with the facts any contradiction of human psychology and human probabilities was admitted. Did some pornographer attack the Queen and defend Rohan? Straightway he was a hero! Had there been a Pantheon he would have had his burial there. Did some anonymous pamphleteer assert his conviction of the Queen's guilt? Straightway he was an authority. Did some obscure and needy man take money to support the immense power and fortunes of the Rohans against the impoverished crown? Straightway (like those who supported Jewish finance in the modern parallel I have quoted) he became a being full of self-sacrifice defending the weak and the oppressed against haughty power. The document whereby the necklace was ordered was signed "Marie Antoinette *de France*," — a signature quite impossible in form and not even remotely resembling in handwriting that of the Queen. No matter. It must be supposed, "for this occasion only," that she wrote thus — once at least. Or, if that lie was too hard to swallow, then she had had Rohan sign thus, or get it signed thus, precisely in order to cover her tracks by an improbable signature. Anything at all was said and believed — especially in foreign countries — provided it implicated the Queen.

The preliminary stages of the trial were long. Oliva was not arrested till late in the winter, at Brussels, fluttering and confused; Rétaux not till the spring, at Geneva.

The Queen endured those months of increasing public insult and increasing doubt. She was in her fourth pregnancy, and, what was more, her character, to some extent her body, had aged somewhat. She had passed that thirtieth year which her mother had foreseen to be critical for her; she had come to what a superstition or a coincidence made her regard as the beginning of bitter years.

Meanwhile in his room at the Bastille, where he was confined, the Cardinal held his court, enjoyed his receptions, and continued to impress the Parisians with all the pomp of his rank. It was not till the end of May that he was taken to the Conciergerie — the last step before the public trial; he went by night upon the 29th of the month. On the next day, the 30th of May, 1786, in the morning, the Parlement met in the Grand Salle, the indictments were read and the pleadings opened.

That trial has been described a thousand times. The Rohans of every degree were packed at the doors of the court. The deference they met with, the immense crowds which, during those long two days, awaited the verdict, the anxiety at Versailles — all these are the theme of every book that has dealt with this best known of historic trials: they need not be repeated here. At the close of the proceedings came the significant thing: the public prosecutor demanded no more than that the Cardinal should apologise for having thought the Queen capable of such things, and should resign the Grand Almonry —on that small point, the forty-nine judges deliberated a whole day long.

It was dark, it was nine o'clock on the 31st of May when their conclusion was announced: some would have condemned him to the mere apology and resignation thus demanded, a few to apology but not to resignation, the majority were simply for acquittal, and at last, by *twenty-six* votes to *twenty-three*, Rohan left the court completely absolved. For the rest the La Motte was ordered to be flogged, branded, and imprisoned at Salpetière. Her husband — in contumacy — to the galleys. Rétaux to be transported. As for Oliva, they declared her not to fall under the matter they had to try — she was free.

In Paris the acquittal of the Cardinal (which meant to the mob simply the condemnation of the Queen) caused an immediate popular outburst of cheering and congratulation. They surrounded his palace. They demanded and obtained its illumination. He was compelled to show himself and to be acclaimed. Then, as must ever be the case with such false heroes, he was completely dropped. Those who had done most to secure the verdict were most in a position to know the perils of further ovation. When the King had stripped him of every possible function and emolument and had exiled him to the Velay, the Rohans themselves were the most assiduous to impose silence upon him and to force him back into obscurity. He lived, unnoticed and unremembered, remote in Strasburg; was advised, on election to the States-General two years later, not to sit; sat, refused the civil oath, emigrated, survived the Queen by some ten years, and died, doing after that no more evil.

No public insult could more deeply have wounded the Queen than this verdict and that demonstration. Her health was touched, but much more her very self was overshadowed as she feared — and she was right — for ever. She had not even, as have we, the resource of history. She did not know how thoroughly history can deal with these Popish plots and Royal Necklaces and Dreyfus Innocencies and the rest, nor how contemptuously time and learning together expose at last every evil intrigue. She only knew — and she was right — that in her time the calumny would never be set right. And indeed this one of the great historical enthusiasms for falsehood was not set right till our own time. Napoleon, musing years after upon the verdict, called it, with his broad judgment and his opportunities for comparison and knowledge, the beginning of the Revolution, the gate of her tomb. Marie Antoinette was of no great judgment — she was contemporary to it all; no experience or research, but only instinct, could guide her — but some such dreadful presentiment of the capital importance of the affair stood fast in her mind: in part it greatly ripened her view of this bad world; much more it oppressed or broke the springs of her spirit, and while there is henceforward in all she did new tenacity and much calculation of effort, there is, much more, an inner certitude of doom.

The King went off to Cherbourg where Calonne, still seeking to re-establish the finances by an extended public employment of labour and by display, had achieved the first stage of that magnificent artificial harbour, the model of all its kind that were to follow in Europe and on the Mediterranean. Everywhere Louis met with easy but fervid acclamation. He had never seen the provinces before. He came back radiant. The new warmth and zeal, which, under another aspect and reacting against other stimuli, were so soon to produce the great change, had already touched the people, and he had bathed, as it were, in a public energy which, till then, cabined in Versailles or wearied by the cliques of Paris, he had never known. All that enthusiasm, his and his people's, he communicated in many letters to the Queen; but she had suffered her blow, and nothing now could undeceive her but that fate was coming. Her relation the Archduke, the last of so many royal visitors at Versailles, had gone. In July her fourth child was born — a girl; and that same summer every stranger that passed through Paris noted the beginnings of the storm. The pamphlets were awake; the press had risen to a continuous pressure of suggestion, anecdote, and attack, and the necessity for facing and solving the violent fiscal problem was no longer a theory to be discussed politically but a thing to be done.

The Court was brilliant in a last leaping flame. Fontainebleau that autumn was glorious with colours and men; the balls at Versailles that winter shone with a peculiar and memorable splendour — but it was the end. There were to be no more glories: — the last ball had been given, the last progress made.

Calonne, whose French audacity might a little earlier have saved the State, dared an experiment which failed — but which, from its nature and the things it could but breed, led on to the Revolution. He determined (and he persuaded the King) to summon, for consultation upon the finances and the betterment of the realm, a council of all those who led in the nobility, the Church, the Parlements, the Services, the great municipalities. This convention was to be named, upon the parallel of the last similar summons — now some two centuries old — an assembly of "the Notables." The Ministry were given the King's decision suddenly, upon the 29th of December. The Notables were to meet upon that day month. More than one critic — especially among the aged — foresaw, the dyke once opened, what a flood would follow; all, wise or unwise, felt that the meeting would be the end of most that they had known and the beginning of quite new perils and perhaps new energies or a new world.

Whether or no the Queen were hurt at a sudden determination in which she had taken no part nor even had a voice, she very rapidly in the next six months rose to hold the Government in her hands: thenceforward to the meeting of the States-General and the opening of the Revolution, her decision and her vigour take part in all those acts — a dozen at the most — which proved ultimately the authors of her destruction.

The Notables met — or rather did not meet — upon the day named, the 29th of January, '87. They came to Paris on the appointed day, they met in the streets of Paris, in drawing-rooms and elsewhere; but those provincial mayors, great judges, and members of the high nobility had to wait and chafe for many days before they were legally convened. Criticism and violence of tongue had time to grow; there was a sense of weakness, of anarchy even, in the petty details of governmental action following on such delay. When they did meet, before their debates had time to develop, one event after another was transforming everything around the Queen.

The Polignacs had quarrelled with her; Madame de Polignac, her life-long friend, had threatened to retire from her post with the Children of France. Many — most — had followed them; all whom the Polignacs had benefited, through the Queen, for so many years. A last and new faction, more intimate, more wounding, more in possession of her secrets, and more dangerous than any other was thus formed.

Vergennes was just dead; the King, should Calonne fail in the great business of Reform which the Assembly of Notables had opened, would be left without a Chief Minister, and the Queen's place was plainly ready for her in his council-room.

More than these, the La Motte had escaped from prison, and had fled (of course) to London.

There was not then, as there is to-day, in London a vast and organised journalistic system by which news is afforded, withheld, or falsified at will. Nay, even had there been such a monopoly, journals had not one-hundredth of the power they have to-day. Again, those who governed England then were usually well-travelled and were acquainted with the French tongue. Again, there existed, what has since failed us, strong independent opinion and a cultivated middle class. The female La Motte was, therefore, not welcomed with those transports of affection or homage which she would receive to-day; but there was already sufficient horror at continental procedure and sufficient certitude in the baseness of all administration of justice abroad to stand her in very good stead. The nourishment of the public conscience upon the sins of foreigners had already begun. La Motte was something of a martyr, and, as she seemed poor, could make some livelihood out of the public folly. She began that series of pretended "Revelations" which were in some few months to be among the principal torments of the Queen. Whether (like Esterhazy by our Press in the parallel I have already drawn) she was bribed to say such things, we have no record. At any rate her publications paid her — for a time.

It has been said that Marie Antoinette helped the La Motte to fly from prison. It may be so. When in a great public quarrel the innocent side is blundering and unwise, its acts of unwisdom are incalculable. Marie Antoinette had certainly sent to have the woman visited in prison. It is possible that, as she had hoped a public trial could help her, so she hoped now the La Motte loose would do less harm than the La Motte imprisoned and gagged, with every rumour free to circulate. Perhaps she was wholly ignorant of the whole matter. Anyhow, the La Motte was loose — and the flood of calumny springing from London flowed against the Queen and did its work. She, at Versailles.

grew every day to be more and more absorbed in the crisis which was developing with such rapidity — for it was already apparent as March proceeded that the experiment of the Notables had failed. Calonne had still his native courage and his peculiar rapidity of manœuvre; he fought his hand hard — but the opposition was too plain, too large, and too strong for him. His plan had been just — he had conceived the reformation of lightening the worst taxes and of arranging the more equal redistribution of the burden upon land — a new redistribution in which no privilege should exist of rank or custom — and, more daring, but still, in the tradition of Turgot, he had planned an adumbration of the Revolution by proposing provincial, local, and parochial assemblies.

Two currents of hostility met him: one that the Notables in the main stood personally for privilege; the other that everyone in France desired more change, and above all, more "democratisation" of the centre of the national machinery.

There was an appetite for debate, for "facts"; a demand for exact accounts and public audit and public acceptance of taxes.

These two currents gained their intensity, however, from the legend which had gathered round Calonne, as the Financier of the Deficit and the Adviser of the Throne. A symbolic character, which was never his but which has endured almost to our own time, was popularly superimposed upon him, a character of mere frivolity, of mere extravagance in time of security, especially of subservience to fancied expensive whims of the Queen.

She, alas! thought to do a public service and a strong one by persuading Louis to the dismissal of his Minister when his failure with the Notables was proved. She won. On the 8th of April, 1787, Calonne fell, to be exiled, to fly (of course) to London, and thence, only too probably, to help swell that river of evil speaking and writing which, since her thirtieth year, flowed so regularly against the character of Marie Antoinette; but which now broke all bounds and filled half the pamphlets.

If in this she acted publicly, decidedly, and to her hurt, in her next equally decisive step the Queen acted even more publicly, more decisively, and more both to her own hurt and that of the alien populace whom she already detested but desired, in such a crisis, to rule. After some mention of Necker, she forced Loménie upon the King.

. . . .

The writing of history, more than any other liberal occupation, suffers from routine. I will not detain the reader of this chronicle with any long digression upon the effect of the French Revolution, upon the nature, the prodigious force, and the universality of what may be called, according to the taste of the scholar, the Catholic reaction or the Catholic renaissance of our day. Still less would I disturb the progress of my story with a divagation upon the ease with which our academies here fall into every trap set them by the enemies of the Faith abroad —whether those enemies be random politicians, high stoics, skeptics of a noble temper, common usurers, or men fanatical against all restriction of the senses. But I will so far delay the reader at this moment as to state plainly a succession of undoubted historical and contemporary truths in no particular order, and to beg him to reach a conclusion by a comparison of them all.

It is in the routine of our universities to say that Catholicism was struck to death by two great upheavals; the Reformation opened it to attack; the Revolution dealt the mortal blow: it is now said to be dying, and especially in France. This is the first truth; that our universities say these things; some regret, some are pleased; but it is believed and said in either camp. Next, it is true that Louis XVI. practised his religion and believed in it. Next, it is true that his Queen, never wholly abandoning the rule of religion — far from it — was now, in 1787, particularly devoted and increasingly exact in her observance; daily, as she daily suffered, more penetrated inwardly by the spirit of the Church. A fourth truth is that no single man pretending to high intelligence in that generation of Frenchmen believed in more than a God: the only quarrel was between those who believed in such a Being and those who denied this last of dogmas. The fifth truth is, that but yesterday all the French hierarchy and all the 80,000 priests of the Church — save, perhaps, three — suffered the loss of all corporate property and all established income rather than vary in one detail from the discipline of Rome. The sixth truth is that the prominent and outstanding names of the French hierarchy or of the Church's defenders before and during this revolutionary crisis were: Rohan, an evil liver, a cheat, a fool, and a blackguard; Talleyrand something even lower in morals than he was higher in wit; the Archbishop of Narbonne — living six hundred miles from his See with his own niece for mistress; Grégoire, a full schismatic and in his way an honest man; Maury, a vulgar politician, like one of our own vulgar politicians to-day, a priest out for a fortune, a sort of "Member of Parliament," a petty persecutor of the Pope in person and of the Papacy, in time a *Cardinal* — and this man Loménie. The seventh truth is that Marie Antoinette (who practised her religion) ardently supported Loménie and befriended him, and that, therefore, Louis (who was devout) accepted him for Chief Minister.

Read these undoubted truths together and decide whether the Faith has advanced or receded in a hundred years.

. . . .

Who was Loménie de Brienne? He had had, these twenty years, a reputation for what is vaguely called in aristocracies "ability." He had presented the address of the Clergy in the Coronation year. He was Archbishop of Toulouse. He suited La Fayette's idea of honesty. He had inordinate passions. He was yet further and later Archbishop of Sens — for the sake of the pickings. He had led with no scruple of honour the opposition to Calonne in the Notables. Mercy favoured him. Vermond, the Queen's old tutor, who owed all to him, supported his claim, and Marie Antoinette imposed him. But who was he?

He was an active, careful, and laborious atheist to whom the King, by a scruple, refused the See of Paris, holding "that the See of Paris is peculiar and had always better be held by a man who believed in God." He was a wit, he loved wealth inordinately — and that was all. He had his reputation with the wealthy, but no action of his remains. Such was the hierarchy of that moment, and to a circle of such men was power restricted. And Loménie de Brienne was made and put into his seat by the advice of Vermond, Marie Antoinette's old tutor, by the advice of Joseph II., a protector of religious doubt; he repaid her by a constant devotion.

It was on May-day, 1787, that this personage was put, with an inferior title, at the head of the finances, a position which — now more than ever — was necessarily the chief post in the French State. On the 25th the Notables, from whom he came and whom he had led, were dissolved. . . .

Fersen, eager to spend one last day in Versailles, had come for a few flying hours. He watched their dissolution as a show . . . he did not return till the eve of the Revolution, and, once returned, he remained a pledged sacrifice, a servant, to the end. . . .

The Notables had done nothing, and Loménie himself proceeded to do much the same; or rather to bring forward for the *third* time as an active proposition — for the millionth as a theory propounded — the scheme of financial reform which every predecessor had, in one shape or another, presented. The destruction of the fossil compartments — walls which separated various antique forms of taxation, a larger total tax, a more equitable distribution; the abolition of imposts uselessly vexatory; *loans* to oil the wheels of change.

The Notables had gone: but to register such decrees a power parallel to that of the Throne must — as we saw in the case of Turgot — concur. The permanent body of legal advisers to the Prince — a conception as old as Rome and morally in continuity with the Empire — the body which had tried Rohan — the Parlement — pleading the absence of a regular budget and of public discussion, refused to register, and within three months of Loménie de Brienne's appointment, the Parlement in session had proceeded from Sabattier's famous pun[1] to affirm that *no*

[1] "Vous demandez l'état des recettes — ces sont les états generaux qu'il nous faut."

permanent impost could be levied upon the nation without the summons and consent of the States-General.

The reader should pause upon that phrase.

The conception that All should rule is cœval with society.

But the words so used by Sabattier were not a mere opinion nor a mere reiteration of justice. They were spoken in that assembly of lawyers which formed the chief body of the State, and once spoken in such an air they were creative.

This memorable declaration of July, 1787, launched the Revolution.

. . . .

Nothing can reinvigorate itself or snatch itself from decay save by a return upon itself and a recapture of its own past. To revive the States-General was to bring back to life the vigour of the Middle Ages, and to renew — at the close of this last long and glorious but exhausted phase in the national life — the permanent energy of Gaul.

When in the eleventh century the great transition from the Dark Ages to mediæval civilisation was accomplished, there came, along with the new Gothic architecture and the new national tongues, as the last fruit of that florescence, an institution known in each province of Christendom by some local name (for the creation was local and spontaneous) but everywhere bearing the same characters, in formation, object, and inner nature. This Institution had for its purpose the affirmation of a doctrine fundamental in the Faith, that sovereignty lies and can only lie with the community. This Institution had for instrument wherewith to enforce that right a conception at once as mystical and as plain as any that the Faith has admitted or revealed in her strict dogmas, the conception of *representation:* two men should speak for thousands; the spirit of a community should enter and be seen through individuals who should speak with the voice of districts; these representatives should *be* the very numbers for whom they stood: an institution as tangible, as real, as visible as the Sacrament; as mysterious as the Presence of the Lord. It was a miracle of faith, but it conquered; and even to-day, woefully corrupt, there resides in Representation something of majesty and a power in moments of great danger or of great national desire to gleam for a moment through the dead body of an Institution whose whole principle of popular sanctity has been forgotten.

The theory of Representation sprang, I say, naturally from that young and happy time when Europe arose from sleep: the century of the Christian reaction against Asia.

The valleys of the Pyrenees, a scene of continual armed endeavours, spurred on by the constant pressure of Islam, first organised the idea.

The cool and cleanly little town of Jaca — an outpost on the Roman road into Spain that led down to the frontiers of the Moors — the little frontier town of Jaca saw the first strict gathering of the kind in the very first of the Crusades: but Jaca was not alone; it was throughout Christendom a natural, a simultaneous growth. The southern cities of Gaul, the great provinces, Languedoc, Bearn, distant and isolated Brittany, the compact England of the thirteenth century, followed; lastly, and not till the opening of the fourteenth century, a united and majestic gathering of Representatives, designed to bring before the Crown at Paris the voice, complaint, or will of all its subjects, emerged.

These assemblies, a *Cortes* in Spain, a *Parliament* in

England, were in France called *Estates* — and that rare one which stood, not for one province of Gaul, but for all combined, was known as the *States-General*. Like every other institution of its kind it was alive with the mediæval passion for Reality. Not abstract statistics nor some crude numerical theory, but the facts of society were recognised in, or rather everywhere translated into, these representative bodies. There were corps of nobles — since the Middle Ages, descending from the Roman centuries and their rich landed class, had nobles for a reality. The priests were separate; the commoners. In some cases (notably in towns) special corporations had special delegates; in all — especially in the States-General of France — the various aspects of the State were present in the shape of innumerable statements and mandates enforced upon the Representatives (and therefore the servants) of clerical and commercial corporations, of territorial units, of municipal authorities.

So long as the high attempt of the Middle Ages was maintained so long these councils flourished. That attempt bent down and failed in the sixteenth century — and with it declined, corrupted, or disappeared the corporate assemblies which were to the political sincerity of the Middle Ages what the universities were to its intellectual eagerness, the Gothic to its majestic insistence upon eternal expression.

In certain places the advent of the Renaissance in the sixteenth century closed the story of representation; in others, under the influence of the Reformation, became a form. In the two chief centres of the West two varied fortunes attached to the two failing branches of that great mediæval scheme. In Protestant England the form of

Representation survived; in Catholic France the memory. By one of those ironies in which History or Providence delights, the English oligarchy, which, in the phrase of a principal English writer, "had risen upon the ruins of Religion," the Howards, the "Cromwells," the Cecils, and the rest, maintained the form of The House of "Commons." The squires used that organ in the seventeenth century to destroy the power of a Crown whose own folly had, through the plunder of the Monasteries, led to its own complete impoverishment and to the enrichment of the gentry. The squires maintained that Crown but kept it as their salaried servant, and thus throughout the eighteenth century the fossil of a representative system was in England not only cherished but actively cherished to serve us as the armour of privilege. Parliament remained intensely national, full of sacred ceremonies and forms, and still using conveniently to the rich some shadow of that theory of national sovereignty which, in breaking with the Faith, the nation had broken with, perhaps for ever: whether for ever or not our own immediate future will show.

For Europe the strange accident by which dry-bones Representation thus survived in England was of vast consequence. This fossil bridged the gulf between the living Parliaments of the Middle Ages and the advent of modern democracy — and by a curious inquiry into the archæology and the extinct functions of English public life, Catholic Europe has begun to reconstruct its own past. For England the consequences of the survival are known to all who have watched the complexion of the Commons and type of membership that House enjoys — and the strange mode of recruitment of the Lords.

In France the fortunes of Representation, that mediæval thing, became, from the moment when the Middle Ages failed, very different. The States-General stood by the side of, and nominally informing, a Roman and centralised sovereignty: they were not, like the English Parliament, an institution immixed in and at last identical with, a wealthy oligarchy; they were an institution that stood by the side of and was at last suppressed by a national despotism. They ceased abruptly (in 1614), but they never lost their soul. Should they hear the call to resurrection they could rise whole and quick, a complete voice of the nation to counsel or to command. In July, 1787, with the protestation of the *Parlement of Paris* and its appeal to the past, that call had come, and from that moment onward it was plain that all France would now soon be found in action. Within two years the thing was decided.

. . . .

What was the Queen's position those two years? She was in the saddle. Her fulness of life, her firmness of purpose, had come upon her quickly. She was already divorced from joy; she was already, and for the first time, mixed constantly with public affairs. It is sometimes written that Loménie de Brienne "gave her a place in the Council." That is nonsense. She chose to enter publicly what, in private, had been hers since the March of 1787 at the latest; what had been partly hers long before. Her strength of utterance, her now formative disillusions (for disillusionment is formative in women), her apparent peril (for peril is formative in those who desire to govern), her recent grievous humiliation and suffering (for these are formative in all), formed her and gave her fixed and constructive power. It was most imperfectly, at moments disastrously, used; but if the reader would understand the violent five years which follow this moment and culminated in the crash of the throne, he must first seize the fact that, though vast impersonal forces at issue were melting and recasting France, and therefore Europe, the personality nearest the executive throughout was that of Marie Antoinette.

In *her* room at Versailles met the coming intriguers during the struggle with the Parlement under Brienne. *She* it was against whom the dishonoured Orleans, with the instinct of a demagogue, intrigued and whispered. She it was who spoke of "a necessary rigour" when the fighting begun; she — we may presume or be certain — who forbade the King to fly in the days of October; she certainly upon whom the great effort of Mirabeau turned; she who planned or rather guided the escape to Varennes; she who principally suffered from the recapture; she who constantly and actively advised Vienna, Mercy, Fersen, Mallet, in the perilous months that followed that failure; she who sustained the Court after the 20th of June; she against whom Paris charged on the 10th of August: hers was that power the memory of which exasperated the Revolution and drove even its military advisers to useless reprisals, and to her death at last.

I do not say that the powers of that awful time were personal or of this world — far from it. Nor do I say that you will not find crowded into that little æon of years a greater crowd of high and individual wills than a century may count in meaner times — there were a regiment of active, organising, and creative minds astir within a mile of Notre Dame. Still less do I pretend that the Queen's judgment, her rapidity, her energy, and her certitude were comparable to any of a hundred or more in that arena. She was nothing compared with their greatest, little compared with their least. But I say that close to the *executive* — to that which, until August, '92, could command soldiers, sign edicts, and, above all, correspond with foreign Powers — its adviser, its constant moderator, at times its very self, was the Queen.

Her last child, the baby of eleven months, was now in the July of 1787, dead. It was the second death of a thing loved that she had known — her mother's the first; it was the first death she had *seen* of a thing loved. In the desertion of her friends, the great part she had to play, the open wound of the necklace verdict, she took that death as but one more poignant sorrow. The little girl had been ailing for but four days: Marie Antoinette shut herself up with her husband and his sister for one day in Trianon to recover from that shock. She returned to act.

She applauded and sustained her husband — or rather Brienne — during the struggle with the Parlement all July. She heard (and despised) the call for the States-General. When the *Lit de Justice*, the solemn ceremony by which the King could enforce the registration of his edicts in spite of the Parlement's refusal, was held on the 6th of August, it was held at Versailles, as it were under the Queen's eye: the Parlement replied by refusing to admit the registration so made.

The Parisian crowd surrounded the Parlement in Paris and applauded: not for this or that, nor for the nature of the taxes protested, nor for anything but for that prime principle — that the *States-General* should be summoned. The Queen ordered economies: they came into force at once, that very week. Those who lost their posts became new enemies of hers: the economies were nothing to the crowd: she gained nothing with the public: she lost more with Versailles. It was dangerous for her to approach the Capital.

If she had hoped, by an economy that seemed to her so important, to affect the Parlement, Marie Antoinette was in grevious error: in error from that lack of perspective and of grip which her position, and above all her character, had left in her. Within a week of it all the Parlement had replied by a renewed refusal to register, a renewed demand for the States-General, and was away at Troyes, exiled but sitting in full power, deliberating and enthusiastically supported by Paris old and new. At Versailles, Loménie de Brienne, the Queen's man, demanded the title, beyond the practical power, of Chief Minister: such a demand led to the resignation of what little brains were left in the Council. In September he compromised with the Parlement, and let it return.

Loménie next formulated decrees which proposed indeed to rely on ordinary taxation — but to an extraordinary extent and on a novel scheme — and to call the States-General *within five years:* he intended (as did the Queen) to adjourn and surely to drop the meeting of the States-General altogether. In November, when a majority in the Parlement was secured by the absence of some, perhaps the purchase of others, he caused the King to meet that body — and then raised its anger again by registering without counting votes and, as it were, by the autocratic power of the King. If, as is possible, the Queen did not advise or countenance this last act, at any rate the whole tone of her correspondence applauds the decision.

The consequences following on this error were immediate.

Orleans, now the Queen's chief enemy, made himself a spokesman of discontent and was exiled to the provinces; he attributed his disgrace to the Queen. Sabattier and Tieteau de St. Just were arrested on the bench itself. The States-General precisely because it had been proposed to consider them "in five years," and because the Parlement had insisted on an earlier date, were more in the public mouth than ever; and as the year closed, Brienne and all Brienne stood for, bethought them of some wide action that should remove all this friction and leave government secure.

That action had the Queen for its authoress. It was an attempt at despotic reform without representation, an Austrian model, and it was named "The New Order."

No year in Marie Antoinette's life had more affected her experience, her character, and her position in the State than this of 1787, her thirty-second, which now drew to an end. She had made a Ministry; she had influenced, supported, in part created a policy; she had reaped the full harvest of pain in the first death of a child, in the growing illness of her eldest son, in the flood of calumny which had succeeded the La Motte's escape from prison. She had come rapidly to actual power, she was exercising it with facility — and every act of hers led more nearly and more directly to the cataclysm before her.

The public hatred of her had immensely grown — in intensity, in volume, but especially in quality, since she had manifestly become the chief adviser of her husband and the creator of a scheme of government. The Polignacs, as I have said, had joined the enemy. Orleans was now definitely the head of her bitter opponents. The drawing-rooms of Paris had joined the populace against her. It had been actually proposed to mock her effigy during the rejoicing at the return of the Parlement from exile. The wits had renewed their nicknames: she was "Madame Deficit" as well as "the Austrian" she had always been — and by the winter all the quarrel in which the Parlement, the crowd, and nearly every permanent force were now ranged against the Crown, saw in her the core of the resistance and the personal object of attack.

The year 1788 at its very opening showed clearly how far the development had gone. That system of "a new order" — a powerful, uncriticised Crown, thorough reform, the negation of ideas — saw, risen up against such feminine and practical conceptions, those much stronger things, dogmas. The civic religion of the French and the creed of the era they were framing emerged. Before Easter the Parlement had denied the right of the executive to imprison at will, as also the right of the Prince to assimilate his edict to a public law, and had demanded the complete freedom of the three lawyers who had been arrested. But — an ominous thing — the Parlement claimed no privileges. It demanded the release of its members as *citizens* and *of human right* against the arbitrary power of the Crown.

Against such a force as this — a creed — the only weapon that "The New Order" and the Queen could imagine was a reform of machinery. In this, as in so much else during the furious struggle of those eighteen months, "The New Order" fore-planned much that the Revolution itself was to achieve: it was modern, it was suited to circumstance, but lacking first principles it was apparent and direct, but lacking nationality and being opposed to the summoning of the States-General it was doomed. The scheme of "The New Order" included a replacing of all this antique, corporate, and privileged power of the Parlement by a High Court more fully reflecting the governing classes of the nation. It was not unwise, and Marie Antoinette — to judge again from her correspondence and from the universal opinion of contemporaries — was largely its originator and wholly its ally. It miserably failed.

The secret plan of it — surrounded with fantastic precautions — was divulged. The threatened Parlement (and it had the whole nation behind it) met at once, and D'Epresmenil explained the peril, and declared once more, but far more directly than before, for the principles upon which the Revolution was to turn, and especially the right of the States-General alone — regularly and periodically summoned — to grant supply. The arrests that followed — arrests which the Queen called with quite singular blindness "acts of rigour" — perilous as she saw, but necessary as she imagined — were the signal for an approach to civil war.

"The New Order" was resisted forcibly in the provinces by the privileged, by custom, by the populace (who feared new taxes), by local patriotism which feared the loss of local character and (what indeed so soon did come) the merging of all in one homogeneous State. All the troops were out; revolt had begun.

In June, 1788, the Clergy — summoned to meet and grant an aid as a last desperate resource for means — replied by an assertion in turn of *their* immutable custom and peculiar right. In July "The New Order" broke down. The demand for the States-General was acceded to by the Crown and by the Queen. On the 8th of August, 1788, they were definitely summoned for the May Day of the following year.

XI

THE BASTILLE

AUGUST 8, 1788, TO SEPTEMBER 30. 1789

THE decision was taken. France was alive with the advent of the States-General. The autumn of 1788 had come. Fersen was with the Queen.

It was more than fourteen years since, a boy of eighteen, Northern, dignified, and grave, his large and steady brown eyes had met hers from far off among the hundreds in the Masked Ball at the Opera. He was then a child. She also was a child, pure, exiled, of an active timidity, and not yet even Queen. I have written what happened then: the rare occasions on which he had come and gone. Now he was here with her at Versailles.

The something permanent which every human life has known had entered in that moment of her girlhood and settled finally within her heart. The accidents of living did little to disturb so silent and so secure a thing. He had been but a chance visitor to Paris — a Swedish lad on his Grand Tour — when they had thus met for ever; during the critical first three years of her reign he had been away in his own country. He had returned, as I have said, in the summer of 1778. The worst of her torments was settled then: she was to be a mother; she might expect an heir to the throne; the adventure, the successful adventure, of America had begun. A position of womanhood and of rule, such dignities and such repose, might have paled or rendered ridiculous the chance passion of extreme youth: they did neither. Whether he came or went, his quiet image — the one fixed thing she had known in a world she could not know — remained. He had been received at once right into the tiny inner circle of the Polignacs before he left for the American War. He had been with the Queen continually, reserved and of that breeding which she longed for, the unpassionate poise of the North. Her child, her husband's child, was born; '79 and its war news came, and Fersen had resolved at last to go. He also by that time, as has been read, knew what had entered his life.

The Queen, as he inhabited the halls of Versailles during his farewells, had followed him with her eyes, and very often they had filled with tears. All the world saw the thing. He had gone off at last to America, to wonder at the swamps and the bare landscape, the odd shuffling fighting and the drag of an informal war. His English gave him work enough interpreting between his own French Generals and Washington; he wrote home from time to time to his father, he busied himself in learning his military trade — but of Versailles or to Versailles there was not a word. During all the three years, '80–'83, that he suffered the new countries, the Queen and he heard nothing the one of the other.

He had returned to Europe; but it was only the journey of his sovereign Gustavus that kept him some months in France, though a colonelcy, more or less honorary, and a pension of some hundreds had been given the young man there. A wealthy marriage, long arranged in England for him, he let slip without concern. The proposal (a year before the affair of the necklace) that he should marry Necker's ugly daughter, he resigned at once in favour of his friend, young Staël, his sovereign's ambassador. With a commission in Sweden as well as in France, it was his own country he preferred. His moments at Versailles were rare, his visits very brief — such as that in which he saw the Notables dissolved (of which scene he records his judgment); in none did he more than appear, silent, for a very few hours or days at Versailles. The girl who had met him, a boy, in '74, was now a woman of thirty and more: chance glimpses alone had lit up the very long space of those years: she had suffered all the business of the necklace, all the rising hatred of Paris, without any too close a word from him; she was entering the Revolution and the way to death when he reappeared: henceforward he did not leave her.

That bond, which time had neither increased nor diminished and which permanent absence and silence had left unfalsified, now became a living communion between them. He was never what is called her "lover"; the whole sequence is that of a devotion as in a tale or a song, and yet burning in living beings: a thing to the French incomprehensible, to men of other countries, to Englishmen, for instance, comprehensible enough — but, whether comprehensible or not, as rare as epic genius.

. . . .

Brienne had fallen: the Queen, and the Queen alone, had put back Necker in his place. Why had she done this? From a desire to rule, and an opportunity for it.

There are those who discover in themselves the capacity to govern, that is to organise the wills of men. Often great soldiers find this in themselves, and are led to govern a whole state at last: such as Napoleon.

There are others to whom cheating, intrigue and cunning are native: such are, at bottom, however high their station, the slaves, not the dictators or the helpers, of their fellow-beings; they have a keen nose for the herd; they will always follow it, and it is their ambition to fill posts where they can give favours and draw large salaries. Of this sort are parliamentary politicians to-day: from such we draw our ministers. They have of poor human nature an expert knowledge such as usurers have and panderers; they are, therefore, not unsuited to choose permanent officials or to recommend to others places of trust and power.

There is a third kind, and to this third kind Marie Antoinette belonged — as many another woman and feminine man has belonged. It neither organises nor intrigues; it desires to do neither, and is incapable of both. All it desires is to be able to say "I govern." The accident of the last two years had permitted her to say this — but, having said it, she could say nothing more. She knew the outcry against Calonne: she undid him. She knew the reputation of Brienne: she made him. She saw Brienne most evidently out of favour with opinion; she unmade him. She heard shouts for Necker — and Necker was summoned to her little room, was regally examined, graciously received and installed.

Those who can govern through a period of peril, that is, those who can organise the wills of men during the short and indeterminate time before any resultant of clashing social forces has yet appeared, note, decide, order, speak, and do — and when it is too late to act, their genius tells them that it is too late. In the early winter of 1788 it was not yet too late. What would one possessed of the power of government have done? In the first place, such an one would have stated the evil publicly in detail and with authority; in the next, chosen not one but a body of men to deal with particular difficulties (as, for instance, a particular *légiste* for the troubles of that absurdity, the Common Law; a particular soldier to suggest a reform of the army, &c.; in the third, used as allies all the positive forces available, all the enthusiasms, all the tide — to this force (by persuasion) how much may not be harnessed? So Mirabeau would have done; so Napoleon did; so some ready eye in 1788 might have planned. The States-General is the fever? You shall have it: in Paris, with splendour. The Commons are the cry? They shall be in full double number and with special new powers — a new dress, perhaps, as well. The nation is crying out for Government? Give them the Crown: the King on horseback day after day.

Had some such judgment controlled that moment, France would have preserved the Monarchy, old institutions clothed in their old names would have been squeezed and fitted into new moulds; France so changing, there would have been some change in Europe — an episode well worthy of memory and noted by special historians. The Bishops of the Church in France would — to-day — have been what Rohan and Narbonne were then; the Faith, already derelict, would by this time very probably have descended to be a ritual for wealthy women or an opinion for a few valueless, weak men: that self-praise and that divorce from reality which is the mark of our backwaters in Europe and of our new countries everywhere would (perhaps) have settled in the succeeding century upon all Europe, and, for the first time in its long history, our civilisation would have missed one of its due resurrections. As it was, God intended the Revolution. Therefore, every error and insufficiency in those directing its inception was permitted, and therefore, on account of such insufficiency, the full force of a military people ran freely, as run natural things, and achieved what we know.

The Queen had nominated Necker from a mere desire to rule, and had therefore simply chosen the man most loudly called for. Necker, on his side, was well worthy of so facile a judgment; he was all that is meant by Geneva.

By his own standards, which were those of a company promoter, he was just barely honest — by those of chivalric honour he was deplorably tainted. Full of avarice, order and caution, a very Huguenot, he sought everywhere an economic solution for political problems; unsoldierly, of course, and in the presence of danger worthless, he was none the less patient in detail and of a persevering kind; very vacillating in the presence of fierce and conflicting desires around him, he was yet tenacious of a general plan. To all these characters he added that kind of ambition which is avid of popularity on condition that it shall face no bodily risk and that it shall labour in words or on paper only. He had his reward: his insignificant figure was for a year the symbol of all the great ferment; his presence with, or absence from, the Council was the test of advance or of retreat in the revolutionary movement. So for one year — then for a few months he is forgotten; then he hears a mob in the street, and flies.

With such a man as figurehead it is not difficult to judge the obvious development of the autumn and winter which produced the first great Parliament. Opinion was invited: the pamphlets poured in. On matters already fixed in public opinion Necker could be decisive, as, for instance, that the Commons in the approaching Assembly should be as numerous as the clergy and the nobles combined — for this was the universal rule in provincial parliaments; but when (two days after Christmas) this point (which had afforded food for violent writing but was in reality certain to be conceded) — when, I say, this point was fixed by King and Queen and Council, Necker so drafted the decision as to make it appear all his own to the populace: while at Court the angry higher nobility said it was all the Queen's. A far more decisive matter — and one that escaped the partisans — was whether the Nobles, Clergy, and Commons should sit and vote together, as the necessity for a Popular Will — for one voice — demanded, or should play the antique fool and, in a crisis so actual and vivid, solemnly vote separately, checking each other's decisions, nullifying the public mandate — all for the sake of custom. Here Necker *could* have decided and changed history: but there was not an opinion sufficiently unanimous to guide him in his nullity. He left that essential piece of procedure to be settled by the Estates themselves when they should have met; he thus (as will be seen) made of the first and most necessary act of the States-General, the insistence of the Commons that all should vote together, an illegal thing — and so coloured all their succeeding action with the colour of rebellion. One thing Necker had done of his own judgment, and it was idiotic. He had summoned the Notables again for a month in the autumn — he was soon glad to be rid of that folly: the decree I have mentioned followed, and in February, 1789 — legally before the end of January — the elections to the States-General began.

No such complete representation of a great nation has been attempted since that day; no such experiment could be attempted save with political energy at white heat and under the urgent necessity of a secular charge. The confused noise which filled the rising spring of '89 was, for once, the voice of ALL; thousands upon thousands of little primary assemblies, of advisory letters, of plaints, of legal suggestions, of strict orders and mandates to the elected (without which no political freedom can exist) of corporate actions by guilds, by townships, by chapters, by every form of political personality, filled and augmented the life of France. So vast was the thing that to this day, amid the libraries of monographs that seem to exhaust the Revolution, all have shrunk from the delineation of this rising ocean of men. There is no final work upon the elections of '89. No one has dared.

April passed. The deputies began to stream into Paris. Paris, the last days of that month and the first of the next, began to overflow into the royal town at its gates. Sunday, the 3rd of May, saw one long procession of every kind and fortune pouring, in spite of the drenching weather, from the capital up into the hills of Versailles. Upon the morrow the opening religious ceremony of the Session was to be held.

. . . .

At about six o'clock of the morning of Monday, the 4th of May, it was still raining — not violently, but still raining; the dawn struggled in wet clouds over the woods and the plain of Paris beyond, and the pavements of Versailles were shining flat under the new day, with large puddles in their worn places. As the light broadened the rain ceased. The uniform and dull low sky began to break and gather: the innumerable crowd moved. Some thousands were sodden after a night spent out of doors; many thousands more, moving from their packed rooms, where a bed was a guinea and the mere shelter of a roof a well-let thing, began to crowd the pavements, the roofs, the cornices; as for the windows, every window had its bouquet of heads at high price, well-dressed heads and eager. The morning rose and grew warm.

The palace of Versailles looks east and north down towards the woods that hide Paris; it looks down three broad, divergent avenues spreading like the fingers of a hand, and starting (as from the palm of such a hand) from a wide space called the "Place d'Armes," which forms a huger outer court, as it were, to the huge Court of the Kings. To the right and to the left of this main square and its avenues, as you look from the palace, lie the two halves of the town: the northern, to the left, has for its principal church Notre Dame; the southern, to the right, has for its principal church St. Louis, which is now the Cathedral; each building is by situation and plan the centre of its quarter. The way from Notre Dame to St. Louis is up the Rue Dauphin, across the great Place d'Armes and then down the Rue Saborg — all in a straight line not half a mile long, with the great Place taking up more than the middle third. From the one church to the other was the processional way of Versailles; it was chosen for that day. From seven onwards the Parlement had been gathering in Notre Dame; not till ten did the royal carriages arrive, all plumed and gilded, swung low and ridiculous: the King and his household, the Queen and hers; the Princes of the Blood — but as for Orleans he was already with the lords in the Church, disdaining his rank and making a show of humility. They all set out in procession for St. Louis, the clergy of Versailles in a small surpliced body leading, the dark Commons next, the embroidered and feathered Nobility, the Priests, the Household, the music, the Bishop; then the Blessed Sacrament in the Archbishop of Paris' hands, with Monsieur and his brother and two more of the Blood at the corners of the canopy; last of all the Queen and her ladies — all in the order I have named; two thousand and more four-front, the length of a brigade —

and every one of them (save the Archbishop who held the Monstrance) with a blessed candle in his or her hand. By the time the head of the line was at St. Louis, the tail had hardly left Notre Dame,[1] and as each detachment took the line, young Dreux Brézé, Master of Ceremonies, on foot since seven, ordered them.

The myriads of people saw them go by. The sun was shining at last: all could be seen, yet the cheers were pointed and full of meaning; the silence also was full of meaning. They cheered the Commons as those six hundred went by, in black without swords — all in black save for a Breton amongst them. Some curiously picked out Mirabeau; they were silent at the lords' blaze of colour, half-cheering only Orleans, his face such a picture! the sacred candle flickering in his hands; they did not (as would a modern crowd) all uncover to the Blessed Sacrament; they cheered the King. Then, as the Queen passed, there passed with her a belt of silence. As she went slowly with her ladies along that way silence went with her; cheering went before and after. At one place only was that silence broken, where a group of rough women suddenly shouted out, as she passed, insulting *vivats* for Orleans: it may be that she stumbled when she heard them.

From the advanced colonnade of the great stables (where the sappers are lodged to-day), upon the roof of the colonnade, there was a truckle-bed and many cushions laid, and on it was lying the broken body of her son, the Dauphin, who would not inherit all these things: he was very visibly dying. His miserable little frame, all bent and careless, lay there at its poor ease. His listless and veiled eyes watched the procession go by.

[1] Carlyle, of course, puts one church for the other, and makes the procession walk wrong way about. The Cambridge History, however, is accurate in this detail.

It is said that his mother, in that half-mile of ordeal, glanced up to where he lay, and smiled.

The sun still shone upon the double row of soldiers — the blue of the Gardes Françaises upon this side, the Red of the Swiss upon that; the crowd was in gaiety — the wet were now dry; the last of the line were now gone and the doors of St. Louis had closed on them. It had been a great show, and all the place and its pleasures were open to the people. Next day the Session was opened in that same hall which had been raised two years before for the Notables.

A member of the Commons, sitting in the back row of his order, would have seen before him, rank upon rank, the dense mass of black uniform menace which his six hundred presented, half filling the floor of the great oblong hall; to left of him, against a row of columns, the clergy of every rank; to the right against the opposite row of columns, the blaze of the Nobles — among them Orleans, his face insolently set towards the Throne. Far above and beyond them all, at the end of the hall, like an altar raised upon its steps, was the last splendour of the Throne. The golden threads of the lilies shone upon the vast canopy of purple velvet that over-shadowed it; seated upon it, alone above his kingdom, the last of the kings possessed a great majesty, in which the known hesitation of his gait, the known lethargic character of his person, were swallowed up in awe: an enormous diamond gleamed in the feather of his hat. Below and around him were grouped the Princes of the Blood and the great officers of State, and in front of the group in a long line sat the Ministry. Necker among these — the only one dressed as the Commons were dressed — appealed to the Commons, while at the foot of the throne, in purple and silver white, a little diamond circlet and a heron's feather in her hair, stood the Queen.

This the Commons could see, under the light that fell from high windows near the roof; it fell over two thousand of the public — guests chosen rather than a true public; they filled the galleries above, they swarmed in the dark aisle beneath, undivided from the three orders — a familiarity shocking to our historians who, craning their necks, have watched as a privilege and with respect the fag-end of the House of Commons or the County Council from a pen.

To the command of Dreux Brézé, all that great hall rose: the King rose also, read his short speech in a firm voice, and put on his hat to sit down. The Nobles covered themselves at the King's gesture: among the Commons there was confusion — they did not know the etiquette, or rather, some did, some did not. The incident was insignificant and comic: a graver thing followed it. Barentin rose, the Keeper of the Seals; he spoke for an hour. Had he spoken for three minutes and spoken but one sentence it would have been all he had to do, for he was there to tell them that *it was left to the Three Orders to sit separate or together as they might choose.* All the Revolution was latent in that order.

The Nobles would vote to sit separate; possibly the clergy: the "National Assembly" — as all thought of it, as all called it — would be turned into a "Lords and Commons" — an absurd, complicated and do-nothing machine with privileges and customs, quaintnesses and long accommodations between this house and that; it would lose touch with the general; the sap of national life would be cut off from it; it would not be able to create; it would be the jest of that which really governed. As in England to-day our various elected bodies are the jests of the plutocracy, so in 1789 the "National Assembly," tripartite, played upon by vanity and ignorance, would have become the jest of the Crown. But in France an institution, once unreal, disappears, and before July the Assembly was, according to this plan, to disappear. It was deliberately conceived as a means of nullifying and destroying the Parlement.

Necker spoke next. He spoke for three hours, and was listened to throughout, for he dealt with finance. His speech was full of lies — but his name had not yet lost the titular place of idolatry. When he had ended his Genevese falsehoods, the ceremony was over and all were free to dine. But with Barentin's words the Revolution had begun.

All May Gaul worked and seethed. The instinct of numbers aimed straight for the objective upon which all turned, and the Commons demanded the accession to one corporate Assembly of the Nobles and Clergy. They negotiated with the privileged houses; they affirmed the principle of combined voting: Necker sent for soldiers. By the end of the month the last attempt at some voluntary arrangement had failed. Meanwhile the King, by some lethargy or through the intrigue of some cabal, had not yet formally received a deputation of the Commons.

What did the Queen make of that May? The days seemed to her first an ugly rumour throughout Versailles, buzzing round the palace — soon an uproar. She stood with the few that actively maintained privilege against the Commons; but, a trifle wiser than they, she brought in their counsels in a moderate form to the King. It was not enough: the troops still came into Paris — Gaul still rose higher and higher; and through the tumult something much more to her, more intimate, infinitely more acute and true, ran and held her as a physical pain will pin the mind and hold it during the playing of some loud and meaningless music: it was the dying of her little son; he lay at Meudon dying.

The end of the French Monarchy was mirrored in the fate of the last bodily forms that were to contain its Idea. The Bourbon heirs, one after another, died before succession. Louis XV., a great grandson, himself delicate from birth, was succeeded by a grandson again, a boy painfully saved by the doctors — a man throughout life partially infirm. The line had come at last to this child, the Dauphin, whose advent had been the opportunity for such strong joy throughout the country and in whom the New Age was to find its first King. All the phases of doom had shown themselves: first, the high promise, then the vague doubts, the mysteries of a general disease; lastly the despairs. For a month, ever since the opening of the States-General, which he had languidly witnessed, it had been but a question of the day on which the boy would die. That day had come.

It was on the 3rd of June, at Meudon. The King and the Queen had come in answer to sudden and graver news of their child; they reached the place in the early afternoon — and they were implored to return. The boy was within, at his agony. The King sank into a chair and cried that his son was dead, and the poor lad's mother, suddenly broken in the midst of so many and such great public alarms, of her government, her resistance and her perils, suddenly knelt down and cried wildly, rocking her head in her hands, burying her face on Louis' knees: she called out to God. They were left thus together, and at one the next morning the Dauphin was dead.

It was as though two majesties or angels challenged each other in those days: the majesty which reigns inwardly and which everywhere makes of a son's death the supreme agony of the world, though sons die hourly; the majesty which reigns outwardly and which commands, once in a thousand years, the passing of societies and kingdoms. For while this death was doing at Meudon, in the Commonwealth the last decisions also were at hand. Two days after the sad procession of ranks and delegates had done honour to the dead child, the Commons summoned for the last time the Clergy and the Lords to join them and form one body to mirror the nation. It was but three days after the little body had been taken to lie at St. Denis among the Kings, that the next step was taken. The Revolution broke with law — it now first began to be the Revolution and to do. The Commons declared themselves to be no longer the "Commons," but — with all of the privileged orders who would join them — they declared themselves to be the "National Assembly": those who would not join them were no part of the body which was to remake the world: their legality was not to avail them: the Commons had "made act of sovereignty," and the strain between two centres of authority, the Crown and the Representatives had begun.

It was this that the Queen must watch and parry and try to understand, now, when the first part of her flesh had gone down into the grave, and her brain, shaken with despairs, must attempt to control and to comprehend the wave; and her eyes, weary of weeping, to read orders, to note faces, and her voice, with which she could not longer call her son, to command. She was in the centre of the resistance for a month, and it failed.

For a few days, in spite of the call for troops which had been heard — and the troops were coming — for a few days more, speech was still formidable and every phase of the debate ringing through the great shed of the Menus was a further affirmation of the new and violent sovereignty of those usurpers, the Assembly. In twenty-four hours a decision was taken by the Crown.

To the assumption of sovereignty by the Commons the Court replied. There was to be a Royal Session on the Monday following, the King present, and all the division between the orders settled by his final voice — as to the Commons declaration it was ignored.

And meanwhile Speech was silenced. Barentin, Keeper of the Seals, had seen to that. He wrote to the King that it was *imperative* the Commons should be silenced until the Royal Session was held. He wrote: "Coupez Court." Have done with the business! A simple way to silence the Commons was found.

It was upon Friday the 19th of June that Barentin had written his letter to the King. Upon the Saturday morning, the 20th, the weather having turned to rain and the streets being deserted, the first stray members of the Commons came up to the door of the Menus to resume their debates. No notice had reached them, nor even their elected Speaker, Bailly, the worthy astronomer. They came with umbrellas dripping above them, the mud splashing their black stockings and black knee breeches, the rain driving in upon their black Court coats. They tried the door: it was locked, and a sentry came forward. They saw, streaked under the rain, a little scrap of writing nailed to the door. The Hall was "closed by royal order," and, within, the sound of hammering marked the carpenters at work preparing for Monday's ceremonial. They wondered: others came; the group grew until at last many hundreds of the Commons stood there without, upon the pavement of the wide planted avenue. Mirabeau was there and Robespierre was there, Sieyès, Bailly—all the Commons. Up at the end of the way the King's great Palace lay silent and, as it were, empty under the rain. No one crossed its vast open courtyard; its shut streaming windows stared dully at the town. The Commons moved away in a herd, leaving the sentry and his comrade to pace and be drenched, and the little scrap of writing to be washed and blurred on the locked door. As they moved off the noise of hammering within grew fainter till they heard it no more.

That very middle-class sight, a great mob of umbrellas wandering in the streets, was full of will: wandering from one place to another they landed at last in a tennis court which was free, just where a narrow side-street of the southern town makes an elbow. Into that shelter they poured: and over against them, watching all they did from above, from his home just across the lane, was Barentin, Keeper of the Seals. He saw the umbrellas folded at the door, the hundreds pressing in, damply; he saw through the lights of the court their damp foot-prints on the concrete of the hall—a table brought: Bailly, the president, standing upon it above the throng and reading out the oath that they "*would not disperse till they had given the nation a constitution*" — then the press of men signing that declaration one by one.

He heard the mob gathering outside and filling the street. Among them at least one witness has left a record of what could be heard through the open doors — how Mirabeau reluctantly signed, pleading popular pressure; how one man only refused to sign, thinking it what it was, rebellion. He was Martin, of Auch.

It was the summer solstice, a date unlucky to the Bourbons.

The King heard all these things — but there was nothing to be done. Sunday passed, and Monday — the Royal Session was postponed. It was not till Tuesday morning, the 23rd, at ten that the procession formed and that Louis prepared to attend it. It was still raining.

All the pomp that could be gathered had been gathered for that occasion, though the very skies were against it. Four thousand men stood to arms, lining that less than half a mile from the Palace to the Menus. Hidden in the woods beyond, camped up on Satory and dispersed in the suburbs around, six regiments more were ready. A vast crowd, wholly silent, watched the Court go by. The Queeh unbroken (but carrying such recent agony!), Artois vivacious and trim, the Ministers hurried, Louis somewhat bent, fat, suffering.

A man who saw that sight has written that he thought to see some great funeral go by: he was right. Of the two million dead which the Revolution demanded from Moscow to the Tagus, the first was passing in the splendid coach of the Kings — I mean, Unquestioned Security. That fixity of political creed and that certitude in social structure, which hitherto no wars had shaken in Europe for century upon century of Christian order, had perished. Men cannot live or breathe without political security, yet for now more than a hundred years Europe has in vain awaited its return.

The King had reached his throne in the great shed of the Menus; the Queen was beside him; the Orders, the Nobles and the Clergy stood ranked on either side; then after some delay the Commons were permitted to enter by a mean side-door and to fill the dark end of the place with their dark numbers. . . . Where was Necker? The Symbol of the New Age was not there; the fatuous Genevese had stayed at home. He had presided at the Council which had drawn up the declaration the King was about to read. He *may* have suggested certain softenings of phrase in it; they *may* have been rejected by the Queen or another—but it was a document the responsibility of which he, in duty, bore; it was for him to resign or to be present: he hedged by his absence and let it be thought that he protested.

With a rumble and a shuffling the twelve hundred of them sat down. When they were all well sat down, Barentin in a loud voice proclaimed: "Gentlemen, the King gives you leave to be seated!" The King turned to the Queen upon his left and bade her also take her throne. She courtesied with an exaggerated grandeur and chose to stand while the whole long speech was delivered—a royal witness to the Crown of which she was now much more the strength and principle than any other there.

The speech was decisive. It willed this and that in strong imperatives — even the voice of the King, into whose mouth these words were put, was firm: he willed very liberal and modern things — but no divided authority — above all, no divided authority! The new and rival sovereign, the Usurper, must resign. The Commons were but the Commons. Of their recent claim no word, but, upon the contrary, an assertion that the States-General might not, even were they to vote in common, determine their own procedure.

As he read, here and there a man would applaud — even from among the Commons.

"Remember, gentlemen, that none of your plans, none of your schemes can become law without *my* express approval

It is *I* that have, till now, given my subjects all their happiness. . . . " And the speech closed with: "I command you, therefore, gentlemen, to *disperse at once. To-morrow* you shall come each into the Hall *assigned* to his order."

When he had read these words the King sat down: the speech was ended. There was but a moment between his ending and his rising again to go. The Queen, very dignified, rose with him. Together, and followed by their train, they left the hall. It was just noon.

The Nobles rose in their turn and left the building: the Bishops preceded them, but of the lower clergy many — half, perhaps — lingered. The body of the Commons refused to move.

They sat massed, in silence, at the far end of the great gaudy shed. Over against them, at the further end, the workmen had begun to take down the scenery of that royal play; the curtains were being lowered, the carpets rolled up, and there was hammering again. Across the empty benches of the nobles and the Hierarchy, in the empty middle of the hall, every exclamation, however subdued, of the bewildered but determined Commons echoed: but the background of that interval was astonishment and silence.

This curious and dire silence, a silence of revolt, lasted perhaps half an hour, when there entered into it the Master of the Ceremonies, young Dreux Brézé.

He was little more than a boy, just married, of a refined and rather whitened sort, tall, covered with cloth of gold. He was not ashamed to stud his hands with diamonds, like an Oriental or a woman; he shone with light against the dark mass of the Commons, and he alone wore a sword. He bore no sign or sacred letter, and his mere office was not awful.[1] He advanced, and in that slightly irritable but well-bred drawl of his he muttered something as though ashamed. They cried "Speak up!" He spoke louder. "They had heard the King's orders. . . ." He repeated the phrase. Various cries and exclamations arose. Then Mirabeau, standing forward, said — What did he say? It is uncertain, and will always be debated, but it was something like this: "We are here by the will of the people and only death can dismiss us." Dreux Brézé walked out with due ceremony, backward.

. . . .

Well, then, why was Death not brought in to sweep the Commons? Here were soldiers all around—foreigners, Germans, and Swiss, in number a full division: why was no shot fired? Because, although apparently no force lay opposed to them save the mere will of less than a thousand unarmed debaters, there did in fact lie opposed to them the potential force of Paris. Close on a million souls, say two hundred thousand men capable of bearing arms, almost homogeneous in opinion, lay twelve miles down the valley, as full of rumour as a hive — at the sound of a musket they might rise and swarm. It was not a calculable thing; Paris *might* after half an hour of scuffle turn into a mere scattered crowd: there *might* be a fierce resistance, prolonged, bleeding authority to death unless a sufficient force contained Paris also, as the debaters at Versailles were already contained. That force was summoned.

Thirty regiments moved. All the last days of June the great roads sounded with their marching from every neighbouring garrison. The rattle of new guns one morning

[1] It had originally been created to provide a salary for one, Pot, who was further dignified with the title of Rhodes—names curiously English.

woke from sleep the unknown Robespierre, who watched them from his window passing interminably under the July dawn; they baited their horses in the stables of the Queen. Of nearly all the troop so gathering one little portion, the half-irregular militia body (militia, but permanently armed) called "the French Guards," was other than foreign. The "French Guards" might not indeed be reliable but, as it was thought, they hardly counted. The rest were for the most part German-speaking mercenaries, the solid weapon of the Crown: and still they gathered.

Neck to neck with the advance of that mobilisation the Assembly raced for power; for every brigade appearing you may count a new claim. In the first hours of their revolt, when Dreux Brézé had just retired, they proclaimed themselves "Inviolable"—that is, in their new sovereignty, they declared an armed offence to that sovereignty to be treason.

The sight of Paris, heaving as for movement on the 24th of June, Wednesday, when the news of the royal session and its sequel came, determined the Duke of Orleans to take a line. He desired to profit by the dissensions. He continually bribed and flattered and supported, by his wealth and through his parasites, the vast and spontaneous surge of opinion, adding perhaps a fraction to its power. He was among the stupidest of the Bourbons, for he thought in his heart he might be king. This null and dissipated fellow led a minority of the Nobles to the Commons and declared their adhesion to the Assembly: that was the Thursday, the 25th — the next day the Court itself, the King, deliberately advised the union of all the orders!

The Court had yielded — for the moment. The Court thought it was better so: the troops were gathering, soon a blow was to be struck, and the less friction the better while it was preparing. . . .

So, as the first week of July went by, everything was preparing: the Electorial College of Paris had met and continued in session, forming spontaneously a local executive for the capital: certain of the French Guard in Paris had sworn to obey the Assembly only, had been imprisoned . . . and released by popular force . . . and pardoned. The last troops had come in; the Assembly was finally formed. On the day when it named its first committee to discuss the new Constitution, the Queen and those about the Queen had completed their plan, and the Crown was ready to re-arise and to scatter its enemies.

There was in this crisis a military simplicity as behoved it, for it was a military thing. No intriguing. Necker, the symbol of the new claims, was to go — booted out at a moment's notice and over the frontier as well. A man of the Queen's, a man who had been ambassador at Vienna, a very trusted servant of over fifty years continually with the Monarchy, a man of energy, strong-stepping, loud, Breteuil was in one sharp moment to take his place. Old Broglie, brave and renowned, was to grasp the army — and the thing was done: the Assembly gone to smoke: the debating over: silence and ancient right restored. And as for the dependence on opinion and on a parliamentary majority for money! . . . why, a bold bankruptcy and begin again.

So the Queen saw the sharp issue, now that all the regiments were assembled. A corps of German mercenaries were in the Park, encamped; their officers were cherished in the rooms of the Polignacs: they were a symbol of what was toward. Paris might or might not rise. If it rose, there would be action; if not, none. In either case victory and a prize worth all the miserable cajoling and submission to which the Court had been compelled while the soldiers were still unready. They were ready now. So the Queen.

On Saturday the 11th of July, at three in the afternoon, Necker was sitting down with his wife and a certain friend to dinner: the excellent dinner of a man worth four millions of money — doubtfully acquired. Ten thousand men lay at arms within an hour of Versailles; at all the issues of Paris were troops amounting to at least two divisions more — mainly German cavalry: one regiment at Charente, Samade; one regiment at Ivry, one, of German hussars, at the Champ de Mars; one, of Swiss infantry, with a battery, at the Etoile (where is now the Arc de Triomphe). Two more, German, south of the river; a whole camp at the northern gate — and many others. No food could enter the city save by leave of that circle of arms. . . . To Necker, so sitting there at table, was brought a note from the King; he opened it: it told him he was ordered out of office and ordered out of the kingdom too. He finished his dinner, and then took horse and coach and drove away along the Brussels road.

There followed three days which very much resembled, to the Queen and the General Staff of the Resistance, those days during which a general action is proceeding at the front and a stream of accounts, true and false, exaggerated, distorted, coming pell-mell and in the wrong order, confuse rather than inform the anxious ears at headquarters far in the rear. Men tore galloping to and fro continually up and down the twelve miles of road between the palace and the gates of Paris. "Paris had risen." "No, only an unarmed mob parading the streets." "Yes, there had been a collision with Lambesc's cavalry." . . . On Sunday, late, a cloud of dust was Lambesc's orderly coming to Versailles with news: there had been no bloodshed. Monday more rumours: "They are forging weapons." . . . "They cannot move: . . . they lack ammunition." . . . "They have formed patrols: . . . the streets are patrolled." Then, at night, fires were reflected on the cloudy sky down the valley — the populace were burning the Octroi Barriers.

It was determined by the chiefs of the army to force the northern gate of Paris and so to subdue the tumult — but there was neither fear nor haste: the tumult was a mere civilian tumult: the thousands roaring in Paris had no arms — and then what about organisation? How can a mob organise? Tuesday came, the 14th of July, a memorable day, and in the forenoon news or rumours reached Versailles that a stock of arms had been sacked. It was the Arsenal — no, this time came details; it was the Invalides that had been sacked—twenty thousand muskets. More news: powder had been found and seized by the mob; in the great square before the Town Hall a jolly priest, sitting astride of a barrel, was seeing to the serving out of powder and of ball — one almost heard the firing. "The Bastille has most of the ammunition in Paris. No mob can take *that!* The pieces have been trained on the street a whole fortnight since." "The Bastille has checked the mob." "No, they have sacked that also, with all its ammunition." "They have captured artillery." "Nonsense! a mob cannot capture guns!" Then again, more definite and certain, longer accounts, eye-witnesses, as the afternoon drew on to evening. One: "It has fallen." Another: "I saw the governor killed. . . . a thousand men in the crowd were hit, but the crowd kept on. . . . How many dead? A hundred, at least a hundred." "They have cannon on Montmartre — the northern gate cannot be forced." Berthier wrote to the King alone: "To-night the troops will master the streets." And meanwhile, like a chorus of human voices to all this roar of powder, the Assembly pouring out decisions and acting the moral sovereign manfully in the face of material arms — sitting "permanently." Even at midnight, when nearly all was known and the popular victory assured, Bailly the Speaker was still sitting there presiding after a sitting of seventy-two hours over the drowsy Commons.

And they had voted! They had voted regrets for Necker; they had voted the responsibility of *all* advisers of the King for these calamities: they had voted bankruptcy "infamous." So many moral broadsides fired at the Queen.

The morning of the 15th came; the firing had ceased, the smoke had rolled away, and with it the issue of the action lay plain. Paris had conquered.

The King alone with his brother, unarmed, unguarded, walked to the Parliament House and announced the withdrawal of the mercenaries; the Queen — bitterness of irony! —had to stand smiling with her children at the central balcony of the palace above the courtyard and to receive the ardent homage of the people for the failure of her great design; in a few months, in October, she was to stand on that balcony again.

All that day and the next the King sat anxiously with his Council debating only one thing — Marie Antoinette's purpose that he should fly. She urged it with vehemence: her jewels were packed and ready — they would fly to Metz and conquer in a civil war; but the majority outweighed

Mr Necker

16 Juillet 1789

Je vous avois écrit, Monsieur, que dans un temps plus calme je vous donnerois des preuves de mes sentimens, mais cependant la confiance que la Nation vous témoigne, m'engage à hâter le moment de votre retour. Je vous invite donc à revenir le plutôt possible, reprendre auprès de moi votre place, vous m'avez parlé en me quittant de votre attachement, la preuve que je vous en demande est la plus grande que vous puissiez me donner

609

Louis

Carra

AUTOGRAPH NOTE OF LOUIS XVI.

Recalling Necker, on July 16th, after the fall of the Bastille

her, notably old Broglie, who feared the issue of German mercenaries against French troops — and the King remained. She with angry tears gave way: it was decided that the King should, upon the contrary, seek Paris on the morrow, accept and legalise the acts of the city, its new popular armed force, its new elected Mayorality, La Fayette the chosen head of the one, Bailly occupying the other.

The royal plan had failed: let the King accept the new conditions and meet Paris half-way. Such were the decisions, and Louis wrote to Necker recalling him — the abortive Ministry of the Resistance was ended.

But that night, in the dead darkness, Artois fled from the coming terror; old Vermond also, the friend and tutor, Enghien, Condé, many another; and the Queen, with passionate love, compelled one now again her friend to fly: the Madame de Polignac. She fled and was saved, bearing with her two ill-spelt, blotted lines in Marie Antoinette's untrained and hurried hand: "Good-bye, dearest of my friends; it is a dreadful and a necessary word. Good-bye!"

In this way did the Assembly enter into its sovereignty, and in this way did Marie Antoinette first find — though she never knew or grasped — but first find the temper of the French people, who, perhaps alone in Europe, can organise from below.

. . . .

That creative summer of '89, in which the Assembly, now victorious, began its giant business, was in the Queen's eyes nothing but a respite for the Throne, or a halt in a retreat between one sharp action lost and the next to be ventured later, when new troops should be at hand and a new occasion serve. That these speech-makers hard by should declare a new creed of Rights, should — in words — abolish Feudal Dues, should debate the exact limits of the King's power — all that was wind. Even the anarchy, coincident with that vast transition, powerfully as it affected her spirit (and her letters show it) with horror, affected it still more with hatred and with a determination so to hold or tame this wild beast, her husband's people, that her son should have his right at last, and that she herself might be free from a ceaseless humiliation.

They were killing men everywhere: they had killed the offensive and corrupt old Foulon in the streets of Paris — he and his powerful, loathsome son-in-law, Berthier: square-jawed, an oppressor grievous to God, Berthier who, so lately, in those abortive three days of the Resistance, had sat at the King's elbow promising that Paris should be held; Berthier had been clubbed to death and shot down as he swung a musket in defence of his big body. In the provinces everywhere the country houses burned.

The Queen waited. She wrote to her brother, to her dear friend Madame de Polignac; she chose (in the absence of that friend) a new governess for the Children of France, the worthy widow of Tourzel, a duchess for the occasion. She waited and did nothing. All September was a wrangling over the King's Veto — his right to refuse a law: she may have known vaguely that to her the nicknames of "Veto" was thereby attached: she did not heed it. In the last days of the month a vigorous attempt to persuade the King to fly was once more made and once more failed. By October new troops had come — their numbers were to prove insufficient for attack but fatally sufficient for enthusiasm, and that enthusiasm of loyal courtiers (breaking out almost within earshot of a Paris fretting at every delay, hungry, mystified) provoked the next disaster.

XII

OCTOBER

SEPTEMBER 23, 1789, TO MAUNDY THURSDAY, APRIL 1, 1790

ON THE 23rd of September the Regiment of Flanders marched into Versailles.

To seize all that follows two things must be clearly fixed: First, that the Queen was now separate from all the life around her; secondly that the accidents of the next fortnight determined all that remained of her life.

The Revolution, now organised, possessed of regular authorities and of a clear theory, was in action, moving with the rapidity of some French campaign towards clean victory, or, upon an error or a check, defeat — a defeat absolute as are ever the failures of high adventure.

The Queen has been called the chief opponent of that Revolutionary idea and of those new Revolutionary authorities: it is an error so to regard her; she did not meet their advance in so comprehensive a fashion. She saw nothing but a meaningless storm whirling about her; she cared for nothing in the great issue but the preservation during the tempest, and the full restoration at the end of it, of all that was to have been her little son's; she feared as her only enemy a violent and beastly thing, a mob, in whose activity she recognised all that had so long bewildered her in the French people; but while she feared it she also despised it as a thing less than human, incapable of plan, able to hurt but certain at last to be tamed. The march of Paris upon

Versailles which was now at hand, with its flaming brutality, its anarchy of thousands and of blood, confirmed in her forever her wholly insufficient judgment. From those days until she died her only appeal was to the foreigner, her only strategy the choice of manner and of time for using an actual or a potential invasion.

It may next be asked why the Regiment of Flanders marching in led to such abrupt and to such enormous consequences? It was accompanied by a section of guns only, and though its ready ammunition was high for a mere change of garrison in those days,[1] it was but one unit more where, three months before, division after division had been massed round Paris and throughout Versailles.

The answer to the question is to be found in the temper of those who watched that entry. It took place in the afternoon with imposing parade; the grenadiers of Flanders filed up the Paris road between the ranks of the Body-guard — a new regiment of the Guard which was still stranger and somewhat hostile to the temper of the crowd. Again, Flanders was a quasi-foreign regiment, comparable to those which the Crown had drafted in before the rising of Paris destroyed the plan of a civil war and had since, on a deliberate pledge, withdrawn. Again the reinforcement coincided with that long verbal struggle upon the acceptation by Louis of the Decrees (of the Rights of Man and the abolition of Feudal Dues)—a verbal struggle apparently futile, but in essence symbolic of the Veto of the Crown. To this it must be added that Paris, in which, in spite of harvest, a partial famine reigned, was again roused for adventure; that now for weeks the opposition of the King to the Decrees of the Assembly had exasperated the leaders of opinion —

[1]They were eleven hundred strong, with about half a dozen reserve cartridges a man and the pouches full; also one waggon of grape for the guns attached to the regiment.

those innumerable writers and those orators who could now voice, inflame, and even guide an insurrection; finally, it must be remembered that there remained but one solid and highly disciplined body intact throughout the insurrections of that summer, the desertions and the siding of the troops with the populace—this was the Army of the East that lay along the frontier under the command of Bouillé. It was of no great size—some 25,000 men, but it was largely foreign (Swiss and German) in composition, was excellently led, well drilled, already *political* in the united spirit of its command. Thither it was feared and hoped the King would fly: a regiment or two to flank his evasion and to escort it would be sufficient: this was the meaning of the Regiment of Flanders.

All this, however, would not alone have provoked an uprising: the departure of the King actually attempted might have done so, but we now know, and most then believed, that though the Queen urged flight, Louis would not consider it. The true cause of the catastrophe; the disturbance, which ruined the unstable equilibrium of political forces that October, was a manifest exaltation or crisis of emotion observable in the officers of the newly arrived regiment, still stronger in the Guards, pervading the whole Court, and nowhere centred more fiercely than in the heart of the Queen. It was as though the tramp of that one column of relief, added to so much restrained and impatient emotion, coming after the silent angers of that long summer, coinciding with a critical intensity of indignation and of loyalty within the palace, was just the final sound that broke down prudence. All the commissioned, many of the rank, betrayed the new glow of loyalty in chance phrases and in jests; chance swords were drawn and shown, chance menaces or chance snatches of loyal songs in taverns led on to the act which clothed all this rising spirit with form, and stood out as a definite challenge to Paris and to the Assembly.

It was customary (and still is) for the officers resident in a French garrison to entertain the officers of a newly-come regiment. The Guards had never done so yet. They were all of the gentry, the general custom of the army affected them little, for in all ranks the gentlemen of the Guard were in theory, to some extent in reality, equal in blood. Nevertheless their officers chose, for the purposes of a political demonstration, the pretext of a custom hitherto thought unworthy of their corps. The Guard had fixed upon Thursday, the first of October, to show this civility to Flanders. In the atmosphere of these days the occasion could not but become a very different matter from such a dinner as the mess of even the premier corps — so acting for the first time — could offer to a provincial body of the line.

In the expenses determined[1] and the place chosen, it was evident that all the Court was moving: the great theatre of the palace, unused for so long and reserved for the greatest and most official ceremonies, was made ready, lavishly; the tables were set upon its stages, the lights, the decorations were the King's; and when the officers of Flanders, all, perhaps (save their Colonel), unready for so much splendour, found themselves in the Salle d'Hercule — the guests of the palace rather than of the Guards — it was apparent that some large affair was before them: they were led to the theatre and the banquet began.

It was just three o'clock: down in the town the Assembly

[1] The dinner alone, apart from wine, ices, lights, etc., was, even in the prices of that day *over £1 a head*, say nowadays £2. Yet the individual hosts were asked for but five shillings each: the difference must have been paid! And the wine!

was voting the last clauses of the Constitution. In the courtyards of the palace the private soldiers of Flanders had gathered, buzzing, at the gates — later, and for a purpose, some few were admitted, but that was not before some hours had passed: they pressed curiously, now and then making way for some belated member of the band, which, with that of the Guards, was to play at the banquet.

The tables were set in a horse-shoe, and two hundred and ten places were laid: more than the two messes were concerned! Eighty seats were for the Guards — for all that could be found connected with Guards — and the Guards were there in full; double their usual number were in Versailles: there were others, strange guests and chosen volunteers. There were others, men whose presence proved a certain plan, officers of the local national militia, the new armed force of the Revolution, but officers picked carefully for their weakness or their secret disapproval of the national movement. So they sat down and began to eat and drink; there were provided two bottles a man.[1]

Outside the great empty theatre the autumn evening closed; within, by the thousand lights of it, the ladies of the Court, coming, as the banquet rose higher, into the boxes to applaud, saw one by one the *white cockades* of the Guards transferred to their guests. The national colours were regulation for Flanders; they were the essential mark of the new national Militia — yet, first one guest then another, eagerly or reluctantly, weakly or defiantly, took on the white cockade of the old Monarchy which the Guards still legally wore. The women folded paper cockades and threw them down . . . at last all seated there were

[1] 210 men, 400 bottles

under the emblem; some say that black for the Queen was also shown. They drank to the King, the Queen, the Heir; the noise of laughter and of enthusiasm grew, the toasts and the cheers were exchanged from the boxes to the stage; the floor of the theatre filled with new-comers—speech and the exhilaration of companionship gained on them and rose. Some there in wine felt now again, like a memory in the blood, the old and passionate French love of the Kings. Some, who had come to Versailles secretly determined for the Crown, now at last gave full rein and let the soul gallop to its end. All were on fire with that Gallic ardour for adventure against great odds, and in all that Gallic passion for comradeship was aflame. Some few of the rank and file were admitted . . . the heavy men of Flanders . . . they also drank. The Queen (the meat being now gone, the fruits come) was seen; whether come by reluctance or willing, in her box. . . . They cried her name, and swords were drawn. They clamoured for her to come down from where she sat there radiant, hearing at last the voices and the mood upon which (so little did she understand of war) she imagined and had imagined her victory to depend.

She came down and passed slowly before them and their delirium, smiling highly, holding in her arms her little son; and the King, less certain of the issue, heavy, splashed with the mud of his hunting, went with her as she proceeded. They passed. The height of their fever was upon these soldiers; one leant over to the band and suggested, "*Pleasant it is to be . . .*" The band consulted; they were not sure of the tune. "Well then, play' '*O Richard! Oh, my King!*'" That everybody knew, anyone could sing it: it was a tune of the day — and with the music madness took them.

They poured out into the cold night air of the marble court, singing, cheering, all armed — defiant of the new world. The whole life of the Palace and its thousands, invigorated, mixed with music and re-heightened the strain. Sundry bugles were blown as though for a charge. The noise of that clamour rang through the town, the populace without the gate was gathering, the Militia armed, and the crowd thus alarmed in the far night could see, beyond the court, under the brilliant windows of the front, a herd of men still cheering madly, the gleam of swords raised, and one dark figure climbing to the King's window to seize and kiss his hand; and against the light within the shadows of the family approving.

The colonel of the Versailles Militia went to the Palace and returned: the crowd dispersed, the cheering of the revellers died away. Next day was sober; yet even all next day the exaltation, though now sober, grew. The national uniform of the Militia was insulted and challenged in Versailles, turned out of the palace. The Queen, ineffably ignorant, gave colours to a deputation of that Militia and begged them, with a smile, to believe that *yesterday had pleased her greatly* — she had seen certain of their officers at the feast — and so little was enough to deceive her! There was another milder meeting (for the men), a mere exchange of glasses, and all Saturday, the 3rd of October, the armament of the Crown, such as it was — some thousands — stood ready and did not forget the valour and the ardent loyalty which their chiefs had lit with such memorable cheers and songs.

But another noise and another life began beyond that fringe of woods which eastward veiled Paris. The million of that place were in a hum: messages from them and to them. Marat had explored the new force in Versailles, the presses in Paris were raining pamphlets — something confused and enormous, a vision of their national King abandoning them, a nightmare of treason; all this mixed with hunger oppressed the mind of the million. I say "mixed with hunger," for though there was by this time plenty of grain there was little flour, and in the lack of bread violent angers had risen: some thought the Assembly (their talisman), the very nation itself, to be again in peril from the soldiers. So all Sunday, October 4, the hive of Paris droned in its narrow streets and gathered; upon Monday, for the second time that year, it swarmed.

. . . .

To the west and to the south of Paris there runs a ring of clean high land against the sky, and it is clothed with forests; one part of it, still charming and in places abandoned, is called the Forest of Meudon, and many who read this have walked through it and have seen at the end of some one of its long rides the great city below.

In the morning of Monday, the 5th of October, 1789, the far corner of these woods near Chatillon rang with shots, and down one alley or another would come from time to time the soft and heavy beat of horses at a canter, as grooms and servants moved with the guns. The King was shooting. A south west wind blew through the trees with no great violence; some rain had fallen and more threatened from the shredded, low, grey clouds above. Of all the company in those alleys and between those high trees, on which the leaves, though withered, still hung, the King alone was undisturbed. His pleasure in horsemanship and his seven miles' ride from the palace, his delight in the morning air, and his keen attention to the sole occupation that called out his lethargic energy, forbade him to consider other things; but all his suite were wondering, each in his degree, what might be happening in the plain below them, or in Paris, or in the town of Versailles which they had left—for it was known that Paris was moving.

All morning long they shot in those woods until, when it was already perhaps past noon and rain had again begun to fall, a sound of different riding came furiously up the main alley which follows the ridge and springs from the high road. It was the riding of a man who rides on a fresh horse and changes post, and is a courier. His name was Cubieres, and he was a gentleman of the Court flying with news, straight in the long French stirrup, with a set face, and his mount belly to the ground. He took one turning, then another, came thundering up to the King and drew rein.

The King, as this messenger reached him, was noting his bag in a little book. The message of Cubieres was that Paris had marched upon Versailles, that the great avenue road was black with tattered women and with men, seething and turning, and demanding food and blood. He brought no rumours, and he could tell the King nothing of the Queen. The King mounted. All mounted and rode at speed. They turned their mounts westerly again, and rode at speed toward Versailles. And as they rode two feelings dully contended in the mind of Louis: the first was anxiety for his wife; the second annoyance at the sudden interruption of his business; and later, as the bulk of the palace appeared far off through the trees, he was filled with that irritant wonder as to what he should do, what his action should be: the trouble of decision which cursed him whenever he and action came face to face. The wind had fallen and now the rain poured steadily and drenched them all.

. . . .

Consider that grey morning in the town also — I mean in the town of Versailles — and how under that same covered sky and those same low shreds of flying cloud the empty streets of Versailles were arming.

Upon the broad deserted avenue before the gates of the National Assembly there were no passers-by; the drip from the brown leaves of the trees, the patter from the eaves of the stately houses, and the gurgling of water in the gutters enforced the silence. Now and then an official or a member in black knee-breeches and thin buckled shoes, delicately stepping from stone to stone, would hurriedly cross over the paving, cloaked and covered by an ample umbrella, as was the habit of those heroes when it rained; but for the rest the streets were empty, the seats shining with wet under the imperfect autumn light. Far off, beside the railing and before the wrought-iron gates of the palace, the troops were beginning to form, for it was already known that the bridge of Sévres had been left unguarded and that the mob was pouring up the Paris road. The troops came marching from one barrack and another in the various quarters of the town, converging upon this central place, and some, the Swiss, were issuing from the outlets of the palace itself, and some, the Mounted Guard, were filing out of the half-moon of the royal stables, where now the Sappers and the 22nd of Artillery may be found. They formed and formed under the weather. The Body-guard upon their great horses, deeply mantled and groomed as for parade, lined all the front; behind them the Swiss on foot filled the square of the courtyard; Ragged Flanders, the Ragged Regiment of Flanders, famous in song for its rags as for its amours and its drums,[1] stood by companies before them all in the wide public place, where all the roads of Versailles converge and make an approach to the Court and form an open centre for the royal city.

The formation was accomplished, food was served, arms piled. They stood there in rank alone, with no civilians to watch or mock them under the rain, and behind them the great house they were guarding stood empty of Monarchy. And before them the wide avenue from Paris, the Avenue, which was the artery of opinion, of energy, and all the national being at that moment, stood empty also, and it rained and rained. The great body of troops, red, yellow and blue in bands, were the only tenants of the scene.

. . . .

Within the Assembly a debate not over-full of purpose had alternately dragged and raged: it had been known almost from the opening of the sitting that Paris would move. Those premonitions which have led the less scholarly or the more fanatical of historians to see in the Revolution a perpetual pre-arrangement and cabal, those warning things in the air which you find at every stage of the great turmoil (rumours flew before the King all the way to Varennes, and the victory upon the right wing at Wattignies was known in Paris an hour before the final charge), those inexplicable things had come, and immediately upon their heels had come direct news from one messenger after another: how the wine merchants' shops had been sacked, how the bridge of Sévres was passed, how the rabble were now

1 "Y' avait un Grenadier," etc.

but five miles off and breasting the hill. That futility, which the Revolutionary Assemblies suffered less perhaps than other Parliaments, but which is inherent in all representative discussion, condemned this engine of the new Democracy to discuss on such a day nothing of greater moment than the order of that day, and the order of that day was the King's letter: for the King had written that he would "accede" to the Decrees (of Rights of Man and to the extinction of the Feudal Dues), but that he would not "sanction" them. And on the verbal discussion between the words "accede" and the word "sanction" legal tomfoolery was fated to batten, while up in the woods of Meudon the King who had written that letter was still shooting peacefully and innocent of guile, and while so many thousands, desperately hungry, were marching up the road having Maillard — as who should say murder — for their Captain, and dragging behind them a section of their guns.

From such futility and from such tomfoolery the debate was just saved by the strength of personality alone. Mounier, in the Speaker's chair, lent energy to them all, though of a despairing kind; and when someone had said to him, "All Paris is marching upon us," and had foreseen the invasion of the palace and perhaps the ruin of the Crown, he had answered, according to one version, "The better for the Republic," according to another version, "The sooner shall we have the Republic here."

At the back of the great oblong colonnaded hall, trim Robespierre, fresh from the Sign of the Fox and from his farmer companions, was, in that vibrating and carrying little voice of his, laying down decisions. There should be no compromise; if they compromised now the Revolution was lost. But he was careful to be strictly in order —

he was always careful of that — and the thing on which he advised "no compromise" was not the mob, but the letter of the King.

A larger man touched nearer to the life, though it was but an interjection; for Mirabeau, ever vividly grasping facts and things, had hinted at the Queen: that mob was marching on the Queen. He had said that he would sign if, in whatever might follow, "The King *alone* should be held inviolate." And there is one witness who affirms that he added in a whisper, which those on the benches about him clearly heard, that he meant specifically to exclude from amnesty and from protection the woman against whom so many and such varied hatreds had now converged, and who stood to a million men for innumerable varied reasons a legendary enemy, but one in her flesh and blood to be hated—the negation of all the hope of the moment and of French honour and of the national will.

. . . .

This woman, upon whom already lay the weight of so much discontent and terror, sat that morning for the last time in Trianon, where the rain was beating against Gabriel's graceful, tall windows and streaming down the panes. Some ill-ease compelled her, though the place was protected, remote and silent, and though the weather was so drear, to wander in her gardens and to cross the paths between the showers. In the early afternoon she was in the Grotto, and it was there that the news came to her, for a messenger found her also as that other one had found her husband. He bade her come at once to the palace and told her that the mob had filled the town.

She came; it was still the middle afternoon, and such light

as the day afforded was still full, when she saw from the windows of the ante-chamber, looking over the full length of the courtyard, beyond the line of soldiers, that eddying volume of the populace and heard the noise of their mingled cries. It was the first time in her life that she had seen the people menacing. She listened to the distant roaring for a long time in silence, with her women about her, until the noise of horse hoofs clattered upon the flags below, and she knew that Louis had returned. He came, booted and splashed, up the great stairs; there members of his Ministry and his advisers were ready. Marie Antoinette entered with them into the Council Room, and as the door was shut behind her there was shut out, though barely for an hour, the instant noise of that peril.

This is the way in which Paris came to Versailles and began its usurpation of the Crown.

. . . .

There is a tall window in Versailles in the corner of the Council Room whence one can see the courts opening outwards before the palace, and so beyond to the wide Place d'Armes. Through that window, streaming with rain under the declining light of the pouring October day, could be seen the tumult.

All the wide enclosure before the palace was guarded and bare. Over its wet stones came and went only hurried messengers—orderlies from the armed forces or servants from the Court. Holding the long 300 yards of gilded railing was the double rank of the Guards, mounted, swords drawn; next the Dragoons, a clear and detached line of cavalry; in front of these, in triple rank, the Regiment of Flanders.

Three armed bodies thus guarded the sweep of the railings and the approach to the palace in parallel order, and beyond them, right into the depths of the landscape, marched a vast and confused mob filling up the three great avenues and crowding half the Place d'Armes; in that mob, met at first in formation but now mingled with the populace, could be distinguished many of the armed Militia of Versailles. At such a distance no distinct voices could be heard, but roaring sound or murmur like the noise of a beach rose from the multitude and outweighed the furious patter of the rain on the glass: at rare intervals a shot was fired, wantonly, but no news of bloodshed came. From time to time a patrol of the Guard could be seen, towering on chargers high above the populace, forcing its way through; swords also, sometimes striking, could be distinguished. This uncertain and menacing sight, blurred in the rain, was all that the palace could distinguish.

Within the King's room were a deputation of women and Mounier, the President of the Assembly, had been received, council upon council was held, that the Queen at least should retire to some neighbouring town, that the King should fly — but nothing was determined, and to that reiterated policy of flight so often suggested since July, now so pressing, the King murmured as he paced back and forth, "A King in flight! . . . " It is said that the horses were ordered; but with every moment the plan became more difficult. Darkness fell upon a sky still stormy; the troops still held their lines, but the noises seemed nearer and more menacing. It was imagined better to withdraw the Guard at least, as the pressure upon them increased.

The order may be criticised, but it may also be defended. La Fayette was marching on Versailles from Paris with a considerable force of partly trained militia. The Guards round whom the legend of the supper had grown, and whose white cockades were an insult to the national colours, exasperated the populace beyond bearing, and were, it was thought, the main cause of the pressure to which the troops were subjected. Wisely or foolishly, the Guard was withdrawn, the line regiments alone were left to contain the mob.

It was eight o'clock, and for two hours further a futile deliberation proceeded in the royal rooms. In those hours first one messenger then another convinced the King of a thing inconceivable in those days—personal danger to himself and especially to the Queen. At ten o'clock he signed the Decrees, the refusal of which were thought to be the political cause of the tumult. At midnight could be heard at last the regular marching of drilled men: La Fayette had arrived with 20,000 from Paris — not soldiers, if you will, men of but three months' training, but in uniform, capable of formation and well armed — the Militia of Paris.

So profound was the mental distance between the surroundings of the King and the leaders of the reform that not a few at Court feared this relieving force, thinking that such a man as La Fayette might be tempted to capture the Monarchy with it and to betray it to the mob! They understood him little. He showed that night some statesmanship, great activity, and an admirable devotion to duty: it was his judgment that failed. He judged falsely of what the crowd were capable; he underestimated his countrymen and he judged falsely of what his Militia could do; he overestimated uniforms and an imperfect drill. He urged that the regular troops, the pressure upon whom after all these hours was now almost intolerable, should be withdrawn; he further urged that he should be permitted with his Militia and with some few of the Guard to police the open spaces and to protect the palace.

His advice—the advice of the only man with a large armed force behind him — was accepted. By two o'clock there was silence and, as it was thought, security. Men slept as they could in such shelter as they might find or in the open. Far off there was the glare of a fire where, in the midst of the crowd, a wounded horse had keen killed and was roasting for food. The hubbub within the palace had died down; nothing was heard but the rhythmic clank of a sentry, or, as the hours passed, the challenge of a relief. The Queen also slept.

What followed has been told a thousand times. Her great bedroom looked east and south; it was the chief room in her wing, which, just beyond the central court, corresponded to the King's upon the northern side. From that room to the Council Chamber and to the King's private apartments there were three ways: the way by the main gallery of mirrors which her household took upon Sunday mornings and on all sorts of grand occasions to join the King for High Mass. A second shorter way through little rooms at the back, which were her own private cabinets; and thirdly, a half-secret passage worked, now in the thickness of a floor, now in the space between two floors, and leading directly from the King's room to her own.

All that afternoon and evening the new strength of her character had conspicuously appeared. Her friends, and her enemies, remarked it equally. There was something in her almost serene during these first experiences of peril; but they were to grow far more severe. Her children she had sent into the King's wing. She was assured of peace at least until morning, and she slept.[1]

Farther along than the tall chapel whose roof so dominates Versailles, towards what is now the limit of the Hotel of the Reservoirs, in the court which is called that of the Opera House, one of the great iron gates which gave entry into the palace grounds stood open on that gusty night of rain. A single sentinel chosen, from the Militia, stood before it. By this gate not a few of the crowd found their way into the palace gardens, and, coming to the Southern wing, vaguely knew, though the interior of the place was doubtful to them, that they stood beneath the windows of the Queen.

Marie Antoinette had slept perhaps three hours when she awoke to hear cries and curses against her name, and staring in the bewildered moment which succeeds the oblivion of sleep she saw that it was dawn. Then next she heard somewhere, confused, far off, in the centre of the buildings, a noise of thousands and cries. Her maid threw a petticoat upon her and a mantle, and delayed her a perilous moment that she might have stockings on as she fled. She made for the private rooms that would take her to the King's wing, when, as the noise of the invading mob grew louder and their leaders (missing her door) poured on clamouring to find and to kill her, one of her Guards half opened the door of her room and cried, "Save the Queen!" The butt of a musket felled him: the Queen was already saved.

The violence of those who thus poured past her door found no victim. She had run through her little library and boudoir, knocked at the door of the Œil de Bœuf and had it hurriedly opened to her: she had knocked and knocked and someone had opened the door fearfully and shut it again

[1] Fersen was in the palace that night. It has been affirmed that he was with her. The story is certainly false

when she had passed through. She saw the Œil de Bœuf barricaded. A handful of the Guard went desperately piling up chairs, sofas and footstools against the outer doors, while she slipped through to the King's room. He meanwhile, as the assault on the palace had awakened him also, had run along the secret passage to her room, and, seeing it empty, had come back to find her in his own.

The eruption of the mob had been as rapid as the bursting of a storm. The immediate forming of the La Fayette's Militia Guard and its victory proved almost as rapid. The first shot had been fired at six, probably by one of the Guards at the central door: within an hour the Militia had cleared the rabble out, even the tenacious pillagers were dislodged and the populace stood, thrust outside the doors and massed in the narrow marble court beneath the King's windows, in part discomfited but much more angry, and with a policy gradually shaping in the common mouth: a policy expressed in cries that "they would see the King," that "the King was their King," that "they must bring back the King to Paris."

The morning had broken clear and fine and quite calm after the rain of yesterday and the wind of the night; its light increased with the advancing hours: the energy of the mob remained—and in the midst of it a long-bearded man, half-mad, an artist's model, was hacking off the heads of the two Guards who had been killed when the palace was rushed.

The Queen looked down upon the flood of the people from the windows of her husband's room. Her sister-in-law was at her shoulder, her little daughter close to her left side, and in front of her, standing upon a chair, the Dauphin was playing with his sister's hair and complaining that he was hungry: and all the while the mob shouted for the King.

The King showed himself. They would see the Queen

too: and La Fayette, still their adviser and still trusted in a bewildered way as a sort of saviour, told her it was imperative that she should come. She went, therefore, to the great central room of all that house, the room which had been the state bedroom of Louis XIV., and stepped out upon the balcony of its central window, holding her children by the hand. The mob roared that they would have no children there. She waved them back into the room, and stood for some moments surveying the anger of the unhappy thousands packed beneath, with the new and serene day rising in the eastern heaven behind them. Her hands were on the rail of the balcony. She hardly moved. There were weapons raised in the tumbling crowd: one man aimed at her and then lowered his musket. La Fayette came forward, took her right hand, knelt and kissed it, and the little scene was over.

How could she have known until that moment that there were such things?

It was certain more and more as the day grew to noon that the Court must obey and that the populace had morally conquered. In a little inner room the King and Queen sat together, and together they decided (or, the King deciding, she could not but decide in the same necessity) that they would return to Paris. She turned to her husband and said: "Promise me at least this: that when next such an occasion shall come, you will fly while yet there is time." Louis, to whom the idea of flight was hateful, let his eyes fill with tears, but did not answer.

. . . .

Louis' decision to return was a wise decision. The popular demand was not to constrain but to possess their King.

THE TUILERIES FROM THE GARDEN, OR WEST SIDE, IN 1789

It was not until later that the changing mood of Paris and its success seemed to make of that moment of October the beginning of the King's captivity; with some little difference in persons and in wills, this yielding to what all the national sentiment demanded might even yet have made of the Crown once more an active national emblem and of the person of the King a leader.

It was half-past one when the carriages with difficulty came to the palace. It was two before the march to Paris began.

The road from Versailles to Paris falls and falls down a long easy valley which the woods still clothe on either side of the very broad and royal highway: the woods rose in that autumn dense and unbroken for many miles. Two things contrasted powerfully one against the other: the howling turbulence of the crowd, the stillness of nature all around. It was as though some sort of astonishment had struck the trees and the pure sky: or as though these were spectators standing apart and watching what tempests can arise in the mind of man.

The season was late; the foliage was but just turning; the gorgeous leaves hung tremulous in that still air: none fell. The masses of colour in the thickets of Viroflay were tapestried and immovable; and all this silence of the world was soft as well. The air had about it that tender, half-ironical caress which it possesses on perfect autumn days in the Parisis, and the sky was of that misty but contented blue which they know very well who have wandered in that valley upon such days. Cleaving through such beatitude, a long line of shrieking and of clamouring, of laughter and of curses, of the shrill complaints of women, of the moans of pain and of fatigue, mixed with the sudden wanton discharge of muskets, went, for mile after mile; the populace drawing back their King to Paris.

It is not seven miles from the Palace to the river — not another four to what were then the barriers of the city. They took for these eleven miles all but seven hours. The coaches crawled and pushed through the swarm of the angry poor. The Queen, her husband and her children, Monsieur, Madame Elizabeth, the governess of the royal children — all sat together in one great coach rumbling along in the midst of insult and of intolerable noise. From where she sat, facing the horses near the window, the Queen could see far off at the head of that interminable column two pikes slanting in the air. The heads of the Guards who had saved her were upon them.[1] She could see here and there, close under those trophies, glints of yellow, where certain of the Foot Guards were marched like prisoners along, with the blue of the national Militia, flanking and escorting them on either side; and, mixed in the crowd, the Mounted Guardsmen were there, prisoners also, with the Mounted Militia holding them. Of all that followed after, she could see nothing but she could hear. There was the rumbling of the wheels of the two cannon, the great sixty waggons loaded with flour, and she could hear the cries that cursed her own name. The afternoon wore on. The sun lay low over the palace they had left; it was dusk by the time they reached the river; it was dark before they came to the barriers of the town.

There, by the same gate of entry which the first of the Bourbons had traversed two hundred years before, the Monarchy re-entered that capital which, for precisely a century, it had, with a fatal lack of national instinct, aban-

---

[1] Or else they were not: there are two versions.

doned. Bailly, the Mayor, met them under torches in the darkness and presented the keys of the city. The Royal Family must needs go on, late as it was and they lacking food, to the Hotel de Ville, that the crowds of the city might see them. It was not until ten o'clock that the unhappy household, the little children broken by such hours and so much fasting, found themselves at last under the roof of the Tuileries.

The Tuileries were a barracks.

The huge empty line of buildings, which, had they been thus abandoned to-day, would have been made a Sunday show, had in that age been put to no use; they had become in the absence of the Court but a warren of large deserted rooms. Furniture was wanting; there was dust and negligence everywhere; the discomfort, the indignity, the friction, were but increased by the hasty swarms of workmen who had been turned on in a few hours to fit the place for human living. No more exact emblem of the divorce between the Crown and Paris could be found than the inner ruin of that royal town house, nor could any deeper lesson have been conveyed — had the last of the Bourbons but heeded it — than the reproach of those rooms.

As for Paris — Paris believed it had recovered the King. The month and more that followed was filled with a series of receptions and of plaudits. The Bar, the University, the Treasury, last of all the Academy — all the great bodies of the State were received in audience and joined in a general welcome. Parliament was at work again before the end of the month, first in the Archbishop's palace upon the Island, later in the great oval *manège* or riding-school which lay along the north of the palace gardens. It was there that all the drama of the Revolution was to be played.[1]

That drama began to work, as winter advanced with a new, a more organised, and, as it were, a more fatal rapidity; and as the volume of the reform grew and its momentum also rose, the Queen sank back further and further into the recesses of her religion.

Her energy was not diminished. Those few months of silence did but restore her power to act with speed and even with violence in the succeeding year, but for the moment, like a sort of foil to the speed of the current around her, she steadfastly regarded the only things that remain to the doomed or the destitute.

The communion of her daughter chiefly concerned her then. To this it was that she looked forward in the coming spring, and this (insignificant as the matter may seem to those who know little of such minds) was the fixed interest of that winter for the Queen.

Her letters during those months betray that momentary isolation. She inclined once more, after the tumults and defeats, to a not very worthy contempt for the slow, insufficient, and absolutely just mind of her husband. There are phrases of violence like the sudden small flames of banked fires in those letters of hers in that season; but her reserve remains absolute. She boasts that she "had seen death from near by." But "she will keep to her plan and not meddle." "My business is to see the King at ease." Then again, later, in Lent she sneers: "One at my side is prepared to take things in a modest way." She follows with a phrase

[1] Those curious to retrace the very sites of history, may care to know exactly where the *manège* stood, since in the *manège*, as a great phrase goes, "La France fit l'eternel." The major axis of its ellipse corresponded to the pavement to the north of the Rue de Rivoli under the Arcades, and the centre of this axis was where the Rue Castiglione now falls into the Rue de Rivoli. Its southern wall slightly overlapped the line of the present railing of the Tuileries Gardens; its northern was about in a line with the northern limit of the property now occupied by the Continental Hotel.

that is reminiscent of the audacity she so recently showed and was again so soon to show: "*I* shall not let the power of the Throne go at so cheap a rate." This letter, which, read to-day after so many years, breathes the too jagged vigour of the woman, has about it an awful character; for she wrote it to a man who, even as she wrote it, was lying dead; her brother and her mainstay, the Emperor. The desire to return to the arena is still in her: she writes once, wistfully, "I must get hold of the leaders." There are other letters, passionate, womanish letters to her woman friends. To Madame de Polignac, out in exile at Parma, letter after letter. In these, as in all the rest, you read her instant of seclusion from the fight. That interval was one of five months.

She in those five months, from the Days of the Dead in November, 1789, to the very early Easter of 1790, was like an athlete who, in the midst of some furious game, stands apart for a moment recovering his breath and relaxing his muscles while the struggle grows more active, separate from him, but acted before his eyes. Soon he will re-enter the press with a renewed vigour. And so did she when after that sad winter she combined with Mirabeau, and the driving force in those two minds tried to work in a yoke together. But for the rest, I say, religion chiefly held her. Her isolation was not so much a plan (as she pretended) as a physical and necessary thing. She was exhausted. She had done with the body for a moment. She was concerned with the soul.

If one could portray graphically the accidents of that tragic life, if a mould could be taken of her great hopes and her great sufferings, if a cast in relief could be made of her passion, you would find, I think, in such a map of her existence two high peaks of exalted suffering and vision: the death of her son — so small in history, so great to her —

would be the first; and the second would be those hours in October when she, to whom such all such things had been mere words, was first in her wealthy life threatened with cold air against her body, the vulgar in her bedroom, and death; when she first saw a weapon levelled at her and first came in physical contact with *violence*, a thing that all save the wealthy and their parasites daily know. These were the two strong, new, and terrible days which had bitten into her experience. These were and remained her isolated memories. The rest, her future evils, came by a more gradual slope: her very death was to her less enormous. Her dumbness during these winter months of '89 and the working inwards of her life was a reaction of repose after the shock of October.

By the vast mass of the Louvre there is a church dedicated to that Saint Germanus who preached against Pelagius in Britain, and who, as an old man, had laid his hand upon the head of the young Saint Geneviève, the goose-girl, near Mount Valerian and had foreseen her glory. This church has much history. From its tower rang the call to arms which roused the populace of Paris against the wealthy oppressor of the Huguenot faction and maddened the poor to take their revenge in the Massacre of St. Bartholomew. It was and is the parish church of the palace. Here, before Lent was over (upon Wednesday in Holy Week), the little girl, her daughter, knelt at her first communion. The Queen stood and knelt in the darkness of the nave, dressed without ornament, her fine head serious, her commanding eyes at once tender and secure.

. . . .

I cannot write of her or hear of her without remembering her thus; and that last power of hers, a power made of abrupt vivacity tamed at last by misfortune into dignity and strength, here, I think, begins. Such a power was not henceforward the permanent quality of her soul — far from it — but it appeared and reappeared. It was strong more than once for a moment in the last hours before she died . . . and how well one sees why such as had perceived in her the seeds of this force of the spirit, even when she was distraught and played the fool in youth, now, when it had blossomed, worshipped her! Upon this last mood her legend is built and survives. She had a regal head.

. . . .

She stood in the nave unnoticed in her black dress without ornament, and saw the little girl go up in white and veiled to the altar-rails. There was no one there. Never since Constantine had the Faith been lower in France; but the Faith is a thing for the individual mind and not for majorities.

They went back homewards. They gave alms.

Meanwhile, though this was her true life for those months, one must speak of what went on without: the rising of the Revolutionary song and the noises at her feet. For out of this swelling energy and increasing peril was to grow her experiment of an alliance with the virile brain of Mirabeau.

There stands, side by side with the activity of mortal life, a silent thing commonly unseen and, even if seen, despised. It has no name, unless its name be religion: its form is the ritual of the altar; its philosophy is despised under the title of Theology. This thing and its influence should least of all appear in the controversies of a high civilisation. With an irony that every historian of whatever period must have noted a hundred times, this thing and its influence perpetually intervene, when most society is rational and when most it is bent upon positive things; and now at the moment when the transformation of society towards such better things seemed so easy and the way so plain, now in late '89, before any threat had come from the King or any danger of dissolution from within, this thing, this influence, entered unnoticed by a side-door; it was weak and almost dumb. It and it alone halted and still halts all the Revolutionary work, for it should have been recognised and it was not. It demanded its place and no place was given it. There is a divine pride about it and, as it were, a divine necessity of vengeance. Religion, if it be slighted, if it be misunderstood, will implacably destroy.

It was the Queen's birthday, the Day of the Dead, November 2, 1789, one of those fatal and recurrent dates to which her history is pinned, which saw the sowing of that seed and the little entry of what was to become the major and perhaps the unending feud of our modern democracies.

The clergy of the French Church were then national to a degree hitherto unknown in the history of the Church in any of her provinces. The national movement swept them all. The Episcopacy represented, in some few of the greatest sees the Revolutionary enthusiasms, in the mass of bishops the resistance to the Revolution which was exactly parallel to the attitude of the lay nobility. The parish clergy reflected with exact fidelity the homogeneous will of the nation. It was a priest who furnished the notes of the Revolutionary movement in the capital of Normandy. Later it was a priest who wrote the last (and the only literary) stanza of the Marseillaise. Even the religious, or what was left of them (for monastic life had never fallen to a lower state or one more dead since first St. Martin had brought it into Gaul), met the movement in a precisely similar fashion, suspected it in proportion to their privilege or their wealth, welcomed it in proportion to their knowledge of the people and their mixing with them. It was the poor remnant of the Dominicans of Paris that received and housed and gave its name to the headquarters of pure democracy, the Jacobins.

The clergy, then, were but the nation. The long campaign against the Faith, which had so long been the business of the Huguenot, the Deist, the Atheist, and the Jew, had indeed brought the Faith very near to death, and, as has so often been insisted in the course of these pages, it is difficult for a modern man to conceive how tiny was the little flickering flame of Catholicism in the generation before the Revolution, for he is used to it to-day as a great combative advancing thing against which every effort of its enemies' energies must be actively and constantly used. The clergy as a body of men were national and willing to aid the nation; the Faith, which should have been their peculiar business, had almost gone — therefore it was that to put to national uses what seemed the grossly exaggerated endowments of religion seemed a national policy in that embarrassed time. Therefore it was that the endowments so attacked could ill defend themselves, for the philosophy of their defence, which lay in their religion, was forgotten. Obviously necessary and patriotic as the policy seemed, it awoke that influence of which I speak, which does not reside in men and which is greater than men, which only acts through men, but is not of them; and Religion — seemingly all but dead — rose at once when it felt upon it the gesture of the civil power.

It was, I have said, the 2nd of November, the Queen's birthday, the Day of the Dead, that the vote was taken upon the confiscation of religious endowments. The light was failing as that vote began. The candelabra of the great riding-school were lit, and it was full darkness before the vote was ended, for five-sixths of all possible votes were cast and nearly one thousand men voted each to the call of his name upon a roll. When the figures were read, a majority of 222 had decided the thing, and, in deciding it, had determined the dual fortunes of Europe thenceforward to our own time. The Revolution, a thing inconceivable apart from the French inheritance, Catholic Dogma, had raised an issue against the Catholic Church. For three weeks had the matter been debated; the days of October had launched it, and while yet the Parlement was in Versailles a bishop — one later to be famous under his own name of Talleyrand — had moved in favour of that Act.

It was a simple plan, and to see how immediate and necessary it seemed we have but to read the figures of the clerical funds and of their iniquitous distribution; yet it failed altogether and had for its effect only one effect much larger than any one dreamt — the creation of enmity in the only Thing that could endure, indefinitely opposed to the Revolution, mobile, vigorous, and with a life as long or longer than its own.

The figures were these: In a nation of 25 millions now raising, by a grinding and most unpopular taxation, less than 18,000,000 in the year, and of that paying quite one-half as interest upon a hopeless and increasing debt was present a body of men, 40,000 in number, whose revenues had always been considered as the retribution of a particular function now universally disregarded; and *these revenues would almost suffice to pay the amount which would save the nation from bankruptcy.* The property from which these revenues were derived was sufficient to cancel the debt and to set the nation free upon a new course of readjusted taxation, an increased and unencumbered activity and, as it seemed to all at that moment, to save the State. Talleyrand himself in his clear and chiselled speech put the matter with the precision of a soldier. The reform would wipe out all encumbrances, permit the destruction of the old and hateful taxes, notably the salt tax, suppress the purchase of public offices, and meanwhile permit the nation in its new course to pay without grievous burden regular salaries to the clergy as civil servants according to their rank, which salaries would abolish the gross inequalities which had arisen in the economic development of fifteen centuries. No ordained priest would have less than what was in those days regarded as a sufficient maintenance. The monstrous revenues of certain sees which were of no service to Religion or to the State, would disappear.

The plan was simple, it seemed most rational, and, as I have said, it was voted—from it was to proceed directly within two months the creation of those Government notes upon the security of Church lands, whose very name is for us to-day a summary of the disaster — the Assignats: the Assignats, which have become a cant term for worthless paper. Before Christmas that ominous word was to appear. Before spring the false step of dissolving the moribund religious orders was to be taken. Before summer the plan to establish a national Church controlled by the State was to be formulated; within a year that simple plan of disendowment had bred schism and the fixed resistance of the King, later it engendered Vendée, Normandv, all the civil wars, and — with a rending that has all but destroyed Europe — a separation between the two chief appetites native to mankind, the hunger for justice in the State, and that other hunger for God, who is the end of the soul. The wound is not yet healed.

Such was the principal act passing during those months of the winter and spring under the eyes of the Queen in her retirement and silence; accompanying that act was much more. The first of the plots had broken out, the first of those recurrent and similar plots for saving the person of the King; the first of the victims, Favras, had been hanged; the first hint, therefore, of a distinction between the King as head of the nation and the King as a person to be preserved had appeared. It was to grow until it threw into the whirlpool of the Revolution the flight to Varennes.

Just before the end of February the force upon which Marie Antoinette now most relied — her brother Joseph — died. Leopold, a character of no such readiness or maturity, succeeded him, and the Queen, reading his letter upon the 27th, knew that she had come to that turn of human life after which, even for the most blest, everything is loss without replacement, until we stand alone at the tomb. Even for the most blest: for her the turn had come just as she and all of hers must sail into the darkness of a great storm.

I have said that it was on the last day of March, Spy Wednesday, that she had stood obscure in her plain black, blotted against the darkness of the nave and watching the communion of her child. Upon the next day, Holy Thursday of 1790, was published by order of the Revolutionary Parliament, that official paper called "The Red Book," which suddenly heralded to all the public all that her Court had been, which gave body and form to all those hitherto vague rumours and legends of extravagance and folly which had been the chief weapons of her enemies. It was as though a malarial, impalpable influence weakening her had suddenly distilled into a palpable and definite material poison. It was as though some weapon of mist, which though formidable was undecided, had become suddenly a weapon of steel. The publication of that list of pensions, of doles, of bribes effected in her fortunes a change like the change in the life of some man whose reputation has hitherto suffered from hints and innuendoes, and who suddenly finds himself with the whole thing published in the papers upon the witness and record of a Court of Law.

Let a modern reader imagine what that publication was by so stretching his fancy as to conceive the delivery to general knowledge in this country of what is done in payment and receipt by our big money-changers, our newspapers, our politicians, and let him imagine (by another stretch of fancy) a public opinion in this country already alive to the existence of that corruption and already angry against it: then he will see what a date in the chances of the Queen's life was this Holy Thursday!

The business now before herself and such as were statesmen around her was no longer to make triumphant, but rather to save the Monarchy.

XIII

MIRABEAU

FROM APRIL 1, 1790, TO MIDNIGHT OF THE 20TH JUNE, 1791

THERE existed in France at that moment one force which, in alliance with the Government, could have preserved the continuity of institutions, among other institutions of the throne. That force resided in the personality of Mirabeau.

Had he survived and so succeeded — for his failure was only possible with death — the French nation might indeed have preserved all its forms and would then have lost its principle and power. It might have been transformed into something of lower vigour than itself, it might have grown to forget action, and the nineteenth century, which was to see our civilisation ploughed by the armies and sowed by the ideas of Napoleon — so that it became a century enormous with French energy and has left us to-day under a necessity still to persevere — might have been a time of easy reaction: a Europe without Germany, without Italy: a Europe having in its midst the vast lethargic body of the French monarchy and dominated wholly by the mercantile activity of England.

This, I say, might, or rather would, have been the fate of the Revolution, and therefore of the world, with what further consequences we cannot tell, had Mirabeau, once in alliance with the Court, survived; for wherever in history the continuity of form has been preferred to a spirit of renascence, such lethargy and such decline has succeeded. But though an effect of this kind would have resulted for Christendom in general, for the Queen and for her family the success of Mirabeau would have been salvation. The air and the tradition of the palace would have survived; she would have grown old beside her husband in a State lessened but preserving many of the externals of power; her later years wise, resigned, and probably magnificent. As it was, the alliance between Mirabeau and the Court was made — but before the first year of its effect had run, Mirabeau was dead: he dead, the slope of change led Marie Antoinette, with rapid and direct insistence, to flight, to imprisonment, and to the scaffold.

It is but very rarely that so much can be laid to the action of one brain in history. What were the characters in Mirabeau's position that made it true of him in this spring of 1790? They were these: that he had through certain qualities in him become accepted as the organ of a popular movement; that, by other qualities more profoundly rooted in him, he was determined upon order; and, finally, that an early maturity of judgment — already hardened before his fortieth year — strong passions often satisfied and their resulting fruit of deadness, much bitter humiliation, the dreadful annealing of poverty working upon known and vast capacity, had rendered him quite careless of those imaginary future things the vision of which alone can support men in the work of creation. He was now a man walking backwards, observing things known, judging men, testing their actions and motives as one would test natural and invariable forces, using the whole either to achieve some end which had already been achieved elsewhere — which was in existence somewhere and had reality — or to preserve things still standing around him, things whose nature he knew. He would have preserved all, and he would have degraded his land. This most national of Frenchmen would have closed to France her avenue of growth. He was "practical": and the chief quality of his people, which is the power most suddenly to evoke a corporate will, he did not comprehend. It was a mystery, and therefore he ignored it. Of things hidden he could divine nothing at all. The Faith, for example, being then driven underground, he utterly despised.

His command of spoken speech, sonorous, incisive, revealing, dominating by turns; his rapid concentration of phrase, his arrangement and possession (through others) of innumerable details, were points that made him the chief of a Parliament: his courage and advancing presence — for he was a sort of lion — peculiarly suited him to the Gauls, and his love of men, which was enormous, forbade the growth of those feminine enmities which are the only perils of our vulgar politicians to-day, and which sprouted from debate even in the high temper of the Revolution, as they must sprout wherever talking and not fighting is the game.

His travel, his wide reading, his communication throughout Europe and in the greatest houses with numerous close, varied and admiring friends, gave him that poise and that contempt for vision which made his leadership, when once he led, secure.

With all this went the passion to administrate, to do, which months of speeches and of opposition to the executive had but swollen. In April his opportunity came.

It was the Queen who made this capital move.

For many months, indeed, he would have come in secret

to the aid of the Court. From the very meeting of the States-General the year before, Mirabeau had known that his place was with Government rather than in the tribune. His past of passion forbade him executive power. Necker, with quite another past — a nasty financial past — had dared to insult him in the early days of the Parliament. All the summer he had begged La Marck, his friend, to speak for him to the Queen, to the Throne. La Marck, who was very close to the Queen and was a companion since Trianon, had spoken, but Mirabeau was still a voice only, and, to women, an unpleasant one. In October he had directly attacked the Queen — she held him responsible for the two dreadful days and the insults of the drag back to Paris. The decrees in November which preserved the Assembly from decay, by forbidding its members to accept office, had closed the Ministry to him: in December he had tried to work a secret executive power through Monsieur and Marie Antoinette's distrust of Monsieur had again foiled him. La Marck had given up hope of helping his friend, the decrees and the debates of the Assembly shook the Throne with increasing violence, the King was counselless, when, after some long debate within herself, of which, in the nature of the thing, we can have no hint or record, the Queen, in the days when the preparation for her child's sacrament was her chief affair, and a fortnight or so before that communion, determined to unite the brain of Mirabeau to the Crown.

She easily persuaded Louis. Before or after that persuasion she spoke to Mercy, and Mercy wrote to that ancestral Balzic land whither La Marck, certain that nothing could be done in Paris, and desiring to check the effects of the revolt in the Austrian Netherlands upon his estates, had betaken him three months before. La Marck at once returned; he crossed the frontier, and in his private house up along the Faubourg St. Honoré, Mirabeau and Mercy met upon an April evening. All was most secretly done, so that none, not the populace, nor the Parliament, nor the courtiers — nor even Necker — should know. These two very separate abilities, Mercy and Mirabeau, recognised each other: for some days yet, the latter and the greater, the storm-tossed one, doubted; he still spoke of "an embassy" for his reward — he stooped to beg favour again of La Fayette. At last he was convinced of the Court's sincerity, and on the tenth of May he wrote for the King — that is, for the Government (there was no other) — that first admirable Letter of Advice which remains the chief monument of his genius. In one year he had proceeded from being an Evil Reputation to be a Speechifier, from a Speechifier to a something inspiring dread: now he was secretly in power; in half-power; his was one of the hands on the tiller. To himself that year had been but a year of debt and makeshift; his principal relief at this vast change was a relief of the purse.

Mirabeau wanted money. He was a gentleman, and his honour wanted it. In his appetite for it he did all a gentleman would do, sacrificing that which men not gentlemen would not part with to save their lives. He approached enemies and friends indifferently. La Fayette, whose militia power offended him and whose nullity drove him wild, La Fayette whom he had attacked and publicly jeered at, he quietly tapped for £2,000 and railed when that cautious Saviour of Two Worlds sent less than half the sum. He had the gentleman's morbid shame of old debts and the gentleman's carelessness in contracting new. He was of the sort that kill themselves rather than finally default, and yet who take the road that makes defaulting sure. To such a man, now rising on the Revolutionary wave, entertaining, ordering secretarial work on every side, playing the part of a public god, the offer of the Court was new life. Yet here again some apology must be offered to the modern reader for the pettiness of the sum which sufficed in those days to purchase so much power upon such an occasion. For the salvation of the Monarchy Mirabeau was to receive, upon the payment of his debts, not half the income we give to a politician who has climbed on to the Front Bench: when he had accomplished his task he was to receive, upon retirement, a sum that would just purchase such a pension as we accord for life to a nephew or a son-in-law fatigued by two years of the Board of Trade. He accepted the terms: but for him, and for those like him, a wage, however shameful or secret, is but an opportunity for intense and individual action. He was the more himself and the less a servant when he had wages to spend. He designed his campaign at once: to see the Queen upon whose energy alone he relied and in whom—though he had never kissed her hand or spoken to her face to face — he divined a corresponding courage; and next, through her, while maintaining his demagogic power, to crush the growth of anarchy by the welding of an army; and at last to restore the Monarchy by a civil war. For order was, he imagined, the chief affair, and anarchy was all that great brain could discover in the early ferment of the time.

He was a man very capable of being a lover: he was an artist who ardently desired an instrument: he trusted his capacity with women, and he far over-priced the power in action, though not the vigour, of the Queen. She upon her side dreaded the meeting and delayed it, though Mercy himself and the new Archbishop of Toulouse, now her confessor, urged it.

Upon the 4th of June the Court had left Paris for St. Cloud to spend, within an hour of the capital and within sight of it, the months of summer. That memorable anniversary of her son's death isolated and saddened the woman upon whom was thus thrown a responsibility too great for her judgment. All the month she hesitated, while the notes from Mirabeau in his new capacity as Counsellor of the Court, coming in continually more insistent, more authoritative, and more wide, made the meeting a necessity. At last, upon the 29th, she decided. A room was chosen, "such that none could know"; he was to come upon Friday, July 3, to the little back door of the garden toward the park; there was a further delay — he was put off to the morrow. He slept at his sister's house at Auteuil, and early on the Saturday morning, taking his sister's son with him for sole companion, disguised, he drove to the little garden door. Everything was silent about him in the summer morning as he drove from Auteuil to St. Cloud, that nephew of his riding as his postilion, and no one by. A certain suspicion weighed upon him. He remembered the delays, the secrecy; he remembered that no friend loved him as much as each loved or hated the Crown. Before he put his hand to the latch he gave the boy a note and said: "If I am not returned within three-quarters of an hour, give this to the Captain of the Militia," and, having said this, he went alone into the garden.

In France and throughout his world the event of those days was the Federation. In ten days all the delegates would meet upon the Champ de Mars for the anniversary of the Bastille: the change in men was to be confirmed in a vast meeting of friendship: the King was to swear and a world quite renewed was to arise. Even in London the blaze of the triumph had struck the street, and the common shows were preparing pictures and models of the feast. Upon this all Europe was turned as the delegates came swarming daily into the simmering July of Paris and as the altar rose upon the great open field by the river. For him, and now for history also, a greater, what might, had Mirabeau lived, have been a more enduring scene, was the secret morning meeting so prepared.

The Queen awaited him in a room apart, the King at her side. She awaited with some hesitation the fierce step and the bold eye, the strong, pitted face of "the Monster," but her rank and a long apprenticeship to reception had taught her to receive. He came in and saw this woman whom he had so much desired to see; he spoke with her for half an hour, and as he left her he kissed her hand. Two things remained with him: the moderation, the over-moderation of the King, but in her a sort of regal determination which was half an illusion of his own, but which most powerfully filled his spirit and which left him enfeoffed to the cause he had so long chosen to serve. He came out to his nephew, where the carriage waited, radiant, all his energy renewed. He had perhaps a clear conception of the Queen in action supporting him, determining the King, eagerly accepting his wisdom and his plans. In that he gave her far too great a place; but great men impute greatness, and Mirabeau was too great for women.

The show of the Federation passed, gloriously; the life of the nation rose to passion and broke bounds. In the matter of the army, by which alone Authority could live,

Mirabeau saw its strength dissolved. The melting of society had destroyed that discipline, the hardest, the most necessary and the least explicable bond among men: the frontier mutinied for arrears of pay, and with the first days of August it was evident that neither for defence nor for the re-establishment of law could the army be available. The army, that one solid weapon of the Monarchy, was now cracked all down the blade. The Army of the East, long, as I have said, the chief resource of the executive, was affected like the rest of the service. There Bouillé, a trained and careful man, wealthy, noble of course, whiggish in politics, and of middle age, held the command and saw from one day to another in all the garrisons of his command the method of soldiers failing. One mutiny followed another; regimental chests were seized for arrears of pay; the non-commissioned officers were no longer with the *cadre* in spirit; officers of the lower grades had been insulted, of the higher reluctantly and more reluctantly obeyed.

It was at this moment that Mirabeau saw fit to give that grave advice for which posterity has judged him so hardly, and which yet betrays the decision of his soul. He determined upon civil war.

Many things might have saved him and the nation from such a policy: notably La Fayette, a plaster head of the Militia might have been made a reserve force behind the failing regulars, and it has been pretended that La Fayette and Mirabeau were now quite separate, and the wealthy young fellow useless to his elder the Statesman, because La Fayette, in opposing Mirabeau's presidency of the Assembly for the Federation, had offended the vanity from which great orators suffer. The cause is insufficient. Mirabeau had lost all hope that La Fayette could act. He passed him by. What as a fact did prevent the immediate prosecution of Mirabeau's policy was the insufficiency of the Queen, and this it was that saved the country and the memory of her adviser from a course that would certainly have preserved the Throne.

Contrasted against the surroundings of her family and her Court, even of her immediate enemies, her decision had shone; contrasted against Mirabeau's will it was pale. She preferred, she even attempted to foist upon him, that project of foreign intervention which, three years later, killed her; and his famous words in his Advice of August 13, seemed to her rhetoric or worse. Its style was "extraordinary": he was "mad." "Four enemies are at the charge," he had written, "the taxes, repudiation, the army, and winter" — she could not bear the style: but he was right. The harvest was in — it was not sufficient; a new and vast increase of assignats was voted — Mirabeau himself most urgently advising it — and on all this, at the end of August, came Nancy.

The chief and the last foundation of force for the King were the Swiss regiments. Those of the Guard in the last supreme moment of the Monarchy all but saved it. At Nancy in that August of 1790 three regiments were quartered, two French, one Swiss, that called "Château Vieux." They mutinied, mainly for pay; after scenes which do not concern this book, they were broken — upon the last day of the month, with a loss to the still disciplined troops opposing them of forty officers and ten times that number of men. The gravity of that day was of a kind we also know, when, in some crisis (with us such crisis has been for generations foreign, not domestic), a much graver thing, a much louder noise, brings to a pitch emotion ready for violence and suddenly presents as a reality what all had desired or feared. Of such are the first shots of a war, the first news of a fatal illness. The French mutineers were disbanded. The opinion of the moment would have tolerated no course more severe: but — and this was the wedge that stuck into the heart of the time and clove men asunder — the Swiss were made such an example of old things as the whole Revolution had come to sweep away. True, their own rich officers were the judges of the Swiss; what was done did not then lie and does not lie to-day on the conscience of the French people; but when of these foreign peasants, driven by poverty to a foreign service and maddened to mutiny by the fraudulent retaining of their pay, *one-half* were made the subjects of a public horror, the country gasped. The town of Nancy, a town of great beauty, the flower of Lorraine, had fought with and had supported the mutineers. It suffered the sight of *half* of the whole Swiss regiment marched out for punishment, half sent to barracks and then reserved for some obscurer fate. Of those so publicly destroyed, two-thirds were for the galleys, near a third were hanged on high gallows before all, to turn the stomachs of the new Citizens of a free state; one was broken on the wheel with clubs, his bones crushed to satisfy the privileged in a social order already infamous, his blood spattered on the pavement of a town which had befriended him. It was an anomaly of hell fallen in the midst of the new hopes and within six weeks of that clamour of good-will upon the Champ de Mars when all such nightmares were to have been buried for ever.

The Assembly voted its thanks for the restoration of order: the vote was moved by Mirabeau. Bouillé commanded an army now silent, and the thing was done.

But the minority of wealthy men that had thus dared applaud the executions at Nancy was now cut off from fellowship with the nation, and the civil war which Mirabeau desired was come in spirit — for the Government, the only possible executive, the Crown, was with that minority.

Necker, lost in public opinion, defeated in finance, thoroughly terrified at the sound of arms, was off across the frontier for ever to Geneva, his Bible and his money-bags. For a few months Mirabeau's strength was to remain increasing, the one central thing — but secretly his power of action was marred, for, while the Court listened and heard him, it did not move. He would have seen the Queen — she would not see him. Already his complicity was guessed by a few — it had been denounced frenziedly and amid Parliamentary jeers and laughter by one young man, since dead: but the rumour had terrified the palace. Mirabeau, still taking the palace's pay, still pouring in upon it Advices which he desired to be commands — (and yet still refused so much as a Royal audience) — grew continually upon the Parliament.

As his power over the Assembly increased, his fret against the hesitation of the Court increased with it; it increased to desperation, and that desperation was the more exasperated because a man of his temper could not grasp — in the absence of personal interviews — what it was that held back the Crown. Yet to a man of another temper the explanation would have been easy. There was a conflict, not only of mediocrity with genius, not only of two wills — the one accustomed to an inert command, the other avid to exercise a vigorous one, but a conflict also of ends to be attained; for that which Mirabeau desired — and which he thought the King and Queen to desire — was a national thing, whereas what the King and Queen now desired was a personal thing. He all the while was considering the Monarchy, an institution necessary to his country: they thought more and more daily of their individual selves: their habits, their wounded right, their children — their religion.

In nothing did the friction of that new machine, the alliance between Mirabeau and the Court, show more than in this matter of religion. To Mirabeau, as to every vigorous spirit of that generation, the Faith was inconceivable. How far, by an effort of fancy, he could picture minds that held it one cannot tell, but one may be certain that he could not but associate such minds with ineptitude. Now the business of 1790, unknown to the men who most mixed in that business, was Religion. France had of herself transformed herself in eighteen months. The Roman conceptions had returned, the municipalities governed, the whole people were moving in a stream together, equality had re-arisen to the surface of things; war, if war came, would be a national thing — the life in each had determined to be based upon a general will. At this overwhelming change the Parliament had assisted; it was their function to express its main features in new laws, and, as to details, to thresh them out in debate and make them fit the new scheme: among these details was the definition of the Clergy's status. The Catholic Church was present — for the peasants, at least — and it must there still be recognised, its powers must be defined, the terms of its recognition must be formulated. These cultivated men of the Parliament — and I include the bishops — had no conception of Resurrection. The Church was an old thing, passive, woven into the lower stuff of the State; it would not again be what a dim tradition affirmed it once to have been. Let it die down quietly in its villages and go. As for the *Institution* of it, the higher-salaried places — its use in Government — why, that was to be Gallican.

Just before the Federation in July, the CIVIL CONSTITUTION OF THE CLERGY had passed the House. Just before Nancy the King had assented, and it was law.

To the men who spoke and legislated, it was a just and straightforward law; to us who know a future they could not know, it was a monstrous absurdity. Priests and bishops "elected" — not by an enthusiasm or by clamour or by a populace ardent, but by paper votes — as we elect our dunderheads to Westminster! Unity, the prime test of life, secured by no more than a letter to Rome announcing election and courteously admitting communion. Every diocese and parish a new creation, created without any consultation of Peter and his authority! Yet such was the sleep of the Faith a century ago that this incredible instrument provoked discussion only; and such protests as came were not protests of laughter or even of anger, but protests of argument — with after-thoughts of money. But the King and the Queen believed.

Had she not suffered, this void of the century in matters of the soul might have left Marie Antoinette indifferent. She had been indifferent to that prig brother of hers when he played the philosopher at Vienna and the fool in the Netherlands. The populace, who guard the seeds of religion, were unknown to her as to the King and to the Parliament. But she had so suffered that she had concentrated upon the Creed: her husband had always held it simply — he was a simple man. Now, when he signed the Civil Constitution and she knew of that act, it was proof that they had done with the national ferment, that their concern was to get away to return and to reconquer; that henceforward no public act of theirs, no acceptation of any Reform, had in it or was meant to have the least validity in conscience. She especially was quite cut off henceforward from the crown she had worn — it was no longer a symbol of her state for her; and if she had continued to wear it, as Mirabeau desired, after a reconquest achieved through civil war, she would have worn it contentedly over defeated subjects rather than over a nation.

All this Mirabeau saw as little as he saw the passion of the village priests, the anger of the women in the country-sides. The resistance (which immediately began) he thought purely political. Priests that would not take the oath were Partisans of the old tyranny and breakdown; the Pope, who was preparing his definite refusal, was a subtle Italian whom he, Mirabeau, must meet by a Gallic brutality. To the King Mirabeau secretly represented the Civil Constitution and the gathering revolt against it as an excellent lever for recruiting the provinces and raising that civil war of the Government against anarchy which was his whole policy; but to the Assembly (and here it was most of himself that appeared) he spoke against the Church's refusal to accept with a violence that astounded, and at times provoked to rebuke, his most extreme admirers. All his spirit during that autumn and early winter of 1790–91 is one of diatribe and fury against the intangible foe he himself had raised.

On the 26th of November he forced the Assembly to vote

the prosecution of priests who refused the oath; on the 4th of January he accused the hierarchy of their old game — "too well known in our history" — of playing for an "ultramontane" authority; ten days later, on the 14th, he broke all bounds: swore that the priests cared little if religion died (and much he cared for it!) so that their *power* was saved. The priests present left the hall. He continued with greater violence, and all the Assembly protested. On the proposition of Camus (himself next door to a Huguenot) it was moved and carried that Mirabeau be no longer heard. When, a bare week after all this, a Letter of Advice reached the King from Mirabeau headed, "*On the Way to make use of the Civil Constitution*," how should the King not be bewildered?

The King read it; he found a stupefying series of counsels. How could so simple a man as he understand the contradiction between Mirabeau's public speeches and secret executive advice? "No time" (he read in Mirabeau's private communication to the Crown), "no time could be more favourable for uniting all the malcontents, the most dangerous ones, and raising his royal popularity to the detriment of the Assembly"; he was to provoke resistance secretly, to refuse executive aid: to throw the odium of the Civil Constitution *and* of the priests' resistance to it on the Assembly. What could a man of Louis' kind make of all this? Had Marie Antoinette been a she-Mirabeau, as Mirabeau half believed her to be, *she* might have followed the plan. Contrariwise, she was a Christian mother, much too untaught and too devout by now to use religion for political intrigue. To emphasise their bewilderment, this Husband and Wife find that their late Confessor — whom they had indignantly rejected for his schism — had taken the oath at the pressing of Mirabeau himself. . . . It is not to be wondered at that Mirabeau's advice in everything hung fire.

There were other glaring contrasts between his public and his private view: there was Mirabeau's high playing of the demagogue rôle. He must roar with the Jacobins: that organisation, the "radical thousand" of Paris, and a hundred and fifty societies at its back throughout France, already directed the storm from the October of '90. He mixed with it, flattered it, became its powerful spokesman in the Assembly, was its President by the end of November; and while he so marked and emphasised with his voice and will almost every one of the succeeding steps that led towards a pure democracy, he marvelled that the Court would not accept his secret counsel and believe his support of the Crown to be his true motive of action all the while. It was indeed his main motive; but men of his stature also require applause, and the double part he filled was acted too brilliantly upon its public side for his private statesmanship — to which all his intellect and much of his heart was really devoted — to obtain full weight at the palace. He was permanently mistrusted, and he met that mistrust by chance phrases of contempt or insult which he may or may not have intended to be repeated to the woman and the office which he desired both to guide and to save.

In one thing, however, his influence still weighed: in that one thing it would have sufficed, had he lived, to save the Queen. I mean in the plan, still debated and still postponed, for the abandonment of Paris by the Crown.

I have said that the main understanding between the Queen and Mirabeau lay in this, that for him a national for her a domestic end was now in view. For months he had urged a public withdrawal from the capital, a public appeal to the armed forces, a withdrawal to some near and loyal town, a town with a palace and tradesmen dependent on it — to Compiègne, for instance, a long day's ride[1] away; thereafter an appeal to the provinces and, if the extremists and Paris would fight, then a civil war and a reconquest of power. He had talked of the Queen on horseback with her son; he resurrected Maria Theresa and imagined bold things. The Queen desired for her husband, herself, and her children merely safety: but she would not leave the King.

Once that summer the Queen and her children had driven out from St. Cloud towards the western woods that overhang the Seine; the King and his gentlemen had ridden westward also in the wooded plain below. Many in either retinue had thought the moment come, but each party returned at evening.

Returned to Paris in the autumn, the rising flood of public feeling made a public appeal and a public withdrawal more difficult with every succeeding month, and month after month it was postponed.

The foreigner, of whom the French had hardly thought during the first months of their enthusiasm, now re-arose before them; many were already anxious for the frontier, and already the irritant of German menace, which was to lead at last from Valmy to Wattignies and from Wattignies to Jena, had begun to chafe the military appetites of Paris. Were war to break out with the spring of the next year — nay, were it only in the air — the escape of the King from Paris would be more difficult than ever.

It was at the close of October,[2] before the Court had left

[1] To be accurate, a little less than fifty miles.

[2] Oct. 20th, not the 23rd, a date accepted since the publication of Bouillé's Memoirs in 1833, but corrected by collation with the original two years ago.

St. Cloud for Paris, that the plan for leaving Paris first took definite shape and that Louis sent Parniers with a message to Bouillé at Metz.

Mirabeau had pointed to Bouillé as the only general to defend that march. Not because Bouillé was on the frontier, but because Bouillé had got his army in hand again, was very capable, did not intrigue. But Bouillé, in Mirabeau's design, was to come westward and to receive the King at Compiègne. The General himself accepted such a plan and urged it. The King still preferred a flight to the very frontier, Besançon for choice, and it is impossible — when his reluctance to leave at all is considered, his whole character, his wife's counsel, and her previous attitude in the letters and appeals of that summer — to doubt that the Queen had moulded that decision. It was not a firm choice. Bouillé's son, coming at Christmas to Paris to sound people and things, found La Fayette of very dubious loyalty, and he doubted the aid of the Militia. He saw Fersen (the young fellow took for granted that Fersen was the Queen's lover); he saw him in Fersen's own house in the Faubourg St. Honoré. They discussed the rottenness of the army, the unlikeliness of immediate foreign aid. It was decided to postpone the thing for three months.

And meanwhile the Queen heard debated before her the alternatives of a flight to the frontier and of a domestic rising nearer Paris in defence of the Crown. She was by all her bent — and was increasingly to be — in favour of foreign support; but Mirabeau's counsel was something to her. At the end of February it prevailed, and La Marck came to Bouillé at Metz with the news that Mirabeau's plan should be considered. Bouillé agreed. There was to be no suggestion of flight: the Court's choice of the frontier was to be abandoned. Compiègne should be the goal of a short and determined march. The soldier rejoiced, as did Mirabeau, that a final decision had been made, that no near presence of foreign aid was expected, and that the idea of a flight to the frontier was given up. March, perhaps the close of it, was to see the thing done, and so with the spring was to be issued the challenge to civil war: then and then only, if necessary, might follow a retirement upon a fortress.

The thing was dangerous and more dangerous. Mesdames, the King's aunts, had left their country house at great pains for Italy: the populace had all but detained them. La Fayette, a month later, had disarmed certain gentlemen of the palace and had insisted that his Militia alone mount guard. It was certain, as March crept on, that the decision must soon be taken, and that the double power of Mirabeau over Court and Parliament could alone force the exit from Paris to a well-chosen town, and so decide the issue of a Restoration of the Monarchy now so grievously imperilled. Mirabeau still grew in power, still spoke in his loudest tones, still watched, and drove all his team of political dupes and Royal clients, still remained strongly double. Swearing to one that he had all ready for the end of Monarchy if the King should fly; writing continually (and more sincerely) to another his plans in aid of such a flight; asking for yet more money (on the 2nd of March); urging a further double-dealing with the Assembly in a secret and verbal message to the King (on the 13th); betraying the Jacobins, his Jacobins, in a private letter (on the 21st). Doing all this with his intrigue fully formed, and the Royal Family already sheltered under the wing of that intrigue, Fate entered.

It was on the 24th of March that Mirabeau wrote his last letter to La Marck. His friend had mining rights in the Kingdom: the new mining laws were down for debate that week. He promised to speak, and on the morning of the 27th he called on La Marck upon his way to the *manège;* he was faint and compelled to rest awhile upon a couch there, but he rallied and went on to the Parliament. It was Sunday. The streets were full of people: he was recognised, followed and cheered.

Upon that 27th of March he spoke more than once: his ill ease was not apparent. On the 28th he was struck. But even so lying in his bed, for the next three days, in spite of an increasing agony, he made of his moments of respite occasions for set words, usually well chosen, pagan, proud, memorable, and a trifle affected. A crowd in the street without kept guard and silence. A crowd was about his bed continually. Talleyrand, reconciled, came; La Marck who loved him, came repeatedly — and a hundred others He spoke, and they spoke, of Death, as a matter for converse, often for jest. La Marck quizzed him: "Oh, you connoisseur of great death-beds!" Talleyrand told him that he came "like the populace, to hear." A man who loved him said well, "that he acted death as a great actor upon a national stage." Astounding courage, and more astounding silence upon the thing he had never cared for or believed all the greatness and all the void of the eighteenth century was here. He admitted God, however, and rallied his good doctor, a materialist — as then were all, and still are most, experts in viscera: the days were sunlit and the sun reminded him of God. So for four days upon the fifth day, the 2nd of April, at half-past eigh in the morning, those watching his last and silent agony, saw that he was dead.

. . . .

Many modern historians have said that the death of Mirabeau affected but little the plans that had been made for flight.

It is an error. The death of Mirabeau changed all, and it was one more of those hammer-blows of Fate exactly coincident with the sequence of the Queen's weird.

It is true that the flight was already long arranged. It is true that its very details were planned for the most part long before Mirabeau died. Nevertheless, had Mirabeau lived, the whole thing would have had a different issue; and for this reason, that Mirabeau dominated all that world — not only the world of the Court but also the world of Parliament, and, in some indirect way, the world of Opinion as well — by Will. Any action that the Court had taken with Mirabeau alive and active would have been bent to Mirabeau's plan, and even if the flight had been, not (as he counselled) to Compiègne, but to Montmédy and the frontier, Mirabeau would have forced at once its success and a consequent civil war. He would have permitted no departure without being privy to it; he would have sworn, shouted, cajoled and persuaded doubly upon either side—for Mirabeau was a soldierly man; he had a plan and could use men by ordering. He could use them for the achievement of a fixed end which was now the salvation of the Monarchy; for he believed the Monarchy to be the skeleton and framework of France—and this creative light of the revolution around him seemed to him a mere mist and dazzle. Great as he was, I repeat it, the Revolution seemed to him to be drifting towards an Anarchy. He was like a landsman who may be brave and domineering but who shudders when he first comes across the temper of the sea.

But what might have happened is but hypothesis. For Mirabeau died; and Mirabeau once dead it was necessarily certain that the Court, left to itself, should attempt to preserve not Monarchy but merely the Court. Mirabeau living, that determination of theirs to save their bodies would have done no harm, and the eagerness of the Queen to get away to the neighbourhood of friends would have been used as human intelligence uses the instinct of animals. Mirabeau dead, that force ran ever along its own blind line, attempting merely to save the persons of the King and Queen and their children. Attempting so small a thing, it happened to fail. But on the failure or success of that attempt the largest things depended.

It was, as we have seen, upon Saturday, the 2nd of April, that Mirabeau died, and had said in dying that there went with him the last shred of the Monarchy.

The Sunday following his death was that upon which the Schismatic Priests said their first Masses in every parish of the city.

. . . .

I have not space to reiterate in this volume the vast issue involved. I have sufficiently emphasised and shall further emphasise the profound truth that every Civil Revolution is theological at bottom, because, at bottom, it must be based upon a divergence of philosophy between the philosophies of the old order and the new. A chance test of philosophy thrown at random into the Revolutionary movement had separated men suddenly and was rifting the State asunder; for a fortnight Paris raged upon the Nationalisation of the Church.

I will not detain the reader. There was here one of those double duties where the wisest get most bewildered and the most sincere go the furthest astray. Let the reader remember (difficult as it is to do so in the religious atmosphere of our time) that with the educated of that day Religion was dead — with the populace of Paris even more dead. The thing was a mere emblem. Its last little flickering light (which we have since seen to grow to so great a flame) was not comprehended, save as a political institution, by the great bulk of the Parliament, by the professions, by the workers; the very beggars in the street despised the Faith, and the shrines were empty. You were a priest or one of the very few Mass-goers? Then you were suspected of supporting the old forms of civil polity! After the Civil Constitution of the Clergy you deliberately refused to take a reasonable oath to the Constitution and the new-born Liberty of Men? Then you were a traitor, and a silly traitor at that. Let it be remembered that at this moment Religion had no warriors. All the vast rally of the nineteenth century was undreamt of. The bishops were place-hunters full of evil living;[1] the Creed an empty historic formula: a convention like the conventions of "party" in England to-day. The reader *must* see this, in spite of all the nineteenth century may have taught him to the contrary, or he will never see the Revolution.

In such a crisis two factors, quite uncomprehended, stood like rocks — they were but small minorities: so are rocks small accidents in the general sea. The one was

[1] Consider Mgr. of Narbonne. His mistress was his own niece.

that little group of people who still practised the united Catholic Faith — and it just so happened that of these the King was one, his sister another, and, from the beginning in her light, easy way, latterly with increasing depth, his wife a third; the other factor was the mass of the humbler Clergy. They felt as by an instinct the note of unity; they refused to subscribe: to all, or nearly all, the bishops it was — for the most part — a matter of rank and policy to resist the *Bill;* to the two-thirds of the country Clergy to resist the *Law* was loyalty to our Lord.

What the King felt in that quarrel we all know. Marie Antoinette, in spite of her devotion, was never able to neglect the human, the purely temporal, the vulgarly political aspect of the quarrel. Her husband, sincerely sympathetic though he was with the French temper, thought mainly of the Divine interests in the matter; though he thought slowly and badly, that was his thought. The populace, the politicians — all the world — saw nothing whatsoever in the Catholic resistance but a dodge devised by privilege to put a spoke in the wheel of the Revolution. And Paris especially, having for so long abandoned religion, raged round the refusal of the priests.

It is pitiful to read how small a rally the Faith could make! *One* chapel in all Paris was hired for the true Mass to be said therein, and handfuls here and there put forward a timid claim to approach the only altar which Rome acknowledged. I say it for the third or for the fourth time, to-day we cannot understand these things, for the Resurrection of the Catholic Church stands between us and them; but to this Paris on that Lenten Sunday, the 3rd of April, 1791, the presence of the Schismatic Clergy, each in his parish, was a plain challenge launched against the Crown, and it was nothing more: the attachment of the Court to the Roman Unity seemed to Paris a mere political intrigue, odious and unnational and stinking of treason. For a fortnight the Parisian anger raged, and the 17th of April was Palm Sunday.

It has become a rule for those who are in communion with the Catholic Church that they should receive the Sacraments at least once a year, and that at Easter or thereabouts; a rule defined, if I am not mistaken, during the struggle with the Lutheran — that latest of the great heresies. This rule the King had satisfied, and on that Palm Sunday had taken Communion in his Chapel from a priest who had not sworn the Civic Oath. All the customary talk of some religious necessity by which he was in conscience compelled to leave Paris is balderdash. The attempt he made the next day, the Monday, to leave the city in order to spend the Easter days in the suburban palace of St. Cloud was purely political. Religion had no part therein. It cannot be determined to-day — unless indeed further evidence should come before us — how much the mere desire to prove a liberty of action on the part of the Court, how much a sort of challenge sure to be defeated, how much a hope that escape would be easier from a suburban point, entered into this plan; but it is quite certain that the Body of the Lord and His Resurrection had nothing whatsoever to do with it. And when upon Monday of Holy Week, the 18th of April, a little before noon, the royal family got into their carriage to drive, as was their constitutional right, to the neighbouring palace, those few miles away where the populace could not surround them, a crowd, organised as were these crowds of the Revolution, held them all around. The scene has been repeated too often to be repeated here; one character marks it—it is one of profound importance. For the first time armed and disciplined force was wholly upon the side of the Revolution.

The Militia which La Fayette had formed were with the people, and the common will of that great mob was present also in the men who bore arms. It had not been so in any of the movements antecedent to this, unless we admit the sharp national anger of the loose and almost civilian "French Guards" against the hired German Cavalry in July, 1789. Hitherto there had been a distinction between the people at large and that portion of the people which was armed and disciplined, a distinction which now broke down because to the French temper on this Monday of Holy Week, 1791, the issue was too grave for such distinctions. The national King must be kept in Paris, the people would not let him leave, much as a man will not let his money go out of his sight or out of his control.

Let it be noted that here, as is invariably the case throughout the history of the French people, the general mass had easily learned a secret thing: all the bamboozlement had failed — as it is failing to-day in spite of the financial press, the Secret Societies, and every other instrument of fraud. The vast crowd which hustled round the King's carriage knew and freely repeated his project of invasion which had now been so carefully and, as it was thought, so secretly plotted for six months.

The French people are accustomed to, and have, as it were, an appetite for, duels in the dark where one of the two combatants must die. There was determination upon the one side — without proof — that the King desired to fly and must be restrained. There was determination upon the other — accompanied by frequent denial — that the King should escape to the French frontier and should be free.

Not the next day, but the day after, Wednesday in Holy Week, the Queen, the Queen herself pulled the trigger. All that blind force of desire for the mere personal safety of her family, which Mirabeau would have controlled, but which in her unguided hands was an unreasoning torrent, impelled her action. She wrote to Mercy that her very life was in danger and that the business must be done with next month at the latest. She mentioned the place of flight, Montmédy.

Eight weeks followed, during which every effort of the royal family was directed to the achievement of a mere flight.

The limits of these pages do not permit me the many details which could make of that early summer a long book of intrigue. When the thing had failed each had his excuses, and Bouillé would have it that with a docile obedience on the part of the Court he could have saved the Court. It may be argued that if the King had gone by way of Rheims he would have escaped. It may be argued that the delay of twenty-four hours (which certainly did take place) made such and such a difference. All these arguments fall to the ground when it is considered that the King did escape from Paris, escaped easily along the road to the frontier, was safe and trebly safe until, as will be seen, two accidents, wholly incalculable and each a clear part of Fate, broke that immemorial Crown of the French Monarchy. The first (as will be seen) was the error —if it was an error— made by young Choiseul on the Chalons road — a mere mechanical one; the second — much more miraculous — was the ride of Drouet, galloping in a dark night under a covered moon wildly through the very difficult ridgeway of Argonne, and even that miracle only just came off by fifteen minutes. It was not delay, whether of twenty-four hours or of a fortnight which brought them back to Paris. It was that other force for which we have no name, but which one may call if one likes, Necessity or Something Written.

. . . .

Fersen, who loved the Queen and whom the Queen loved, had stood in the centre of the plot, had seen all the conspirators, and brought to its climax everything. He was now to risk his life. The great travelling-carriage called a berline (which easily held three people upon either side), was waiting in its shed in the stables of the house he had hired, as the summer solstice — a date fatal to the Bourbons — was approached. Fersen himself in disguise was to drive them, disguised also, from their palace by night in a cab to where that travelling-coach awaited them. Their passports were ready; the children's governess, the Duchess of Tourzel, was to play the part of the chief personage and to be called the Baroness of Korff. The Queen was to be the governess of her children, and the King her valet, his sister a maid; the children were to be Madame de Korff's children, and the Dauphin was dressed as a girl and called by a girl's name.

. . . .

There are a few square yards in Paris which should be famous in history. Here Joan of Arc fell in her failure to force the Western gate of the city. Here to-day is the hotel called the Hôtel de Normandie, frequented by foreigners, and opposite is a money-changer's booth. Here the Rue St. Honoré crosses the Rue de l'Echelle. There[1] at mid-

[1] To be accurate, the exact spot was a few steps to the south of the present crossing, and much about the middle of the modern Rue de l'Echelle, and opposite No. 6 of that street

FACSIMILE OF FIRST PAGE OF THE ADDRESS TO THE FRENCH PEOPLE

Written by Louis XVI. before his flight

night on the 20th of June, Fersen, dressed as a coachman, was waiting with his cab to drive them to the travelling-coach which awaited them at the eastern boundary of the city. He had already visited the palace to make all sure. His disguise was good, his acting excellent. His love compelled him. He took snuff with the other cabbies. He waited resignedly. The lights went out, midnight approached, and first one, then another of certain beings approached him down the dark alley that led from the courtyards of the palace. The King came, and the Royal children, their governess, and the King's sister. Last of all, and after some delay, the Queen. All of them had escaped safely from what was the chief barrier around them all — the Militia Guard. When they were well in their cab, Fersen, that devoted man, drove them in a leisurely manner to the gates of the city, found the berline drawn up on the highroad, and with it two Gentlemen of the Guard who had come, disguised in old yellow liveries, to act as postilions, while a third had ridden on to the first post-house. Fersen had the berline driven by his servants, himself upon the box, and so reached, in that earliest of all dawns of the year, the first post and relay, the suburban post-house of Bondy.

There was light in the North. He saw before him at that hour the free road to the frontier; the country and the simple minds of subjects; the happy past returning; the end at last of all that Parisian fever, and the chastisement perhaps of all that Parisian violence — at any rate, the solution of the whole affair. His friend was free.

. . . .

The King had but to reach the garrisons of the east, and Austria would move, the last of the regular French armies would advance: now that the royal person was no more in danger from such a march, the march on Paris would begin.

But it was the summer solstice, a moment ill-omened to the Bourbons.

XIV

VARENNES

FROM MIDNIGHT OF MONDAY, JUNE 20, 1791. TO JUST AFTER SEVEN ON THE EVENING OF SATURDAY, JUNE 25, 1791

IT was no longer night; it was near day, the brightening air smelt of morning. The links of the harness-chains clattered a little as the relay horses were backed against the pole of the big carriage. Fersen sauntered to the carriage window of that side upon which the Queen sat. He called out loudly her supposed mistress's assumed name, "Madame Korff," saluted her and turned to go on his lonely cross-country ride to Bourget and the Brussels road, by which he also purposed to fly. But, even as he turned, they say that she held his hand a moment and slipped upon his finger a ring. It was a ring of yellowish gold, broad and heavy, and having set in it an unknown stone. It is still preserved. Here is the story of the ring: —

. . . .

It was again the 20th of June — the summer solstice that strikes, and strikes again, and again at the Bourbons and at the soldiers of the Bourbons. Nineteen years had passed since the dawn when Fersen had left the Queen at Bondy, seventeen since he had broken his heart at her death, and had become silent. His campaigns had forbidden him to show prematurely the effect of advancing age; indeed, as men now count age, he had not reached the

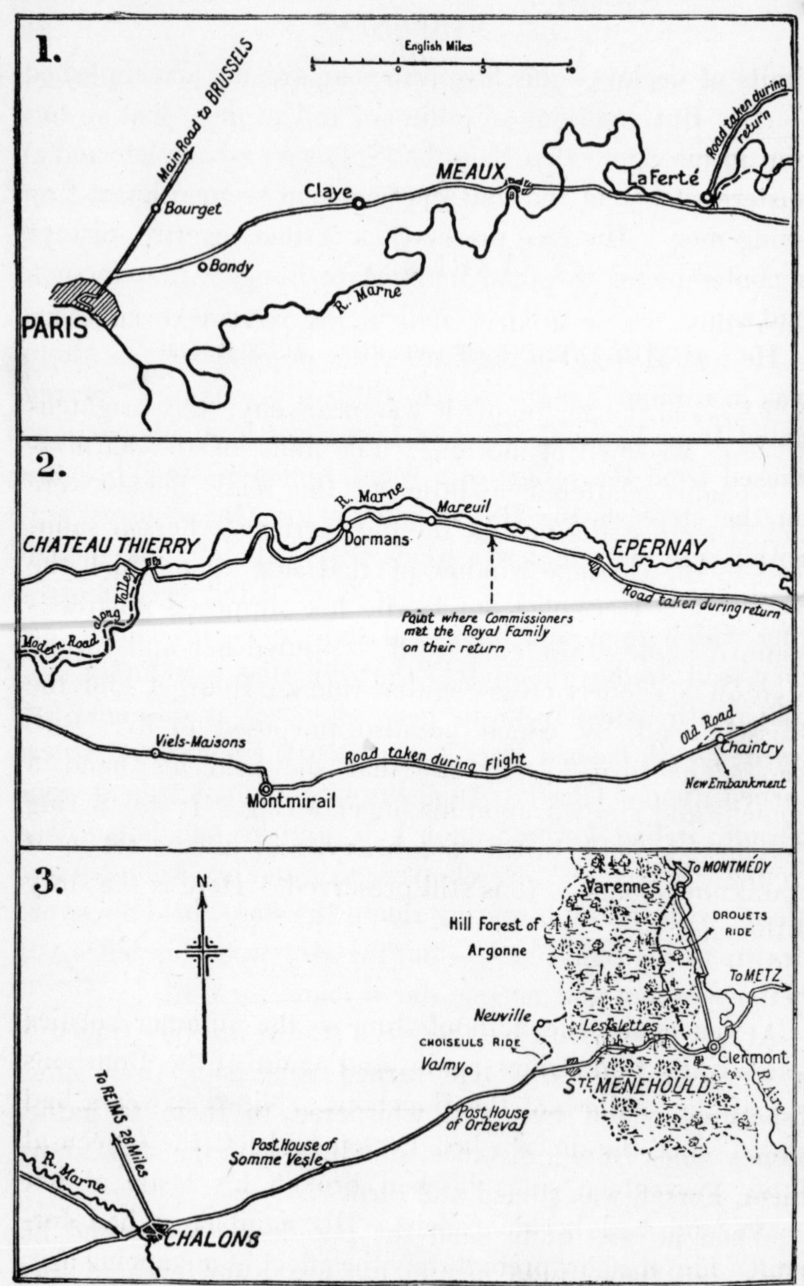
1.
English Miles
5
0
5
10
Main Road to BRUSSELS
Bourget
Bondy
PARIS
Claye
MEAUX
R. Marne
La Ferté
Road taken during return
2.
CHATEAU THIERRY
R. Marne
Dormans
Mareuil
EPERNAY
Road taken during return
Modern Road along Valley
Point where Commissioners met the Royal Family on their return
Viels-Maisons
Montmirail
Road taken during Flight
Old Road
Chaintry
New Embankment
3.
N.
To MONTMÉDY
Varennes
Hill Forest of Argonne
DROUETS RIDE
To METZ
Neuville
Les Islettes
CHOISEULS RIDE
Valmy
Clermont
R. Aire
Sᵀᴱ MENEHOULD
Post House of Orbeval
Post House of Somme Vesle
To REIMS 28 Miles
R. Marne
CHALONS

MAP OF THE FLIGHT TO VARENNES AND THE RETURN

limits of decline—his fifty-fifth year was not accomplished. . . . But emotions so inhuman and so deep had so torn him in his vigour that there had followed a complete and an austere silence of the soul: he had long seemed apart from living men. His face preserved a settled severity, his eyes a contempt for the final moment of danger: that moment had come.

He was Marshal of the Forces; the populace of Stockholm was in rumour, for the North still had vigour in it, impregnated from France. He had been torn from his carriage, chased from the refuge of a room, and now stood bleeding on the steps of the Riddenholm alone (the Squires were within the church, barricaded: they had left him outside to die). The populace, hating him, hated even more a ring which they saw large and dull upon his finger, for they said among themselves that the ring was Faëry, and that death issued from its gem whenever it was held forward; Death flashed from it and struck whomsoever it was turned upon. Charles Augustus himself had seen it upon parade; it had lowered upon him, and he had fallen dead from his horse. . . . Fersen, so standing, wounded and alone, with the mob roaring round the steps, held his sword drawn in his right hand—but the ring upon his left was a better weapon, and no one dared come forward.

At last a traitor (since there is a traitor in every tragedy), a servant of his who had turned fisherman, drew other fishermen round him and whispered to them to gather stones: thus, from a distance, standing upon the steps above them, Fersen was stoned and died.

When he was quite dead the populace drew round his body, but they would not go too near, and even as they approached they shielded their eyes from the ring. But this traitor, Zaffel, bolder than the rest, went forward also with an axe, and, shielding his eyes also, he hacked the finger off. The people cheered as they would cheer a man that had plucked a fuse from a shell. He ran, with his head still turned, to the riverside, and he threw the finger with the Queen's ring upon it far out into the stream.

Next day Stockholm was as calm as though there had been no evening tumult. Zaffel at early morning took his boat out upon the cold lake water by a pleasant breeze, and pointed up river: he had a plan to fish. When he had left the many islands of the town behind him and had passed into a lonely reach of pine-trees, he felt a gentle shock upon the keel, and the boat stood still. . . . He went forward to the bows and looked over; he could see nothing but very deep green water bubbling below. As he came back aft the masthead caught his eye, and there, clasping it, was a severed hand; the blood which was apparent at the wrist was not running. The hand grasped the trunk of the mast with rigour, and Zaffel, as he saw it, shuddered, for one finger of that hand was gone.

The boat went forward in spite of the tide and aslant the wind, with the sheet loose and the sail at random, and he in the boat could feel for hours that the impulsion of its course was from the masthead to which he no longer dared look upwards. The boat cut steadily across the eddies of the Moelar. At times he tried the tiller, but he found the fixed movement unresponsive to his helm.

There is no darkness in the North at this season, but a twilight which, if there are clouds, fades from the grey of evening to the grey of dawn; he had sat cold, crouching in the stern of his boat, throughout all the hours of the day, and now this grey twilight was upon him. In the midst of it he saw far up-stream a white rock from which, as it seemed to him, some phosphorescence glowed unnatural, and in the midst of that light, upon a ledge of the stone, was the ring. He took it, as at a command; then at last he dared look up at the masthead. He saw the hand, now whole, relax and change and disappear, and he felt the boat go free, turn and drift down stream.

When he was back upon the quays of Stockholm, all his body trembling with a fast of twenty-four hours and with the cold of the morning, his neighbours, as they caught the mooring rope, asked questions of him. He answered them with meaningless songs, and then, as the vision returned, with pointings and terror. He was mad.

They took him off to the Bethel beyond the stream. On the Knights' Island, within the church of Riddenholm, the Squires who had deserted Fersen upon the day before were at that moment gathered round the coffin to do honour to his burial; and upon the pall they noticed (some curious, some indifferent) the broad band of yellowish gold and the unknown stone.

When it came to the burial, the grave-diggers dared not put it into earth as they should have done; they gave it to his family. With them it still remains, to do evil and disturb his sleep.

. . . .

From Bondy the great carriage went forward under the growing light of the day. At Claye a cabriolet with the Queen's waiting women joined them and followed the berline. That increasing light forbade the family to sleep; they settled in comfort upon the broad and padded seats of white velvet, leaning back into them, and every word they said revealed the enlarging confidence of their souls. The King felt himself already upon horseback; the Queen and the Duchess repeated the rôles they were to play on whatever little public occasions the rapid journey might involve them in. The Duchess as Madame Korff, in whose name the transport had been made out; the Queen as her governess — and so forth. They went rapidly in that mixed landscape of wood and market-garden, and half-continuous village which still marks the confines of Paris and of the influence of Paris. Now they were in the open country, with Paris quite forgotten, now in a district with a dialect of its own — sure test of honesty and of freedom. The countrysides were awake, the mowers were in the field, the road was down among the narrow pastures of the Marne, and at last in Meaux, where for the first time they halted for a relay.

So near to Paris, the wealthy equipage and its suite attracted no curiosity, while prudence still restrained the travellers from showing themselves in the market-square, fatigued as they may already have been by a continuous travelling of now over five hours — for it was past six and the town was astir by the time the berline and the cabriolet had rumbled in. To this concurrence of good accidents the neighbourhood of the capital added another element, for the posting station of Meaux was so used to the continual passage of considerable travellers (how many of the emigrants had it not re-harnessed!) that not only was the whole place incurious, but also the relay was rapidly effected. It was not a quarter of an hour before they were off again upon the Chalons road.

By the route they had chosen, which had the advantage that it was somewhat shorter and, what was of even more importance, less frequented than the main way through Château Thierry and Epernay, the distance before them to Chalons, the next large town, was somewhat over seventy miles. It would fill the whole morning and more. They fell to talking to one another with some little anxiety as to what might happen when Chalons, with its considerable population, its newspaper and its activity, was reached. But their immunity at Meaux, the advent of a pleasing, shaded and tolerable day, the remote countrysides through which they passed after branching off the main road at La Ferté, dulled their fears, or rather exorcised them. They fell to eating—a sort of picnic without plates, cutting their meat upon their bread, and drinking their wine from a cup passed round. No sunlight fell upon the green blind of the off-side window to fatigue their eyes; no reflections of excessive heat as the morning rose shone from the road upon the white velvet of the cushions: they were in comfort and at ease.

By eight they were upon the side-road they had chosen; by ten, at the hour when the peasants were reposing under the high quadruple rank of roadside trees, with their scythes at rest beside them, they came to the post of Viels-Maisons. They were behind their hour — a trifle — but they were by this time quite secure in mind. The governess had given the children air, and had walked with them up the long hill by which the road leaves the Marne valley. The pace had been hardly business-like, perhaps to save fatigue; the King had sauntered from the carriage more than once, to stretch his legs at the post-houses; there were even occasions upon which he had spoken to the little groups of peasants that surrounded the carriage as the new horses were put in. For a moment, indeed, some anxiety —

very probably baseless — had arisen amongst them at sight of a horseman who seemed to be following the carriages; the children and their governess, who were on the back seat, had noticed a rider far down the road behind them, but he turned off and was seen no more.

In the stables of Viels-Maisons was a postilion of the name of Picard; his action is worthy of note to anyone who would comprehend the nature of this journey, the emotions which it aroused in those who witnessed it, and the tangle of authority amid which the flight was driven. His action is worthy of note, especially to those who would see, as it is necessary to see, the Champenois peasantry who form the background of all the picture. He first, at this long distance from Paris, fifty miles and more, recognized the King.

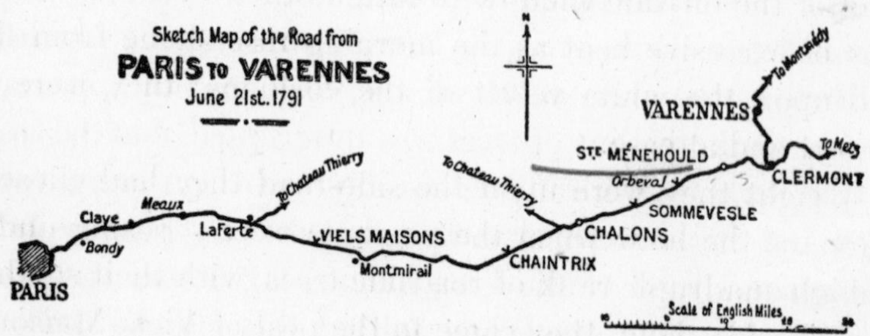

He might have sold the knowledge; he might have gambled on the royal family's success, have whispered his recognition, and have waited for his reward. He might have presupposed the final success of the National Government, and have taken immediate steps to earn its gratitude by denouncing the King: This peasant did none of these three things. He held his tongue.

The carriages rolled onward. At midday when, at one of the posting stations in that great bare, dusty plain, an isolated place, the King had strolled out again, in the interval of the harnessing, to joke with a knot of poor yokels and to give charity to them, Monstier, one of the Guards who were acting as drivers, ventured a timid remonstrance, and Louis said what should never be said within the hearing of the gods — that he was now safe from all accidents. When he had said this he continued to talk to the poor about him: he talked of their crops and of the hay that he saw tedding.

It is possible that some one of these wondered a little overmuch at the grand people; it is possible there had been rumours: but if any beggar or mower among them guessed, he also held his tongue — and the carriages rolled onward.

. . . .

The day, still veiled and moderate, was at its height; it was two o'clock, or a little later, when the road which had hitherto borne every mark of age, took on the appearance of new work, the line of trees was interrupted, and the stones of the kerb were clean and freshly sawn. A green valley, then but imperfectly drained, though but slightly below the general level of the Champagne, lay across its course. . . . An older track had skirted this marshy land, but for now six years the road had cut straight across the doubtful soil upon a great embankment, which was one of those new engineering works of which the reign, for all its financial embarrassment, had been full. Upon this embankment stood (and stands) the posting-house, and upon such a site little else could stand. There were at that time but two other roofs: a blacksmith's forge and a tavern. The post was called "the Petit Chaintry"; it is Chaintrix to-day, and a hamlet still. Here lived an elderly man, Lagny, a widower, with his daughters and one son-in-law, by name

Vallet, a dangerous lad, for he had travelled, and had been himself brought up in the noise and curiosity of an inn; nay, he had seen Paris, and had marched with the Federals upon the Champs de Mars the year before. Only rarely did Vallet visit his wife's home—but there is a fate and a God. In this lonely plain of Champagne where no one travels, where few then knew Paris, even, let alone the Court, this man happened on that one day to be at the stables of his father-in-law's posting-house; he happened also to be by nature—the nature of a townsman—garrulous and touched with melodrama. He recognised and worshipped the King. From that moment the secret was dissolved — and in loyalty perhaps half an hour was consumed.

No record remains of the spreading of the news, but proof remains of the result. Vallet insisted on riding himself upon the leaders; he rode hard, and twice he let his horses down, breaking harness; so that an hour perhaps was lost by his hard riding. Before even the berline and its attending cabriolet left Chaintry, Lagny and his daughters had been told. The royal family had not denied the recognition; they had even, in reward for the loyalty displayed, bestowed gifts upon the innkeeper. It is certain that the news must have spread through the countryside.

In such an atmosphere of recognition, nay, of open dependence upon the loyalty of those who knew them, they traversed the remaining twelve miles of road and entered Chalons, where alone they feared arrest and in whose crowds only detailed forethought and plan could have preserved them unknown. That plan and that forethought had been wholly absent; a vague instinct of its necessity had in the morning haunted the fears of the travellers, but now, after the safety and isolation of the many long hours from Meaux, it was forgotten.

They entered the big town at four o'clock; the two carriages drove clattering through its streets; they pulled up at the posting-house in the Rue St. Jacques. Viet, the post-master came out to see to the horses. A crowd gathered, and to every one in that crowd and to Viet, and to any one of the town who cared to ask, the presence of the King was perfectly well known. It was discussed with approval or disapproval; indeed, the journey would have ended here, but that Viet himself, true to the character of the peasant (for he was peasant-born), refused all risk. Officially he knew nothing; he would neither detain nor speed the King; he was obstinately silent. Whether Louis won, or his enemies, he, at least, would be safe.

As he was buckling the last of the fresh horses, a man dressed with care and with some appearance of wealth, approached him, and insisted upon what was, by the Constitution, his duty, but Viet gave him no change and was still silent. The man dressed with care and with some appearance of wealth, failing to move this very minor functionary, went off to the Mayor, Chorez by name; there was no time to lose; horses are unharnessed and others harnessed in but a little delay. The Mayor was as silent as Viet: he took refuge in that common excuse of temporisers and cowards—he demanded "proof." It is probable that the well-dressed man with some appearance of wealth went off upon the frontier road. We do not know, for we do not even know his name; but when a little before five o'clock the berline had halted a moment at the foot of a rise, surely it was the same man who passed it rapidly and muttered to the royal family as he passed: "You have planned ill!"

The town of Chalons lies upon the border of an extensive plain peculiar in French history. Here, as tradition will have it, Attila's army was destroyed by the Romans and the Barbarians whom the Romans had trained. It is a wide and desolate space, which the prosperity succeeding the Revolution has transformed, but which, as we watch it to-day from a distant height, still bears something of its ancient poverty — to the eye, at least — so level is it and so treeless. Far off to the eastward runs the wooded wall of Argonne, very faint and small; at the base of this, the town of Ste. Ménehould.

From Chalons to Ste. Ménehould, by the straight road bridging the plain, is a long day's march, twenty-five miles or more: and there is very little between. The passage of this bare, direct and dusty stretch was, the fugitives might imagine, the very last and the least of the risks they were to run. Chalons, which alone they feared, had not detained them, the emptiness of the countryside renewed, or rather rendered absolute their confidence. Within an hour they would be at the bridge of Somme-Vesle, an utterly deserted spot, with nothing but the stables of the post to mark it.

. . . .

At this point of their successful journey let the reader note in what order the guarding of the flight had been conceived by Bouillé.

The first stages of it — till beyond Chalons — were to be quite bare of soldiery, lest suspicion should arise and Paris receive the alarm; but once well past Chalons, the hundred miles and more accomplished, small posts of cavalry, mostly German mercenaries, were to be placed upon one pretext and another, at intervals along the way, until at *Varennes*, Bouillé's own son should meet the fugitives with his troop, and eastward from Varennes the remaining miles to Montmédy, which was their goal, they would need no special guard; they would be in the thick of Bouillé's army. The first of these small posts was one of German mercenary *Hussars* under the Duc de Choiseul, a nephew of the old statesman of Louis XV. It was to expect the King at Somme-Vesle at *one* — giving as its excuse for its presence escort for a convoy of bullion — but an exact keeping of the time-table was urgently necessary, for it would be perilous for the foreign troops to hang about indefinitely in these eastern villages.

It was at the lonely post-house of Somme-Vesle, then, that the first soldiers were to be looked for by the King; there, as it had been arranged, the first Hussars would be seen, posted upon the lonely road; these would close up immediately behind the carriage for a body-guard. With each succeeding stage of the shortening trial troop after troop would join that barrier and increase it, Dragoons at Ste. Ménehould, more at Clermont, till, before the evening gathered, the Royal Family would have between them and the National Government of Paris or the young patriots of the villages of the Marne, a guard of their own soldiers, an escort warding them into the heart of the frontier army that was to be their salvation.

The hour passed quickly — it was not yet six, when the King, who had watched with his old interest in maps every detail of the road, and had followed it with the guide-book upon his knee, heard the brake upon the wheels;

a slight descent ended, and the carriage drew up. A long farmhouse, with stable door and garden gate shut tight and with no head at a window, stood, French fashion, all along the kerb. They looked from the window, noted the desertion of the fields, the silence of the house, and the broad paved way, and asked with a growing anxiety what they feared to know, the name of the place.

The third Gentleman of the Guard, Valory, who had at each stage gone before them to have the horses ready, came to the door and told them it was the posting-house of Somme-Vesle: of soldiers not a sign; a few peasants, slouching off to the fields.

. . . .

Long before the King, with his delays of loyalty and his breakdowns, had reached Chalons, just upon three, under that veiled sky and upon a dip of that monotonous, dead straight, white road, close to the bridge and posting-house of Somme-Vesle, half a troop of Hussars were up and mounted. They were Germans, but their foreign gutterals were not heard by the sleepy ostlers of the place, for, in some disorder, the little knot of mounted men were at attention. At their head, upon his finer horse, sat Choiseul, and with him Aubriot, a lieutenant of Dragoons, and old Goguelat, used to commissariat, to organization, and to plans. They pointed westward up the Chalons road, looking along its right line between the parallel perspective of its trees. Choiseul especially strained his eyes to see whether no rising dust or no distant specks of a large vehicle and a cabriolet following might announce the advent of the King, but there was no sign upon the road. He had so sat his horse for hours.

It was eleven when his light travelling-carriage had

trotted up to the stables,[1] his German soldiery had joined him before noon, and by one, as the time-table of the plan had been given him, the berline should have been there.

Two o'clock passed. An anxious hour of waiting brought no news. Yet another hour of growing anxiety upon the soldiers' part, of growing suspicion in the inn. And now it was three o'clock; but there was no sign upon the road.

Already the hoofs of these fifty mercenaries had been clattering and pawing for three hours and more round and about the long white wall of the posting-house. The ostlers, the few and sleepy ostlers, were not fond of such visitors, nor were the peasants in the fields.

De Choiseul had much to think about beside the punctuality of the fugitives as he sat his horse there, straining his eyes along the road. The people of the place had asked him familiarly, in the new revolutionary manner, what this body of horse was for. They might have added: "Why was it foreign, mercenary horse?" Such a question was certainly implied. . . . Why had an army of the frontiers thrown out a point of its cavalry-screen towards its base against all the known rules of war, instead of towards the frontier which it was to line and defend? . . . If it was for orders or for manœuvring, why did they stick close to this one posting-house? . . . Troops, even unsuspected troops, had been known to commandeer food-stuffs without payment: and the peasantry were sullen.

All these things were passing in the minds of the French peasants there, and Choiseul, who was also French, knew what was passing through their minds. There was some-

[1] He had come from Paris, where he had made the last arrangements, and with him and in his carriage he had brought Leonard, the Queen's hairdresser. This garrulous fellow he had sent forward down the road to Montmédy, and his mysterious hints at important secrets did much to spread the news.

thing more: the countryside was armed. The Revolution had made of every village a tiny, ill-trained but furnished military post; of every market town a section with two guns and a team of gunners; of every city a rough volunteer garrison, with ammunition and with arms, without discipline for a campaign, but in a momentary scuffle possessed of the power to wound.

Had even this been all, what Choiseul did might not have been done; but it was not all. There had always been present in the minds of these officers upon the frontier the permanent indecision of fears of the King. The date of the flight had been postponed and postponed. Choiseul himself, who had been in Paris with the King twenty-four hours before, was aware of that indecision and those fears.

It was three, and half-past three, and later; it was four — and still nothing appeared. The road still lay empty and silent; the posting-house became, if possible, a trifle more curious; the group of peasantry increased: the men were hustled. Why did not these foreign soldiers unsaddle? What was the urgency? Choiseul had his reply ready, his casual piece of news: "They were expecting treasure, and he was ordered to furnish an escort." Why, then, let them trot up the road to meet it! . . . With every quarter of an hour the strain grew greater.

Four o'clock passed, and half-past four. It was for Choiseul to judge exactly (as it has been for how many another soldier commanding thousands where he commanded fifty) beyond what point resistance would mean disaster. From time to time a peasant crossed a distant field, bearing, perhaps, a message to his armed peers; from time to time an ostler would ask a question of one of the Hussars and disappear; bearing, perhaps, a message of his own, and Choiseul thought, "If the country was raised behind him, in Argonne, the King is cut off and lost!"

Among so many Germans a French soldier was easier of approach. The post-master of the place, lounging by, made up to speak to Aubriot. What he said was this: "So the King is expected to pass? . . . At least, the people are saying so." . . . He sauntered away.

It was near five. By Choiseul's watch it was a trifle later still. The situation could no longer be borne, and the moment for retreat had come. Ten to one the King had not started after all. . . .

As Choiseul left he saw that fresh horses were put into his travelling-carriage; he ordered into it his valet and the Queen's hair-dresser, Leonard, whom he had brought from Paris; he gave them a note which said that it had been necessary for him to abandon Somme-Vesle, and that, moreover, he doubted if the Treasure would come that day. He himself was going to rejoin the General, and new orders must be issued on the morrow. This note was to be *shown* to the officer in command at Ste. Ménehould, and *given* to the officer in command at Clermont. Thence they were to post for Montmédy. This note written and handed, open, to his valet and Leonard, Choiseul saw the carriage go; and when he had seen it well away he turned rein, ordered his weary Germans, and bent reluctantly eastward along the road which his command had traversed that morning.

So they rode back till, at Orbeval, Choiseul took a guide, crossed Neuville Bridge and plunged into Argonne, lest by following the highroad right into Ste. Ménehould they might raise that alarm which at every cost it was his duty to allay. . . . In vain. The country was already awake: that rumour, that something in the air which no historian has ever traced, had preceded him, and a woman in Ste. Ménehould had said to a soldier in a tavern that "the King would pass that way."

In this way was the post of Somme-Vesle abandoned. It was in the neighbourhood of half-past five when the cavalry marched out and up the slight eastern slope of the road; just hidden by the brow of hill behind them as they left the spot where they had waited it for so long, the King's berline had begun the last climb before the descent to the post-house. Fifteen minutes economised on the Royal Family's delays would have saved them.

. . . .

The berline waited, as it had waited so often that day; the horses were changed in as humdrum a fashion. Within the carriage a doubt had fallen on the fugitives. . . . It was a lonely house in a lonely dip of the plain with a vast, straight, empty road rising upon either slope before it and beyond. They drove on to Orbeval, but in a mood now changed; they passed Orbeval and approached the long hill-forest of Argonne.

It was already full evening; the clouds upon the western horizon had lifted; the reddening and descending sun shone for the first time that day against the rise of the Argonne woodland ridge and upon the bare, rolling folds of corn-land and of mown pasture at its base.

Under the level shafts of that sunset the belated berline approached Ste. Ménehould. They passed the lonely tavern upon the height called "At the Sign of the Moon"; they saw for a moment upon their left a mill not yet grown famous, the mill of Valmy; the shadows lengthened, and just as the sun disappeared they rattled full speed into the main square of the town.

The green blinds were up to admit the cool of the evening. The Queen looked from her window, without concealment, and saw the gossiping and curious crowd which a French town collects upon its public place at the end of day. She saw the soldiers—some of them, she thought, saluted; she saw their officer. He came up and addressed her respectfully, in his garlic-accent of Bearn. He certainly saluted fully, and she bowed her acknowledgment of the salute. She saw and heard no more, unless perhaps she saw, on the King's side and through the open window of it, a young man still heavy with the swagger of the dragoons (for he had served), and still insolent with the brave insolence of soldiers; clear in eye, hooked in nose, bronzed, short, alert and, as it were, itching for adventure. If she did see this figure, she saw it for but a moment: the horses were in, the whips were cracking, the carriage was on the move; he had thus for a moment passed her window, coming in from the fields, where he had been mowing; he had passed for a moment, and was gone. It was Drouet, the acting post-master of the place, and the son of the old post-master. He had noted that the yellow coach was huge and heavy; he had found just time to say to his postilions, "Don't kill the cattle"; then he had gone off: it was but a moment of time.

They were off, a top-heavy haystack of a thing, rolling full speed up the hill beyond the river, and right into the advancing darkness. As they went, rising high with the road, through the orchards and into the forest and the hills, they heard, far behind them one pistol shot, and then another, the distant noise of a crowd, high voices, and the shuffling of horse-hoofs. But the cries grew fainter, and they had soon left all far behind. They gained the complete silence of the high wood, under the stars. They began the ascent of Argonne.

But already in Ste. Ménehould all was known. The girl who had said "It was the King," was now but one of many. The popular Council had met, and hardly had it met, and hardly had the crowd outside in the square appreciated the rumour, when those came in from Neuville village who had an hour or two before watched the movement of Choiseul and his Hussars, and the retirement of the cavalry over the bridge of Neuville into the forest, seeking Varennes. Their report added certitude to the general clamour: "Choiseul and his Hussars had hung about the posting-house of Somme-Vesle for hours!" "They had taken a guide and were in the woods behind Ste. Ménehould at that moment." The troops in Ste. Ménehould itself must have the same purpose. There was no doubt at all it was the King. And to this news there was added news, that Choiseul and his Hussars were keeping in touch with the main road, scouting back from time to time, ready and watching.

The handful of cavalry at Ste. Ménehould were French, not German. When Leonard had passed through, half an hour before, and had shown Choiseul's note to the officer in command, that Captain had bid his men unsaddle and take their ease. They were now filled with the evening's fraternity and wine. There was an attempt to gather them against the townspeople. It failed. And as the twilight lessened one resolution after another was taken in the Town Hall, with the rapidity that marked the action of the Revolution everywhere, from Paris to the smallest village. The municipal drum beating and the tocsin noisy against the hills, vote after vote proceeded. The Captain of the troop was arrested; the troop itself disarmed. The despatch of a courier to pursue and intercept the King was decided, and that courier chosen and named.

It was upon young Drouet, for his horsemanship and his courage, that the choice fell. He took with him a companion, Guillaume, an innkeeper, such as he himself was, once a dragoon, as he himself had been; they saddled the last two horses left in the stable and thundered off up the long hill that rises from the town into Argonne, down the sharp ravine of the Islettes and onward along the great eastern road — the road to Metz — whither all thought the King was bound. An hour ahead of them on that same road rattled the cabriolet and rolled the huge berline.

There was a moon, but the clouds covered her. The darkness of this, the shortest night of the year, deepened for its brief hours, but there was still a glow in the north as they neared, towards ten o'clock, the post of Clermont. Drouet heard voices in the darkness before him; it was his own postilions on their way back from the end of the stage, and Drouet hailing them heard that the travellers, when the relay horses were harnessed, had given the order to leave the main Metz road, and to turn up northward to Varennes.

The military temper of this people! The halt had not lasted a moment, but in the moment Drouet had formed his plan.

He had not, it seemed, a stern chase before him, a mere gallop up the Metz road. The quarry had doubled and along its tracks were Guards. There were troops at Clermont as there had been at Ste. Ménehould; there would now be troops every few miles until the headquarters of the treason should be reached; it was his business to warn the citizens against Bouillé, to avoid the outposts of that commander, to cut by a corner way across the elbow ahead of the royal

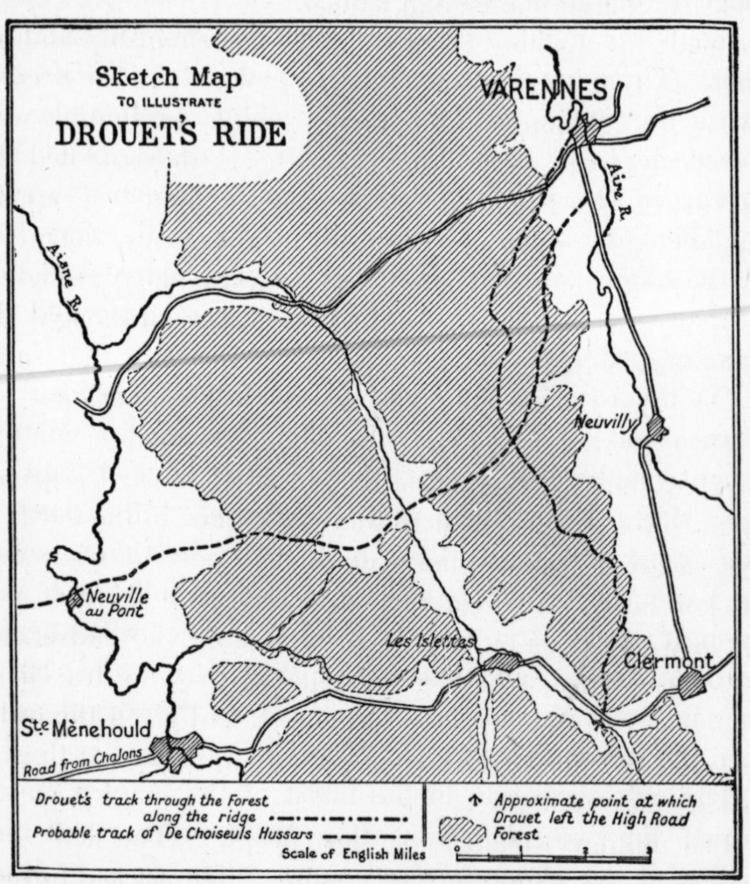

carriages, to intercept them and to thwart all. He took at once, therefore, to the wood upon his left; he took it where now the railway most nearly approaches the road, about half a mile beyond the level crossing — and plunged with his companion into its long, deep dries. He galloped up the steep to a farm he knew upon the summit, risking holes and fallen trunks of trees. Once there he followed, along the crest of the ridge, a green lane of immemorial age that runs along the summit. It was well past ten. Up on the ridge of the forest these two men galloped steadily and hard through the night, with high trees like a wall on either side. Three hundred feet below, upon the open plain that skirts the wood, the berline swayed at speed along the paved highroad. So the race ran. The fugitives slept unwarned and deeply as they drew on to Varennes through the silent darkness. On the hills above, with every beat of the hoof upon the turf, the two riders neared and they neared. Upon who should win that race depended the issue of civil war.

On the issue of that race all the future depended: all France and all Europe. The riders had eleven miles of rough woodland in the dark to cover, an hour at most for their ride. Below them on the highroad, with a start of two miles and more, their quarry was hurrying, rolling to Varennes. If the wheels and the smooth road beat them, it was Austria over the frontier, France without government, defeat, and the end of their new world; but if they in the woodlands beat the wheels on the smooth road, then the Revolution was saved.

Through a clearing in the midst of the tangled undergrowth the two riders saw before them, as they still rode furiously, the glimmer of a known white stone, a landmark; they sheered down a ride to the right: the wood ended abruptly, and they saw below them the lights of Varennes — one or two at that late hour, and the twinkle of the town lamps in the square of the town. The grasses of the forest were dull no longer under the anger of their ride: they clattered on a highroad for a moment, next in the narrow street of Blainville Hill. They came down upon the bridge head and saw the dark line of the river; they halted the sweating beasts and strained to listen. They heard no sound, except the panting of their mounts; there was no rumbling of wheels, no distant approach of riders, no noise of cavalry. It struck eleven as they waited so. They had been beaten, and the berline had already passed the town and its one bridge; or the wheels had not yet rumbled in, and they had won. It struck eleven as they waited so.

Guillaume crossed the bridge to the main square to see what he could find, whether indeed they had come too late, and whether between them and the fugitives was now cast abroad that compact screen of cavalry which had failed at Somme-Vesle and at Ste. Ménehould. Drouet stayed on the hither side of the bridge, inquiring among the taverns of the upper town if any had seen a large travelling-coach go by. It seems that no one had noticed such a thing. . . . Yet the berline was there.

He saw it suddenly, up the steep hill; he saw the two great lights of it, and he heard the postilions protesting that the stage was finished, that they were not bound to go down the hill, that their mistress at Clermont needed the horses early next morning for the carrying of her hay. But even in the midst of the discussion, though he could not see the horses in the darkness under the houses, he could hear the skid upon the wheels, and he knew that the heavy vehicle had begun to move. He ran down at once to a little inn called "The Golden Arm," burst in upon a group of rustic politicians, and warned them in one word that a large carriage would next moment go braked and sliding past; that carriage would hold, he said, the King, their public King — in flight for the frontier.

. . . .

The military temper of this people! Here were a handful of men in the black darkness of the now moonless night, with not five minutes in which to make the decision that should transform the whole polity in which they lived. Yet they saw in a flash — and Drouet saw clearest of them all — first, that the high town was not occupied with troops, and that therefore the commanding officers and those awaiting the King must be in the low town beyond the river; secondly, that but one communication connected the King and his rescuers, and that that communication was the narrow bridge across the Aire, the river of Varennes; thirdly, that they could gather in those few minutes no forces, even of the smallest, wherewith to hold the bridge, and that the least noise, until the bridge was held, would give the alarm.

There stood at the bridge head a great van for the removal of furniture, packed, with its pole upon the ground, waiting for the dawn, when it should be harnessed and started upon its road. In a moment they had drawn it across their end of the narrow bridge and blocked the approach. In the same moment certain of their companions had warned the officials of the town, and these, especially Sauce, the Procurator, saw to the rousing of every house upon the hither side of the river.

All this was done with such rapidity that the officials were astir, the bridge barricaded, and two men already armed, before the royal carriage had skidded half-way down the hundred yards of hill. At that point an archway running under an old church blocked the road; at that archway the two armed men posted themselves, and just as the outrider of the fugitives had come into the narrow pass, the challenge was given which ended the hopes of the Monarchy. For the two sentries thus improvised challenged, the outrider dismounted, voluble, the horses of the cabriolet were thrown back upon their haunches, the huge coach-and-six behind it slithered somehow to a stop upon the steep road, and the Queen suddenly realised that the crash and the disaster had come. She heard the threat to fire. She looked from her window, as the Duchess fumbled for the passports, and uttered one of those phrases memorable in history for their anti-climax: she begged the gentlemen who had stopped them to go through the formalities quickly, *as she was desirous of reaching the end of her journey as quickly as might be.*

The two armed men had increased now to eight; to this little group was added a German soldier or two wandering aimlessly upon leave, uncommanded and perfectly drunk. The ladies in the cabriolet had got out and had been thrust into the inn; but even when matters had gone so far, that incertitude and fear of responsibility, which had saved the family thrice already in their flight, all but saved them again. The passports seemed regular, and had it not been for the wild energy of Drouet, his threats and his violence, the journey would have proceeded, the van would have been rolled back from the bridge, the relay of horses in the square of the lower town would have been harnessed, Bouillé's own son, who had been waiting in a hotel beyond the river all day and was waiting there now in the dark, expectant, would have accompanied them out of the borough. . . . With the dawn, which was now not two hours off, the vanguard of Bouillé's cavalry would have ensured their safety forever. But Drouet stormed, shouted perpetually the words "High treason!" and gained all that he desired, which was delay. "If there were any doubt," said Sauce, "to wait for morning would do no harm. The horses needed rest, the night was dark." He lifted the lantern in his hand and put it closely and curiously into the face of the Queen: "You must get down, Madame; you must get down." He would not endorse the passport until the morning.

Even during the few words of this conversation, the crowd had continued to increase, and with the crowd the armed men. It occurred to the King to command; he did it paternally, with a "Now, then," and a "Come, come," bidding the postilions go forward. Nothing happened. He looked out of the window and saw that the postilions had dismounted, and there came again, now from a great number of levelled muskets, the threat to fire. There was but one faint and last chance against discovery: to pretend no more than an inconvenience, and to do as they were bid.

The family got down wearily (for twenty-four mortal hours they had been cramped upon that journey), entered the house of Sauce the Procurator, just opposite, and waited for the morning. Meanwhile in the street outside the clamour of Ste. Ménehould was repeated, the tocsin sounded and the drum, and the men of the town armed by tens and by hundreds, and at last all the population, children and old men and women, were crowding the street, and filling it with perpetual noise.

It was not yet light when the Hussars, Choiseul and his Hussars, came blundering out of the wood. Mercenary troops have great advantages. If the troops are foreign the advantages are greater still; but a disadvantage attaches to such troops, which is the need of interpreters. They could understand nothing of what was going on around them, they could not understand the speech that was made, urging them to save "their" King.

They were ordered to charge, and did so, clearing the street, and they formed after the short charge in front of the mean house which held the royal family. There could be no further doubt in the townsmen's minds; it was indeed the King.

The Hussars and the King and the Queen, his gaolers, the Municipality, all were in a general agreement that with dawn the royal family should continue its journey. But meanwhile the incalculable element, the populace, swelled out of all knowledge. When the first light showed in the streets far more than the population of Varennes was there. They poured in from the countrysides; the men going to the fields to catch the grass with their scythes before the dew was off it heard the news and came; those coming in for market to the lower town heard the news and came; the Men of the Forest came. And the rumour that Bouillé was on the march with his army, at the head of the hired German cavalry, did but increase the crowd.

It was full day. For a second time under the increasing menace the Hussars were ordered to charge. They hesitated, and against them, now in rank, were the armed men of the local National Guard. The sun had risen. Goguelat tried to force his way forward, trusting that if he did so his Hussars would follow. But these looked on in a kindly German way, bewildered, and the officer of the National Guard shot Goguelat, who fell from his horse. The crowd, already morally impassable for its determination and its arms, was now physically so. All down the street to the bridge and all round, up the courts and alleys, one could see nothing but the crowd; and the proportion of Militia uniforms among them, the number of bayonets that showed above their shoulders, increased as the hours passed, as four o'clock struck, and five, and six.

The King's green coat had been seen a moment at the window; the cheers that met it (for they were cheers, not groans) were now swelled by the voices of some ten thousand armed men, and already the cry was raised "for Paris." . . . Already had the scouts of Bouillé's Uhlans appeared far off upon the sky-line of the eastern hills.

He could never have passed the bridge in time. Nothing but artillery could have cleared the town. The general and popular decision was made and grew; no discipline, no individual command could meet it. The cry of "Paris" filled the air, now with a meaningless noise, now with a comic rhythm, such as impatient audiences make in theatres or soldiers on the march. There were negotiations, but with every mention of "Montmédy," the shout of "Paris" grew louder.

The couple of guns, which the National Guards of the town were allowed by law, had at their head, as was only right, a gunner. It was this gunner who brought the good news out at last and said that the King had consented to return.

By seven the whole swarm of thousands, with the berline wedged in the midst, were off back westward again upon the Paris road, a vast dust about them, songs, and — what is more curious — speed, but a speed which was soon crushed under the pressure of such a multitude. As they lost the horizons of Varennes, the last sight they saw behind them was the main body of Bouillé's German cavalry as it came over and formed upon the hill beyond the river, baffled. By ten, in a violent heat of the sun, the throng had crawled to Clermont; the first, the only doubtful and the fatal stage of the capture and the return was accomplished.

. . . .

What had happened that the King's mind should change? For all those hours in Varennes every official had desired the continuation of the journey; all the "responsibles" had withstood the growing anger of the populace, when suddenly, Radet, the gunner, had announced a capitulation, and, almost as suddenly, within the half-hour before seven, after all those dark and morning hours of delay, the King had consented to return.

What had happened was this: Two men had come with authority from Paris, from the Parliament — Bayou and Romeuf were their names; they had reached Varennes in the morning, the first exultant, the second reluctant; each came burdened with that Authority by which the French live, and both had entered the house of Sauce. The Queen had stormed, and had dashed their written message of Authority to the ground, but even the reluctant Romeuf had picked it up and laid it again reverently before her. Authority by which the French live lay now in the National Parliament. It was this which compelled the King. To this he had yielded.

. . . .

The military temper of this people!

The Parliament learnt the flight of the King at about eight or nine o'clock in the morning following that midnight adventure. Bayou was commissioned to "pursue, capture, and report" in the forenoon of that day the 21st of June.

He started eleven hours behind the King. The King, driven by Fersen, had passed the barriers of Paris, as we have seen, just after midnight of the 20th.

It was close on noon when Romeuf had shot like an arrow through the Porte St. Martin, galloping hell and leather along the great frontier road. Louis was at Chaintry then, *fifty miles* ahead. An hour after Bayou, Romeuf, who had been sent also, followed upon another trail: he was a royalist and hated the job, but he obeyed orders; at last he caught the right scent from witnesses and rumour, and was thundering off with a heavy heart, but a soldier, down the same way.

Bayou rode and he rode, a ride to test his breeches. Seventy miles, eighty miles, is a ride for any man. Bayou, relaying at every post and covering, in between, his fifteen miles an hour or more, galloped into Chaintry just before six in the evening, and there at Chaintry — where at midday Louis and Marie Antoinette had graciously revealed themselves to old Lagny — Bayou found a suspicious man, one De Briges, very evidently employed to follow and to aid the fugitives. Bayou dismounted, held that man prisoner, and dined, but not before he had sent on, by his written Authority, Lagny's boy helter-skelter up the road to rouse Chalons beyond.

Romeuf was less speedy, but a fine rider for all that. He was an hour behind Bayou, he reached Chaintry on account of missing the scent at starting two hours behind him, when Bayou, having dined and sent forward that messenger, was already off in a carriage to Chalons following the trail. They met at Chalons — a town all informed and astir — thence forward, the two together, Bayou eager, Romeuf in despair for his friends (but discipline constrained him), drove — not rode, past the bonfire glare and howling of Ste. Ménehould, all night through Argonne, till by morning they came — with their Authority — to Varennes.

And in this day and night of hard-riding Frenchmen, a third must be mentioned: Mangin, druggist and lawyer of Varennes, had galloped from Varennes at dawn, had left his horse collapsed at Clermont, had relayed and relayed, still riding, urging back to Paris to give news to the Parliament.

He passed in a flash the carriage of Bayou, careless of it; long before six he was at Ste. Ménehould, changed horse, was off to Orbeval, changed horse, was off to Somme-Vesle, changed horse, was off to Chalons, riding and riding hard, nearly fifty miles and not yet eight o'clock. He ate and drank and mounted, re-horsed, and on: what skin! All the long road all day, gallop and change and gallop under the sun: twelve hours in the saddle when he came to the deep Marne, sixteen when he dashed into Bondy. . . . A companion, who had met him, rode on to share his triumph. . . . Mangin shook him off. . . . The suburbs of Paris . . . the barrier — eighteen hours of it before he got his foot to ground and staggered into the Assembly! Lord! what a ride!

It was ten at night; the hundreds of candles guttered and glimmered over a handful of exhausted men upon the benches of the Parliament; Mangin handed his message to the Chair, and his ride was done. Good Lord, what a ride!

. . . .

Beauharnais was in the Chair: remarkable for this, that his widow married Napoleon.

Beauharnais read the message: "The King was taken!"

As Parliaments go that Parliament was drastic and immediate; it came to its conclusion in two hours — a space of time that meant thirty miles to a courier. It nominated, somewhat after midnight, three commissioners: Barnave, Pétion, Maubourg — of the centre, of the left and of the right — and with them Damas for military orders. Each young, each growing in fame — Barnave and Pétion already famous — they left together with the morning.

It was Thursday, Corpus Christi. Every village of the Marne Valley was garlanded and upon holiday, the church doors stood open to the humming air of midsummer, the peasants, most of them at games, some few in procession or coming out from Mass, upon that great feast made every stage of the road alive; as the sun rose to noon, the population of the villages on either slope of the river valley poured in like rivulets down the chalky lanes, swelling the mob upon the great highway. By the afternoon the throng had so largely increased that the carriage of the Parliamentary Commissioners could no longer go at the trot, it was walked, as was walked, surrounded by a larger, dustier, much fiercer crowd, that other carriage, the berline, which was crawling to meet them across the flat miles of Champagne.

The hills grew higher, the dale narrower, as their slow progress brought them past Dormans, and gradually, with the multitude about them, to Mareuil. The setting sun was on the famous vineyards and on the fringe of forest far above: they were anxious, perhaps, whether they would meet the returning fugitives while yet it was light, and so be spared the risk of confusion and perhaps disaster in the darkness.

But that meeting could not now be far off. Rumour

first, then couriers, going before the gradual advance of the King's captors announced his advent, and the three Commissioners wondered what they would see. Reports had already moved them, true details in the midst of much fable, of invasion and of fancied massacres and fires . . . the mob at Chalons, the sleepless night of consultation, the irruption of a violent militia from Rheims, the terrible slow march on the Epernay road with its jeers and anger and threats of death; the violent jostle at Epernay itself — the fear that the prisoners might never reach the capital. They had heard composedly of these things, with clearer and clearer detail as the later passages of the long agony were given: they were now very near the meeting.

The hot day had fallen to its end, and evening was come quite pure over the high plateaus that bound the valley; it was darker upon the water-meadows of the valley floor when they saw before them, a long way off, the dust, and heard the noise, when they came near and smelt the incalculable crowd that roared round the carriages of the King.

The advent of the Commissioners of Parliament threw an abrupt silence over the French, ever avid for worship: these three dissimilar men, one of whom alone approached greatness, were taken as transubstantiate with the National power. In such an attitude, near the doors of the berline, in the centre of the compact thousands that were massed, hats off and reverent in gaze, between the hillside and the river, Pétion read the Decree of the Assembly.

With excuses upon their part and voluble instance from the King, Pétion and Barnave managed to get themselves into the carriage, for the Queen took the Dauphin on her knee, the Princess stood before her aunt, and Pétion decorously straightened between the Duchesse de Tourzel

PÉTION

and Madame Elizabeth, faced Barnave, who sat, more generously large between the King and Queen.

At last the Commissioners could watch that driven group. Three nights without sleep, two of agony; three days, one of flight, two of intolerable heat, insult, violence, and a snail's-pace progress, had left them feverish, and yet — as sufferers are when all is quite abnormal — interested in tiny things, and careless. Their linen was dirty in the extreme— the Queen's grey dress stained, torn, and roughly mended, the King's brown coat a very dusty brown; but their faces were clean — they had washed at Epernay — and they were not unlively.

It got darker and darker; the noise of the crowd outside calmed a little, though from time to time a great rustic head would lumber in at the window to stare at royalty. The Queen, who had talked rapidly from the moment she had seen her deliverers, Madame Elizabeth, who had caught and pressed Pétion's arm and clung in a foolish ecstasy of terror, kept up a ceaseless chatter — and the King, against his wont, joined in. They had not meant to leave the country — far from it. "No" (from the King); "I said so positively. Did I not?" (appealing to his wife). "We are really anxious about the three Guardsmen. We went to Mass at Chalons this morning — but it was constitutional, I assure you." Only once did the reserve of an earlier (and a later) time appear upon the Queen; it was when Barnave hinted that one of the men on the box was Swedish, when Pétion added that the man who had driven the coach from the Tuileries was a Swede — called? . . . he pretended to hesitate about the name: the Queen had said, "I am not in the habit of learning hackney coachmen's names," and, after saying it, was, for perhaps the first time in two hours, silent. Then she forgave them — forgave Barnave at least — and talked on in lower tones. She was getting to like Barnave. The little boy, playing with the buttons on Barnave's coat, made out the letters on them. "It says 'we will live free or die.'" He was proud to read such small letters so well. He repeated the phrase, but no one of his elders answered him.

Pétion, upon the back seat, felt an arm upon his in the darkness. He remembered the same arm as it held him close when he had met the berline two hours before. He saw under the moonlight the white and small hand of Madame Elizabeth lying near his, and it occurred to him[1] that this very pious, very narrow, very distant girl either suddenly loved him or feigned love in order to corrupt his republican ardour — for he was already republican.

It is objected with indignation that women of birth do not so demean themselves with country lawyers. The indignation is fatuous, but the objection is well founded. Women of birth have indeed so profound a repugnance for his class that even the bait of a great fortune, though it often compels them to a marriage, will hardly overcome the loathing, and if they must yield to passion it is more commonly to favour a groom than a solicitor. But this woman had no such frailties. She was saintly, foolish, well bred and bewildered. She may have made herself as pleasant a companion as it was in her power to be, for by such easy arts the rich, when they fall, will always try to appease their conquerors. More than that she certainly did not do. The Queen knew better in what way to command her captors; she fixed upon Barnave, and within the first day of their companionship she had drawn him from that other camp into hers.

---

[1] He has recorded this sensation at length in print.

They slept at Dormans — so much as they could sleep with the mob howling all night in the square outside. Next day, Friday, the third of that return, the fourth of that martyrdom, they continued the Paris road. The day was yet hotter than the yesterday had been, and the violent and the out-o'-works from Paris began to join the crowd. At evening the tower of Meaux stood up before them against the red sky.

There, at Meaux, Marie Antoinette took a turn with Barnave; long, quiet looks, a familiar and continued conversation, a stroll in the garden alone and decent confidences during the night, finally captured Barnave. He was, from the moment of their return to Paris, the Queen's.

He suffered no conversion in opinion, he did not forget his early political principle, he simply became indifferent to it and a servant of something that lived and suffered and exercised also upon some few — and he was one — a charm, perhaps of voice, perhaps of carriage, but, at any rate, of sex.

He worked henceforward absolutely for Marie Antoinette. He achieved so little that his name will hardly appear again in this record of her fall, but his name should be retained as a proof of what she still was to men.

He has long been accused of treason. He would have told you that he betrayed a formula, a phrase, to be the more loyal to a soul and body which he had come, as by a revelation, to understand. But Barnave was wrong: not to bodies or things, but to ideas, are men rightly subject: religion resides in dogma: loyalty must express itself in a creed, and the Word is God. These reasonings against reason, these preferences of the thing to the idea, are dangerous to honour.

Henceforward Barnave was near her always: advised her secretly, wrote to dictation from her lips: ran risk and peril, and at last died by the same hands which had killed her also upon the scaffold.

This bishop's Palace at Meaux, the halls that Bossuet had known, was their last resting-place. The sun was well up, it was already warm when they left the town for the slow stretch of thirteen hours to Paris.

The weather would not change. The same intense and blinding heat pursued and tortured them; but it was now less tolerable than ever, both from the length to which the strain had been spun out, and from the increasing crowds which lined the old paved road in a wider and wider margin as they neared the capital. The flat hedgeless fields seemed covered with men — as the prisoners saw it through their low windows — to the horizon. The murmur beyond had swelled into a sort of permanent roar, which mixed with the songs and cries of the few hundred that still kept pace with the carriages, and now that they had left the valley of the Marne and entered the dry plain that bounds Paris to the north, the drought and the dust were past bearing. The approach of evening afforded them no relief. At the gate of the city, where at least they might expect the contrast of the familiar streets and the approach to repose, they were disappointed. The driver had orders to skirt the barrier round to the western side. So for some two hours more this calvary dragged on: the ragged marchers themselves were exhausted, many clung to the sides of the coach. Some few had climbed upon its roof and jeered and threatened those three Guards, who sat silent in their yellow liveries not replying, awaiting their chance of escape at the end of this endless journey.

BARNAVE

When the last slope into the town was climbed, the travellers, as they crossed the flat summit where is now the Triumphal Arch of Napoleon, could see at last before them, beyond lines of trees and about the innumerable heads, the windows of their palace sending back the evening light in a blaze, and to the left that huge oblong roof of the riding-school where sat the Parliament.

Meanwhile, as the berline passed the barrier the bellowing and the songs, the tramping and the press of moving poverty, white with dust and parched to drunkenness, ceased suddenly. It was like a stream of anarchy breaking against that curious homogeneity of attitude and clear purpose which marked the capital upon every principal day of the Revolution and cut it off sharply from the provinces and even the suburbs around.

This new and purely Parisian crowd which they now entered, silent, dark-coated and with covered heads — largely of the middle class — thronged all the length of the Champs Élysées and packed the Place de la Concorde. The myriad fixed eyes of it saw the convoy show black against the western light upon the summit of the hill; they watched it creeping down the avenue between the double line of soldiery, each section of which, as the King passed, reversed arms as at a funeral soldiers reverse arms.

There was no sound. The spontaneous discipline which makes Paris a sort of single thing, living and full of will, so controlled this vast assemblage that neither a cry was raised nor a hat lifted. The note of the whole was silence.

During the full half-hour of that long approach down the hill this silence endured; the carriage was at the gates of the Tuileries Gardens, had entered them. Within the riding-school, the *manège* where sat the Parliament, to benches that rapidly emptied as the curiosity of the Deputies drew them away, Fursy was droning out a report upon fortified places of the first, the second, and the third class. Outside, the crowd still denser but silent as ever, the berline passed and the sections saluted — a reversed salute, on either side; it was within a furlong of its goal when, from a platform outside the Parliament building, a young member of the Royalist right drawing himself well up that he might be observed, lifted his hat and very gravely and pronouncedly made obeisance to the Crown.

The spell was broken. There was a scuffle, a hubbub, a general war; the slowly moving crowd crested into weapons as a deep swell at sea will crest into foam. The postilions of the berline urged their horses; a hundred yards to go, and the hedge of soldiery was forced and the mob was upon the carriage. The three Guardsmen sat still untouched, with death upon them; but the horses floundered through the deafening cries and strugglers, trampling and rearing; the great vehicle was hauled and piloted in; the wrought-iron gates clanged behind it. It was past seven and the journey was ended.

A week had gone. On Monday night they had watched with Fersen; all Tuesday fled; on Wednesday night and morning suffered at Varennes, and in the slow drag-back to Chalons; on Thursday at Epernay met the Commissioners, all Friday suffered their captivity till Meaux was reached— and now, as the light of Saturday began to fall, the hunting was over.

XV

THE WAR

FROM SATURDAY, JUNE 25, 1791, TO HALF-PAST EIGHT ON THE EVENING OF JUNE 20, 1792

A MAN, callous or wearied by study, might still discover in the pursuit of History one last delight: the presence in all its record of a superhuman irony. In Padua, where the Polignacs had taken refuge with their loot, the Emperor Leopold, returning from Tuscany, was at that moment their host and guest. With them and their circle he discussed the enormities of the French and the approaching escape of his sister and the King; for he was cognisant of that plan; he knew that since the death of Mirabeau the idea of relying upon French arms against the Parliament had been abandoned, and that an invasion by foreign allies was the scheme of the Court.

Leopold certainly designed, when the first part of that scheme was accomplished and the King was in safety on the frontier, to strengthen the royal armies with his own and to advance upon the Revolution. Varennes, I repeat, was everything. The King once free of Paris, and the armies would have been over the frontier. The King a captive in Paris, and compelled to pose as the acting and national Executive, war was another matter. The French nation could act as one force.

So insecure and dilatory were the communications of the time that for a whole fortnight nothing but guesses reached

Padua. Upon the second of July these guesses urged Leopold to write; but at last, upon the 5th, a fortnight after the flight, came definite and official news. The King had succeeded. He was safe in Metz with the army of Bouillé. The Queen was safe beyond the frontier in Luxembourg.

Leopold sat down and wrote at once a sort of pæan, a cry of triumph and of immediate action, and offered his treasury, his army, his everything to his sister for the immediate march against the French people.

She, in Paris, watched and guarded every way, had found it possible to write to Fersen two notes which, when he destroyed these many monuments of her love for him, he copied with his own hand. Her main preoccupation is that he should not return by stealth. She tells him he is discovered, and that his part in the flight is known; she begs him to keep safe. But it is probable or certain from one phrase in these notes that in the bitter anger of the moment she desired to be rescued by a chivalry under arms, and would appeal to war.

That determination in turn she abandoned, and from the month of August onwards until nine months later, the armed struggle began, one plan, lucid, and especially lucid when one considers that it proceeded from so imperfect a judgment as hers, possessed her and was continually expressed: she demanded a congress backed by arms, the immediate threat of a vast but silent force, and no word of hostilities. Nevertheless and largely, as we shall see, through her, war came. It came with the spring and these few months after Varennes are but the lull before the noise of the first guns.

I would here admit into the text of this book one of those discussions which, in History of a living sort, should but rarely be admitted, and belong rather to an appendix.

I admit it because a conclusion upon it is vital to any comprehension of the Queen and of the European position which ended in the struggle between France and Europe.

No historical quarrel has been more warmly debated than this. Did the old society, notably the Germanies, and at last all the privileged of Europe, down to the very merchants of the city of London, attack the Revolution to destroy it? Or did the Revolution break out in a flame against them, and compel them to the action they took and to the generation of war which ended in Waterloo?

In the current negation of morals the question has been thought by many to lack reality. Yet such is the nature of man that if he cannot give a human answer upon the matter of right and wrong, and a decision upon his *motive*, all his action turns to dust, and he can neither approve nor disapprove any human act. Now when man can neither approve nor disapprove, things cease to be, so far as his intelligence is concerned; and without morals even his senses are dead. Therefore is it, and has it always been, of supreme importance to every great conflict of History that the one side or other should justify itself in motive. And therefore has this discussion raged around the origins of the Great War.

There is one sense in which the debate can never be resolved. It can be argued for ever as a metaphysical proposition; just as a man may argue whether a spherical surface is concave or convex, and fall at last into mere legomachy, so it may be eternally debated as to which of the two combatants was legitimately defending his existence. It is evident that both were in this position.

Again, there is a fruitless and eternal debate opened if we are to consider separately every chief personality concerned.

Did Brissot really want war? Did Danton want it? Did the Emperor want it? Did Berlin want it? Did Spain? Did the King, Louis? Did Dumouriez? The varying ignorance of each character named, the varying intensity of the emotions and necessities of each, the divergence of particular objects in each individual case make such a synthesis impossible. But if one looks at the field in general and considers the common action of men between the return from Varennes and that April day when Louis was compelled to read out the Declaration of War before the French Parliament, a true picture, I think, arises in the mind, which — when, if ever, the Revolution ceases to incline to judgment — will be the final judgment of History. It is as follows:—

All desired war: all feared it. All attempted to postpone it. But, as all energy of its nature polarises, these energetic hatreds and fears gathered round two centres. The one in France had for its heart the young men from the south and all their group, soon to be called the "Girondins," who, when the new Parliament gathered at the close of the summer of Varennes, rapidly came to lead it. These men, Gallic in temper, more and more desired to bring to the issue of arms sooner rather than later what they thought must end — could not but end — in war. Round this clear opinion, by the time winter had come, what was living and active in France increasingly gathered. It is a phenomenon repeated a hundred times in the history of the French people. We shall certainly see an example of it in our own generation. The hand once upon the hilt of the sword draws it.

Over against this current of opinion the Emperor (Marie Antoinette's brother), the King of Prussia, the English

Oligarchy. The Spanish Bourbons also tended to war; their decision was not due to an increase of determination—they were determined on the main question all along—but to the gradual settlement of details long in negotiation between them. These details settled, and the mutual suspicions and jealousies of the Allies sufficiently though partially appeased, the privileged bodies of Europe certainly marched against France, and to the Girondin crusade was opposed something which was intended not to be resistance but rather a rapid and successful act of police. The thing had got to end, and, though the Powers only crossed the frontier in the succeeding summer, all the Courts of Europe and all the privileged bodies of the old Society were contented and glad that the fight was on. Nor were any more contented than the governing class in England, who had helped to engineer the campaign and who could not but reap the fruit of it, though it was profoundly to their interest not to bring into the field the insufficient armed forces at their command.

In the appreciation of this situation an element must be remembered without which the modern student goes all astray. The Allies were bound to win. We to-day, looking back upon those amazing twenty years, forget that truth. Valmy, though still almost inexplicable, has happened, and we take it for granted. The long straggling regiments of Napoleon, the butchers' boys turned generals, the vulgarian dukes and marshals, the volunteer gunners and the rest of it, won; and their victory is now part of the European mind. In that winter before the war broke out, as '91 turned into '92, it was not so.

The elements obvious to every thinking man, especially to the cold and therefore profoundly insufficient judgment of alien observers in Paris itself (of such coxcombs as Gouverneur Morris, for instance), were elements which made the final and rapid defeat of the Revolution certain, and gave that approaching defeat all the qualities of what I have called it, an act of police. The Allies might be jealous and suspicious one of the other, but there can be no doubt once an accord was come to — and it was reached in the early months of '92— that against the anarchy into which the French people had fallen, and the hopeless indiscipline of their swollen armies, the operations of the invaders would soon become but a series of executions, and a summary and severe suppression of armed mobs. The enthusiasm of the Girondins, and soon of all France, was the enthusiasm of rhetoricians and that self-doubting expectation of the impossible which is proper to inebriate moods. Nor was there one commander of experience west of the Rhine who anticipated victory for the French, nor one commander east of the Rhine who dreaded the failure of the Kings. It was mere sound— as poetry and music are mere sound — that urged the French to war. And those who in theory combated the policy of war, of whom Robespierre was the most remarkable, those who, from their concrete experience, desired to fend it off (with the army in such a state! with the military temper of the people so hopelessly wild!) that is, you may say, every general officer — foresaw at the best some sort of compromise whereby the Revolution would end, after some few battles lost, in some sort of a Limited Monarchy. It was the appetite for a Limited Monarchy which made so many acquiesce in such a campaign in spite of the certainty of defeat. It was the fear that the great ideal of the Revolution might tail off into a Limited Monarchy that made the most ardent democrats oppose the policy of what could not but be a disastrous war.

Meanwhile, during the earlier months of this development, the French nobles who had crossed the frontier (the Émigrés), and notably the brothers of the King, were an element of peril to either side, lest, a small and irresponsible body, they should provoke hostilities before either side demanded them. The Émigrés were active because they had nothing to lose, and careless of this moment because for them negotiation was unnecessary. To restrain this activity was the chief anxiety of the great interests which were slowly coalescing into that invincible instrument of war whose mission it was to restore order under the King of Prussia and the Duke of Brunswick. As the months proceed, as the coalition forms, this disturbing element is of less and less importance. In the early summer of '92, when war is once declared, the Émigrés fall into line with the rest of the Allies; and when the invading army crosses the frontier, the Émigrés cross with it in the natural course of things and merge in the general flood.

. . . .

Such was the general development of the European situation between the month of July, 1791, and the month of April, 1792.

What, during that period, was the particular disposition of the Queen?

She was very active. She had determined upon a lucid plan, and of all the brains that were thinking out how and when, if ever, the struggle should come, hers was perhaps the most tenacious of its purpose.

We have a dozen letters of hers between the return from

Varennes and the end of the year. One of great length, written to her brother in September, is accompanied by a memorandum and exactly details her plan. With the exception of two which were written, as a blind, for publication, and which in a private note she ridicules and disowns, every word she writes is consistent with her thesis. She proposes that the International Congress should be called. In her later letters she begs that it may be called near the frontier, as for instance, at Cologne. Before it is summoned, and during its session, there must be gathered an overwhelming military force ready to invade at once. But not a syllable must be breathed that could be taken as menace. In this plan Marie Antoinette was considering the personal safety of her husband and her child; and the whole theory of the action she advised pivoted upon a certain conception of the French people which was now so fixed in her mind that nothing could dissolve it; her theory was that the French were not a military people; that they spent energy in words, and that before a plain evidence of force they would always give way; she carried that theory of hers, little as it later accorded with the brute facts of actual war, unmodified to the scaffold.

I have repeatedly insisted in this book upon the inability of Marie Antoinette to perceive the French mind. As a young woman her misconception of her husband's people dealt with no more than personalities, ladies' maids, duchesses, and the rest. When Gaul moved, and when she began her attempt at power in 1787, along through the communal millioned action of the Revolution, this misconception became a strong creed, a vision as it were. She saw the French people intensely active, cruel, cowardly, and unstable: much in them of the cat and the fox, nothing of the eagle. She perceived their great mobs and their sudden united actions — but these phenomena were to her sporadic; she saw them — she did not reason upon them, nor argue from them some peculiar regimental talent in the populace; and if you had told her that these appearances of marching thousands were due to a power of organisation from below — a national aptitude for the machinery necessary to arms and to diplomacy — the words would have seemed to her simply meaningless. She could not so much as conceive humanity to be capable of organisation save by the direct action of a few placed above it.

Of military qualities she understood nothing. She confused order, silence, and similarity of buttons with discipline. She had no conception of ferocity as the raw material of valour. Safe out of Paris she would without a moment's hesitation have ordered the invasion, and she would have expected its successful issue in less than six weeks. Even in Paris she would have bargained to conquer with a "whiff of grape-shot" or some such rubbish; but in Paris, without one regiment to hand *and without regular artillery*, she felt that the very bodies of her family were in peril from "monsters and from tigers" — the words are her own: hence only did she hesitate and demand an armed congress rather than an invasion. To that armed congress and its menace she had no doubt at all that the French would yield.

A metaphor will explain the situation clearly. A human being, caught by some fierce animal but not yet mauled, appeals in a whisper to a comrade near by to load, and, if possible, by some demonstration of human force or of will to make the wild best loose its hold; he begs that comrade to do nothing merely provocative lest the animal should rend him upon whom it has pounced: but, of course, that comrade is to fire at the first active gesture of attack the brute may deliver. Of the ultimate victory of his armed comrade the man in peril feels there can be no doubt at all; he only advises a particular caution on account of his own situation and impotence.

Moreover, she was convinced, and says it in so many words, that the French would give way at once before the presence of a great and silent but determined force upon their frontier.

So clear is the plan in her mind that she is bitterly impatient of the necessary caution and delay of diplomacy, and of the long process of negotiation whereby Berlin is brought into the agreement, the tergiversations of Madrid are discounted and the exact balance between desire for war and power to wage it are sounded. Here and there the peevishness of her early womanhood appears in the complaints she makes, almost as though she had been abandoned by her brother and his armies.

At last, in February, 1792, this long correspondence is ended. The French nation has, upon the whole, accepted, its young rhetoricians enthusiastically acclaimed the approach of war. She, true to her plan, proposes that her brother shall meet this growing enthusiasm by positive demands, definitively formulated, dealing with the internal affairs of the French people, proceeding from Vienna and demanding instant reply. We now know that she herself drafted these demands, and on the 16th of February Mercy writes to tell her that the Emperor will order the French Parliament to maintain French Monarchy, in its full rights and liberty, to withdraw the French armies from the frontier, to respect the imperial rights of the Alsatian feudatories; and that he will at once back up this ultimatum with an additional force, beyond that already gathering, of 40,000 men. She acknowl-

ce 8 7bre

qu'il y a longtems mon cher frere que je n'ai pû
vous ecrire, et cependant mon coeur en avoit
bien besoin, je sais toutes les marques d'amitie
et d'interet que vous ne cessé de nous donner
mais je vous conjure par cette meme amitie, de
ne pas vous laisser compromettre en rien pour
nous, il est certain que nous n'avons de ressource
et de confiance qu'en vous. voici un memoire
qui pourra vous montrer notre position
au vrai, et ce que nous pouvons et devons esperer
de vous. je connois tres bien l'ame des
2 freres du roi, il n'y a pas de meilleurs
parents qu'eux, (je dirois presque de frere)
si je n'avois pas le bonheur d'etre votre soeur:
ils desirent tous deux le bonheur la gloire
du roi uniquement, mais ce qui les entourent
est bien different, ils ont tous fait des calculs
particulier pour leur fortune et leur ambition
il est donc bien interessant que vous puissiez
les contenir; et surtout comme mr. de mercy
doit deja vous l'avoir mandé de ma part

FACSIMILE OF FIRST PAGE OF MARIE ANTOINETTE'S LETTER

Written on September 3, 1791, to the Emperor, her brother, proposing armed intervention

edges the plan and confirms it. A fortnight later, upon the 1st of March, Mercy can give her the last great news: Prussia has formally consented to move, though demanding, of course, from the French Monarchy after its victory, compensation for the cost of the campaign — which will surely be willingly accorded.

It was on the 1st of March, I say, that this final news was written, when, as so continually chances throughout Marie Antoinette's life, a special fate appears and intervenes. On the 1st of March the King of Prussia has agreed to march with Leopold, and all is ready for that armed demonstration which would, as she was convinced, calm this great storm about her. On that same day, the 1st of March, Leopold lay dead. Doctors assure us that he was not poisoned.

Two things followed upon that death: first, the heir, her nephew, a sickly boy of twenty-four, now held in Vienna all the power that in those days accompanied the Crown, and he in his weakness was now the master of the armies his father had summoned.

Secondly, there must be a long delay for the business and the trapping of his election and his crowning.

Her plan meanwhile had failed. It was to be not a silent threat of arms, but war. The French temper had taken Leopold's command as a challenge. The ultimatum she had suggested or drafted was met by a total change in the Executive of France. Dumouriez was made the chief man in the new Ministry and was personally in charge of Foreign Affairs. The guns were certainly ready. For ten days after Dumouriez' nomination she drew from him his designs; and on the tenth day wrote secretly to Mercy in cipher betraying his plan of campaign upon the Meuse. Three days later the last of her friends who could command an army, the King of Sweden, stabbed a fortnight earlier, died; and on the 20th of April her husband, "the Head of the French Executive," read out in a firm voice a declaration of war against her nephew, "the King of Hungary" — for he was not yet crowned Emperor. Having so read it in a firm voice he went back home, and Marie Antoinette and he must now bethink themselves how the madness of the people, when the invasion should begin, might be fended off — at least from their own persons and from their heir, until their saviours should show the white Austrian uniforms in Paris and march the grotesque Prussian march within sight and hearing of the Tuileries. On the 30th of the month she advised Mercy that the first proclamation of the invaders had best be mild.

. . . .

Such had been the plan of the Queen, and such its fortune; and by such a fate had she been shadowed. For the sake of clarity I have omitted during this recital all save her negotiation. I will briefly return to the drift of the Revolutionary progress around her, and show how this also led up to that fatal conclusion, from the failure of the flight to Varennes at the end of June, 1791, to the declaration of war in the following April.

. . . .

When spirits are at high tension and in full vision, as it were, often a shock brings back the old, sober, and incomplete experience of living. Such a shock the flight to Varennes had afforded. While the royal family were yet absent there had been talk against the very institution of the

Crown; and some rich men had spoken of the Republic; the Revolutionary exaltation ran very high. The flight was arrested: the royal family were brought back, and in a sort of mechanical, unconscious way reaction gathered force; after all (the politicians thought) the nation must not lose, could not afford to lose, might lose its very soul in losing, the web of inheritance which had come to it from so many centuries.

This force of reaction exploded when, during the Feasts of the Federation, three weeks after the return of the royal family, a popular outbreak upon the Champ de Mars was repressed by the declaration of martial law, the use of the Militia under La Fayette, and the authority of the Mayor of Paris.

The Revolution, going the way we know it did, the hatreds, the threats of vengeance covertly growing from that day (which the poor and their champions had already christened among themselves the "Massacre of Champ de Mars") take on a great importance; but to the people of the time the tumult and its armed repression did not seem of any great consequence save as the beginning of quieter things. The end of the summer was principally occupied in some speculation as to what the new Parliament would do when it should be convened in the autumn. That Parliament was restricted in power: the National Assembly which had made the Revolution was to be dissolved. This second body was to do no more than elaborate the details of laws; it was called, and remains to history, "The Legislative."

By an ironical accident, this very Parliament of one year, from which the great and by this time well-known leaders of the early Revolutionary movement were specifically excluded (for no man might sit in it who had sat in the

National Assembly) had thrust upon it the duty or the burden of the Great War. Such was the Revolutionary time and air, that from anywhere genius sprang; and through these men of the Legislative — so many of them young, nearly all of them unknown — chosen only to sit in an ephemeral assembly for a year—there blew such inspiration as Plato thought to blow through poets, but which, in times of social creation blows through rhetoricians too. Chief among these was the group of men from the South who were later called the Gironde. It was their business to demand and to withstand the first assault of Europe, and indeed before the Parliament met at all, it was certain that the assault would come, for in the August of 1791, in the midst of the reaction which overshadowed Paris, and while the principal leaders of the Revolution were exiled or in hiding, there was drawn up that compact between the German monarchs which is called the Declaration of Pillnitz.

This document has too often been put forward as an example of the hesitation and moderation of the Kings. Such a view of it is an academic reaction from the old, popular, and vague but in the main just conception that privilege made deliberate war upon the Revolution: a conception which often took Pillnitz for the inception of that counter-crusade.

The matter can be presented quite simply to the reader: The Emperor, Marie Antoinette's brother, whom we have seen so eager, had the flight to Varennes succeeded, to move his armies at once, combined at Pillnitz with the King of Prussia in an appeal to all monarchical governments that they should use such strength as might give back to the King of France his old arbitrary power, and re-establish him therein. The two allies swear publicly that they will use all necessary force, when such an appeal bears fruit, to support this universal assault upon the French people, and meanwhile they will direct their troops to the best striking points from which the military action of that people may be paralysed.

There is the Declaration of Pillnitz in a few words; and while one partisan may insist upon its caution or nullity, another upon its insolence and provocation, all must agree who read history quietly and without a brief, that it was a violent and public declaration of hostile intention as it was also the first definite public act from which hostilities sprang.

The Parliament met in September. Its proposed secondary value soon proved to be primary; the splendid definition, rapidity and precision of the National Assembly was well reflected among these younger and less tried men: but much more powerful than Parliament was the growing exaltation of the populace.

That had many roots: the oblivion of the French (after forty years) of what war might mean, the impatient passion for *any* solution which all feel during a moment of strain, most of all the moral certitude (and how well founded!) that if the enemy delayed they delayed only for their own purpose, and that war must certainly come — all these pressed to the final issue: the noise of the cataract could already be heard.

As to the acceptation of the Constitution by the royal family, their reluctance, the Queen's anger, it but little concerns the story of her fate. At bottom she and Louis also were willing enough by this time to sign anything and to swear anything. The war must come, and the war would solve all. The Queen herself, who was now, as I have shown, in the thick of the intrigue, put it simply enough to the man she most loved, to Fersen, in a note that has been preserved and which she wrote before the end of September. "It would have been more noble to refuse (the Constitution) . . . it is essential to accept (it), in order to destroy any suspicion that we are not acting in good faith."

So far as concerns that unhappy and devoted life, one incident deserves a very special mention. Twice in the autumn there had been talk of yet another flight: the plan was not impossible, but it had been dropped, partly because the King might have had to fly alone, partly because the Queen was confident that a show of strength and a vigorous menace upon the frontier would be enough to change all. In the new year the proposal for their escape took on a more serious form, and Fersen reappeared for the last time, and for the last time saw the Queen.

It was upon Saturday the 11th of February, 1792, that he started upon that perilous journey, and it was his business to discuss in detail and by word of mouth whether escape was still possible. Upon Monday, the 13th, at evening, he passed the barrier of Paris. He saw the Queen before he slept, and next day at midnight spoke secretly to her and to her husband together. He carefully noted before them the routes that might be followed: the method of escape: perhaps (as had appeared in several plans) the string of forests that run up from Paris north-eastward toward the marches of Flanders.

The King and the Queen wasted no little time in that midnight hurried parley in reproaches against the ingratitude of all, and in bewailing their isolation. The next day Fersen left with nothing done. He returned indeed to Paris four days later, but he dared not enter the palace. The whole thing was futile and every plan had broken down.

He never saw her again.

A fortnight later he wrote his King, in Sweden, detailing all that they had told him.

Before he could reply or act, the King of Sweden had been shot in a masked ball at Stockholm, and some days later, as the reader knows, he had died.

. . . .

The Declaration of War had not only broken the original plan of the Queen; it had changed from a general and partly passive to a particular and active terror the life of Paris around her. Nothing had yet appeared to show as a reality what all knew in theory, the extreme peril of the nation, the military certitude inspiring the Allies, the despair increasing among what was left of the French Regulars. There had indeed been desertions immediately following the declaration of war, especially desertions of the German mercenaries, in bulk. A skirmish, or rather a panic upon the frontier, had also given evidence of the rot in the jumble of armed men whom the Revolution could summon. The first tiny action — it was hardly an action at all — had seen mutinies and the massacre of officers. Paris once more rose and fermented, and there was a surging around the walls of the palace. The enemy had not yet crossed the frontier; but in the short breathing-space before he should appear, and while the royal family were holding a fortress, as it were, for their own security until that enemy should arrive, Parliament put as a sort of ultimatum to the King a demand for the execution of two decrees: one against the Clergy who would not subscribe to the Civic Oath; a second in favour of the formation of a camp of 20,000 volunteers under the walls of Paris.

The error of uniting in one requisition two such diverse

pleas only posterity can recognise. For the men of the time there was a plain link between either demand, for the recalcitrant Clergy seemed to them nothing more than anti-nationalists, and it seemed to them that nothing but an anti-national desire for the occupation of Paris by the foreigner could make the King hesitate to permit the formation of the camp of volunteers.

It was upon the 19th of June that the King published his veto against both these bills or projects of the Parliament, behind which lay the violent opinion of active Paris.[1]

What follows is well known. Paris rose, and rising poured into the palace. It was the 20th.

The 20th of June: the anniversary of the flight: the summer solstice fatal to the Bourbons.

It has been said that the rising was artificial and arranged. The same nonsense is talked of the St.Bartholomew. No one who has seen such things can believe them artificial. They are corporate things. There was little violence, though there were many arms among those thousands upon thousands; and as they poured through the rooms, which opened one into the other like a gallery, they were not much more (save for their rough clothes and their arms) than the same populace which had demanded for generation after generation, and had obtained, the right to see, to visit, to touch their public King.

The Court had forgotten the popular conception of the Monarchy; but the populace necessarily preserves a longer memory than the rich. The thing was a menace, upon the whole not ill-humoured: a violent recollection that the King was the servant of the common weal, and its symbol, something to be handled, met, and perhaps ordered. The mob,

[1] And what was more significative, the whole of the little wealthy reactionary minority was opposed to the projects, and signed a petition in proof of its opposition.

in whom atheists can see no more than a number of poor men, cried out its significant cries, against "Mr. and Mrs. Veto," making a popular jest of this public power. But in those moments when one jest perhaps might have put the King at the head of popular emotion again, he and his wife remained no more than what the decline of the Monarchy had made them; individuals in peril, and courageous; not the Nation incarnate.

If any Angel had for its function the preservation of the French Crown and Nation, that Angel, watching such a gulf between the people and the Monarchy, must have despaired of the latter's hope and of the former's survival: nevertheless, despite that divorce, the French people after grievous wounds have survived.

. . . .

The last group which that roaring torrent of the rabble saw was the Queen and her children, her friends, especially Madame de Lamballe and the governess, the Duchess of Tourzel, a soldier or two, a minister and one or two others, crowded in the recess of a window behind a great table which had been pushed into the embrasure to defend them. The little heir to that Monarchy which had failed to understand sat on the table, very much afraid, and the Queen put on his head with loathing the red cap of liberty which the mob demanded. The day was sweating with heat, the cap was thick and dirty, and Santerre, who was there, passing them forward by bands in front of the table, a popular leader of the crowd, seems to have ordered that it should be removed. It was already nearly dark; it was half-past eight before that violent but not tragic tumult had subsided, and before the last of the street people went back out of the palace, which they thought rightly a public thing, on to the public paving which at least was still certainly theirs.

Outside, during all that night, all the talk was of the war. When would the invaders cross the frontier and when would the first shock come?

XVI

THE FALL OF THE PALACE

FROM HALF-PAST EIGHT IN THE EVENING OF THE 20TH JUNE, 1792 TO EIGHT IN THE MORNING OF THE 10TH AUGUST, 1792

THE noisy, good-natured, and very dangerous mob had gone at last; their final stragglers, gazing, curious and tired, at the pictures and the gilding (the trappings of their Public King in his great Public Palace), had wandered out. A few steps on the wide stone stairs of the central pavilion were still heard lazily descending. The dishevelled family was at rest.

A little group of Deputies remained behind, and talked in low and careful voices to the King and Queen — principally to the Queen, for she was voluble. She was suave, though somewhat garrulously suave. "Would not some of these gentlemen come and see her put the Dauphin to bed?" A familiar appeal made by the very wealthy to the middle class rarely fails. They followed respectfully and a little awkwardly to where, in a small bed out of her room, the child slept. She had him ready for bed in a few moments; then she said to him smiling:

"Tell the gentlemen you love the Nation, darling."

The drowsy child repeated mechanically, "I love the Nation."

The Middle Class were enchanted. She laid him down, doubtless with every maternal charm; she turned to go before them, certainly with an exaggeration of that excessive carriage which had delighted so many foreigners and dependants for now twenty years and had done much to lose her the respect of her French equals at the Court. The select committee of the Middle Class came after.

"See what damage they have done: look at these doors!" The Deputies stooped solemnly to examine the broken panels and the hinges torn from their screws, the oak splinters showing dark against the white paint and the gold. They admitted serious damage—they regretted it.

"Who is the proper authority to take note of this?" They looked at one another; then one of them, remembering the Constitution, Liberty and the rest of it, said:

"Nowadays the proper authority before which to bring such misdemeanours is a Justice of the Peace."

"Very well, then," she replied sharply, "send for one."

A servant was despatched and returned with a Justice of the Peace. He gravely took written notes of all:

"*Item:* the lower left panel broken;

"*Item:* the upper left panel cracked;

"*Item:* the lower right hinge of the door torn off, and the post splintered."

All was done in order, and they returned to find the King.

The King was annoyed. They noticed him grumbling and moving his lips and teeth. He was even a little excited, but his training in names and faces, which is the acquired talent of high functionaries, served him well. He spoke with authority, knowing each of them and addressing them in turn, and after speaking of the mob he particularly complained that roughs climbed the palings of the Tuileries gardens and disturbed his privacy. The Queen interrupted from time to time to reproach them. "Why had they not prevented the procession of the mob through the palace?

Why, at least, had they not given warning? The Department had done its duty! Why not they?" The King continued in another tone, till, at last, some of them coming nearer home asked him for news of the armies. His dignity as the Executive (which he still was) forbade him any full replies: he had good news, very good news. . . . He could tell them no more.

They suspected [we *know*] that there was no news at all . . . only a few packed, ill-ordered garrisons awaiting the attack; a long line in the field all the way from Belfort to sea, numbering but 80,000 men, and half of that an ill-clothed helter-skelter of broken companies: divided counsel, no plan, and, a few marches east, that slow concentration of the allies upon Coblenz which now drew to its close.

So the Deputies left them: the sky was still full of light on this slowest night of the year, and Paris after the uproar of that bacchanalian Wednesday, the 20th of June, was silent.

. . . .

Meanwhile the South had risen.

On that same Wednesday evening messengers from Montpellier had reached Marseilles; on Friday they were feasted, and when the banquet was over, one of the Montpellier men, Mireur, with a voice of bronze, rose to sing them a new song. It had come from the frontier, he said; as for the air he did not know whence it was, but he thought (wrongly) from the opera "Sargines." He sang it, and the men that gathered outside the open windows to hear upon that summer evening, the guests within, and soon all the city, were swept by the MARSEILLAISE.

The next day the Municipality of Marseilles met,

determined upon spontaneous action in company with all the South: they decreed the raising of a volunteer battalion in spite of the Crown; the next, the Sunday, when all were abroad and could read, the walls were placarded with the appeal to join. Monday and Tuesday the names poured in: a committee was chosen to pick only the best in character and health. Its work was at once accomplished; within twenty-four hours five hundred had been so chosen out of the throng of volunteers; within forty-eight they had been enrolled, drilled for hours, and separated by companies under officers of their choice. Three days of rapid organisation and continued drilling followed: the route was traced, a time-table drawn up, the expenses estimated and provided. A section of guns (harnessed to men) with its caisson was drafted; the stores and baggage were concentrated too. Upon Monday, the 2nd of July, at nightfall, a week after the first appeal, through a crowd of all the city that pressed on every side, they marched out by the northern gate of Marseilles singing their song. Next morning, just as the arid eastern hills began to show against the beginnings of the dawn, they entered Aix and had accomplished the first stage of their advance. "The Executive" — that is, the Crown — had warned every authority to disperse them and all such others, but the wind on Paris was from the South, and they and their song could not be hindered.

. . . .

Meanwhile, in the German town of Frankfort, there hummed a continually increasing crowd: the Emperor was to be crowned. Here, therefore, were all those who had a business with Austria, and here was, among others, a Swiss Huguenot, Mallet du Pan, upon whom more than upon any other in that town the King of France and the Queen in her extremity depended. He was a journalist, very keen about accounts and probity in small money matters, of the bourgeoisie, sedate and perpetually attempting to understand the French people, now from this side, now from that: they interested him hugely. His work, however, was not to pursue this fascinating study, but to save the persons of the royal family he served: in this task he showed that same discipline and devotion which his compatriots were later to show under arms. He bore as his chief principles, as his last instructions, two orders: one order to keep the farce of the war going, and never to let it be hinted publicly or breathed that there was collusion between those who sent him and the invading Austrian power. The other order was this: to produce a manifesto to be signed from the camp of the invading army, and to strike, as it was hoped, blind terror into the leaders of the National movement: the time had come (so it was imagined at the Tuileries) to threaten the worst and so tame Paris.

He took his journey (but was scrupulous to give an exact account), left his family in Paris, passed through Geneva, his home, and now, by the end of June, was here at Frankfort.

He had chosen his centre well, for upon Frankfort converged all news, and from Frankfort went out all orders: orders to Coblenz whence the armies were to march to the relief of the Tuileries; news from Brussels, which was of the first moment, for here Mercy d'Argenteau, the expert upon France, was ready every day to advise; here was the danger of attack from France most felt, and here, most central of all, was Fersen.

Fersen heard regularly from Paris, wrote as regularly. Since the death of the King of Sweden his official position had been less, but those whose business it was to discover truth, the diplomats, knew that the last and most intimate thought of the royal family was to be reached through that channel alone. Austria and Prussia, Frankfort, that is, hardly acted upon his advice as to war (and in his diary he bitterly reproaches them for their neglect), but they sucked his knowledge — and to-day it is through him that we know, somewhat late, the principal truths upon those last few weeks of the French Monarchy.

What did the Court of the Tuileries demand, and what will was behind it in so demanding?

Mallet du Pan was there at Frankfort with no credentials but a sheet of note-paper, and written on the top of it in Louis' hand two lines of writing unsigned. "*The person who shall present this note knows my intentions; entire confidence may be put in what he says.*" What instructions had he?

Fersen was stationed at Brussels with an organised letter-service between the Tuileries and himself, written in secret ink, full, confidential and direct. All that he told Mercy or another went to Frankfort. What message was thus continually conveyed?

The demand from the Tuileries was an urgent demand for immediate invasion, and forerunning it, a drastic proclamation from the armed force at Coblenz: the will which inspired that demand was the will of Marie Antoinette.

A man in flight could cover the distance from Paris to Brussels in two days; an urgent runner in three. Normally the courier with his post-bag arrived on the morning of the fourth day. From Brussels to Frankfort worse roads, varying frontiers, and the German lethargy between them compelled news to a delay of close upon a week.

The ferment in Paris was rising; the Federals of the South were on the second day's march northward when, in the middle of the first week of July, the Queen, whose policy, or rather passion, could bear no more delay, wrote to Mercy and to Fersen separately two letters of great weight. These letters have never yet been given their due. The student should note them closely if he is to understand all that followed.

The originals have, perhaps, not come down to us, but either man, Fersen or Mercy, noted their intents, and we thus know them.

These letters Lasserez brought into Brussels, riding on the morning of Sunday, the 8th of July, and on the next day Mercy and Fersen, meeting, consulted on their purport. The Queen, with whom the project of such an engine was familiar, now definitely demanded a separate and nominal threat against the town of Paris, and a menace that the whole city should be held hostage by the invading German armies against the safety of her husband, herself and her child. This clause her judgment of the French character assured her to be efficacious; this clause she insisted should be added to the Manifesto which was even now preparing.

It was upon July the 9th, I say, that the two men met and consulted upon the Queen's orders: that day they sent off command or counsel to the Rhine.

On the 14th, while, in that same Paris, Louis was once more swearing to the Constitution upon the Champ de Mars, while hour for hour, far off on the Rhone a priest receiving the Marseillaise Battalion was adding his famous verse "of the Children"[1] to their famous hymn, in Frankfort the last of the Emperors was receiving with incredible

[1] "Nous entrerons dans la Carrierè," &c., the best verse and the only poetry of the lot.

magnificence the Crown of the Empire. The note inspired by Marie Antoinette was at the gates of his town.

It entered: Mallet saw it. "Paris is to be destroyed by fire and the sword if the royal family are harmed": it was approved. From Frankfort it went back as a new clause to Coblenz; there it was incorporated in the Manifesto and signed. Immediately, the ink barely dry, it was published (upon the 25th of July) to the world, above the signature of the Duke of Brunswick and in the name of that perfect and mechanical army which Prussia in especial could move with the precision of a physical law upon the capital that phrase had doomed.

This was the origin of that famous Clause VIII. which ordered, if the Tuileries were forced, nay, if submission to the Royal Family was not at once made, that Prussia and Austria would take "an unforgettable vengeance," that Paris should be given up "to military execution and subversion, and the guilty rebels to the death they deserve."

Such was Marie Antoinette's one piece of formulated policy — the first in which she had been able to act as clearly as she saw; it was also her last interference in political affairs. It had been lit by her hand, this match that fired the hesitating war: it had run its train through Brussels to Frankfort and back to Coblenz, lingering in no one place for a full day: now it had touched powder. Three days later the Manifesto was spoken of in Chalons; secret copies were in print, the King received it.

All Paris knew it, though not yet officially, when upon the evening of Sunday, the 29th of July, the dusty 500 of Marseilles with their guns, crossing the bridge at Charenton, saw the distant towers of Notre Dame above the roofs of Paris and reached their goal.

Let soldiers consider the nature of this exploit, and politicians consider what that civilisation is whose comprehension I have shown throughout these pages to have so vainly fatigued so many aliens.

The French of Marseilles had trained for but three days. They had left the Mediterranean in the height of a torrid summer; their organisation was self-made, their officers self-chosen, their discipline self-imposed. They had covered five hundred miles of route, dragging their cannon, at the rate of precisely eighteen miles a day; they planked across the bridge at this the end of their advance, solidly, in formation, still singing their song, and at the roll-call every name was answered. . . . Their small numbers have made them appear to some historians insignificant (or a legend), to others rather a symbol of the military power in the populace which was to sack the palace than the attack itself, but they were more; they were, as tradition justly represents them, the framework of the force that decided the critical day of the Revolution, as their song was its soul.

They marched in next morning by the St. Antoine Gate, with their drums and colours before them, the crowds of the suburbs blackening the site on which the Bastille had stood; and half Paris, as it were, going out to meet them. They passed over to the Island, formed at the Mairie where Pétion the Mayor greeted them; re-crossed the river (followed by the crowd) and took their places in the barracks assigned to them, upon a corner of what is now the Boulevard des Italiens; from that evening the struggle between the City and the Monarchy had begun, and the few days' delay that was to follow was but a manœuvring for position on either side, that of the populace and of the Tuileries.

This last had now for long been steadily arming and was already strong. The King, the executive, held the arsenals, the regular army and a good half, even, of the autonomous Militia. What was of more importance, the Crown and its advisers could rely not only upon the machinery but upon the devotion of the one well-disciplined corps which had not gone to the front: the Body-guard. These excellent mercenaries, nearly all Swiss by birth and nearly all ignorant of the French language, were precisely such material, human for courage and mechanical for obedience, as should overcome almost any proportion of civilians — especially such as might be spoilt by playing at soldiers. A recent law passed by the Legislative Assembly forbade their presence in Paris. The "Executive" parried such mere word of the "Legislative" by posting them in suburbs between which and the palace were only woods and fields. When danger was imminent, in the last hours of the truce, they were marched in and occupied the Tuileries, law or no law.

Two objections to the strength of the King's position against the populace are urged (Napoleon, no mean judge, and an eye-witness, thought it the stronger, and *his* estimate of the King's forces brings them to about 6,000 men); these are, first, that no building can be held in the face of artillery, for the popular force had guns; secondly, that it was but defensive, and that the assault, though repulsed, might return. The first of these is based on a misconception of the terrain and supply, the second upon a general ignorance of arms.

For the first: there was no position whence artillery, even were it available in time, could be used against the long walls of the palace save by passing through narrow streets easy

EAST FRONT OF THE TUILERIES

The side attacked by the mob, in the last state before the Commune of 1871, after the clearing away of the streets and houses in front of it

for infantry to defend, and as a fact the guns were not available to the populace either in sufficient amount or (what is of more importance) with sufficient training and supply. Guns, popularly manned and ill supplied, emplaced in the labyrinth which flanked the palace could be captured (and in fact were captured) by the trained infantry defending it. The short range alone would make certain the destruction of their teams by sharp-shooting from the upper windows.

The second objection — a reply to which shows how considerable were the King's stake and chances — is met by the military consideration that nothing more needs a special organisation and training than a successful rally. An assault, if it is of any consequence, must be pressed hard; if it is fully repulsed, its head and energy are crushed at their highest vigour; the defeat is more crushing than that of a defensive which retires in time. This is generally true of soldiers in the field. It is always true of civilians. The doubts and defections that accompany a civil war, the conversion of the great body of cowards and the still larger majority of indifferent men, the claims of regular domestic life, the absence of a commissariat, the near presence of women and children, the contrast which the return of quiet after the blow presents to the pain and terror of a renewed struggle, make it, as it were, impossible for a defeated mob to return, after an interval, against the regular force which has repelled it; moreover, the regulars, once victorious, can pursue, scatter, and destroy the unorganised mass, while its leaders are arrested and judged; nor is there an example in history of a popular rising which, when it has once broken against the defence of a regular force, has not been broken for good.

The strategy of the Court was therefore sound, their

calculation of victory was reasonable, and their chances of the best when the defence of the palace was organised in these first days of August. It was calculated that the populace even with artillery could do little against the palace: that the trained men would crush the mob once and for all. Had that defence succeeded, the advent of the foreigner, perhaps allied with one of the royal armies, was secure. That the defence of the palace failed was due partly to the lack of homogeneity in the garrisons, more to a lack of united leadership, but most of all to the unexpected, incalculable and hitherto unequalled tenacity and determination of the insurgents.

With every day the tension increased. The Federation delegates who had come from all over France to the Feast of the 14th of July, many of whom lingered in the city, clashed in the streets with courtiers, and with those who, whether by temperament or service, were still supporters of the Crown.

Just when the Marseillais were entering Paris, Brunswick had broken camp and the march of the Allies into France had begun. Less than a hundred miles of flat road along the Moselle valley separated Brunswick from the outposts of the defence: Paris itself was hardly further from him than is York from London. Rapidity would put the first garrisons of the frontier into his hands within a week and even the tardiness which the Prussian calculation and the Prussian confidence involve, could hardly (it was thought) delay for a fortnight the news that the frontier was passed.

In the passionate quarrel the enemy's character of invader was forgotten. Not only to the Court but to many who could now remember nothing but the ancient tradition of the Monarchy, the enemy seemed a saviour. Bands parading the pavement by night threatened their fellow-citizens with Brunswick, songs threatening vengeance against the revolutionaries were heard abroad after carousals, and a continuous series of petty street fights, increasing in gravity, enlivened the attention of either side.

Hardly were the Marseillais in Paris, for instance, when, that same evening of their arrival, after a banquet, a violent quarrel between them and a body of armed royalists had broken out. They carried their side-arms only, but blood was shed, and as the victims upon the defeated side of this brawl were carried to the Guard-room in the palace, the Queen, seeing blood, thought that the final struggle had begun. She was relieved to see the King go down amongst the wounded, staunching the blood of one with his handkerchief. Her women, fearing what she had feared, began crying each for one of hers. "Is my husband wounded?" "Is mine?" She could not forbear from one of those insults which had lost her the affection of so many, and from one of those reflections which proved how little she conceived the French nobility. "Ladies," she said to the noblewomen about her, "your husbands were not there." She had no further opportunity to revile them: it was perhaps the last expression of her contempt for a people whom she believed to have grown incapable.

Either side continued to arm. The heat, growing steadily in intensity, had bred by the 3rd of August a very thunderous calm, when the King announced to the Assembly the terms of Brunswick's Manifesto. It was received in silence, and those who least knew and know the city thought and still think that the news was met with indifference. But during that night, while a furious storm struck Paris time and time again with lightning, one workman's suburb, St. Marcel, sent word to another, St. Antoine: "If we march to the palace, will you?" In the midst of the thunder, messengers returned saying: "We will!" And in the night as they went and came, they passed men bearing the dead whom the lightning had struck and killed. Very late and before the growling of the thunder had ceased, certain of the Marseillais must go to the walls of the palace and shout the chorus of their song.

Next day they asked for ball-cartridge. Sergent, the official guardian of the Militia ammunition-reserve, had been struck in the face when he had gone, as his duty compelled him, to the palace a fortnight before; he had been struck because his politics were known. Should the insurrection fail, his signature for rebel ammunition would be his death warrant. Nevertheless, remembering that blow, he signed; and the arsenal served out ten rounds a man to the Battalion of Marseilles. They crossed the river so armed, and were received at the Cordeliers,[1] which was Danton's fief, and Danton restrained them till such poor and hasty organisation as could be undertaken should be effected. It was the end of the week which had seen their entry into Paris, and nothing had been done. The Tuileries continued to arm, the populace to convene, and between the combatants the Parliament daily lost its power and grew bewildered.

On Sunday, at Mass, always a public occasion in the palace, men passed and re-passed each other in the gallery, and there were quarrels. This also was the last time in which the Monarchy was treated as a general thing — with the next morning its isolation began. On Monday the King was begged to fly, at least to Compiègne: the road was

[1] Now the Clinical Museum opposite the faculty of Medicine in the University.

guarded and it was an easy ride if he went alone round by Poissy and the north. He refused. On Tuesday the last preparations were made in the suburban garrisons of the Crown soldiers. On Wednesday, the 8th, in the morning, the Swiss Guard was warned that on the morrow before dawn it must be accoutred.

The Parliament, more and more bewildered, vacillated and was hardly heard as the two antagonists rose from their places to fight. The deputies refused all action. It had been proposed to them to condemn La Fayette for a hurried journey he had taken to Paris after the last insurrection to defend the King. They had refused by a very great majority. Now, on this 9th of August, the fatal eve of the struggle, they debated an academic point — whether the King should abdicate or no; they adjourned it to dine . . . and after dinner they did not meet.

But all the while upon that Thursday evening, troops were afoot along the Rueil road; the doors of the Palace were open to men who entered one by one, armed and were stationed; the sound of carpenters was heard in the Long Gallery of the Louvre, sawing the planking of the floors, by night, to make a gap between the Louvre and the Tuileries;[1] mounted police rode up in squads to the courtyard and took their stations; there was also the rumbling of waggons. In the sections south of the river and eastwards St. Antoine and St. Marcel were moving; wherever the people had strained at the leash too long, the popular assembles sat in their close halls choosing the men who should take the Guildhall by right of the City's decision and in spite of the law, and proclaim the insurrection.

The last of the day declined and the night came, but

[1] The gap was six feet broad. Too narrow, for the insurgents next day leaped it and bridged it, and by that entry forced the Tuileries.

the unnatural heat would not decline, and the open windows all about, the lights shining from them, and the vigil which so many kept, gave the effect of an illumination.

. . . .

That night, short and stifling as it was, was drowsy; a necessity for sleep oppressed the city. Danton himself, in the thick of the rising, attempted a moment of repose; he had hardly lain down when he was roused again. The watchers in the palace felt midnight upon them and would have slept. The barrack-beds which filled the attics in their regular lines were strewn with men; the gentry who had volunteered, certain also of the Militia, lay silent in the darkness, their muskets slung beside them, their large allowance of cartridges served. Below in the great rooms and on the stairways groups of mixed soldiery lay huddled, servants armed, and policemen: every kind of man. The Regulars who formed the core of this force, the Swiss, lounged in their bare guard-room or sat silent upon the stone benches of the yard; some few files of them stood at ease upon the stairs of the lesser hall.

Upon this silence there crashed at about a quarter to one o'clock the noise of cannon. The report was hard and close at hand — it came from the Pont Neuf at the further end of the Louvre, and the united fabric of the long walls trembled to it; the heavy pictures and the mirrors shook. The six thousand who garrisoned the Tuileries expected an immediate advance of the insurrection: for a moment the whole palace was roused. Those battalions of Militia which had been camped in the garden for a reserve began to file in by the central doors: the cavalry mounted to take up their stations at the narrow issues of the Louvre, and everywhere the lights moving before the windows of the vast façade showed the ordering of men.

This general stir had hardly arisen when it was perceived that this first shot had been but a signal, for to the call of that cannon no other succeeded, but almost immediately the steeples of the city trembled to the first notes of bells.

The deep and heavy bells, that had for centuries raised the alarm of invasion or of fire, began to boom just east of the University; they were answered by the peal of St. Anthony over the river, by the tocsins of St. John and St. Gervase; St. Laurence rang, and southward upon the night boomed the huge tower of the Abbey, which had heard the same sound nine hundred years before, when the dust of the Barbarian march hung over Enghien, and smoke went up from burning farms all down the Seine. The Cathedral followed: thenceforward no one could hear the striking of the hours, for the still air of the night pulsed everywhere with the riot of the bells. Two sounds alone could pierce the clamour: the high bugle-call to which the French still mobilise, and the sullen fury of the drums. The horses, therefore, of the defenders in the courts of the palace, the continual clattering of their hoofs upon the paving, the clink of metal as the lines were formed, the tramp of the reinforcements arriving—all the movement of the six thousand who gathered to support the Crown, was set to this music, and the air they breathed was full of the noise of the bells.

Yet for some hours after the posts had been taken the advent of the rebels was expected in vain. Paris seemed empty, or full only of this increasing and ominous sound. Of men there was no trace. The stone courtyards before the palace and the streets that led to the Square of the

Carrousel were silent. They lay open and deserted under the sky, and so remained even when the first stars paled and when there was already a hint of dawn. A doubt rose among the Royalists, first whispered, then openly spoken, and leading at last to jests: the insurrection had missed fire; the bells had failed. No voice of the insurgents had been heard, nor had any rider brought news of their approach, when the last of the stars had gone and the Militia companies, still remaining as a reserve in the western gardens, saw the day rise gorgeously beyond the palace they were to defend.

In a small room whose window looked toward the east, the Queen, with some few of her women, waited for the day. The ceiling was low, and its air of privacy gave some little respite from the strain of the eve and of the morrow. She lay upon a sofa, but she could not sleep; she spoke but rarely and that in low tones, and vaguely watched the night. With the first grey of the morning she rose, unrested, and bade them dress her boy, the child who alone in that great house had slept throughout the alarms. Then, under the growing light, she saw the Princess Elizabeth near her, who called her and took her to a window whence she might watch the rising of the sun. They stood together beside the open casement gazing at the city in silence.

Early as was the hour (it was but little past four) the tone of the air already promised a blinding summer's day. The end of darkness had lifted no mist from the gardens. The last heats of yesterday blended with the new warmth of the sunrise that stretched bright red across the far suburbs where the populace stood to arms; behind the confused high roofs and spires of their capital the two Princesses saw advancing at last great beams of power and, enflaming the city, an awful daybreak. The younger woman was afraid and spoke her thought, saying that it looked like some great disaster, a burning spread before them.

Now that it was broad day the vigour of the Queen returned. She became again the will of the defence, and its leader — if it had a leader. She had not expected defeat even in the worst silences of the night; with the new day she was confident of success.

The commander of the Paris Militia, one Mandat, who had lately come by rote to that function, she knew to be sound. He had garrisoned the bridge-head by which alone the transpontine mob could cross the river to the palace; his cavalry also held the narrow arch at the Guildhall, by which alone the east end could come. Pétion now became the mayor of Paris, who had been summoned to the palace for a hostage, had gone — the Parliament had demanded him — but Mandat remained and his presence sufficed for her. Upon that presence she relied: when she came to seek him she found that he too had disappeared. The Town Hall had summoned him twice, and twice he had refused. At the third summons he had gone, suddenly, unescorted, "to account for his command." She began to wonder, but her hope was still maintained. She crossed to the room where she could find her husband, and she engaged upon the last act which freedom permitted her to command.

Still pursued by memories of what the Court had been, she determined to show the King to his subjects, and to present a sight which should exalt his soldiery and linger in history as the appeal which saved him.

The King obeyed her summons: he had better have remained to repose, for she found him but recently awakened from a stupor into which he had fallen at the end of the night when all his garrison had risen to the alarm.

The servitors, the gentlemen, the Militia, and the strict Swiss beside them saw, as they stood drawn up in a rambling line upon the western garden terrace, the figure for which they were to die.

He appeared at the main central door, weary, dishevelled, and, as it were, aged. His violet coat recalled the periods of mourning. The shadow in which he stood enhanced the sombre colour of his clothing and the pallor of his freckled face; his stoutness and his habitually sanguine temper rendered that pallor unnatural and suggested catastrophe or disease. His paunch was obvious, his hair deplorable. With such an introduction to their loyalty he wandered heavily from end to end of the line. There was a laugh — by one light-head he was covertly insulted as he passed — he was certainly of less and less moment in their eyes with every step he took in this unhappy review. When it abruptly ended, old Mailly went down stiffly on one knee and tendered his sword, then stiffly rose again. Again in the ranks some one laughed. From this scene the King returned to his room in silence.

She also, the Queen, returned from it angry and in tears, the more embittered that she herself had designed the thing.

The first news that met her on her return to the palace was the death of Mandat. As the details were told her she understood, though vaguely, what a blow had fallen. He had reached the Town Hall "to account for his command," but had found there, not the hesitating constitutional body which he expected and which had a right to summon the head of the Militia. He had found instead a ring of new

AN EARLY VIEW OF THE APPROACH TO THE TUILERIES FROM THE CARROUSEL

Showing the three courtyards

faces, the insurrectionary Commune: the Revolution, maddened and at bay, had glared at him across the lights of the hall. As he went down the steps to the street, blinded by that vision of terror, some lad shot him dead, and with that deed the whole plan of the defence crumbled. The bridge-head and the archway were abandoned.

The crowds of the south and east gathered as the morning advanced; their way was now clear, and yet, to those watching from the palace windows, it still seemed as the sun rose higher that the movement had failed. Seven chimed above the central portico; it chimed slowly upon bells of nearly a hundred years; the half-hour sounded, and still the courts of the Carrousel lay empty. But the deserted air was ominous. No street cries rose from the neighbouring market-stalls. There was no sound of workmen upon the new building of the bridge[1] down river; the regular sawing of stone and the ring of hammered iron were silent.

. . . .

At last a head showed above the high wooden palings that separated the courtyard from the square. Then another, the heads of ragged street-boys, who peered over, standing on their companions' shoulders. A stone was thrown. One of the sentries aimed, and in a twinkling the dirty, beardless faces disappeared. As yet no shot had been fired.

A noise like that of swarming bees came confusedly from the quays, muffled by the intervening wing of the Louvre. It approached, still dull and blanketed by the vast building; for a moment it was swallowed up in the deep passage beneath the Louvre; then, with an immediate and overwhelming roar it burst into the square of the Carrousel.

[1] Now called the Pont de la Concorde.

Some one in command must have dashed upstairs, to where from the higher attic windows he could overlook the hoarding: such an one saw the Carrousel crammed with a violent whirlpool of men that seethed and broke against the great oaken gates of the yard. Even as he looked the gates gave way or were opened — which he could hardly distinguish in the press. The inner court filled as the torrent of arms surged through the entry. At a window of the upper floor certain gentlemen who had volunteered knelt, with their muskets upon the crowd below.

They waited for the order to fire.

XVII

THE TEMPLE

THE vanguard of the mob came pouring in.

They swarmed through the arches under the Long Gallery and the main body of them still came swinging up to it along the riverside.

The sun, well up and brazen, touched the metal about them and sent dancing gleams from pikes and curved hooks bound to staves. Before that uneven crowd the long shadows of morning stood out sharply, thrown along the uneven paving of the narrow quays. They sang or jested: they jostled and could not order themselves. There were no soldiers among this first batch of the insurrection, nor even a body of the half-trained Militia, nor had they any guns. So they swarmed through the public archways under the Long Gallery, so they packed and surged in the square of the Carrousel. Before them were the walls of the central courtyard of the palace and a great gate shut against them.

Of the fourteen guns that the palace commanded, five faced them in this court, ready to fire should the crowd burst in. Three were advanced in the emptiness of the square; two, in support, were just outside the main door, whence the central staircase of the Tuileries swept up to the royal rooms. At that door the lads who had climbed the outer walls of the courtyard could also now see some few of the Guard drawn up in formation outside the palace door and already retiring; the rest were massed behind these in the hall: the solid body of Swiss who were the kernel of the defence.

These thousand mercenaries and more, immovable men, had in their attitude something at once of the grotesque and the terrible. Stiff and strict as lifeless things in their red and white, tight hose and musket erect and firm, they were ready first for the volley, then for the charge, and every man (in that time, when ten rounds was thought a day's provision) carried forty rounds upon him. The pale, unmoved faces of the mountaineers were here and there diversified by some livelier face, their rough-cut hair by the careful barbering of the wealthy, for there were gentry of the King's who had borrowed uniforms of the Guard and had slipped in among them and now stood part of the silent rank.

The roaring of voices in the Carrousel beyond the walls of the courtyard increased continually; the other noise of the sea of Paris rose with it every moment, and on the first floor where the Royal Family and some few advisers sat, all this gathering crowd outside the courtyard walls was watched by those who were responsible for the unity of the nation in face of the advancing invasion, and for the person of what was still the King. Chief of those so responsible was Roederer. He stood there for that new public authority, the elected county-body which alone had legal power; he considered only the necessary survival of the King.

Already, at dawn, he had advised that the King should leave the defence to others; now, hours later, as the mob and its noise swelled and swelled, he insisted once more. It was but a personal act whose value in the military thing that followed only those present could judge, nay, only those who knew, as only contemporaries can know them, the personal forces at work. There was no capitulation here. . . .

But in the judgment of the greatest master of war, Louis leaving the defence by those few yards determined the issue; for it was Napoleon, himself perhaps a witness, who said that if the King had then been seen on horseback before the palace, his troops would have had the better of the fight. But the King did what he thought was necessary for the moment of peril, and guarded his family. He said, "Let us go." As he passed through the corridors of the palace down to the main doors upon the garden side, he said to those who heard him, "We shall be back soon." He believed it and they also. None saw in this precaution an element of defeat, and yet that sort of shadow which doom throws before itself as it advances vaguely oppressed the palace.

The King, the Queen, and their children, Madame de Lamballe and Madame de Tourzel, the governess, the handful of ministers and friends, had nothing to do with the military scheme of the defence. Louis had thought it prudent, and his advisers also, that those few steps should be taken between the palace and the Parliament House that lay beyond the palace garden, and as they went along the broad garden way between the formal trees, few thought, if any thought, that those few minutes in the privacy of their grounds were final. Later, all called it the beginning or the presage of defeat.

The King walked solidly on in front by himself, murmuring from time to time that the leaves had begun to fall very early that year. The Dauphin, holding the Queen's hand, trotted by her side and amused himself by pushing away with his feet those same dead leaves, until, the sickly little chap growing weary, a Grenadier of the Royal Militia, which formed their little escort, lifted the Prince in his arms against his blue coat. The Queen's face, mottled red and white in the violence she did herself by that retreat, was now disfigured by tears, and the crowd beyond the palisades of the garden, seeing Royalty thus taking refuge, broke through a gate and made a hubbub round the Parliament door. But a couple of dozen members made a way through them and met the royal party, assuring them of an asylum within. With some little pushing, complaints, and speechifying, they got them into safety, and the King so took his place beside the Speaker in that great oval of the riding-school in the early but hot and sunlit morning, the Queen and the children behind him upon the bench of the Ministers; and there the Grenadier gently put down the child.

Vergniaud was in the chair, and, when the King had spoken his few words to the Parliament, it was Vergniaud who assured him of the protection of the laws. But there was a prejudice too strong in volume, of too recent a date, and too lively in character, to permit of the open presence of royalty at their debates. Royalty must, at least in name, withdraw, and Louis and his wife and the children and some few of their attendants, consented to enter a little box where the shorthand reporters of a certain journal had usually their place. It overlooked the hundreds of the Assembly from a little above their level, and was so placed at the south-eastern corner of the great ellipse that the sun, creeping round, was bound to beat upon it through the high-arched southern windows as the day wore on. The grating was removed, they were attempting some repose in that strict lodgment, when the sudden sound that all so tensely

CONTEMPORARY PRINT OF THE FIGHTING IN THE COURTYARD

awaited broke out beyond the garden trees. The firing had begun. It was a little after nine.

Cabined as they were within the little box, whose outer wall gave upon the gardens of the Palace, they could hear, trembling through the stone and noisy through the open windows on that hot August morning, the rattle of the musketry of the defence. The Marseillais had come up in their turn; they had come into the courtyard. They had parleyed with the Swiss. The gentry at the broad windows of the first floor, each group twelve front, three deep, had opened fire to stop that parleying. But of what so passed the Parliament and the little party in the reporters' box knew nothing. They heard but one discharge of cannon, booming dull, and after that a silence. The debate in the hall of the Parliament ceased. It was the moment when the Swiss had rallied and when the defenders of the palace had swept the populace from the Carrousel, and had so thought to have ended the day. There were many in that hall who thought it ended also: mobs are thus often defeated in a few moments. The silence lasted.

Two more discharges of cannon might have been — and were perhaps thought to be in the anxious house and by the much more anxious group that strained their ears in the reporters' box — the last volley against a flying crowd. It was not so: these cannon were the two pieces of Marseilles leading a return of the mob, and thenceforward, with every moment for a quarter of an hour, for twenty minutes, the fusillade and the roar of approaching thousands swelled like the calculated swell of an orchestra. The Queen heard, where she sat in the corner of the tiny lodge, the whistle of grape, the thud of solid shot against the walls, the crash of glass and all that increasing roar which told her that the populace had returned like a tide, flooding the courts of the palace and invading its very doors. For some very few moments they heard that struggle maintained.

Then it was that Roederer, rightly or wrongly, a lawyer, not a soldier, determined that the day was lost. In the spirit which had made him, in his capacity as a high official of the Local Government, twice advise the King to retire, and the second time succeed in that advice, in that same spirit he now advised a capitulation. Perhaps he hoped by such a compromise (could it arrive in time) to save the Monarchy. More probably he deemed the Monarchy secure, and thought only by this capitulation to save the House in which the Parliament sat and in which the Crown had taken refuge from direct assault by the mob. At any rate there was written, and presumably in the King's presence, the hurried word or two which ordered the Guard to cease firing, and that scrap of paper Louis signed.[1] It was the last act of the French Monarchy.

This order was conveyed to the upright and soldierly D'Hervillé: it filled him with contempt and anger. He took the paper, pocketed it, forced his way round with difficulty to the further side of the Tuileries, saw that the defence, though now beaten back to the very doors, was still maintained, and so far from communicating the King's command, determined, as many a soldier before has done in such a fix, to disobey. He continued to direct the battle.

Though the populace had rushed the doors and in part the river wing of the palace, a furious hand-to-hand still raged. The staircase was not yet carried; that wing of the populace which had leapt the gap in the flooring and had boarded the Pavilion de Flore from the Long Gallery had

[1] The authenticity of this document is discussed, or rather alluded to, in the reproduction of it which appears as a frontispiece.

not yet fought its way into the Tuileries. The great body of the insurgents was still massed outside in the square; a steady fire was still maintained upon them from the windows of the palace. It was not until the rooms were at last flooded by the advancing mob and the staircase was held, that D'Hervillé faltered. He was turned. The assault had begun to verge upon a massacre. Of one-half company of the popular Militia, all but five had been hit at one door alone in the upper rooms. Before the main door within a few yards of it, 400 men — if we may trust those who most desired to hide the full numbers — 400 men at least lay heaped. Within, the mob was taking its revenge and the sacking had begun before D'Hervillé showed that scrap of paper to the Guard. This second command, also, the Swiss obeyed, as they had obeyed the first command to die.

They fell back out of the palace in order, this remnant of a high discipline; they passed down the main broad avenue of the Gardens steadily: the covering volleys of their retreat came very sharp and clear just outside the windows of the Parliament. Those within heard their steady tramp, until at last that tramp turned to a scuffle; there were crunchings upon the gravel, confused scrambles upon the lawns, choked cries and fugitive running; they had broken by the round pond.

Far off along the riverside one could still hear a rhythm and a tramp of men. It was the marching of the Marseillese with their prisoners: for they had made prisoners and disdained to massacre. They had saved somewhat more than a company of the Guard and bore them escort. The fight was done.

It was just after ten o'clock. In those two hours, or little more, of doubt, in that one hour of combat, there had perished many thousands of men and the tradition of nine hundred years.

. . . .

The day passed without wind or air, a day of increasing clamour. The conquering populace entered by deputations, and with the rhetoric of the poor and of their leaders before the bar of the *manège.* They demanded and obtained the suspension of Louis "till the National Convention should be called." They brought spoils religiously to that bar, "lest they should be thought thieves." They harangued and they declaimed — by the mouth of leaders.

Far off in the chapel of the palace a young man at the organ played the "Dies Iræ" for his whim. Those who had so lately been the masters sat huddled in the box of the *Logographe.*

If the modern reader would have some conception of it, this "loge" of the shorthand reporter, let him think if he is rich, of a box at the opera, or, if he is poor, of a cabin upon a steamer, such was its size.

Louis XVI. and one or two of his armed gentlemen, the Queen, the little children and their governess, sat packed hour after hour in that little den; through the torn grating of it they could see the vast oval of the riding-school, its sweep of benches under the candle-light. It was a huge pit from whence in a confusion of speech and clamour rose the smoke of their fate.

The summer night had been so tedious and so burning that in their ten-foot square of a hutch the refugees had hardly endured it. The little child had fallen into a stupid sleep upon his mother's knees, and a sweat unnatural to childhood so bathed his exhausted face that the Queen would

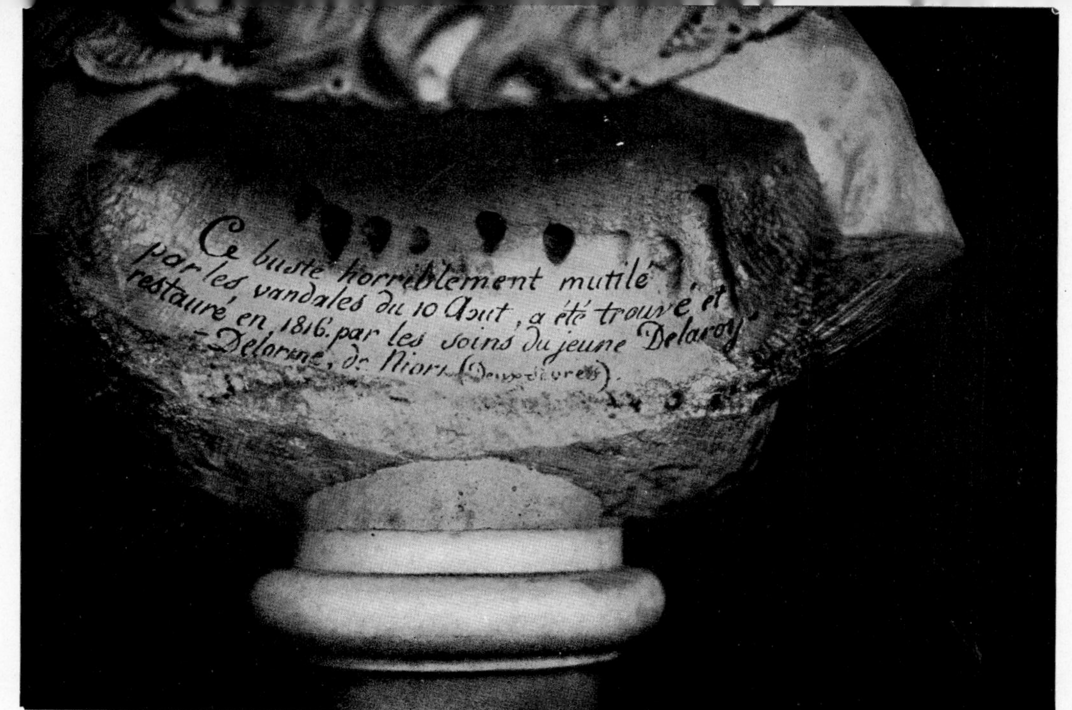

A RELIC OF THE SACK OF THE PALACE

Inscription on the broken bust of the Dauphin

not let it remain. She turned for a handkerchief to a gentleman of theirs: he gave her his — but there was the blood of a wound upon it.

Midnight had passed, and they still sat thus packed and buried; before them still rose the sonorous cries of the invading mob, the interjections of the Parliament, the rhetoric of the last speeches. The hundreds of lights still flamed in the double chandeliers of the enormous hall; the roof and the planks of the half-empty benches around the arena still sent back echoes.

It was two in the morning before the doors could open on them, and with the sweep of cooler air came the roar of the populace still on guard after all these eighteen hours. The crowd pressed against the railings as a strong escort hurried the King and Queen across a little corner of the gardens to the deserted monastery next door. There were large candles thrust into the barrels of chance muskets: the night was calm and they could burn. By that faint and smoky light, which but just caught the faces of the crowd beyond, they hurried in to the door of the Feuillants.

For many months no one had trodden the corridor of the place; the bricks of the flooring beneath their feet lay unevenly. The blank and whitewashed walls, cracked and neglected, were pierced by four such similar little doors as monasteries use for an entrance to their cells, and in those four bare cells the Parliament had hurriedly provided what furniture the old house afforded.

The Dauphin had awakened for a moment in the fresh air, and had smiled; he had said, so that those near could hear him: "I am to sleep in mamma's room to-night!" His mother had promised it him as a reward during the dreadful day; he slept when the doors closed on them, and his sister slept too. The Queen was too angry for repose.

She saw the monk's bed of the cell, little and hard; she saw the mouldy green paper on the wall; she stamped for one last futile time into the King's presence beyond the partition to cry that things should surely have turned differently.

"The Marseillese should have been driven back!"

Louis had never failed to meet her anger when it rose, by a stolid truth. "Who was to drive them back?" he said.

Then she, who had not understood the armed nature of the struggle, but only her own fierce desire, turned back and threw herself upon the narrow bed of her refuge.

The day already glimmered. One could see the trees of what had been but yesterday her royal garden, and one could see the palace beyond through the dirty windows of the little room. The sun rose and showed her her misery more clearly. She could not sleep. It was not till the light in the east had risen above the many roofs of the Tuileries and had already thrown a slit of bright shining aslant into the room, that there fell upon her less a slumber than an unhappy trance of exhaustion.

There was silence while she slept. The mob had gone home exhausted. The carts, which had worked all night round the palace and in the gardens picking up the wounded and the dead, lumbered no more, and their crunching upon the gravel of the alleys had ceased. No wheels rattled in the Rue St. Honoré as yet, and the few that still maintained the sitting in the Parliament were attended by no more in the Tribunes than a few sleepy beings watching to the end. Outside in the still air all that could be heard was the early piping of birds.

For that little space Marie Antoinette lay broken but forgetful of the dreadful day.

Her sister-in-law, in whom self-sacrifice was permanent, watched her pitifully so lying for one hour and another. Then she woke the children and dressed them for the new day, silently, so as to spare their mother's sleep, but that sleep did not endure. The Queen raised herself unrefreshed, and, when she saw the children, remembered their promise and their fall and said: "It will all end with us! . . . "

With the morning some succour began to arrive from their own class, who pitied them, especially from foreigners. Lady Gower's little son, younger than the Dauphin, was yet of the same measure. The child could therefore wear the change that was sent him from the English Embassy. The King was supplied by a captain of his Swiss, a man as corpulent as himself. The Queen could get linen at least from the Duchesse de Gramont. Her watch and purse were stolen, left behind or lost, but there was plenty of money; one of her women had no less than twenty pounds upon her: there was no need to look further.

At ten an escort brought that broken family back to the reporters' box. And so daily the long fatigue was endured and the mean lodging of the night. All the Saturday, all the Sunday, the debates continued in their presence. They saw, they half-understood the quarrel between the city, which had determined to be master of their persons, and the Parliament, which refused to forego its sovereignty. They heard the decree passed that overthrew the statues of the Kings throughout Paris. They heard that the palace of the Luxembourg was to be their sumptuous prison; then the long argument against that building, the perpetual demand of the city for their custody; the suggestion of this place and that: the Archbishop's palace — at last the Temple.

They saw the deputation of the city, with the Mayor at its head, insisting; they heard the Parliament give way, and knew by Sunday evening, that Paris would hold them hostages.

On the morrow — a fatal 13th — their Court was removed from them: a few friends only were allowed to remain. Under the wan light of evening two great carriages — still royal, but their drivers' livery gone and a dull grey replacing it — stood before the door of the Feuillants. The act of imprisonment had begun.

The heavy coaches rolled along the paving. The scene was that of a crowd freed from labour at such an hour, thousands on either side, and a dense escort pushing its armed column through. The sunset and the long twilight were full of halts and summonses; Pétion, with his head thrust through the window, was insisting on a way for Authority: there was a noise of men struggling, sometimes to see, sometimes to save their feet, snatches of songs, cries.

The distance was not quite a mile and a half. For over two hours the coaches pushed and fought their passage up to the Place Vendôme, where the statue of Louis XIV. lay fallen: past the wide boulevards whose width did nothing to disperse the crowd: down at last along the narrow lane of the Temple, till they came to the great pillars of the porch.

All this while the Queen sat silent. Her husband and she and her royal children were still given honour — sat on the front seat of the great carriage; but the ladies who yet followed the Court, the governess of the Children of France, were indignant that Authority should have passed to the

THE TOWER OF THE TEMPLE AT THE TIME OF THE ROYAL FAMILY'S IMPRISONMENT

officials, and that these should sit wearing their hats of office before France-in-Person. So also when the Royal Family walked across the courtyard to the steps of what had once been Artois' Palace of the Temple, the deputation of the Commune there present to receive them kept their heads covered and insisted upon their new authority, calling Louis "Sir," not "Sire," and preserving in his sight that austere carriage which he had thought the peculiar appanage of kings.

They went up the great staircase, lit splendidly as for a feast, lit as it had been for Artois in the days she so well remembered: the doors shut as upon guests assembled. They followed their warders down a short, walled way through the open night, and saw before them at last, with lamps in every old crochet of the corners, and every window ablaze, the enormous mass of the Tower.

. . . .

To the north of the square keep which was the main outline of the Tower, a second building, an afterthought of the latter Middle Ages, had been added. It leant up against its larger neighbour, forming a kind of pent-house; its four storeys were far lower than those of the stronghold—the rooms into which each storey was partitioned were necessarily smaller and less convenient than those which they were to occupy later in the main tower: it was nevertheless necessary to lodge them here for the first few weeks, because this annex alone was furnished. It had been the residence of the Archivist in charge; its main room had been his drawing-room; the whole was ready for an immediate occupation.

To these Princesses and their train there was a portentous novelty in such a place. The King, a man, and one fond of hunting in all weathers, self-centred, negligent of his person, careless of any luxury save that of the table, saw nothing sharp in these surroundings: indeed, his sex, especially when it is leisured, can take what it finds in a campaign or accident with no great shock. But the women, who had in every moment of their lives been moulded by magnificence and ease, could not understand the place at all. Varennes had been a hurly-burly; the wretched three days just ended at the Feuillants a violent interlude; for the rest their pains and terrors of the past three years had been played upon a gorgeous scene. They had slept for a thousand nights of peril in very soft and bulging beds whose frames were thick with gilding, beds whose canopies were splendidly high and curtained like thrones. They had been surrounded for a thousand days of peril by silent servants trained and dressed in gorgeous livery for their work. They had looked out on great ordered gardens, and had walked over the shining floors of the palace. That was their protection: a habit of grand circumstance and continuous exalted experience against which the occasional horror and the strain of their lives could make no impression.

To-night, in the unaccustomed stillness of the Temple enclosure, they sat silent in the knowledge that these low roofs and common walls must be a kind of home for them. All was at first insupportable; the King's sister, sleeping on a ground floor, in a room which once the cooks of the house inhabited: next to her through the wall, the Guard Room; the Queen, the royal children and their governess, cooped up in a couple of small bedrooms fifteen feet square or less, preparing their own beds and the Dauphin's, were in a new, worse world. The poor Princesse de Lamballe, with her own great virtue of fidelity surviving all her inanities, put a truckle bed for herself in the dark little passage between the two rooms and slept there, as a dog sleeps at the door of its mistress. Nor did even this society endure. A week had not passed when the officers came by night to read a new decree, and to separate the Duchesse de Tourzel and the Princesse de Lamballe from their masters, saying: "There must be no one here but Capetians." Then the complete isolation of their lives, a new habit, of settled hours and monotonous exactitude, began.

This life reflected as in a quiet mirror the chaos of the enormous struggle which was being fought out beyond the walls of the Temple. They were prisoners and yet unrestricted; confined by public authority and yet permitted the refinements of their rank. Surrounded by guardians, but by guardians none of whom as yet insulted them, many of whom were secretly their friends, some few their devoted servants, traitors to the State in the crisis of a great war but traitors through devotion to a national tradition.

Twenty courses at a meal were not thought too many; a dozen servants, paid fantastic salaries, did not suffice them; their expenditure, if not the half-million voted, was yet at the rate of many thousands a year; the doctor and the drawing master may visit them, and the Duchesse de Gramont may send them books. Their wine, though the King alone drank it, was of the best, commonly champagne (at that time not the fashionable wine of the rich, but rather the ritual of feast days); they had good furniture at their demand, an ample library of many hundred volumes; and in general such comfort as such a situation could afford. But a violent contrast marked their lives, the contrast between this luxury and the anarchy of manners around them. Their guards, often gentlemen, were now courteous, now obsequious, now offensive, according as chance sent men of varying politics or character by turn to be on duty at the Tower.

The alternate fears and expectations of the Revolution, the doubtful chances of the frontier battles, the unsettled quarrel of the political parties among the conquerors — all these permit the inconsistencies of that moment upon the part of the Commune and the Parliament. They permit within the Tower that mixture of the prison and the home whereby an increasing severity of rule and an increasing vexation did not forbid the costly furniture, the very complete library, the exquisite cooking which make up the curious contrast of their lives.

The order of their day was simple and unchangeable. The King would rise at six, shave, dress, and read till nine. The Queen and the Dauphin were up by eight, at which hour the servants and the guard came into the rooms. At nine they breakfasted. During the morning great care was taken by Louis himself with the lessons of the boy. The Queen and her sister-in-law dressed for the day. They walked in the large gardens where the mob from far off could watch them from behind the railings of the Square; dined at two o'clock, played cards. The King would sleep in the afternoon, would sup again at nine, and read till midnight.

A week after the Princesse de Lamballe and the Duchesse de Tourzel had left them, before the end of August, the first of the indignities offered to the person of the Monarch came to him thus: They took away his sword. It was but an ornament, yet in all that long line of ancestry no other had had his sword unclasped. And this man, who could never have used a true sword, let alone that toy, felt the loss like a wound. Much at the same time, that is before the end of August, entered three new people into the prison—Tison and his wife, new gaolers who had to act as spies upon them; and Cléry, who was to act as the valet of Louis, who was devoted to him, and who has left us what is certainly the clearest and probably the most accurate account of the prison life of the family.

In those same days they heard whispered to them by one of the guards, Hue, the first news they had had upon the matter that never left their thoughts. The invasion was successful. Brunswick was well on his way — it was impossible that he should be opposed.

For yet another week no incident disturbed the common run of their quiet; the physical impressions which build up most of life were neighbouring and small; the daily noise of hammering in the great tower next door where their permanent apartments were preparing; and the daily reading, the daily games of backgammon, and, daily, the sumptuous meals; the modest dresses, changed (as is the custom of the gentry) for the evening; the daily intercourse with such two commissioners from the City Council as happened to be on guard. From their windows they could see the rapid demolition of the small huddled buildings round the Tower, and Palloy's great encircling wall rising between them and liberty on every side.

But beyond these exterior things their minds dwelt continually upon the matter which had held all their thoughts for a year. They remembered, in their isolation, the frontier, the Argonne (which is a wall), and beyond it the bare plains of the East: moving densely over these the convoys, the guns, and the packed columns of the invasion. They had failed to hold their Parisian fortress till the advent of that slow machine, but they could still hope serenely: they had known regulars since their childhood: they saw in the advance of Brunswick something inevitable; they were certain of this success, and they waited.

. . . .

How truly the history of the Revolution is the history of war can never sufficiently be stamped upon the mind of the student. The Terror when it came was, as I shall call it, nothing but martial law established during a reign: the steps by which the fury of the time advanced towards it corresponded exactly to the fortune of the French armies.

Upon the 2nd of September, as the prisoners walked in the garden, they heard a roar throughout the city. The populace beyond the railings threw stones: they were hurried back into their prison. For a moment before dusk they saw the wild and fanatical face of Mathieu, once a monk, who shouted at them: "The Émigrés have taken Verdun, but if we perish you shall perish with us." In the increasing hubbub all around, the little Dauphin cried and was disturbed; and all night the Queen could not sleep. She could not sleep as the noise rose and roared throughout Paris. . . . It had almost come. The armies were almost here, and once again the dice were being shaken for the murder of the prisoners, or for their deliverance.

It was on that day, and pricked by the spur of such news, that Marat's frenzied committee gathered a band, and began the massacre of those caught in the public prisons—all those suspect of complicity with the invasion and of the desire to help the foreigner in destroying the new liberties

THE PRINCESSE DE LAMBALLE
A rough miniature preserved at the Carnavalet

of the nation. Among these hundreds, roped in suddenly upon suspicion from among the rich or the reactionary of the older world, was the foolish, tender and loyal woman who had determined to share the fortunes of the Queen — the Princesse de Lamballe. When they had taken her a fortnight before from the side of her friend she had but been thrust into another prison to await these days.

The 3rd of September broke upon the captives, a dull uneasy morning in which the clamour of distant disturbance still occasionally reached them from the centre of the city southward, then came nearer.

They were told that on that day there would be no walk in the garden. They sat therefore all the morning in their rooms. They dined as was their custom; their dinner was over, it was not quite three o'clock, and the King and the guard for the day stood together at one of the great tunnel-like windows of the first floor, for the windows were not yet blinded as they later were. The guard by his side was one Danjou, a young man of thirty-two, very eager upon the new world which he believed to be then arising; full of a vision of freedom; a good sculptor — for that was his business — intense in action, he was, above all, brave. Energy bubbled out of him, and he had, what goes with energy, a clear head and rapid decision. The King and this man stood together exchanging that kind of easy conversation which Louis had by this time learnt to hold with men of every rank. They were watching the workmen pull down the houses near by, and the rising of the wall which was built to enclose the gardens of the Temple. Now and then, as a great beam fell with its great clouds of dust, the honest and slow King would laugh and say: "There goes another!" Their conversation was on this level when they heard an increasing noise outside the gates. To the Royal Family it meant but one more mob rolling by. Danjou, who was a free man fresh from outside and knew better, was silent and anxious: he was aware that the massacres had begun.

At first it was a set of drunken songs far off, and then a clamour in the streets. At last, quite close, separate cries and loud demands, and hammering at the gates; and next a nasty crowd burst in. They were not very numerous, but they were drunk and mad with blood; and they dragged with them the body of the only woman killed during all those horrors, a corpse stripped, perhaps mutilated, and separate from it a head with powder on the hair. This head, thrust upon a pike, some of the foremost raised before the window; and Louis, slow of vision though he was, recognised it for the Princesse de Lamballe. His wife was at the table behind him. The window was high, deep and distant. Louis cried suddenly, "Prevent the Queen . . . !" But, whether she had seen or had not seen that dreadful thing, the Queen had fainted.

Without, Danjou, acting as promptly as a soldier, was standing on the steps, giving the mob all the words that came to him of flattery, rhetoric, or menace; and getting them at last to scramble down from the heaps of broken brick and rubble they occupied, and to go, taking their trophy with them. Within, her sister and her husband attended the Queen.

She was quite broken down. The night fell, but again she could not sleep. She passed the dark hours sobbing with pain, until yet another day had dawned upon her. And still a long way off in Paris the massacres continued. Still, through the first week of September and the second, advanced the army of the invaders which was to save them as it came victorious; or at the worst it came at least to destroy their enemies and the city which had dared to imprison them.

News did not reach the prisoners save at such intervals, or in such broken whispers, or by such doubtful signs that they could make little of it: but whether they knew much of that news or little, the army was irresistibly advancing: the French troops which were to oppose it were increasingly falling in value: the passes of Argonne were forced — all but one. Dumouriez was turned; and by the 20th of September Prussia and Austria were present, armed, four days' march from the gates; and there was no force at all between them and Paris. That same day the Parliament in Paris met the menace by declaring the Republic.

Upon the morrow the most extreme of the extremists, Hébert, the cleanly and insane, looked in to mock them coldly; while outside the booming voice of Lubin proclaimed in a most distinct proclamation, phrase by phrase, that the French Monarchy was no more. The King went on reading, the Queen went on sewing; for such was the occupation of either as they heard those words. The slow hours of the equinox passed without news or disturbance in the city; but meanwhile, out where the armies were, a prodigious and as yet unexplained thing had happened. Austria and Prussia and the Emigrants had failed. The strong cities which they had easily taken, the passes of Argonne which they had almost as easily forced, the contemptuous and just strategy by which they had marched round the worthless forces of the National Defence and now stood between it and Paris — all these by some miracle of war had availed them nothing: and in a muddy dip before the windmill of *Valmy* the whole campaign had failed.

. . . .

I wish I had the space here to digress into some account of that inexplicable day. I know the place, and I have well comprehended the conditions of soil and of gunnery under which the Prussian charge failed even before its onset. Nor could any study more engross, nor any examination prove more conclusive, than an analysis of the few hours in which this accident of European history was decided upon the ground which, centuries before, had seen Gaul, and therefore Europe, saved from Attila. But neither the limits nor the nature of my subject permit me; and it must be enough to say that on the 21st of September at Valmy, a few yards from the road whereby the King had fled to Varennes, by the failure of one charge the invasion failed. In a few days the retreat of the army that was to rescue or to avenge the King and the Queen had begun; and from that moment the nature of their imprisonment changed.

. . . .

Upon the 29th of September pens, ink and paper were taken away from the prisoners, and on the evening of the same day there once more entered the cleanly and insane Hébert, who read to them the order that Louis XVI. should be separated from his family and imprisoned in another set of rooms in the Tower.

Those relations which had been at first ridiculous, later tolerated, and though affectionate not deep, between the Queen and her husband, her dislike of his advances towards the Liberal movement, her angry amazement at his patriotism in the early days of the revolt — all these which are too often read into her last emotions in his regard, must be in part forgotten when we consider how they all lived together behind those thick walls. Every human soul that left the group was something lost to them forever. Of the two that had last left them, the head of one, shown murdered, had been seen at the window. And moreover, this order to separate the King meant almost certainly some form of approaching disaster. The children also were a bond. For they knew nothing of whatever early phantasies, whatever recent disagreements there had been between the wife and the husband, and they must now have their father hidden from them.

He was taken away. Upon the next day, the 30th, as once before during their imprisonment, the Queen refused to eat and sat silent. To that silence there succeeded a fit of violent anger in which she screamed at the guards. It was when Cléry came to get some books for his master.

It is reported that Simon, one of the Municipals who was later to be the gaoler of her child, said as he saw the distress of the women, that it nearly moved him to tears, and that turning to the Queen he told her that she had had no tears when the palace fought the people upon the 10th of August. It is said that the Queen answered: "You do not understand." And when he added: "You should be glad at least that the traitors are caught" — by which phrase he meant the popular vengeance and the massacres in the prisons, the repulsion of the invasion and the rest of it — the Queen would not answer a word.

Upon the 1st of November, the day before her thirty-seventh birthday, she saw again a visitor to her prison, a dark face which it appalled her to see: it was a face stamped with all the associations of Varennes. It was the face of Drouet.

He spoke to her as a deputy from the Municipality (to which he now belonged), to ask whether she had anything to complain of. She resolutely maintained her sullen silence; she turned her face away and treated him as though he were not there, and he on his part threw his arms up in a gesture of resignation, then bowed to her and went out.

The royal people had colds in November and waited through a shivering month what could not but be the approach of some very evil thing. Upon the 6th, one of those scraps of news — positive news and ill — which reached them like patches of clear light in the midst of murky fears and rumours, was granted to the prisoners. The Committee of Parliament had reported upon Louis' case: an indictment was framed; he would certainly be tried.

To such an advance of misfortune they could only oppose the fixed hope that in some way or other the regular armies of the Old World *must* break through. They had been checked at Valmy, nay, they had retreated. But surely they *could not but* return, and brush aside at last the raw and formless rags of the French volunteers. *They could not but.* The old regulated armies, the peace of mind, the brilliant uniforms, the vast prestige of German arms, the leadership of gentlemen — sanity, cleanliness, and the approval of educated men — these *must* at last destroy those mere composite mobs, half regulars, half levies, half sodden, half mutinous, ill-fed, ill-clothed, officered as best might be, untutored and untutorable, which their gaolers had flung together in a sort of delirium, hotch-potch, to make a confused covering against the governing classes of Europe who were advancing in defence of all the decencies of this world.

As the Royal Family so hoped against hope, that ill-conditioned crowd — old soldiers relaxed in discipline, young enthusiasts who drank, sickly and grumbling volunteers, veterans hoping for revenge against the harsh experience of years (a dangerous type), company-officers of a week's standing, put side by side with others of twenty years, captains in boyhood and lieutenants at forty — this welter was jumbled all together under the anxious eye of Dumouriez, along a valley of the frontier, on the muddy banks of the river called Hate — La Haine.

I know the place: low banks that rise in the distance into hills are overlooked far up stream and down by the fantastic belfry of Mons and its huge church dominating the plain. Dumouriez, deeply doubting his rabble but knowing the temper of his own people, poured the young men and the old across the line of the river, leading them with the Marseillaise. Among the villages of the assaulted line Jemappes has given its name to the charge. By the evening of that same day, the 6th of November, the Austrian force was destroyed, a third of its men lay upon the field or had deserted, the rest were beating off in a pressed retreat, eastward and away. The rabble should have failed and had succeeded.

I have said that for Valmy no explanation has as yet been given. For Jemappes there are many explanations: that the Austrians had attempted to hold too long a strategic line and were outnumbered at the chief tactical point of the battle: that their excellent cavalry (the French in this arm were deplorable) had not been allowed to hold their left long enough: that one passage of the river was accidental and could not have been foreseen (a bad commentary on any action!). But the true cause of that temporary yet decisive achievement was to be found in two forms of energy: rapidity in marching and in the handling of guns — but such criticisms do not concern this book.[1]

Of this victory, coincident with the beginning of the King's agony, Marie Antoinette for days could know nothing, and even when the rumour reached her it was but the victorious shouting in the streets and a name or two whispered by a servant that gave her a passing impression that her champions had suffered a further check — no more. Yet before that tide should flow back and finally swamp the French packed in Leipsic, twenty years must pass, and not till then should the Kings and the lords at last see Paris from a hill.

There is one detail in connection with Jemappes which the reader must know because it does so illustrate the myriad coincidences of the Queen's life.

That child whom she had seen and adopted during her early childless years, when her fever of youth and exasperation was upon her, that child which for a moment had supplied to the girl something of maternity, had now grown to manhood. The birth of her own daughter had long ago driven out any recollection of the whim: the peasant boy of St. Michel was forgotten. He had grown into his teens full of the bitterness which irresponsible and spasmodic patronage can so vigorously breed. During the days of October he had been recognised among the wildest of those who attacked the palace in Versailles; he had shouted for the Nation; he had enlisted and was there at Jemappes, an obscure volunteer among the thousands whom Dumouriez forced forward upon the frontier. He was present upon the 6th of November upon the bank of the Haine

[1] These two military qualities are present to-day capitally among the French, and may at any moment reappear in the discussions of modern Europe.

Au Citoyen Suppleant pour le Procureur General Sindic du département

Citoyen

Je viens de recevoir les ordres que vous m'avez adressez. Je vais prendre toutes les mesures pour qu'il n'arrive aucun retards à ce qu'ils prescrivent. Le charpentier est averti pour la pose de la machine, laquelle sera mise en place à l'endroit indiqué.

Il est absolument nécessaire que je sache comment Louis partira du temple. aura-t-il une voiture. ou sy ce sera dans la voiture ordinaire aux exécutions de ce genre.

après l'exécution que deviendra le corps du justicié.

Faut il que moi, et mes commis, nous nous trouvions au temple à huit heures comme

SANSON'S LETTER

Asking the authorities what steps he is to take for the execution of the King

when the mixed battalions charged, singing: a bullet struck him and he fell down dead. She, the Queen, was there a prisoner in her dimly lit room at night — separated from the father of the children who slept near by: her mind was big with the new doom of his Indictment and Trial which the dull day had brought her. Eighteen years before she had caught up that peasant baby in the Louveciennes road and kissed it, her eyes full of tears, and in her heart a violent yearning half-virginal, half-maternal: he, however, lay dead that same night in the Hainault mud with the autumn rain upon his body: his name was Jacques Amand.

. . . .

With December there was some little respite, for a new Municipality had been elected that was a trifle more moderate than the old, but in general this life of hers with its calm, its dread and its monotony, continued. Now it contained some act of humiliation, as when all razors and sharp-edged things were taken from the King (upon the 7th), now some indulgence, as when (upon the 9th) a clavecin was allowed the Queen — and it is said that from curiosity she played upon this, later, the new notes of the Marseillaise.

For a few hours the Dauphin was taken from her. It was her turn to ask questions of the guards, and theirs to be silent; she asked distractedly: they did not reply: but the child returned.

The affair of the trial proceeded rapidly. The briefs were gathered, the Kings' counsel met the King day after day in the apartment below, and she stayed above there alone with her children and was still. She had no communications with him at all save when at Christmas, after he had drafted his will, he wrote to the Convention and caused a short message to be conveyed to the Queen. It was perhaps during these days that she wrote upon a fly-leaf which is still preserved in St. Germain, "*Oportet unum mori pro populo.*"

Louis, as the new year broke, saluted it sadly. Within a fortnight he had been pronounced guilty at the bar of the Parliament before which he was arraigned — guilty, that is, of intrigue with the foreigner and of abetting the invasion. Upon the 17th of January, 1793, it was known in his prison that the penalty would be death. Again did Marie Antoinette hear in the room below the step of Malesherbes, her husband's counsel, coming upon that day to confer with the King, but this time he came to speak not of defence but of death. A respite was denied to Louis. Upon the 20th his prayer for three days in which he might prepare to meet God was again refused, and his execution was fixed for the morrow. His sentence was read to him in his prison: he heard it quietly: and thus upon that 20th of January (a Sunday), a murky evening and cold, when it was quite dark the princesses heard in the street a newspaper-seller crying the news that the King must die; the hollow word "*la mort,*" very deep and lugubrious, repeated and repeated in the chanting tones of that trade, floated up from the winter streets.

It was eight o'clock when they were told that they might go down with the children and see the King.

The family met together and for a little time were silent.

. . . .

The spell was on them which we never mention — one which the inmost mind refuses — I mean that fear . . .

During this long isolation of theirs they had become

20 janvier 1793. 1°

Je demande ~~a la Convention Nationale~~ un delai de trois jours pour pouvoir me preparer a paraitre devant la presence de Dieu. je demande pour cela de pouvoir voir librement la personne que j'indiquerai aux Commissaires de la Commune, et que cette personne soit a l'abri de toutte inquietude et de toutte crainte pour cet Acte de Charité qu'elle remplira auprés de moi. je demande ~~a la Convention Nationale~~ d'estre delivré de la surveillance perpetuelle que le Conseil General a etabli depuis quelques jours.

Je demande dans cet intervalle a pouvoir voir ma famille quand je le demanderai ~~desirerai~~ et sans ~~temoins~~ temoins. je desirerois bien que la Convention Nationale s'occupat tout de suitte du sort de ma famille, et qu'elle lui permit de se retirer librement et convenablement ou elle le jugeroit a propos.

Je recommande a la bienfaisance de la Nation touttes les personnes qui m'etoient attachées, il y en a beaucoup qui avoient mis touttes leur fortune dans leurs charges, et qui n'aiant plus d'appointements doivent estre dans le besoin, et meme de celles qui ne vivoient que de leurs appointements. Dans les pensionaires il y a beaucoup de vieillards de femmes et d'enfants qui n'avoient que cela pour vivre.

a la Tour du Temple le Janvier 1793

Louis

La Conv.on Nat. passe à l'ordre du jour.
P. Val du 20 Janv.r 1793. —
Page 322.

AUTOGRAPH DEMAND OF LOUIS XVI. FOR A RESPITE OF THREE DAYS

very fixed upon the matter of the Catholic Faith, but that fear pervaded them as the Church has said that it must always pervade the last hours. This human curse, too sacred for rhetoric and too bewildering to occupy a just and reasonable prose, I will abandon, content only to have written it down — for it was the air and the horror of that night.

For not quite two hours they sat together, not speaking much, for all understood, except the little boy: he was sad as children are, up to the usual pitch of sadness, for any loss great or small which they do not understand: he saw his own sister, a child older than he, and all his grown-up elders thus crushed, and he also was full of his little sorrow. He knew at least that his father was going away.

The King, seated with his wife on his left and his sister at his right hand, drew the boy towards him and made him stand between his knees. He recited to him, as it is proper to recite to children, words whose simplicity they retain but whose full purport they cannot for the moment understand. He told the child never to avenge his death, and, since oaths are more sacred than repeated words, he took and lifted up his small right hand. Then, knowing that the will of the sufferer alone can put a due term to such scenes, he rose. His wife he pressed to his shoulder. She caught and grasped to her body her little children — to hold so much at least firm in this world that was breaking from around her. She knew that Louis desired them to leave, and she said, after she had wildly sworn that she would stay all night and the children with her (which he would not have):

"Promise that you will see us again?"

"I will see you in the morning," he answered, "before . . . I go. At eight."

"It must be earlier," she said, not yet releasing him.

"It shall be earlier, by half an hour."

"Promise me."

He repeated his promise, and the two women turned to the great oaken, nail-studded door; helping the fainting girl, and taking the child by the hand they went out to the winding stair of stone. It was a little after ten.

When the iron outer door had shut and he knew the women and the children to be above, out of hearing, Louis turned to his guards and gave this order, that in spite of what he had said, the women should not be told in the morning of his departure, for that neither he nor they could suffer it.

Then he went into the turret chamber where the priest was, and said: "Let me address myself to the unique affair."

But above, from the room whose misery could just be heard, the Queen, when she had put her boy to bed and kissed him bitterly, threw herself upon her own bed all dressed, and throughout the darkness of the whole night long her daughter could hear her shuddering with cold and anguish.

That night there was a murmur all around the Tower, for very many in Paris were watching, and through the drizzling mist there came, hour by hour, the distant rumble of cannon, and the sharp cries of command, and men marching by companies up the narrow Temple lane.

It was the very January dark, barely six of the morning, when a guard from the King's room came up the stair. The Queen from above heard him coming. Her candle was lit — her fixed gaze expected him. . . . He entered, but as he spoke her heart failed her: he had not come for the summons, he had but come for the King's book of prayers. She waited the full hour until seven struck in

A. le 23 janv

Procès-verbal de l'inhumation de Louis Capet.

Le Vingt un janvier mil sept cent quatre Vingt treize, L'an deux de la République françoise, Nous soussignés administrateurs du Département de Paris chargés de Pouvoirs par le Conseil Général du Département, en Vertu des arrêtés du Conseil Exécutif provisoire de la République françoise, Nous Sommes transportés à neuf heures du Matin en la demeure du Citoyen Picavez Curé de Ste Madeleine; Lequel ayant trouvé chez lui, Nous lui avons demandé, s'il avoit pourvu à l'Exécution des Mesures qui lui avoient été recommandées la Veille par le Conseil exécutif et par le Département pour l'inhumation de Louis Capet: il nous a répondu qu'il avoit exécuté de point en point ce qui lui avoit été ordonné par le Conseil exécutif et par le Département, et que tout étoit à l'instant préparé

REPORT OF THE COMMISSIONERS

That all is duly arranged for the burial of Louis Capet after his execution

the steeples of the town, and the pale light began to grow: she waited past the moment of her husband's promise, till eight, till the full day — but no one came. Still she sat on, not knowing what might not have come between to delay their meeting: doors opening below, steps coming and going on the stairs, held all her mind. But no one sent for her, no one called her. It was nine when a more general movement made her half hope, half fear. The sound of that movement, which was the movement of many men, passed downward to the first stories, to the ground, and was lost. An emptiness fell upon the Tower. Then she knew that her hope had departed.

For a moment there were voices in the courtyard, the tramp of many men upon the damp gravel, the creaking of the door, more distant steps in the garden, and the wheels of the coach far away at the outer porch. Then the confused noise of a following crowd dwindling westward till nothing remained but a complete silence in those populous streets, now deserted upon so great a public occasion.

For yet another hour the silence endured unbroken: ten o'clock struck amid that silence, and the quarter. . . . The Queen heard through the shuttered window the curious and dreadful sound of a crowd that roars far off, and she knew that the thing had been done.

Life returned into the streets beneath, the loud shrill call of the news-men, crying the news accursedly, came much too shrill and too distinct against the walls. All day long, on to the early closing of the darkness, the mists gathered and lay thick over Paris and around her high abandoned place.

XVIII

THE HOSTAGE

FROM THE 21ST OF JANUARY, 1793, TO THREE IN THE MORNING OF THE 2ND OF AUGUST, 1793

THAT night the prisoners in the Tower did not sleep, saving the little Dauphin: he slept soundly; and it is said of his mother, that, watching him, she murmured that he was of the age at which his brother had died, at Meudon, and that those of her family who died earliest were the most blessed. In the last silences of the January night, till past two in the morning, the woman Tison, who was in part their gaoleress and in part a spy upon them, heard them talking still, and when she came to them Madame Elizabeth said: "For God's sake leave us."

Cléry, the dead master's valet, was taken away, still noting as he went the new look in the Queen's eyes. And in this same week there came the mourning clothes which they had asked of the authorities and which had been granted them. The Princess Royal fell ill. The Queen would no longer walk in the garden now, and the child, lacking exercise — and with bad blood — suffered. Her legs swelled badly. The authorities allowed the man who had been the family doctor of the children in the old days to come and visit them now. Brunier was his name, and in the old days Marie Antoinette had affected to ridicule his middle-class energy: she thought he lacked respect to the clay of which she and her children were made. She was glad enough to see him now, and he

Première

Archives Nationales.

Rég. A. 2. f° 17. N° 103.

+

Au nom de la tres Sainte Trinité du Pere du Fils et du S. Esprit. Aujourd'hui vingt cinquieme jour de Decembre, mil sept cent quatre vingt douze. Moi Louis XVI du nom Roy de France, etant depuis plus de quatre mois enfermé avec ma famille dans la Tour du Temple a Paris, par ceux qui etoient mes sujets, et privé de toutte communication quelconque, meme depuis le onze du courant avec ma famille. de plus impliqué dans un Procès, dont il est impossible de prevoir l'issue a cause des passions des hommes, et dont on ne trouve aucun pretexte ni moyen dans aucune Loy existante, n'ayant que Dieu pour temoin de mes pensees, et auquel je puisse m'adresser. je declare ici en sa presence mes dernieres volontés et mes sentiments.

Je laisse mon ame a Dieu mon createur, je le prie de la recevoir dans sa misericorde, de ne pas la juger d'apres ses merites, mais par ceux de Notre Seigneur Jesus Christ, qui s'est offert en sacrifice a Dieu son Pere, pour nous autres hommes quelqu'indignes que nous en fussions, et moi le premier.

Je meurs dans l'union de notre sainte Mere l'Eglise Catholique Apostolique et Romaine, qui tient ses pouvoirs par une succession non interrompue de St Pierre auquel J. C. les avoit confiés. je crois fermement et je confesse tout ce qui est contenu dans le Symbole et les commandements de Dieu et de l'Eglise, les Sacrements et les Mysteres tels que l'Eglise Catholique les enseigne et les a toujours enseignés. je n'ai jamais pretendu me rendre juge dans les differentes manieres d'expliquer les dogmes qui dechirent l'Eglise de J. C. mais je m'en suis rapporté et rapporterai toujours si Dieu m'accorde vie, aux decisions que les superieurs Ecclesiastiques unis a la Sainte Eglise Catholique, donnent et donneront conformement a la discipline de l'Eglise suivie depuis J. C. je plains de tout mon cœur nos freres qui peuvent etre dans l'erreur, mais je ne pretends pas les juger, et je ne les aime pas moins:

Paraphé et lu au conseil général de la commune ce 21 Janvier 1793 l'an 2 de la République à une heure après midi [illegible]

FIRST PAGE OF LOUIS XVI.'S WILL

was devoted. He was allowed to call in a surgeon and to bring in linen. Nor was he their only communication with the external world, for though the sound and the news of it did not reach them, yet they were not, as modern prisoners are, denied companionship. Upon the pretext or with the real excuse that the mourning clothes did not fit, a dressmaker whom they had known was allowed in; and in general, as will be seen in a moment, there were methods of communication between them and those who desired to know every moment of their captivity and every accident of their fate. From the close of January onward into the summer, five months, it is possible to establish no precise chronology of their actions, but it is possible to decide the general tenor of their lives: save in one particular, which is that we cannot determine to-day what exactly were the relations between the Queen and those who would rescue her or who could give her news of the outer world — especially Fersen.

We have of course several accounts furnished by eyewitnesses, notably the account of Turgy, who was their sole servant in their prison; but these accounts, and that account especially, are tinged with the quite obvious atmosphere of the Restoration. Quite poor people, writing at the suggestion of a powerful government at a time when every laudatory or illuminating detail upon the imprisonment of the royal family had its high money value, must, however honest, be somewhat suspect. For the most honest man or woman the conditions of the Restoration were such that there would be an inevitable tendency to exaggeration; and we have no evidence available of the exact characters of the witnesses. Still the witnesses are witnesses, and though an elaborate code of signals (which some of them pretend) probably did not exist, yet we know both from Fersen himself and from the way in which affairs were conducted on either side, that not a little communication was established between the widowed Queen and the Royalists outside. To more than that general statement no historian can commit himself, unless he be one of those belated university types who will trust a printed or a written document beyond their common sense.

It must be remembered that during the first two months after the death of the King, that is, during all February and March, 1793, the exalted and the noble minds of the Gironde were still at the head of that executive power which is in France (since the French have no aristocracy) the whole of government. Nay, they remained technically the heads of the Executive until the end of May, 1793, though their power was touched by the establishment of the Revolutionary Tribunal on the proposal of the Radicals in March, and undermined by the establishment of the Committee of Public Safety on the proposal of Danton in early April.

The Girondins and the Municipality of Paris were at odds. The Municipality itself was not homogeneous.

The guarding of the Queen, which was the business of the Municipality, was not uniform. The Municipality had to choose many men to relieve each other in relays; and of these, two, Toulan and Lepitre, tended, at least after a little experience of their prisoners, to show them sympathy. One of their officers, Michonis, did more, and would have saved her.

From time to time a newspaper would be smuggled in to these princesses; it is said that music played from a window whence they could hear it, conveyed signals, and at any rate it is certain that Fersen had some news of them.

Now Fersen at this moment, in early February that is, bad as his judgment of French affairs was, appreciated their situation in a phrase. He called the Queen "a hostage," and this describes very accurately the meaning of her captivity.

I repeat, no one can understand the Revolution who does not treat it as a military thing, and no one can understand military affairs who imagines them to be an anarchy. Of necessity a brain directs them, for if in military affairs a plan be lacking, the weakest opposing plan can always conquer. It was not cruelty nor love of vengeance that dominated the position of the prisoners. They were an asset.

But though their value was recognised and their imprisonment was part of a diplomatic arrangement, yet there were different policies regarded them. The Radicals, the Mountain, were at once the most enthusiastic and the most practical of the Revolutionary groups. They were not in power, they had not a permanent majority in the Parliament though they had Paris behind them; but they saw clearly that France was in to win: they saw clearly (first Danton, then in succession to him Carnot) that every general action lost, every fortress in a chain surrendered, was the approach not of some neutral or balancing arrangement, but of a full, complete and ruthless reaction in Europe without and in France within. It had come to winning all or losing all. The nobler Girondin blood that still controlled the Republic, knew too little of the vices of men to follow that calculation. The Girondins still believed that in some mystic way the steady adherence to the Republican ideal — the volunteer soldier as against the conscript, the citizen controlling the soldier, the locality governing itself —man absolute — was a thing so high that no human circumstance could wound it. They thought it bound to survive through some force inherent in justice.

Within three weeks of the execution of Louis all Europe was banded against the Republic, and one may say, morally, all the Christian world, for even the distant and ill-informed Colonials of Philadelphia and Virginia had recoiled nervously at the news of a king's execution. The pressure of that general war against the Republic was to give, by what fools call the logic of events, a most powerful aid to the practical and savage determination of the Mountain: it was to squeeze to death the idealism of the Girondins.

While yet these last were in power there were plots for the escape of the prisoners, plots which failed; and their treatment, even in minor details (as the allowing them to take their own form of exercise and the leaving of them as much as possible alone) was easy. Little objects left by the King were conveyed to the Queen from the upper room, and Jarjayes, a friend, saw that they reached the King's brothers. Had the impossible attempt of the Girondins performed the miracle which they who had called on this miraculous war demanded, had the patchy volunteer forces of the French found it possible to conquer in those early months of '93, the treatment of the prisoners would have gone from better to better; their release by negotiation would soon have arrived, if not by negotiation then from mere mercy. This same Jarjayes, who had been Marshal of the camp and was husband to one of the Queen's women, found things so easy that he could weave a definite plot for the escape of the royal prisoners. Why it failed we do not know, though of course the Royalist evidence we have ascribes it to a special virtue in the Queen. who refused to be separated from her children. In the first week of March the first plan failed, on account of a violent reaction towards severity on the part of the authorities following the first military reverses in the Netherlands. The second is better attested, and there is here a sufficient concurrence of witnesses to believe that some hesitation of the Queen's did cause its final failure. She would have had to flee alone, and it is on the whole just to decide that she refused; for we have it on the authority of a fairly honest man that the Princess Royal had some memory of this incident of her childhood and had spoken to him on it, while Chauveau-Lagarde (who was later the Queen's counsel during her trial) has left a copy of a note of hers saying that she would not fly alone without her children. Of other supposed communications between her and Jarjayes we have only his copy of her writing.[1] At any rate, with the last days of March all this early phase of the Queen's widowed captivity comes to an end. Dumouriez and the French armies lost the great and decisive action of Neerwinden upon the 18th of the month, and in the last week of it, though the Committee of Public Safety was not yet formed to establish martial law throughout the Republic and to save the State, yet new rigours began.

The woman Tison and her husband — half the gaolers, half the spies of the family, as I have said — were not permitted to leave the Tower of the Temple. Pencils were forbidden. Upon the 25th of March a chimney fire was

[1] I can but pay little attention to evidence of that kind. In the case of Fersen there are reasons for his destroying the originals: he was the recipient of her passionate affections. Moreover, we know his nature well: he had all the Northern simplicity, and with that intense passion of his, he would have thought it sacrilege to ascribe a single word to her that she had not written, or to make fiction out of her beloved soul. Moreover, he cared little whether posterity knew or did not know the things he chose to bequeath to his heirs. In the case of inferior men, with an obvious axe to grind, and proud, whatever their loyalty, to be intermediaries between the Hostage and her rescuers, the evidence of mere copies which they alone can certify is of very little value.

a pretext for the appearance of Chaumett coming from the Commune of Paris. He returned the next day with the Mayor Pache, and with Santerre, the man of the fall of the Bastille, the rich leader of the popular militia; in those same hours Dumouriez at the head of the defeated French Army was receiving the general of the Austrian forces and negotiating treason. He was about to join hands with the enemy and to propose a march on Paris. The first demand for the Queen's trial was made — by Robespierre: a week and Dumouriez' treason was accomplished: the chief general of the Republic had despaired of France and had gone over to the Austrian camp with the design of marching on Paris, and at least restoring order; his army had refused to follow him, but the shock was enormous. Paris won; the Girondins lost. The Committee of Public Safety was established. The Terror was born; and the Revolution, acting under martial law, went forward to loose everything at once or to survive by despotism and by arms.

. . . .

Thence onward Marie Antoinette's imprisonment becomes another matter. On the 20th of April there came into her prison men whose tone and manner would never have been allowed before: the chief of the "Madmen," as the populace called them, the intense Republicans who would believe anything of a Bourbon, Hébert, came into the prison. He came at night. By coincidence or by design her terrors for the future were to be terrors of the night. It was near eleven when his dandy, meagre figure and thin, pointed face appeared to terrify her, and for five hours the whole place was searched and ransacked. Her little son, already ailing, she had to lift from his bed while they felt the mattress and the very walls to see what might be hidden. They took from Madame Elizabeth her stick of sealing-wax, her pencil — which had no lead to it — and they took with them a little scapular of the Sacred Heart and a prayer for France — but the France for which the princesses had this written prayer was not the nation.

On the 23rd they came again and found nothing but an old hat of the King's, which his sister kept as a sort of relic and had put under her bed. It was taken for granted (and justly) that communication had been established between the prisoners and the kings outside. A denunciation of Lepitre, Toulan and the rest, failed, but Toulan and Lepitre were struck off the list of guards.

With the end of May the populace, supported and permitted by the new Committee of Public Safety, conquered the Moderate majority, and the Committee of Public Safety was left without rivals; it began from that moment to direct the war with the leonine courage and ferocity, the new and transcendent intelligence, the ruthless French lucidity which ultimately at Wattignies saved the State.

Upon the victory of Paris and the Mountain the destruction of the Moderates, the establishment of martial law, the despotism of the Committee of Public Safety, came the last phase of the Queen's imprisonment — and with it, by a most evil coincidence or portent, the growing illness of the little heir, her son. Sharp pains in his side, convulsions, the doctor sent for in the early part of May, and again toward its end, and again in June, things going from bad to worse with him.

To these prisoners, shut away from men, the movement of that world was unknown. They only knew that something was surging all round the thick, obliterating, impenetrable walls of their tower.[1] On the day when the populace conquered the Girondins, all they knew was that they were not allowed even upon the roof, from which, upon most days for some hour or so, they might take the air and look down upon the slates of revolutionary Paris far below, and during June when the new power of the Committee and of martial law, of the Terror, of the determination of the Revolution, of the city, was fixing itself firmly in the saddle, they knew nothing of what was passing, save perhaps from a growing insolence in their guards.

In that same month yet another plot for their escape failed. It depended upon two men; the one a certain Batz, on whom our information is most confused and our evidence most doubtful, as indeed his own character and his own memories were doubtful and confused (he was a sort of enthusiast who had already attempted many impossible things); the other, a character quite clearly comprehended, one Michonis. Batz was a kind of baron; Michonis was, like Toulan and Lepitre, of the Municipality and had regular authority. He will be seen again in the last plot to save the Queen. Of whatever nature was this uncertain attempt, it also failed. Shortly after the woman Tison diversified their lives by going mad with great suddenness and suffering a fit. She was removed, and the incident is only of note because certain pamphleteers have called it a judgment of God. Yet her wage was small.

Upon the day after that unusual accident, the growing suspicion of the popular party against what was left of Moderate administration in Government broke out in a furious denunciation of actual and supposed conspiracies.

---

[1] The walls, to be accurate, were nine feet thick, and the windows were like tunnels.

It was feared that the great mass of suspects now gathered into the prisons possessed some engine for revolt. An extreme policy in diplomacy and in arms, as in internal government, finally prevailed, and with the 1st of July this ardent severity took the form of a decree, passed in the now enfeebled and captured Parliament, that the Dauphin — the greatest asset of all — should be separated from his mother and put, though in the same building, under a different guard.

. . . .

It is not to be imagined that so large a transformation of policy between the execution of the King and the decree for the separation of the Dauphin had, in any part of it, a mainspring other than the war. I have said that the steps of the spring, the destruction of the Gironde by the Mountain, the capture by Paris of the Parliament were but the effects of the collapse of the volunteer rush at Neerwinden, the treason of Dumouriez and the new — and necessary — martial law that henceforward bound the Republic. All the last rigours of the imprisonment depended upon the same catastrophe.

The enemy that had been checked at Valmy, had been attacked in the winter but half-prepared, the enemy that had suffered the French gallop to overwhelm the Netherlands and to occupy Mayence — was returning. The Republicans were out of Belgium, the armies of the Kings were flooding back upon the Rhine. The Rhine and Alsace depended upon two things, Mayence and, behind it, shielding Alsace, the lines of Weissembourg that stretched from the river to the Mountains. Mayence was to fall, the lines of Weissembourg were to be pierced. As for the Belgic frontier, there a line of fortresses could check for a moment the advance of the Allies — for the French fortify: they are in this the heirs of Rome; and whenever they suffer defeat the theory of fortification is belittled; in their resurrection of military power the spade goes forward, borne upon the shoulders of Gaul.

In this July of 1793 the Belgic frontier only perillously held. The sieges were at hand and the fall of the frontier strongholds was at hand. These once conquered, it was proposed by Austria, Prussia and England to dismember the territory of the Republic. To all this I will return.

It was upon the 1st of July, with the enemy advancing, that it was proposed to take the Dauphin from the Queen.

Upon the evening of the 3rd the order was executed.

It was but just dark when the guard challenged a patrol at the gate of the Tower; the patrol was the escort of six Municipals who had come from the authorities of the city to take the person of the child.

The women within the prison had had no warning. The same fate which had been kind to them in making a silence all around their lives during these dreadful months and in hiding from them the dangers that rose around was cruel to them now, leaving them unprepared for this sudden and tearing wound. There was a candle in the room and by its light the little girl, the Princess Royal, read out aloud — from a book of Prayers it is said — to her aunt and her mother, the Queen. These two women sewed as they listened; they were mending the clothes of the children. The little boy slept in his bed in the same room: his mother had hung a shawl to hide the light from his eyes. Save for

Présents
Guiton
Dumas
Lindet
Hérault
Danton
Jeanbon St. André
~~Lindet~~
Cambon
Barère
Berlier
Couthon

Séance du 1er juillet 1793, l'an 2e de la République française.

Sur la dénonciation faite au comité d'un complot tramé contre la liberté publique, et dont le C. arthur Dillon paraît être le chef.

Le comité arrête que le Maire de paris demeure chargé de prendre toutes les mesures convenables pour l'arrestation dud. arthur Dillon ainsi que des deux individus dont la désignation est faite par la notte qui sera remise par copie aud citoyen Maire, ~~après avoir été paraphée par les Membres du comité~~.

Qu'il sera de suite procédé à l'apposition des scellés sur leurs papiers.

Arrête également que le jeune Louis fils de capet sera séparé de sa Mère, et placé dans un appartement à part le mieux défendu de tout le local du temple.

Il sera le présent arrêté mis au carton des pièces secrètes avec la dénonciation qui y demeurera annexée, après qu'expédition du tout aura été transmise au C. Maire de paris.

Cambon fils aîné

Hérault

T. Berlier

L B Guyton

Jeanbon St. andré

G. Couthon

B Barère

Danton

ORDER OF THE COMMITTEE OF PUBLIC SAFETY

In Cambon's handwriting, directing the Dauphin to be separated from his mother

his regular breathing there was no sound to interrupt the high monotonous voice of the little girl as she read on, when suddenly her elders heard upon the floors below the advent of new authorities and of a message. The steps of six men came louder up the stone stairs, the doors opened as though to a military command, and the princesses saw, crowding in the corner of the small room, a group whose presence they did not understand, though among them the Queen recognised Michonis. The reading stopped, the women turned round but did not rise, the child stirred in his sleep. One of that group spoke first before the Queen could question them. "We have come," he said, "by order of the House, to tell you that the separation of Capet's son from his mother has been voted."

Then the Queen rose. Never until now had she abandoned before any but her hushand, or perhaps in the very intimacy of the Council, the restraint which she believed her rank to demand. The violence of her blood had been apparent in many a petulant and many an undignified gesture; she had raised her voice against many a Deputation; she had sneered more than once against women of a poorer kind; she had thrown at La Fayette the keys which he demanded on their return to the palace after the flight to Varennes. But she had never yet lost command of herself. Upon this terrible night for the only time in her life she did completely lose all her self-command. Something confused her like a madness and all the intensity of her spirit came out nakedly in defence of the child.

She stood up by the little bed; all her complexity of pride and all her training in intrigue deserted her; she cried out; she took refuge in such weapons as the women of the poor, whom no law protects, use to defend their sanctities. Her voice rang, became shrill and shrieked in the little room, violent and rising; she threatened death; next moment she implored. Her little daughter and her sister-in-law caught her methods. They joined in the imprecations and in the prayers. The child was awakened by the noise, by the shuffling of so many awkward and heavy feet in the doorway, by the passionate outcries around him; he awoke and gazed; then when he saw his mother he clung to her, and she kissed him repeatedly and held him as though he were again part of herself and as though none could take him from her without taking her life also, and all the while her prayers and execrations showered upon the armed men as they stood hesitating apart and waiting.

How long this scene continued we cannot tell. It may have been the best part of an hour.[1] At last some one of the deputation found decision and cried, "Why will you make this scene? No one wants to kill your son! Let him go freely; we could take him — if you force us to that!"

She lifted the little boy up and dressed him, his eyes still dazed with sleep. She lingered over him with conventional benedictions, repeated and prolonged. Her hands could not let him go. Fearing some further violence, a member of the deputation muttered a suggestion for the Guard, but the Queen's active passion was exhausted, she would be violent no more. She herself, perhaps, loosened his little hands from her dress and said, "Come, you must obey. . . ." Then they took him away; the great door was shut upon him; the women within, trembling beside the cot, could still hear the child pleading with a lessening voice

[1] The Duchesse d'Angoulême, the little girl then present, said, years after, that it lasted a full hour, but such memories are untrustworthy.

in the distance until another door clanged below and the rest of the night was silent.

. . . .

God has made a law whereby women are moved by strength and by weakness, but in different ways: by strength as a necessity for their protection, so that they demand it in men and in things and yet perpetually rebel against it; and by weakness as an opportunity for the exercise of all their nature, so that suffering (if it is sudden) or disaster calls out in women all of themselves: and this is especially true of mothers and sons.

That child, that boy, had seemed at first so rosy and so well in the old days at Versailles; his health had so contrasted with the sickly advance of Death upon his elder brother. He had been the hope of the Throne. Then there had come upon him the curse of the *men* of his family, he had grown weaker and more weak, he had had nervous fits of rage, a nervous fear of noise unnatural to his age. Some had thought him deficient; all had noted with anxiety or with malice his increasing weakness during the period of the Royal Family's imprisonment. Fits had seized him. But a few weeks before he had had convulsions; and all June during the relief of which I have spoken, fears for him had already arisen: it was a rapid tragedy of childhood that was soon to end in death.[1] His mother's devotion — having him now only for its object in the isolation of those stone walls — had become the whole of her being. That he had grown so dull, so failing, so more than common sickly, so odd, did but heighten in some way the

[1] I take for granted the death of Louis XVII. in prison: it is certified, it is clear, and even were it not so, the progress of his disease compels such a conclusion: but this book is not the place for a discussion upon the question, nor could so considerable a debate be discussed even in an Appendix.

mystic feeling in her. He was the KING. . . . She was observed to pay him a certain reverence, and she served him at table (as spies thought at least) with the gravity of a ceremonial. All this at one abominable stroke she lost.

She would watch him—oh, unhappy woman! — through chinks and chance places when the little chap was taken out to get the air, with gaolers, upon the roof for some few minutes of the day. He, of course, easily and at once forgot. He soon learnt to repeat the phrases he heard around him, laughed when his guardians laughed, and even asked, as he heard them ask, "whether the women still lived?" He played at ball a little with his gaolers; but he weakened still and he decayed. That child was the head of an authority older than Islam, and the heir to a family name older than the Sagas, and in his little drooping body were all the rights of the Capetians.

The Queen saw him, I say, for a few moments — now upon one day now upon another — by chance, as he took the air with his gaolers. She had nothing more to lose — and her soul was broken.

. . . .

Those who were to destroy the new society of the French, to rescue or to avenge the Queen, were now once more at hand and now almost arrived.

Their way to Paris lay open but for two last perilous and endangered defences; to the right the lines of Weissembourg, to the left Maubeuge.

There are two avenues of approach westward into the heart of Gaul and two only. The great marches of the French eastward, which are the recurrent flood-tides of

European history, pour up by every channel, cross the Alps at every pass, utilise the narrow gate of Belfort, the narrower gate of the Rhone, the gorge of the Meuse, the Cerdagne, the Samport, Roncesvalles. But in the ebb, when the outer peoples of Europe attempt invasion, two large ways alone satisfy that necessity at once for concentration and for a wide front which is essential to any attack upon a people permanently warlike.[1] These two ways pass, the one between the Vosges and the Ardennes, the other between the Ardennes and the sea. By the first of these have come hosts from Attila's to those of 1870; by the second, hosts from the little war band of Clovis to the Allies of 1815. Both avenues were involved in this balancing moment of '93: the first, the passage by Lorraine was still blocked by the defence of Mayence and the lines of Weissembourg,[2] the second, the passage by the Low Countries was all but won. Of the string of fortresses defending that passage Maubeuge was now almost the last, would soon be the very last to stand.

It was not upon Mayence and the lines of Weissembourg (though these to soldiers seemed of equal importance), it was upon the bare plains of the north that Paris strained its eyes in these perilous hot days — the long flat frontier of Hainault and of Flanders—and it is here that the reader must look for his background to the last agony of the Queen.

The line of defence, stretched like a chain across that long flat frontier, was breaking down, had almost disappeared. Point after point upon the line had gone; it held now by one point remaining, and the ruin of that was

[1] These words "concentration" and "a wide front" may seem self-contradictory. I mean by concentration a massed invasion, if you are to succeed against a military people; and by "a wide front" the necessity for attacking such a people in several places at once, if you are to succeed. For a force marching by a single narrow gate (such as is the valley of the Meuse) is in peril of destruction if its opponents are used to war.

[2] The lines of Weissembourg did not, of course, physically block the entry; they lay on the flank of it: but until the army behind them could be dislodged it made impossible an advance by that way into Lorraine.

imminent: the Republicans were attentive, in a fever for the final crash, when the last pin-point upon which the defence was stretched should give way and the weight of the invaders should pour unresisted upon Paris. When that march began there would be nothing for those who had challenged the world but "to cover their faces and to die."

Of what character is that northeastern frontier of France and what in military terms was the nature of the blow which was about to fall?

It is a frontier drawn irregularly due southeast for a hundred miles, from the sea to the difficult highlands of Ardennes and the waste Fagne Land. As it runs thus irregularly, it cuts arbitrarily through a belt of population which is one in creed, speech, and tradition: there is therefore no moral obstacle present to the crossing of it, and to this moral facility of passage is added the material facility that no evident gates or narrows constrain an invading army to particular entries. From the dead flat of the sea-coast the country rises slowly into little easy hills and slopes of some confusion, but not till that frontier reaches and abuts against the Ardennes does any obstacle mark it. It is traversed by a score of main roads suitable for a parallel advance, all excellent in surface and in bridges and other artifice; it is thickly set with towns and villages to afford repose and supply. Lastly, it is the nearest point of attack to Paris. Once forced, a week's rapid marching from that frontier brings the invader to the capital, and there is nothing between.

Such advantages — which, it is said, tempt unstable brains in Berlin to-day — have rendered this line, whenever some powerful enemy held its further side, of supreme defensive importance to the French. Until the formation of the Belgian State it had been for centuries — from the battle of Bouvines at least — the front of national defence; here the tradition of the seventeenth century and the genius of Vauban and his successors had established a network of strongholds, which formed the barrier now so nearly destroyed in this summer of '93.

These fortresses ran along that frontier closely interdependent, every one a support to its neighbours, forming a narrowing wedge of strongholds, from where Dunkirk upon the sea was supported by Gravelines to where the whole system came to a point in the last fortress and camp of Maubeuge, close up against the impassable Ardennes.

Maubeuge was the pivot of that door. Upon Maubeuge the last effort of the invaders would be made. The rolling up of the defending line of strongholds would proceed until Maubeuge alone should be left to menace the advance of the invasion. Maubeuge once fallen, all the Revolution also fell.

So much has been written to explain the failure of the Allies and the ultimate triumph of France in that struggle, that this prime truth — the all-importance of Maubeuge — clear enough to the people of the time, has grown obscured.[1] The long debates of the Allies, the policy of the Cabinet in London, the diversion upon Dunkirk, all these and many other matters are given a weight far beyond their due in the military problem of '93. The road from the base of the Allies to their objective in Paris lay right through the quadrilateral of fortresses, Mons, Condé, Valenciennes, Maubeuge. Mons was theirs; Condé, Valenciennes and

[1] The great authority of Jomini laid the foundation of this misconception, one which the reader might (perhaps erroneously) find implied in Mr. Fortescue's admirable account of this campaign; but the truth is that it is impossible to accumulate detail—as a military historian is bound to do—especially where long cordons are opposed to each other, without losing sight of the vital points of the line.

Maubeuge blocked their advance at its outset. A deflection to the left was rendered impossible by the Ardennes. A deflection to the right, possible enough, added, for every degree of such deflection, an added peril to the communication of the advance, laying the flank of the communications open to attack from whatever French garrison might have been left uncaptured. All these garrisons must be accounted for before Coburg could march on Paris. Mons, as I have said, was in Austrian hands and in Austrian territory; Condé, nay, Valenciennes, might fall successively to the invader; but so long as Maubeuge remained untaken the march upon Paris was blocked.

There were not wanting at that moment critics who demanded an immediate march on the capital, especially as the summer waxed, as the peril of the Queen increased, and as the immobility of the allies gave time for the martial law of the Terror to do its work, and to raise its swarms of recruits from all the countrysides: these critics were in error; Coburg at the head of the Austrian army was right. Poor as was the quality of the French troops opposed to him, and anarchic as was their constantly changing command, to have left a place of refuge whither they could concentrate and whence they could operate in a body upon his lengthening communications, as he pressed on to Paris through hostile country, would have been mad cavalry work, not generalship. Maubeuge with its entrenched camp, Maubeuge open to continual reinforcement from all the French country that lay south and west of it, was essential to his final advance. That Maubeuge stood untaken transformed the war, and, in spite of every disturbing factor in the complex problem, it should be a fixed datum in history that the resistance of Maubeuge and the consequent charge at

Wattignies decided '93 as surely as the German artillery at St. Privat decided 1870. Maubeuge was the hinge of all the campaign.

Coburg, as the summer heightened, set out to pocket one by one the supports of that last position; he easily succeeded.

. . . .

In Paris a vague sense of doom filled all the leaders, but a fever of violent struggle as well. . . . The Queen in her prison saw once again (and shuddered at it) the dark face of Drouet and heard his threatening voice.

All France had risen. There was civil war in the west and in the north. A Norman woman had murdered Marat. Mayence was strictly held all round about with the Marseillese raging within; and as for the Barrier of Fortresses to the north, Coburg now held them in the hollow of his hand.

. . . .

A fortnight after the Dauphin had been taken from the Queen, the fortress of Condé fell; it had fallen from lack of food. The Council of Maubeuge heard that news. Valenciennes would come next along the line—then, they! They wrote to the Committee of Public Safety a letter, which may still be read in the archives of the town, demanding provisions. None came.

It is difficult to conceive the welter of the time: distracted orders flying here and there along the hundred miles of cordon that stretched from Ardennes to the channel: orders contradictory, unobeyed, or, if obeyed, fatal. Commands shifted and reshifted; civilians from the Parliament carrying the power of life and death and muddling half they did; levies caught up at random, bewildered.

surrendering, deserting; recruits too numerous for the army to digest, a lack of all things. No provisions entered Maubeuge.

July dragged on, and Maubeuge could hear down the west wind the ceaseless booming of the guns round Valenciennes. Upon July 26th, Dubay, the Representative on mission for the Parliament, sent to and established in Maubeuge, heard an unusual silence. As the day drew on a dread rose in him. The guns round Valenciennes no longer boomed. Only rare shots from this point and from that were heard: perhaps it was the weather deceived him. But all next day the same damnable silence hung over the west. On the 30th he wrote to the Parliament, "We hear no firing from Valenciennes — but we are sure they cannot have surrendered." They had surrendered.

So Valenciennes was gone! . . . Condé was gone. . . . Maubeuge alone remained, with the little outpost of Le Quesnoy to delay a moment its necessary investment and sure doom.

The officer in command of Maubeuge awaited his orders. They came from Paris in two days. Their rhetoric was of a different kind from that in which Ministers who are gentlemen of breeding address the General Officers of their own society to-day. The Committee of Public Safety had written thus: "Valenciennes has fallen: you answer on your head for Maubeuge."

Far off in Germany, where that other second avenue of invasion was in dispute, the French in Mayence had surrendered.

. . . .

So July ended, and immediately upon the 1st of August the defiant decree was thrown at Europe that the Queen herself should be tried. So closely did that decision mix with the military moment that it was almost a military thing and at half-past two on the morning of the 2nd, the order reached her: she in turn was to go down the way so many had begun to tread.

She showed no movement of the body or of the mind. Night had already brought her too many terrors. The two women were awakened. The decree of the Convention which ordered the transference of the Queen to the Conciergerie for her trial was read. She answered not a word, but dressed herself and made a little package of her clothes; she embraced her daughter gently, and bade her regard Madame Elizabeth as her second mother; then stood for a moment or two in the arms of that sister-in-law who answered her in whispers. She turned to go and did not look backward, but as she went out to get into the carriage which was to carry her across the City, she struck her head violently against the low lintel of the door. They asked her if she was hurt, and she answered in the first and only words that she addressed to her captors that nothing more on earth could give her pain. The carriage travelled rapidly through the deserted streets of the night, the clattering of the mounted guard on either side of it. It was her one brief glimpse of the world between a prison and a prison.

As the Queen drove through the night, silent as it was, there reached her those noises of a city which never cease, and which to prisoners in transition (to our gagged victims to-day as they cross London from one Hell to another) are a sort of gaiety or at least a whiff of other men's living. These noises were the more alive and the more perpetual in this horrid August dark of '93 because a last agony was now risen high upon the Revolution; then news had been of defeats, of cities fallen, of Valenciennes itself surrendered: so that the next news might be the last. All night long men sat up in the wine-shops quarrelling on it; even as her gaolers drove her by, she saw lights in dirty ground-floor windows and she heard from time to time snatches of marching songs. It was the invasion.

XIX

THE HUNGER OF MAUBEUGE

FROM THE MORNING OF AUGUST 2, 1793, TO MIDNIGHT OF SUNDAY, OCTOBER 13, 1793

THE Queen descended from her carriage. She was weak, but erect. The close heat of the night and her sleeplessness and her fatigue had caused great beads of sweat to stand upon her forehead. Up river along the quays there had already showed, as she crossed the bridge on to the Island of the Cité, a faint glimmer of dawn, but here in the courtyard all was still thick night. The gates of the Conciergerie opened rapidly and shut behind her.

Her gaolers led the way down a long, low, and dark corridor, stiflingly close and warm, lit here and there with smoky candles. She heard the murmur of voices, and saw at the end of the passage a group of the police and of magistrates at the door of the little room that was to be her cell. She entered through the throng, saw the official papers signed at the miserable little table, and heard the formal delivery of her person to the authorities of the prison; then they left her, and in their place came in a kindly woman, the wife of the porter, and with her a young girl, whose name she heard was Rosalie. The Queen sat down on the straw-bottomed chair and glanced round by the light of the candle beside her.

It was a little low room, quite bare: damp walls, the paper of which, stamped with the royal fleur de lys, hung mildewed, rose from a yet damper floor of brick set herring-bone-wise; a small camp-bed covered with the finest linen alone relieved it, and a screen some four feet high, between her and the door, afforded some little shelter. Above her a small barred window gave upon the paving of the prison yard, for the cell was half underground. Here Custine — who had lost the North and was to be executed for the fall of Valenciennes — had been confined till his removal but a few hours before to make way for the Queen. Here is now the canteen of the prison.

It was very late. The new day was quite broad and full, showing the extreme paleness of her face and her weary eyes. She stood upon a little stuff-covered hassock, hung her watch upon a nail, and began to undress, to sleep if she might sleep for a few hours. A servant of the turnkey's, a girl called Rosalie, timidly offered her help; the Queen put her gently aside, saying: "Since I have no maid I have learnt to do all myself." They blew their candles out and left her to repose.

On the fourth day, the 6th of August, they came again and took from her further things which a prisoner might not enjoy; among them that little watch of hers in gold. She gave it to them. It was the little watch which she had worn when she had come in as a child to Compiègne on her way to the great marriage and to the throne. It was the last of her ornaments.

A routine began and lasted unbroken almost till August ended. In that little low cell, more than half underground, dimly lit by the barred window that stood level with the flags outside, day succeeded day without insult, but without relief, and here at last her strait captivity began what the Temple hitherto could never do. Her spirit did not

LAST PORTRAIT OF MARIE ANTOINETTE
Presumably sketched in the Temple ; now at Versailles

fail, but her body began to weaken, and in her attitude and gesture there had entered the appearance of despair. . . . Outside the Committee wondered whether their daring might not bear fruit, and whether, to save the Queen, the frontier might not be relieved. But no offer came from the Kings, and the hostage of the Republicans remained useless on their anxious hands. . . . In Brussels Fersen heard and went wild, talked folly of an immediate march on Paris, cursed Coburg and all rules of war; but Coburg was not to be moved — he knew his trade, and still prepared the sieges.

She had no privacy. All day long a corporal of police and his man sat on guard in a corner of the room. All night her door, in spite of its two great bolts, was guarded. For the rest her wants were served. She asked for a special water from the neighbourhood of what had been Versailles, and she obtained it. They hired books for her. They permitted her good food and the daily expense upon it of a very wealthy woman.[1] The porter's wife and the maid were very tender to her. They put flowers on her small oak table and they marketed at her desire. Her other service wounded her; first an old woman who was useless, the turnkey's mother; next a young virago, Havel by name, whose rudeness disturbed her. They would let her have no steel — not even the needles with which she was knitting for her little son, nor a knife to cut her food; but more than all there sank into her the intolerable monotony, the fixed doubt, the utter isolation which made the place a tomb. The smallest incident moved her. She would watch her gaolers at their picquet and note the game, she would listen to distant music, she would greet with a dreadful reminiscence of her own the porter's little son, and cry over

[1] What would come to a pound a day in our money, and at our scale of living—for the uncooked food alone.

him a little and speak of the Dauphin — but this last scene was so vivid that at last they dared no longer bring the child. She kept for consolation all this while, hidden in her bosom, a little yellow glove of her boy's, and in it a miniature of him and a lock of his hair.

. . . .

Meanwhile Maubeuge:

On the day which had seen the Queen enter the Conciergerie the Commander of Maubeuge issued the first warning of danger. The aged, the women and the children were invited to leave the shelter of the fortress and to betake themselves to the open country. That order was but partially obeyed — and still no provisions reached the town.

Now that strong Valenciennes had fallen, the Allies had their business so thoroughly in hand that some debate arose among them whether the main garrison of Maubeuge should be assailed at once or whether the little outlying posts should be picked up first: the large and the small were equally certain to capitulate: there was ample leisure to choose.

Coburg was for the main attack on Maubeuge — but he was not keen — the wretched little force at Cambrai would do to begin with — or even the handful in Le Quesnoy. It was simply a question of the order in which they should be plucked.

The young Duke of York, acting as he was bidden to act from Westminster, proposed to divert some 40,000 men to the capture of Dunkirk; for it must be remembered that all this war was a war of Conquest, that the frontier towns taken were to compensate the Allies after the Revolution had been destroyed, and that Dunkirk was historically a bastion of importance to England, and that all the advance was to end in the annexation of French land.

This march upon Dunkirk has been condemned by most historians because it failed; had it succeeded none could have praised it too highly. Politically it was just in conception (for it gave Britain some balancing advantage against the Austrians their allies), and as a military project it was neither rash nor ill-planned. The force left with Coburg was ample for his task, and nothing could be easier than for the Austrian army alone to reduce (as it did reduce) the worthless garrisons opposed to it, while the English commander was doing English work upon the right.[1]

The combined forces spent the close of the week after Valenciennes had fallen in driving off such of the French as were still in the open under Kilmain. A few days later forty-seven battalions, of whom a full seventh were English and Irish men, marched off under York for Dunkirk, while Coburg at his ease sat down before the little town of Le Quesnoy, the last fortified support of Maubeuge upon the west. Upon the same day he brushed the French out of the wood of Mormal, the last natural obstacle which could protect Maubeuge when Le Quesnoy should have fallen. It was the 17th of August — but already in Paris there had passed one of the chief accidents of history: an accident from which were to flow all the tactics of the Great War, ultimately the successes of Napoleon, and

[1] Even as it was and in spite of his failure before Dunkirk, the Duke of York had plenty of time to come back and help Coburg after that failure, and to have joined him in front of Maubeuge (before the French attempted the relief of that town. The English commander could easily have been present at Wattignies, and would probably or certainly have prevented that miracle. But no one foresaw the miracle. Coburg did not ask York to come till the 7th of October. York did not march till the 10th, and even then he thought he had the leisure to while a week upon forty miles!

immediately the salvation of the Revolution: Lazare Carnot had been admitted to the Committee of Public Safety.

. . . .

In Paris the Queen endured that August: and, isolated from the world, she did not know what chances of war might imperil her through the fury of a defeated nation or might save her by the failure of the Terror and its martial law.

As she thus waited alone and in silence the pressure upon the Republic grew. Lyons had risen when Marat died. Vendée was not defeated: before the month ended the English were in Toulon.

As the hot days followed each other in their awful sameness she still declined; her loss of blood never ceased, her vigour dwindled. A doctor of great position, the surgeon Souberbielle,[1] visited the cell and denounced its dampness for a danger: nothing was done. She lived on, knowing nothing of the world beyond and above those dirty walls, but vaguely she hoped or imagined an exchange and to be reunited with her children — to survive this unreal time and to find herself abroad again with living men. No change or interruption touched the long watch of her soul until, when she had already passed three weeks and more in nothingness, that inspector of police who had already befriended her in the Temple, Michonis, entered; and a certain companion, spare and wild-eyed was with him. It was a Wednesday; the last Wednesday in August; the month had yet three days to run.

---

[1] He was famous for his operations for the stone; sat upon the jury that condemned the Queen, was summoned for his art to Westminster Hospital, wondered in old age why the Restoration would not give his European fame a salaried post; thought it might be a fear of his infirmities of age; danced high vigourously before the Committee of medical patronage to prove, at ninety, his unimpaired vivacity, was refused any public salary, and died — some years later — a still active but disappointed man," fearing that his politics had had some secret effect in prejudicing the royal family against him."

These two were in league, and fantastic fortune had put an official of the city at her disposal for escape.

The whole scene was rapid — she had barely time to understand the prodigious opportunity. She noticed in the hand of Michonis' companion a bunch of pinks — perhaps she half recognised his face (indeed, he had fought in defence of the palace), she failed to take the flowers and he let them fall behind the stove — and the while Michonis was covering all by some official question or other. It was not a minute's work and they were gone: but in the flowers, when, after her bewilderment, she sought them, she found a note. Its contents offered her safety. Michonis (it ran) trusted as an official, would produce an order to transfer her person to some other prison; in the passage he would permit her to fly. The note asked for a reply.

She had no pen or pencil, but she found a plan for answering, for she took a pin and pricked out painfully these words on a slip of paper: "I am watched; I neither write nor speak; I count on you; I will come." The policeman of her guard — not the corporal — had been bought. He took the slip of paper from her and gave it to the porter's wife, her friend. Next day Michonis called for it, knew that the Queen was ready, laid all his plans, and on the Monday, by night, appeared at the door of the Conciergerie with his official order for the removal of the Queen.

Even in these few hours there had been time for treason. The policeman had revealed the message to the authorities. The faces Michonis saw at the gate of the prison by the sentry's lamp when he came up that Monday night, were not those he expected or knew. His plot was already in the hands of the Government and he was lost.

Within, the Queen waited in an agony of silence for

the sound of her deliverers; the hours of the morning drew on and the summer dawn of the Tuesday broadened; no steps had sounded on the stones of the passage: everything had failed.

Her deliverer suffered. She herself was closely examined and transferred to another cell where she must wait, in a more rigid compulsion, for the end.

No other human fortune[1] came to Marie Antoinette from that day until, seven weeks later, she died.

. . . .

West and a little north of Maubeuge, but twenty miles away, the watchers a month and more before had heard the ceaseless guns round Valenciennes. Then had come the silence of the surrender. Now they heard much nearer, west and a little to the south, the loud fury of a new and neighbouring bombardment as the shot poured into Le Quesnoy. Soon, as they knew, those guns would be trained on their own walls. Little Le Quesnoy was the last of the line but one, and they, in Maubeuge, the last of all. The Monday, the first Monday in September, the Tuesday, the Wednesday, the Thursday, the Friday, all that week the garrison at Maubeuge listened to the endless sound which never faltered by day or by night, and they still wondered how long it might endure: there were but 6,000 in the little place and their doom was so certain that their endurance seemed quite vain. Sunday, and the guns never paused or weakened; the second Monday came and they still raged — but on the ninth day when the marvel seemed to have grown permanent, on the Tuesday (it was the day that the Queen was thrust into her second and more vigorous

[1] I reject the story of her communion.

imprisonment) again — as with Valenciennes — the ominous silence came: Le Quesnoy was treating, and Maubeuge now made ready for its end.

The free troops to the south and east (two poor divisions) moved doubtfully toward the entrenched camp of the fortress — knowing well that they must in a few days be contained: there was no food: there were not even muskets for them all.

Around them by detachments the French forces were being eaten up. The little garrison of Cambray had marched out to relieve its neighbour — 6,000 men, three-quarters of the infantry regulars, three squadrons, and a battery of guns. The Hungarians rode through that battery before it could unlimber, refused to accept surrender, broke the line, and hacked and killed until a remnant got off at a run under the guns of Bouchain. Declaye, their general, survived; he was in Paris within forty-eight hours, tried within another forty-eight and on the morrow beheaded.

For a fortnight these contemptuous successes on the fringe of Coburg's army continued, and the main force meanwhile was gathering supplies, calling in detachments, organising train, and making all ready for the last and decisive blow that should shatter Maubeuge. In Maubeuge they hurriedly and confusedly prepared. Such grain as they could gather from neighbouring farms was seized, many of "the useless and the suspect" were expelled, the able-bodied civilians were set to dig, to entrench, and to complain, and over all this work was a man worthy of the place and the occasion for, on a high morning, the 15th of September, but a day or two after the surrender of Le Quesnoy, there had gallopped into Maubeuge a representative of the Parliament well chosen by the Terror to superintend such an issue: he rode straight in the long stirrups of the cavalry with harsh, eccentric, and powerful, clean face; a young man, dark and short and square: it was Drouet.

The two divisions hung nervously, the one east, the other west of the fortress, making a show to dispute the passage of the river against forces three times their own in number and indefinitely their superiors in training and every quality of arms; on the 28th[1] of September, at dawn, Coburg crossed where he chose both above or below the town; of the French divisions one was swept, the other hunted into the fortress — before noon the thing was done, and the French force — happy to have escaped with but a partial panic — was blocked and held. With the next day the strain began, for the Austrians drove the surrounding peasantry within the walls and in the same hour burnt the stores accumulated outside the walls. On the third day the first of the horses within Maubeuge was killed for food.

Drouet, for all his high heart, doubted if the Republic could deliver them and knew the sudden extremity of the town. He imagined a bold thing. On the 2nd of October, the fourth day of the siege, he took a hundred dragoons — men of his own old arm — and set out cross the Austrian lines by night: he designed a long ride to the Meuse itself and the sending of immediate news to the Committee of the danger of Maubeuge; he feared lest those civilians in Paris should imagine that a week, ten days, a fortnight were all one to the beleaguered town and lest they should frame their plan of relief upon the false hope of a long siege. So he rode out — and the enemy heard the hoof-beats and caught him. They put that tall man in chains; they caged

[1]Not as Jomini says, the 29th.

him also and made him a show. In Brussels, Fersen, with a dreadful curiosity went to peep at his face behind the iron bars; in Paris the woman whose chance of flight he had destroyed at Varennes sat and awaited her judges.

. . . .

Three days passed in Maubeuge and all the meat, salted and fresh, was sequestrated. The manuscripts in the monastery were torn up for cartridges; everything was needed. On the next day, the 6th of October, hay and straw were commandeered. On the next, the 7th, a census of the food remaining showed, for over 30,000 adult men and all the women and children besides, barely 400 head, and of these more than three-quarters small sheep in poor condition. Upon the 10th such little grain as the town contained was seized by the Commandant. The next day the whole population was upon half-rations and the townsmen were struggling with the soldiery. Upon the morrow again, the 12th, counsel was taken of the desperate need to advise the Government that the place was all but gone, and it was designed that by night such as might volunteer should bear the news or perish in crossing the lines.

. . . .

That evening, the evening of the 12th, after dark, Marie Antoinette was led out from her cell for that preliminary Interrogation which, in French procedure, preceeds the public trial. They led her from her little cell, through the narrow passages, into a great empty hall. Two candles, the only lights in that echoing darkness, stood upon the table.

She was in a deep ignorance of her position and of Europe.

The silence of the room corresponded to the silence within her: its darkness to the complete loneliness of her heart. She did not know what were the fortunes of the French army, what advance, if any, had been made by their enemies —whom she still regarded as her rescuers. She knew nothing of the last desperate risk upon the frontier which the Republic ran; she knew nothing of the steps by which she had been brought to this position, the demand in Parliament for her execution as the news from the front got worse and worse: the summoning of the Court: the formation of the Bench that was to try her. Least of all did she know that the extreme mad group whom Hébert led had gone to her little sickly son suggesting to him (probably believing what they suggested) nameless corruptions from her hand: to these they believed he had been witness, nay, himself a victim; she did not know that to these horrors that group had caused the child's trembling signature to be affixed. . . . He had sat there swinging his legs in the air from the high chair in which they had placed him to question him: he had answered "Yes" to all they suggested. . . he was her little son! She, imprisoned far off from him, knew nothing of that hellish moment. She was utterly deserted. She saw nothing but the dark empty room and the two pale candles that shone upon the faces of the men who were soon to try her: they marked in relief the aquiline face of the chief Judge, Herman. The other faces were in darkness.

Certain questions privately put to her were few and simple, a mere preliminary to the trial; she answered them as simply in her own favour. Her dress was dark and poor. She sat between two policemen upon a bench in the vast black void of the unfurnished hall and answered, and, when she had answered, signed. She answered conventionally that she wished the country well, that she had never wished it ill, she signed (as they told her to sign) under the title of the "widow of Capet." They named two barristers to defend her, Chauveau Lagarde and Tronçon Ducourdray, and she was led back to her cell and to her silence. Next day the 13th, these lawyers were informed and came to consult with her.

. . . .

Upon the 13th by night, twelve dragoons volunteered to take news out of Maubeuge, a sergeant leading them. They swam the Sambre and got clean away. They rode all night, they rode by morning into Philippeville and begged that three cannon shots might be fired, for that was the signal by which Maubeuge was to know that they had brought news of the hard straits of the city beyond the Austrian lines. They rode on without sleep to Givet, and there at last they heard that an army was on the march, straight for the relief of the siege.

Carnot had gathered that army, bringing in the scattered and broken detachments from the right and the left, concentrating them upon Avesnes, until at last he had there to his hand 45,000 men. Carnot was there in Avesnes and we have records of the ragged army, some of them fresh from defeats, most of them worthless, pouring in. There were those who had one shoe, there were those who had none; they were armed in varying fashion; they were wholly under-gunned. The boys straggled, marched, or drooped in, the gayer of them roaring marching songs, but the greater part disconsolate. With such material, in one way or another, Carnot designed to conquer. Maubeuge had been upon half-rations since the beginning of the week, it might ask for terms in any hour, and between him and it stretched the long high line of wood wherein Coburg lay entrenched impregnably.

. . . .

The nominal command of the hosts so gathered was in the hands of Jourdan, a travelling draper who had volunteered in the American War, whom the Committee of Public Safety had discovered, once more a draper, and to whom it had given first the army of the Ardennes, then this high post before Maubeuge. He was a man of simple round features and of easy mind; he had but just been set at the head of the Army of the North: left to himself he would have lost it — and his head. But the true commander was not Jourdan, it was Carnot. Carnot came to represent only the force of the Parliament of which he was a member and the force of the Committee of Public Safety of which he was the brain; but once on the field he exceeded both these capacities and became, what he had always been, a soldier. His big and ugly, bulging forehead with its lean whisp of black hair hid the best brain and overhung the best eye for tactics of all those that preceded, and formed the final effect of, Napoleon's armies.

The great Carnot in Avesnes that night stood like a wrestler erect and ready, his arms free, his hands unclenched, balancing to clutch the invader and to try the throw. He, with that inward vision of his, saw the whole plan of the struggle from south to north, and overlooked the territory of the French people as a mountain bird overlooks the Plain. He knew the moment. He knew it not as a vague, intense, political fear, nor even as a thesis for the learned arms and for the staff, but as a visible and a real world: he saw the mountains and the rivers, the white threads of roads radiating from Paris to all the points of peril, of rebellion or of disaster; he saw the armies in column upon them, the massed fronts, the guns. He saw the royal flag over Toulon and the English fleet in harbour there, he saw the bush and the marsh of Vendée still unconquered, he saw the resistance of Lyons (for he had no news of its surrender); above all he saw those two doors against which the invader leaned, which were now pushed so far ajar and which at any moment might burst open — the lines of Weissembourg; and here, right to his hand, the entrenchments that covered the last siege of the northern frontier. He saw reeling and nearly falling, the body of the Republic that was his religion, and he saw that all the future, death or life, lay in Maubeuge.

The Sunday night fell over Paris and over those long Flemish hills. The morrow was to see the beginning of two things: the trial of the Queen and the opening of a battle which was to decide the fate of the French people.

XX

WATTIGNIES

MONDAY, the 14th of October:—

Oct. 14, 1793. 6 a. m. The fate of the Queen and of the Republic had each come to a final and critical issue when the light broke, dully in either place, over Paris and over the pastures of the frontier. There the army lay to arms in the valley, with Coburg entrenched upon the ridge above them, and beyond him the last famine of Maubeuge; from dawn the French lines could hear, half a day's march to the northward, the regular boom of the bombardment. But Carnot was now come.

. . . .

Oct. 14, 1793. In Paris, 8 a. m. In Paris, when it was broad day, the chief court above the prison was prepared.

The populace had crammed the side galleries of the great room and were forming a further throng, standing in the space between the doors and the bar. The five Judges, Herman the chief, filed on to the Bench; a little below them, and on their right, a jury of fifteen men was empanelled. It was on the courage, the conviction, or the fanaticism of these that the result would turn.

They presented, as they sat there awaiting the prisoner, a little model of the violent egalitarian mood which had now for a year and more driven the military fury of the Republic. Among them would be seen the refined and somewhat degraded face of a noble who had sat in the earlier Parliaments, and who had drifted as Orleans had drifted — but further than had Orleans. There also were the unmistakable eyes of precision which were those of an

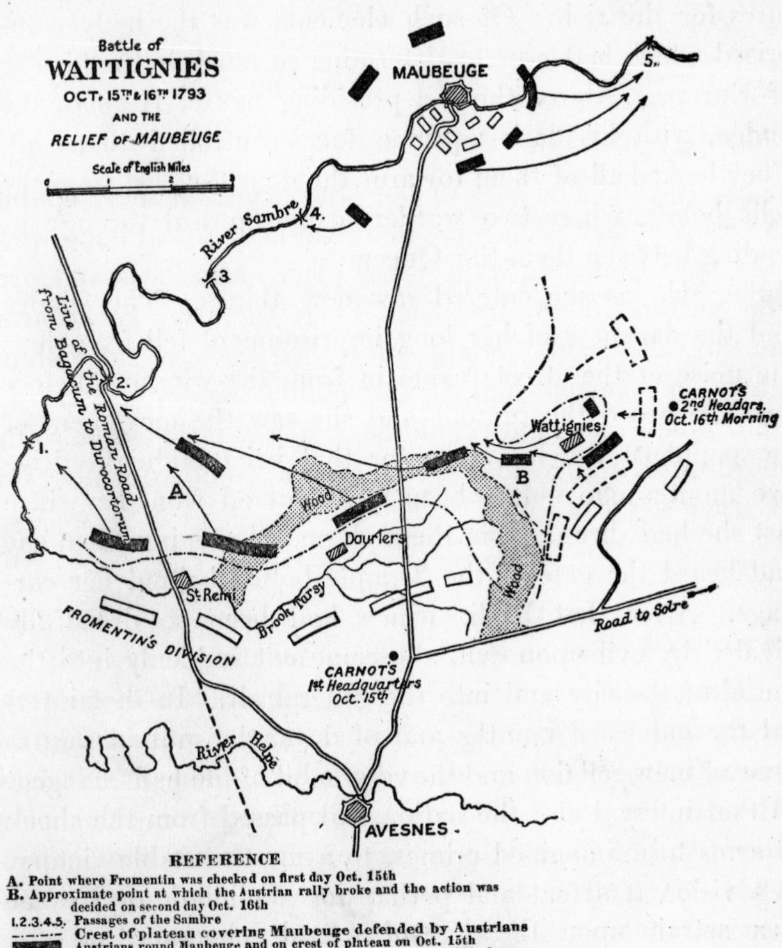

REFERENCE

A. Point where Fromentin was checked on first day Oct. 15th
B. Approximate point at which the Austrian rally broke and the action was decided on second day Oct. 16th
1.2.3.4.5. Passages of the Sambre
Crest of plateau covering Maubeuge defended by Austrians
Austrians round Maubeuge and on crest of plateau on Oct. 15th
French line just before assault on Oct. 15th, also garrison of Maubeuge
Reinforcements arrived from French centre and left in the night and lines of their assault
Austrian retirement on Bridges of Sambre after their line had been turned at Wattignies Oct. 16th

optician, a maker of instruments. There were, resting on the rail of the box, the firm hands of a great surgeon (Souberbielle). A few of the common people were mingled with these: contractors also, prosperous men, and master-carpenters. There was a hatter there, and a barber, a man who had made violins, and another who painted pictures for the rich. Of such elements was the body comprised which had now to determine so much in the history of Europe. Above them a presiding figure, Herman the Judge, with his dark aquiline face, controlled them all. They looked all of them towards the door that led from the cells below, where two warders came upward through it, leading between them the Queen.

She also as she entered saw new things. The silence and the darkness of her long imprisonment fell from her: the noise of the streets came in from the windows before her; she heard the rumour and she saw the movement of the populace which — save for that brief midnight drive two months ago — had been quite cut off from her since last she had shrunk from the mob on the evening when she had heard the gate of the Temple bolted behind her carriage. After that hush, which had been so dreadfully divided by evil upon evil, she came out suddenly into the sound of the city and into the general air. In that interval the names of months and of days, the mutual salutations of men, religion and the very habit of life had changed. In that interval also the nation had passed from the shock of arms to unimagined crimes, to a most unstable victory, to a vision of defeat and perhaps of annihilation. France was astrain upon the edge of a final deliverance or of a final and irretrievable disaster. Its last fortress was all but fallen, all its resources were called out, all its men were under arms, over the fate of the frontier hung a dreadful, still silence. In the very crisis of this final doubt and terror the Queen stood arraigned.

The women lowered their knitting-needles and kept them still. The little knot of Commissioners sitting with Counsel for the State, the angry boys in the crowd who could remember wounds or the death of comrades, stretched forward to catch sight of her as she came up the stairs between her guards: they were eager to note if there had been any change.

She had preserved her carriage, which all who knew her had regarded since her childhood as the chief expression of her soul. She still moved with solemnity and with that exaggerated but unflinching poise of the head which, in the surroundings of Versailles, had seemed to some so queenly, to others so affected; which here, in her last hours, seemed to all, as she still preserved it, so defiant. For the rest she was not the same. Her glance seemed dull and full of weariness; the constant loss of blood which she had suffered during those many weeks spent below ground had paled her so that the artificial, painted red of her cheeks was awful in that grey morning, and her still ample hair was ashen and touched with white, save where some traces of its old auburn could be, perhaps, distinguished.

She was in black. A little scarf of lace was laid with exactitude about her shoulders and her breast, and on her head she wore a great cap which a woman who loved her, the same who had served her in her cell, put on her as she went to her passion. The pure white of this ornament hung in great strings of lawn on either side, and round it and beneath it she had wound the crape of her widowhood. So dressed, and so standing at the bar, so watched in silence by so many eyes, she heard once more the new sound which yesterday she had first learned to hate: the hard and nasal voice of Herman. He asked her formally her name.

She answered in a voice which was no longer strong, but which was still clear and well heard in that complete silence:

"Marie Antoinette of Austria, some thirty-eight years old, widow to Louis Capet, the King of France."

To the second formal question on the place of her first arrest, that:

"It was in the place where the sittings of the National Assembly were held."

The clerk, a man of no great learning, wrote his heading: "The 23rd day of the first month of the fourth year of Freedom," and when he had done this he noted her replies, and Herman's short questions also: his bidding to the jury that they must be firm, to the prisoner that she must be attentive.

Into the clerk's writing there crept, as there will into that of poor men, certain grievous errors of grammar which in an earlier (and a later) time would not have appeared in the record of the meanest court trying a tramp for hunger; but it was the Revolution and they were trying a Queen, so everything was strange; and this clerk called himself Fabricius, which had a noble sound—but it was not his name.

This clerk read the list of witnesses and the indictment out loud.

When these formalities were over they brought a chair. The Queen sat down by leave of the court and the trial began. She saw rising upon her right a new figure of a kind which she had not known in all her life up to the day when the door of the prison had shut her out from the noise and change of the world. It was a figure of the Terror, Fouquier Tinville. His eyes were steadfast, the skin of his face was brown, hard and strong; he was a hired politician, covered with the politician's outer mask of firmness. Within he was full of the politician's hesitation and ner-

GATEWAY OF THE LAW COURTS THROUGH WHICH THE QUEEN WENT TO HER DEATH

The right hand one of the three gateways in the railings

vous inconstancy. A genuine poverty and a politician's hunger for a salary had been satisfied by the post of Public Prosecutor. He earned that salary with zeal and with little discernment, and therefore, when the time came, he also was condemned to die. It was he now in this forenoon who opened against the Queen.

His voice was harsh and mechanical: his speech was long, dull, and violent: rhetorical with that scenic and cardboard rhetoric which is the official commonplace of all tribunals. The Widow Capet was Messalina; she was a leech; she was a Merovingian Tyrant; she was a Medicis. She had held relations with the "Man called King" of Bohemia and Hungary; she had urged Capet on to all his crimes. She had sent millions to aid her family in their war against the French people. She had woven the horrid plot of the 10th of August, which nothing but incredible valour had defeated. She was the main enemy which the new and angry Freedom for which he spoke had had to meet and to conquer.

Apart from its wearisome declamation the accusation was true; save that — through no fault of her own, poor woman! — she had not aided the foreign cause with gold, all the story was evident and publicly known. She sat as near this orator as is a nurse to a bedside. She heard him with her suffering and disdainful face quite fixed and unmoved, save at one point: the mention of her son.

Fouquier Tinville was sane: he saw the crass absurdity of Hébert's horrors, he barely touched upon them very hurriedly (and as the rapid and confused words escaped him, her lips twitched with pain), but even as he did so, he knew he had given the defence a hold.

It is held on principle in French Courts that an impartial presentation of the truth cannot be obtained unless witnesses are heard in a chance sequence, not divided into friends and foes, as with us, but each (such is the theory) telling what he believes to be the truth. Even in these political trials of the Terror (which were rather Courts-martial or condemnations than trials) the rule was observed, and when Fouquier sat down the file of witnesses began.

The parade was futile. For plain political facts known to the whole world no list of witnesses was needed, nor could their evidence be of the least avail. Moreover, that evidence was lacking. The witnesses defiled one after the other, each vaguer than the last, to prove (and failing to prove) things that were commonplaces to all Europe. Long past midday the empty procession continued through the drowsy hours past one o'clock and two; remembering trifles of her conduct true and false. To every assertion as the Judge repeated it (true or false), she answered quietly by a denial; that denial was now false, now true.

Even if the Revolutionary Tribunal could have subpœnaed Mallet or the Emperor or Fersen, it would have meant little to the result. Her guilt, if it was guilt so to scheme against the nation, was certain; what yet remained in doubt was the political necessity of such a trial at such a moment, the limit of hardihood in her Judges and the possible effect in a democracy of public sympathy at some critical phase of the pleadings — and much more potent than any of these three, because it included them all, was the news that might come at any moment from the frontier and from the hunger of Maubeuge — no news came.

Last of these witnesses Hébert, all neat and powdered, presented his documents and put forward his abominations, his fixed idea of incest. The public disgust might here have turned the trial. There was a stir all round: her friends began to hope. As for the officials, they could not stop Hébert's mouth, but Herman was careful to omit the customary repetition: he was hurrying on to the next witness when a juryman of less wit than his fellows and filled with the enormous aberrations of hate, pressed the charge.

The Queen would not reply. She half rose from her chair and cried in a high voice: "I appeal to every mother here," and then sank back again.

The crowd in the galleries began to move and murmur, the women raised their voices against the angry orders of the ushers and of the Bench demanding silence. Away, dining beyond the Seine, Robespierre, hearing of it, broke a plate at table in his anger, and thought Hébert's lunacy had saved her. A further witness, though he spoke of the flight to Varennes, could hardly be heard, and spoke quite unheeded; and when he had concluded, the Court abruptly rose in the midst of the commotion, hubbub and change.

The Queen was led to her cell, keeping, as she left her place, in spite of her hopeless fatigue, the steady step wherewith she had entered; and as she passed she heard one woman in the press sneering at her pride.

It was three o'clock. The first act in that long agony had lasted, without food or breathing time, for seven hours.

. . . .

While the Republic thus held the old world prisoner in Paris, and tortured it in the person of the Queen, out on the frontier in the water-meadows of Avesnes, the Republic lay in its chief peril from the old world free and armed. Coburg and every privilege

Oct. 14, 1793. Before Maubeuge, 8 a.m.

held the crest of the hills invincibly, and Maubeuge was caught fast, unreachable beyond the entrenchments of that ridge.

Carnot, looking westward down the valley of the Helpe, saw the deep orchards laden with October, nourished by the small and very winding stream. He saw the last French frontier hamlets and their mills. St. Hilaire, Dompierre, Tenieres, dwindling away to where, far off in its broad trench, ran the Sambre.

Before him also in this valley, as he looked westward down it, he saw stretched for some ten miles the encampment of his army: bivouac after bivouac, one beyond the other along the lines, and smoke rising from them. Tall hedges, not yet bare, divided the floor of the valley and the village grounds: here, also, Cæsar had marched through against the Nervii: for this corner of Europe is a pack of battlefields. Malplaquet lay just before the army; within a march, Fleurus; within sound of cannon, Jemappes.

Up above them beyond that wood of Avesnes, the line of the heights along the sky, was the enemy. It had loomed so dark before the late, dull and rainy dawn, that they had seen the notches in that line which were the emplacement of guns. The early afternoon had shone upon the sides of the hills, and the French outposts had seen the outposts of the evening busy in the little villages that mark the foot of the slopes: St. Vaast, Dourlers, Foursies. And all day long boomed to the north behind the hills the sullen guns before Maubeuge. At any hour that dull repeated sound might cease, and it would mean that the last fortress had fallen.

All that day Carnot passed in silence. The troops,

some last detachments of which had but just marched in, lay dully in such repose as soldiers can steal: a jumble of forty patchwork battalions, militia, regulars, loud volunteers, old stark gunners; they listened to the distant and regular thunder of the siege. In some stations the few horses were grooming: in others, fewer still, the rare guns were cleaned.

An hour before dusk the six generals were called to Carnot's tent, and here and there the bugles roused the troops called for reconnaissance. These few detachments crossed the woods, pierced gaps in the hedges,[1] to prepare the advance of the morrow, noted and exchanged shots with the outposts of the evening, and at evening they retired. As they retired Carnot gave orders to the guns. Out of effective range, vague and careless of a target, they fired and proclaimed the presence of a relieving army to the besieged.

Oct. 14, 1793. Before Maubeuge, 4 p. m.

Maubeuge, in that still evening, during a lull of the siege-pieces, heard those French guns, and Ferrant and the general officers with him counselled a sortie. Only Chancel stood out, but Chancel was in command of the camp of Maubeuge, and his authority was unassailable. He did not distinguish the French fire, he thought it Austrian; no instinct moved him. Therefore, all the next day, while the battle was engaged, the garrison of Maubeuge failed to move; and later, for this error, Chancel was tried and killed.[2]

The troops fell back again through the wood of Avesnes and slept the last sleep before the battle. In

[1] So on the same field had Cæsar been compelled to clear the hedgerows. So little does the French peasantry change in a thousand years, and so tenacious is each French province of its customs.

[2] And the other version is that Chancel was for moving but that Ferrant would not. Choose.

Paris during that same evening, the long trial of the Queen proceeded.

. . . .

Oct. 14, 1793. In Paris, 5 p. m. At five, just at that hour when Carnot was recalling his scouts and ordering that warning cannon, the Court gathered and the prisoner was recalled.

In her cell she had not been silent.

As a great actress in an interval between her hardest lines will refuse repose and will demand rather comment or praise, so had she filled this little respite of two hours with questions and with doubts professed. She had dwelt upon the forms of the trial, she had begged her counsel to reassure her. She had despised the evidence. She had said she feared but one witness — Manuel — and indeed all who could have spoken as eye-witnesses to a hundred notorious truths were now over the frontier or dead.

With her entry the trial was resumed and the file of witnesses continued. It was as monotonous and as vague as before. Even Manuel, whom she had feared, was vague, and the very servants of the prison (though they had been witnesses to conspiracy) were uncertain and rambling. And this fatuity of the witnesses, who were so solemnly and so strictly examined, did not proceed from the turmoil of the time alone, nor even from the certitude which all then had (and which history has now) upon the past action of the Queen in cherishing the hope of foreign domination and in procuring it: rather did it proceed from the fact that these dreadful days were filled not with a judicial but with a political action, and that the Court was met, not to establish truths at once unprovable and glaring, but to see whether or no the Revolution could dare to condemn the prisoner. It was an act of War and a challenge to What lay entrenched up there before Maubeuge, training its guns on the last hope, the ragged army in the valley of Avesnes below.

If all the witnesses which history possesses to-day, if Boville, Fersen, Mallet, could have been brought into that Court and have had the Truth dragged from them, it would have affected the issue very little. One thing could alone affect that issue, the news of victory: and no news came. All reports from the frontier had ceased.

The lights in the Court were lit, smoky and few. The air, already foul from the large concourse, grew heavy even for the free; for the sickened prisoner it became intolerable as the night hours drew in — six dark, interminable hours. She heard the succeeding witnesses distantly, more distantly. Her head was troubled, and her injured eyesight failed her. It was very late. The droning of the night was in her ears. She vaguely knew at last that there was a movement around her and that the Court was rising. She asked faintly for water. Busne, the officer in guard of her, brought it to her and she drank. As he supported her with some respect down the short passage to her cell he heard her murmuring: "I cannot see. . . . I cannot see. . . . I have come to the end. . . ."

She lay down when her doors had received her, and just before midnight she fell asleep. She slept deeply, and for the last time.

. . . .

Tuesday, October 15.

A little before dawn the French bugles upon the frontier roused the troops of Avesnes; their calls ran down the line, they passed from the Diane to the Générale, the woods before them sent back echoes, and soon the army moved. Far off upon the left Fromentin, upon the far right Duquesnoy, began marching forwards and inwards converging, but the main body in the centre took the high road, which, if it could force its passage, would lead them straight to Maubeuge.

Oct. 15, 1793. Before Maubeuge, 6 a. m.

The sun was still level over the glinting wet fields when Carnot came to the summit of the long swell whence could be perceived, over an intervening hollow, the village of Dourlers, and above it the level fringe of trees which held the Austrian cannon; an impregnable crest upon whose security Coburg and the Allies founded the certitude of victory. The guns began.

Among the batteries of the French (too few for their task), two batteries, one of sixteen-pounders, the other of twelve, were the gift of the city of Paris. By some accident these, though ill-manned, silenced the Austrian fire at one critical and central point above Dourlers itself and close to the highroad. Whether the French aptitude for this arm had helped to train the volunteers of the city, or whether these had such a leaven of trained men as sufficed to turn the scale, or whether (as is more probable) some error or difficulty upon the opposing slope or some chance shot had put the invaders out of action, cannot be known. Carnot seized upon the moment and ordered the charge. As his columns advanced to carry Dourlers he sent word at full speed to either wing that each must time itself by the centre, and forbade an advance upon the left or right until the high road should be forced and the centre of the Austrian position pierced or confused.

As he stood there, looking down from the height where the road bifurcates, all the battle was plain to him, but his sapper's eye for a plan watched the wings much more anxiously than they watched the centre before him. The stunted spire of Wattignies a long way off to the east, the clump that hid St. Remy to the west, marked strong bodies of the enemy, and, in the open plateau beyond, their numerous cavalry could crush either extremity of his line (which at either extremity was weak) should either be tempted forward before the centre had succeeded. The front was long — over five miles — he could not enforce sagacity nor even be certain of intelligence, and as he doubted and feared the action of his distant lieutenants, he saw the centre advancing beneath his eyes.

The Austrian cannon had abandoned the duel. The French line approached Dourlers, deployed, and began the ascent. A sudden and heavy fire of musketry from the hollow road and from the hedges met the sixteen thousand as they charged; they did not waver, they reached the garden walls, and closed until, to those watching from the hill, the attempt was confused and hidden by a rolling smoke and the clustered houses of the village. It was past mid-morning.

. . . .

In Paris they had wakened the Queen, tardily.

She wondered, perhaps, to see De Busne not there. He had suffered arrest in the night, he was detained to see if he could tell the Court or the Committee some secret gathered from his prisoner. It was under another guard that she left her cell.

Oct. 15, 1793. In Paris, 7.30 a. m.

It was nearly nine before the Court assembled in the

dull light, and later before the futile drag of evidence was renewed.

Whether sleep had revived her, or whether some remnant of her old energy had returned to her for such an occasion, no further weakness was perceived in the Queen. She sat, as she had sat all the day before, until her faintness had come upon her, very ill, pale, and restrained, but erect and ready for every reply. Moreover, in that morning the weary monotony of such hours was broken by an incident which illuminated, though it made more bitter, the last of her sad days; for after D'Estaing, the Admiral, had been heard to no purpose, another noble, also a prisoner, was called; and as she saw his face she remembered better times, when the struggle was keen and not hopeless, and when this bewildering Beast, that called itself now "Freedom," now "The Nation," had been tamed by the class which still governed Europe outside and which in that day controlled her kingdom also. It was Latour du Pin, the soldier who had been responsible for the repression of the mutiny at Nancy, three years — three centuries — before.

He still lived. Against no man had '93 a better ground for hate, and indeed the time came when the Revolution sent him down also to meet his victims under the earth; but so far his commanding head was firm upon his shoulders. He enjoyed, as did all the prisoners of that time, the full use of his wealth. He was clothed, and fed in the manner of his rank. He entered, therefore, with pride, and with that mixture of gaiety and courage, upon which, since the wars of religion, all his kind had justly plumed themselves; and as he entered he bowed with an excessive ceremony to the Queen.

The Judge asked him the formal question: Whether he recognised the prisoner? He bowed again and answered: "Indeed I know this Lady very well"; and in a few moments of his examination he defended himself and her with a disdainful ease that brought Versailles back vividly out of its tomb.

Revived or stung by such a memory, the Queen replied to question after question exactly and even with some power: upon her frivolities, her expenses, her Trianon — all the legends of debauch which were based upon that very real and very violent fugue of pleasure in which she had wasted her brilliant years. The close of that dialogue alone has a strict interest for history, when Herman came at last to the necklace. Trianon had been on his lips a dozen times, and as he spoke the word he remembered that other fatal thing: —

"Was it not in Trianon that you first came to know the woman La Motte?"

"I never saw her!"

"Was she not your victim in the affair of the necklace?"

"She could not be, for I had never known her!"

"You still deny it?"

"I have no plan to deny. It is the truth, and I shall always say the same."

It is a passage of great moment, for here indeed the prisoner said precisely what was true and precisely what all, even those who would befriend her, least believed to be true. She would pretend a love for the French and a keen regard for their glory — even for the success of their armies. She would pretend to have obeyed the King and not to have led him; to have desired nothing for her son but only the welfare of the people. Trapped and abandoned, she thought every answer, however false, legitimate; but in that one thing in which her very friends had doubted her, another spirit possessed her and her words were alive with truth.

After that episode no further movement followed. There was opened before the Court (as the law compelled) her little pocket and the trinkets taken from her on the day of her imprisonment: the poor relics of her affection—the lock of hair, the miniature — were laid before the Judges. They heard Simon, the cobbler, in whose house her son was lodged — perhaps she looked more curiously at his face than at others — but he had nothing to say. They heard the porter of the Temple and sundry others who had seen, or pretended to have seen, her orders for the payments of sundry thousands — but all that business was empty and all those hours were wasted: it was not upon such vanities that the mind of Paris and of the crowded Court was turned, but upon the line of Flemish hills a long way off and upon the young men climbing up against the guns.

Paris and the mob in the street outside that Court of Justice and the hundreds crammed within it strained to hear, not Valazé, nor Tiset, nor any other useless witness but some first breath of victory that might lift off them the oppression of those days; nay, some roaring news of defeat, and of Coburg marching upon them: then, at least, before their vision was scattered by the invader, they could tear this Austrian woman from her too lenient Judges for a full vengeance before they themselves and that which they had achieved should die. At the best or at the worst, they panted for a clear knowledge of their fortune; but on through the day and well into the afternoon, when the

Court rose for its brief interval, no hint or rumour even had come to Paris from before Maubeuge.

. . . .

Carnot had come down the hill from the fork of the roads; he, and Jourdon beside him, followed behind the assault, bringing the headquarters of that general plan some half-mile forward. So they knew that the village of Dourlers was held. It was noon before the place was secured, and now all depended upon the action of the extreme wings.

Oct. 15, 1793. Before Maubeuge, 10:30 a. m.

It was certain that the struggle for this central village would be desperate: all depended upon the extreme wings. If these (and both of them) could hold hard and neither advance too far up the slope nor suffer (either of them) a beating-in, then the work at Dourlers would be decisive. And, indeed, the village was won, lost, and won, and lost again: all the hard work was there. The French carried it, they went beyond, they were almost upon the ridge above it. In the upland field below the crest of wood the Austrian cavalry under Muffling struck them in flank, and they were disordered. They were back in the village of Dourlers, and the fight for it was from house to house and from window to window. Twice it was cleared, twice lost. The French carry to an immortal memory a lad of fourteen who slipped forward in those attacks, got in behind the lines of the Hungarian Grenadiers who held the market place, and, in lanes beyond, drummed the charge to make his comrades think that some were already so far forward, and thus to urge them on. Many years after, in digging up that ground, his little bones were found buried sidelong with the bones of the tall Hungarian men; and he has now his statue beating the charge and looking out towards the frontier from the gateways of Avesnes.

I have said that the horns of that crescent, the extreme wings, were ordered to be cautious, and warned that their caution alone could save the fight; for if they went too far while Dourlers in the centre was still doubtful, that centre would certainly be thrown back by such a general as Coburg, who knew very well the breaking-point of a concave line. The fourth attack upon Dourlers was prepared and would have succeeded when Carnot heard that Fromentin, upon the far left, upon the extreme tip of the horn of that crescent, had carried his point of the ridge, and, having carried it, had had the folly to pursue; he had found himself upon the plateau above (an open plateau bare of trees and absolutely bare of cover), with his irregulars all boiling, and his regulars imagining success. Weak in cavalry, commanding men untrained to any defensive, he found opposed to him the cavalry reserve of the enemy — a vast front of horse suddenly charging. That cavalry smashed him all to pieces. His regulars here and there formed squares, his irregulars tried to, they were sabred and galloped down. They lost but four guns (though four counted in so undergunned an army), but, much worse, they lost their confidence altogether. They got bunched into the combes and hollows, the plateau was cleared. They in their turn were pursued, and it would have been a rout but for two accidents: the first accident was the presence of a fresh reserve of French cavalry; small indeed, but very well disciplined, strict and ready, certain Hussars who in a red flash (their uniform was red) charged on their little horses and for a moment stopped the flood of the enemy. The check so given saved the lives though not the position of the French left wing. It was beaten. It was caved in.

The second accident was the early close of an October day. The drizzling weather, the pall of clouds, curtained in an early night, and the left thus failing were not wholly destroyed: but their failure had ruined the value of the central charge upon Dourlours. The final attack upon that central village was countermanded; the Austrians did not, indeed, pursue the retreat of the French centre from its walls and lanes, but the conception of the battle had failed.

. . . .

In the Court-room, in Paris, during those hours, while the Judges raised the sitting, the Queen sat waiting for their return; they brought her soup which she drank; the evening darkened, the Judges reappeared, and the trial began anew.

Oct. 15, 1793. In Paris, 5 p. m.

The witnesses called upon that last evening, when the lights were lit and the long night had begun, were for the most part those who had come personally into the presence or into the service of the Queen. Michonis especially, who was rightly under arrest for attempting her rescue, appeared; Bruiner appeared; the doctor who had attended to the children in the Temple. The farce went on. The night grew deeper, the witnesses succeeded each other. All that they had to say was true. Nothing they said could be proved. One put forward that she had written some note asking if the Swiss could be relied upon to shoot down the people. She had said and written one hundred of such things. Her counsel, who were mere lawyers, worried about the presentation of the document — meanwhile night hastened onwards, and the stars behind their veil of an October cloud continually turned.

. . . .

Upon the frontier the damp evening and the closed night had succeeded one the other, and all along the valley of the little river it was foggy and dark. The dead lay twisted where they had fallen during that unwrought fight, and a tent pitched just behind the lines held the staff and Carnot. He did not sleep. There was brought to him in those midnight hours a little note, galloped in from the far south; he read it and crumpled it away. It is said to have been the news that the lines of Weissembourg were forced — and so they were. The Prussians were free to pass those gates between the Ardennes and the Vosges. Then Maubeuge was the last hold remaining: the very last of all.

Oct. 15, 1793. Before Maubeuge, 10.30 p.m.

Jourdan proposed, in that decisive Council of a few moments, held under that tent by lantern light in the foggy darkness while the day of their defeat was turning into the morrow, some plan for reinforcing the defeated left and of playing some stalemate of check and countercheck against the enemy; but Carnot was big with new things. He conceived an adventure possible only from his knowledge of what he commanded; he dismissed the mere written traditions of war which Jourdan quoted because he knew that now—and within twelve hours—all must certainly be lost or won. He took counsel with his own great soul, and called, from within his knowledge of the French, upon the savagery and the laughter of the French service. He knew what abominable pain his scheme must determine. He knew by what wrench of discipline or rather of cruelty the thing must be done, but more profoundly did he know the temper of young French people under arms to whom the brutality of superiors is native and who meet it by some miraculous reserve of energy and of rebellious smiles.

Those young French people, many half-mutinous, most of them ill-clothed, so many wounded, so many more palsied by the approach of death — all drenched under the October drizzle, all by this time weary of any struggle whatsoever, were roused in that night before their sleep was deep upon them.

Carnot had determined to choose 7,000, to forbid them rest, to march them right along his positions and add them to the 8,000 on his right extreme wing, and then at morning, if men so treated could still charge, to charge with such overwhelming and unexpected forces on the right, where no such effort was imagined, and so turn the Austrian line.

There were no bugle-calls, no loud voice was permitted; but all the way down the valley for five miles orders were given by patrols whose men had not slept for thirty hours. They roused the volunteers and the cursing regulars from the first beginnings of their sleep; they broke into the paltry comfort of chance bivouac fires; they routed men out of the straw in barns and stables; they kicked up the half-dead, half-sleeping boys who lay in the wet grass marshes of the Tarsy; and during all that night by the strength which only this service has found it possible to conceive (I mean a mixture of the degrading and the exalted, of servitude and of vision), from the centre and from the left — from the men who were shot down before Dourlers and from the men who had fled before the Austrian cavalry when Fromentin had failed—a corps was gathered together, under the thick night, drawn up in column and bidden march through the darkness by the lane that led towards the right of the position.

With what deep-rooted hatred of commandment simmering in them, those fellows went after thirty hours of useless struggle to yet another unknown blind attempt, not historians but only men who have suffered such orders know. They were 7,000; the thick night, I say, was upon them; the mist lay heavy all over the wet land; and as they went through the brushwood and chance trees that separated the centre from the right of the French position, they heard the drip of water from the dead, hanging leaves. Their agony seemed to them quite wanton and purposeless. They were halted at last mechanically, like sheep, at various points under various sleeping farms in various deserted tiny, lightless villages. The night was far spent; they could but squat, despairing, each company at its halting-place waiting for the dawn and for new shambles. Meanwhile it was thick night.

. . . . . .

Oct. 15, 1793. In Paris, 11.30 p.m.

It was nearing midnight in Paris, but none yet felt fatigue, neither the Judges nor their prisoner; nor did any in the straining audience that watched the slow determination of this business suffer the approach of sleep. The list of the witnesses was done and their tale was ended.

Herman leant forward, hawk-faced, and asked the Queen in the level judicial manner if she had anything to add to her defence before her advocates should plead. She answered complaining of the little time that had been afforded her to defend — and the last words she spoke to her Judges were still a vain repetition that she had acted only as the wife of the King and that she had but obeyed his will.

The Bench declared the examination of the witnesses

closed. For something like an hour that bronzed and hollow-faced man next by her, Fouquier Tinville, put forward the case for the Government; he was careful to avoid the mad evidence Hébert had supplied. When he sat down, the Defence spoke last — as had since Rome been the custom or rather the obvious justice of French procedure; so that the last words a jury may hear shall be words for the prisoner at the bar — but this was not a trial, though all the forms of trial were observed. Chauveau-Lagarde spoke first, his colleague next. When they had ceased they were arrested and forbidden to leave the building, lest certain words the Queen had whispered should mean some communication with the invader.

The summing up (for summing up was still permitted, and it would be a century of Revolutionary effort before the pressure of the Bench upon the Jury should be gradually raised) was what the angers of that night expected and received. It was three o'clock in the morning before the four questions were put to the jury. Four questions drawn indeed from the Indictment but avoiding its least proved or least provable clauses. Had there been relations between the Executive and the foreign enemies of the State, and promises of aid to facilitate the advance of their armies? If so, was Marie Antoinette of Austria proved to have been privy to that plan?

The Jury left the hall. A murmur of tongues loosened rose all around. The prisoner was led out beyond the doors of the chamber. For one long unexpected hour she was so detained while the Jury were still absent; then a signal was given to her guards and they led her in.

The cold violence of formal law still dominated the lawyers. Herman put forth the common exhortation of judges against applause or blame. He read to her the conclusions of the Jury: they were affirmative upon every point of the four. He asked her with that same cold violence of formality, after the Public Prosecutor had demanded the penalty of death set down for such actions as hers in the new Penal Code, whether she had anything to say against her sentence. She shook her head.

Oct. 16, 1793. In Paris, 4 a. m.

She was at the end of human things. She stood and saw the Judges upon the Bench conferring for a moment, she stood to hear her sentence read to her, and as she heard it she watched them in their strange new head-dress, all plumes, and she fingered upon the rail before her with the gesture ladies learn in fingering the keys: she swept her fingers gently as though over the keys of an instrument, and soon the reading of the sentence was done and they led her away. It was past four o'clock in the morning.

On the terrace of his castle in Germany that night George of Hesse saw the White Lady pass, the Ghost without a face that is the warning of the Hapsburgs, and the hair of his head stood up.

. . . .

Oct. 16, 1793. Before Maubeuge, 4 a. m.

The long dark hours of the morning still held the troops that had marched over from the left to the right of the French position before Maubeuge. The first arrivals had some moments in which to fall at full length on the damp earth in the extremity of their fatigue, but all the while the later contingents came marching in until, before it was yet day but when already the farms about knew that it was morning, and when the cocks had begun to crow in the steadings, all rose and stood to arms.

ce 16 8bre a 4 h ½ du matin

C'est a vous ma sœur, que j'ecris pour la derniere fois, je viens d'etre condamnée
non pas a une mort honteuse, elle ne l'est que pour les criminels, mais a
aller rejoindre votre frere, comme lui innocente, j'espere montrer la meme
fermeté que lui dans ces derniers momens, je suis calme comme on l'est
quant la consience ne reproche rien, j'ai un profond regret d'abandonner
mes pauvres enfants vous savez que je n'existois que pour eux, et
vous ma bonne et tendre sœur, vous qui avoit par votre amitié tout
sacrifiée pour etre avec nous dans quelle position je vous
laisse. j'ai appris par le plaidoyer meme du procés que ma fille etoit
separée de vous. helas la pauvre enfant je n'ose pas lui ecrire elle
ne recevroit pas ma lettre je ne sais meme pas si celle-cy vous parviendra
recevez pour eux deux, icy ma benediction, j'espere qu'un jour lorsqu'ils
seront plus grands, il pourront se reunir avec vous, et jouire en
entier de vos tendres soins. qu'ils pensent tous deux a ce que je
n'ai cessé de leurs inspirer; que les principes, et l'execution
exacte de ses devoirs sont la premiere baze de la vie, que leur
amitie et leur confiance mutuel, en fera le bonheur. que ma fille
sent qu'a l'age qu'elle a, elle doit toujours aider son frere, par les
conseils que l'experience qu'elle aura de plus que lui et son amitie
pourront lui inspirer; que mon fils a son tour rendent a sa sœur, tout
les soins les services, que l'amitie peuvent inspirer; qu'ils sentent enfin tout
deux que dans quelques position ou ils pourront se trouver, ils ne seront
vraiment heureux que par leur union. qu'ils prennent exemple de
nous. combien dans nos malheurs, notre amitie nous a donné de
consolation, et dans le bonheur ont joui doublement quant on le
partager avec un ami, et ou en trouver de plus tendre de plus uni
que dans sa propre famille. que mon fils n'oublie jamais les derniers
mots de son pere que je lui repette expressement, qu'il ne cherche jamais
a venger notre mort. j'ai a vous parler d'une chose bien penible a mon
cœur; je sais combien cet enfant, doit vous avoir fait de la peine
pardonnée lui, ma chere sœur; pensée a l'age qu'il a, et combien il est facile

FIRST PAGE OF MARIE ANTOINETTE'S LAST LETTER

The mist was deepening upon them, a complete silence interpenetrated the damp veil of it, nor through such weather were any lights perceptible upon the heights above which marked the end of the Austrian line.

. . . .

The Queen went down the stone steps of the passage: she entered regally into the cell made ready. She called without interval for pen and paper, and she sat down to write. She felt, after that transition from the populous court to the silence of these walls, an energy that was not natural and that could not endure, but that served her for an inspiration. She had tasted but a bowl of soup since the morning — nay, since the evening before, thirty hours — soon she must fail. Therefore she wrote quickly while her mood was still upon her.

Oct. 16, 1793. In Paris, a little before four in the morning.

She sat and wrote to her dead husband's sister the letter which, alone of all her acts, lends something permanently noble to her name. It is a run of words exalted, dignified, and yet tremendous, nor does any quality about that four-fold sheet of writing, yellow with years, more astound the reader than the quality of revelation: for here something strong and level in her soul, something hitherto quite undiscovered, the deepest part of all, stands and shines. The sheet is blurred — perhaps with tears: we do not know whether ever it was signed or ended, but before the morning came she laid herself upon her bed in her poor black dress, her head was raised somewhat upon her right hand, and so lying she began very bitterly to weep.

The priest of St. Landry, the parish church of the prison, entered to minister to her: she spoke just such few words to him as might assure her that he had sworn the civic oath and was not in communion. When she knew this she would not hear him. But he heard her murmuring against the bitter cold, and bade her put a pillow upon her feet. She did so and was again silent.

The hours wore on, the scent of newly lighted fires came from the prison yard and the noise of men awakening. The drip of the fussy weather sounded less in the increase of movement, and on the pavement of the quays without began the tramp of marching and the chink of arms; from further off came the rumble of the drums: 30,000 were assembling to line her Way. The two candles showed paler in the wretched room. It was dawn.

. . . .

Oct. 16, 1793. Before Maubeuge, half-past six in the morning.

The 16th of October broke upon the Flemish Hills: the men who had endured that night-march along the front of the battle-field, the men who had received them among the positions of the extreme right, still drooped under the growing light and were invigorated by no sun. The mist of the evening and of the night from dripping and thin had grown dense and whitened with the morning, so that to every soldier a new despair and a new bewilderment were added from the very air, and the blind fog seemed to make yet more obscure the obscure designs of their commanders. The day of their unnatural vigil had dawned and yet there came no orders nor any stirring of men. Before them slow schistous slopes went upward and disappeared into the impenetrable weather which hid clogged ploughland and drenched brushwood of the rounded hill; hollow lanes led up through such a land to the summit of the little rise and the hamlet of

WATTIGNIES; this most humble and least of villages was waiting its turn for glory.

The downward slope, which formed the eastern end of the Austrian line, the low rounded slope whose apex was the spire of the village, was but slightly defended, for it was but the extreme end of a position, and who could imagine then — or who *now* — that march through the sleepless night, or that men so worn should yet be ready for new action with the morning? No reinforcement, Coburg knew, could come from behind that army: and how should he dream that Carnot had found the power to feed the fortunes of the French from their own vitals and to drag these shambling 7,000, wrenched from west to east during the darkness: or how, if such a thing had been done, could any man believe that, such a torture suffered, the 7,000 could still charge?

Yet, had Coburg known the desperate attempt he would have met it, he would have covered that ultimate flank of his long ridge and reinforced it from his large reserve. But the deep mist and the dead silence harshly enforced during the night-march had hidden all the game, and in front of Wattignies, holding that round of sloping fields and the low semicircular end of the ridge before the village, there were but 3,000; the infantry of Klebek, of Hohenlohe, and of Stern; for their cavalry they had behind them and alongside of the village farms a few dragoons; certain Croatian battalions stood in a second line. These, in that morning, expecting nothing but perhaps the few troops as they had met easily the day before, waited under the mist in formation and heard no sound. The morning broadened; the white vapour seemed lighter all around, but no voices could be heard, nor did there come up through its curtain any rumble of limber from the roads below.

. . . .

As the Queen so lay disconsolate and weeping bitterly, stretched in her black gown upon the wretched bed and supporting her head upon her hand, there came in the humble girl who had served her faithfully and who was now almost distraught for what was to come. This child said:

Oct. 16, 1793. In Paris, about seven in the morning.

"You have not eaten all these hours. . . . What will you take now that it is morning?"

The Queen answered, still crying: "My child, I need nothing more: all is over now." But the girl added: "Madam, I have kept warm upon the hob some soup and vermicelli. Let me bring it you." The Queen, weeping yet more, assented.

She sat up a moment (but feebly — her mortal fatigue had come upon her — her loss of blood increased and was continued), she took one spoonful and another; soon she laid the nourishment aside, and the morning drew on to her death.

She must change for her last exit. So much did the Revolution fear to be cheated of its defiance to the Kings that the warders had orders not to lose sight of her for one moment: but she would change. She would go in white to her end.

The girl who had served her screened her a little, and in the space between the bed and the wall she crouched and put on fresh linen, and in place of her faded black a loose white muslin gown. Her widow's head-dress also, in which she had stood proudly before her Judges, she stripped of its weeds, and kept her hair covered by no more than the linen cap.

The Judges came in and read to her her sentence.

RÉQUISITION au Commandant-général de la force armée parisienne.

AU NOM DE LA RÉPUBLIQUE.

L'ACCUSATEUR PUBLIC, près le Tribunal criminel-révolutionnaire, établi à Paris par la loi du 10 mars 1793, en exécution du jugement du Tribunal de cejourd'huy requiert le citoyen commandant-général de la force armée parisienne, de prêter main-forte et mettre sur pied la force publique, nécessaire à l'exécution dudit jugement rendu contre Marie antoinette Lorraine autriche Ve de Louis Capet et qui la condamne à la peine de Mort laquelle exécution aura lieu aujourd'huy a Dix heures du Matin sur la place publique de La Revolution de cette ville. Le citoyen commandant-général est requis d'envoyer ladite force publique, cour du Palais, ledit jour, à huit heures précises du Matin

FAIT à Paris, le 25 du 1er mois de ~~179~~ l'an second de la République française, une et indivisible. Ce vu sept Mercredy 16 8bre Cinq heure du Matin

ACCUSATEUR PUBLIC.

A. Q. Fouquier

FACSIMILE OF THE DEATH WARRANT OF MARIE ANTOINETTE

The executioner, awkward and tall, came in. He must bind her hand. "Why must you bind my hands? The King's hands were not bound." Yet were her hands bound and the end of the rope left loose that her gaoler might hold it: but she, perhaps, herself, before they bound her, cut off the poor locks of her hair.

They led her out past the door of the prison: she was "delivered" and signed for; on the steps before the archway she went up into the cart, hearing the crowd howling beyond the great iron gates of the Law Courts, and seeing seated beside her that foresworn priest to whom she would not turn. . . . Nor were these the last humiliations: but I will not write them here.

Oct. 16, 1793. In Paris, at half-past ten in the morning.

Up and down the passages of the prison a little dog whom she had cherished in her loneliness ran whining and disconsolate.

The cart went lumbering on, past the quay, over the bridge under the murky drizzle. The windows beyond the river were full of heads and faces; the edges of the quays were black with the crowd. The river Seine ran swollen with the rains; its tide and rolling made no mark upon the drenched water-walls of stone. The cart went lumbering on over the rough wet paving of the northern bank. It turned into the Rue St. Honoré, where the narrow depth was full of noise. The long line of troops stood erect and close upon either side. The dense crowd still roared behind them: their prey sat upon the plank, diminished, as erect as the constraint of her bonds and her failing strength would allow. Her lips, for all their bent of agony, were still proud; her vesture was new: her delicate high shoes had been chosen with care for that journey — but her face might have satisfied them all. The painted red upon her cheeks was dreadful against her utter paleness: from beneath the linen of her cap a few whitened wisps of hair, hung dank upon her hollowed temples: a Victim. Her eyes were sunken, and of these one dully watched her foes, one had lost its function in the damp half-darkness of the cells: it turned blank and blind upon the rabble that still followed the walking jolt of the two cart-horses and the broad wheels. At the head of those so following, an actor-fellow pranced upon a horse, thrusting at her by way of index a sword, and shouting to the people that they held the tigress here, the Austrian. In the midst of those so following, an American, eager to see, elbowed his way and would not lose his vantage. From the windows of the narrow gulf the continued noise of wonder, of jeers, and of imprecations reached her. She still sat motionless and without speech: the executioner standing behind her holding the loose end of the cord, the forsworn priest sitting on the plank beside her but hearing no words of hers.

It is said that as the tumbril passed certain masts whence limp tricoloured pennants hung she glanced at them and murmured a word; it is to be believed that, a few yards further, at the turn into the Rue Royale, she gave way at the new sight of the Machine set up for her before the palace gardens.

This is known, that she went up the steps of the scaffold at liberty and stood for a bare moment seen by the great gathering in the square, a figure against the trees of what had been her gardens and the place where her child had played. It was but a moment, she was bound and thrown and the steel fell.

Oct. 16, 1793. In Paris, at a quarter past twelve, noon.

. . . .

On the low mud and slope of Wattignies the mist began to wreathe and thin as the hours approached high noon. Through gaps of it the three Austrian regiments could see trees now and then in the mid-distance, showing huge, and in a moment covered again by new whorls of vapour. But still there was no sound. In front of them toward Dimont, to their left round the corner of the slope in the valley of Glarges, with every lift of vapour the landscape became apparent, when suddenly, as the mist finally lifted, the wide plain showed below them rolling southwards, a vast space of wind and air, and at the same moment they heard first bugles, then the shouts of command, and lastly the rising of the Marseillaise: Gaul was upon them.

Oct. 16, 1793. Before Maubeuge, about eleven in the morning.

The sleepless men had been launched at last, the hollow lanes were full of them swarming upward: the fields were ribbed with their open lines, and as they charged they sang.

Immortal song! The pen has no power over colour or over music, but though I cannot paint their lively fury or make heard their notes of triumph yet I have heard them singing: I have seen their faces as they cleared the last hedges of the rise and struck the 3,000 upon every side.

These stood, wavered, fell back to re-form: then saw new masses of the Republicans, roaring up from Glarges behind their flank, broke and were scattered by the storm. The few heavy guns of the Austrians there emplaced were trained too late to check the onrush. The little pieces of the climbing and the surging men were dragged by laniards, unmasked behind gaps in the hurrying advance, crashed grape and were covered again for a moment by the living cover of the charge. The green at the hilltop was held, the poor yards and byres of Wattignies were scoured and thundered through, and Carnot, his hat upon his sword, and Duquesnoy his face half blood, and all the host gloried to find before them in their halting midday sweat when the great thrust was over, the level fields of the summit, the Austrian line turned, and an open way between them and Maubeuge.

Two charges disputed their certain victory. First the Hungarian cavalry galloped and swerved and broke against the dense and ever denser bodies that still swarmed up three ways at once and converged upon the crested edge of the upland plain; then the Royal Bourbon, emigrants, nobles, swept upon the French, heads down, ready to spend themselves largely into death. They streamed with the huge white flag of the old Monarchy above them, the faint silver lilies were upon it, and from either rank the cries that were shouted in defiance were of the same tongue which since Christendom began has so perpetually been heard along all the battle fronts of Christendom.

Oct. 16, 1793. Before Maubeuge, just past noon.

. . . .

These also failed: a symbol in name and in flag and in valour of that great, once good, and very ancient thing which God now disapproved.

The strong line of Coburg was turned. It was turned and must roll back upon itself. Its strict discipline preserved it, as did the loose order of the Republican advance and the maddened fatigue of the young men who had just conquered: for these could work a miracle but not yet achieve a plan. The enemy fell back in order, sombre, massed and regular, unharassed, towards the Sambre. The straggling French soldiery, wondering that the fighting had ceased (but wisely judged incapable of pursuit), possessed the main road unhindered; and that evening drank with their comrades in Maubeuge.

In this way was accomplished what a principal critic of the art of war[1] has called "The chief feat of arms of the Republic."

It was somewhat past noon.

. . . .

Upon that scaffold before the gardens which had been the gardens of her home and in which her child had played, the Executioner showed at deliberation and great length, this way and that on every side, the Queen's head to the people.

Oct. 16, 1793. In Paris, just past noon.

[1] Napoleon Buonaparte.

APPENDICES

APPENDIX A

THE OPERATION ON LOUIS THE SIXTEENTH OF FRANCE

THE somewhat lengthy attempt to determine the exact date which changed the course of Louis XVI.'s life, to which I have been compelled in the text, would have been unnecessary had the document which proves both the operation itself and the moment of it been published.

It is certain that Maria Theresa knew in the last year of the old King's reign the nature of the trouble.[1]

Louis XVI.'s hesitation in the matter endured through the month immediately succeeding his accession; though in the December[2] of that year he seems to have come very near to a decision. It is certain that the Emperor was to act with authority in the matter; and it is probable that Louis XVI's long and disastrous hesitation was in part occasioned by his brother-in-law's delay and postponement of his voyage to Versailles.

Mercy was informed thoroughly of the main object of the Emperor's visit just before it took place,[3] and Maria Theresa at the same time specially emphasised to her Ambassador this capital business which her son had undertaken.[4]

[1] MARIA THERESA to MERCY, *3rd January*, 1774. — "Je ne compte presque plus que sur l'entremise de empereur, qui à son arrivée à Versailles, trouvera peut-etre le moyen."

[2] MARIE ANTOINETTE to MARIA THERESA, *17th December*, 1774. — "Le roi a eu il y a huit jours une grande conversation avec mon médecin; je suis fort contente de ses dispositions et j'ai bonne espérance de suivre bientôt l'example de ma sœur."

[3] MERCY to MARIA THERESA, *18th March*, 1777. — "Relativement au séjour que fera ici S. M. l'empereur, et à toutes les circonstances qui pourront en résulter, il ne me reste pas la moindre incertitude sur les hautes intentions de V. M., et ses ordres seront remplis avec tout le scrupule et le soin qu'exige l'importance d'une pareille conjuncture dont il peut résulter tant de différents effets."

[4] MARIA THERESA to MERCY, *31st March*, 1777. — "Vous pouvez bien croire que ce point est un des plus importants a éclaircir, s'il y à espérer de la succession ou point, et vous tâcherez de mettre au clair cela avec l'empereur."

We know that the operation was performed by the King's surgeon, Lassone, and the point is to determine, in the absence of direct evidence, the date upon which Lassone operated.

I say "in the absence of direct evidence," for, though that evidence exists, it is not available. All papers left by Lassone, including the *procès verbal* of the operation on the King, were ultimately brought into the collection of Feuillet de Conches. This collector has been dead twenty years, and Dr. Des, among others, asked, just after his death, for the production of this all-important document; but it was refused, and I believe it is still refused. It is a great loss to history. Moreover, one does not see what purpose can be served by such reticence, if, as I believe, it is still maintained.

As it is, we must depend upon a few veiled and discreet allusions in the contemporary correspondence of Mercy, the Queen, and the Empress. The principal of these consist in nine passages, the first of which is as follows: —

> "Le 27 je me rendis de grand matin à Versailles, ou, après avoir parlé d'affaires avec le comt de Vergennes, j'allai à l'hôtel garni qu'occupait l'empereur. Le premier médecin Lassone avait été pendant une heure chez S. M., et elle était alors dans son cabinet avec l'abbé de Vermond."

This letter was written on 15th June, 1777. Mercy, who had been in very bad health, sends to Maria Theresa his account of the Emperor's visit. In this letter he mentions, under the date Tuesday, 27th May, a long interview which the Emperor had with Lassone, he himself, Mercy, being present, and also Vermond, the Queen's former tutor. Later in the day the Emperor spent two hours alone with his brother-in-law, discussing, in Mercy's phrase, "confidential details." It was at this momennt, presumably, that the Emperor persuaded the King. It will be seen, therefore, that he put off mention of the matter until late in his visit, at the end of the month of May. Maria Theresa, having by that time had opportunity of hearing by word of mouth things that could hardly be written, writes that she is content so far as things have gone, but is waiting to hear about everything from her son on his return.

She also writes to Marie Antoinette on the 29th June, 1777, as follows: —

"J'en attends les plus heureuses suites, et même pour votre état de mariage, sur lequel on me laisse espérance: mais on remet le tout au retour,[1] ou on pourra me parler."

It is evident that nothing was done during the Emperor's actual stay, or in his presence. On the 29th of August, Maria Theresa, having seen her son, is still by no means certain.[2] One must allow a fortnight (more or less) for news to reach her from Versailles. We may be confident, therefore, that whatever was written to about her the middle of the month of August was not yet wholly reassuring, though this may not prove that no operation had taken place; it may only go to show that success was not yet certain.

It is on the 10th of September, in a letter from Marie Antoinette to Maria Theresa that the first note of confidence on the part of the Queen appears. It was premature, but matters were now certain.[3]

We may, therefore, take it for certain that things were settled *not earlier* than the middle of August, *nor later* than the end of the first week of September; and it may be predicted that when Lassone's paper sees the light it will bear a date within those three weeks.

---

[1] "The return," of the Emperor, that is.

[2] Maria Theresa to Mercy, *29th August*, 1777. — "Je le souhaite à l'egard du roi, mais je n'en suis pas rassurée."

[3] "Ce nouveau-né" — she writes of her sister-in-law's child — "me fait encore plus de plaisir par l'espérance que j'ai d'avoir bientôt le même bonheur."

Mercy sees by January[4] that everything is long settled. The Queen knew herself to be with child in the first week in April, and news was sent to her mother on the date which I have given in the text.

---

[4] "Je dois aussi ajouter la remarque très essentielle que la reine continue à se conduire très-bien avec le roi, qui de son côté persiste à vivre maritalement dans le sens le plus exact et le plus réel."

APPENDIX B

ON THE EXACT TIME AND PLACE OF DROUET'S RIDE

THE reader or student acquainted with various records of the French Revolution may be tempted to regard the account of Drouet's Ride in my text as containing too much detail for accurate history; especially as no historian has hitherto done more than vaguely allude to it. I will therefore in this Appendix show the way in which I found it possible to reproduce every circumstance of Drouet's movements from the time when he left Ste. Ménehould until the time of his arrival at Varennes.

The berline left Ste. Ménehould shortly after eight. It had to climb to Germeries Wood[1] on the crest of the forest, four hundred feet in four miles. It could not possibly, therefore, have reached the summit till after nine, and however fast was the run down on to Islettes (just over five miles from Ste. Ménehould) that village cannot have been reached before 9.15. From Islettes to Clermont is just four miles, and mostly slightly rising. The best going could not cover the distance in twenty minutes, which puts the earliest possible entry into Clermont at twenty-five or twenty to ten. The change of horses took from ten minutes to a quarter of an hour. Put it at the lowest, and one has for the earliest possible time the berline can have left Clermont that it must have been within ten minutes of ten o'clock.

From Clermont to Varennes is nine miles: a straight road, descending slightly on the whole, but not quite flat.

[1] The summit is 860 feet above the sea; the town about 460 feet.

Under the best conditions that day the berline had not covered ten miles in the hour; let it gallop at *twelve* (a pace it was quite incapable of, save in short spells) and Varennes would still be three-quarters of an hour off.

Now Varennes was entered just on a quarter to eleven. The berline cannot, therefore, have left Clermont later than ten; and cannot have arrived earlier than ten minutes to ten; so this departure of the Royal Family from Clermont for Varennes, of Drouet's postilions back from Clermont for Ste. Ménehould, took place sometime in those ten minutes.

Now Drouet reached Varennes before eleven. He reached it round about by the forest — not by the main road — and he reached it by a gallop through a pitch-dark night in dense wood without a moon.[1] The shortest line as the crow flies from the last bend of the road before Clermont to Varennes Bridge is ten miles; any deviation through the wood, even in a straight line, would make it nearly twelve. It is very difficult to cover twelve miles in an hour under such conditions, but even if you allow Drouet that pace he must leave the high roadabout ten.

All this synchronises to within a very few minutes. The postilions leave Clermont to turn back home in the ten minutes before ten; they go fast, for they are riding light; a mile or so up the road they meet their master. It is just here that the forest on the northern side of the ravine touches the modern railway and comes nearest to the road. Drouet takes to the forest certainly not before ten and equally certainly not ten minutes after.

So much for the hour at which he took to the wood.

Now what road did he pursue in the forest? Only one is possible. The forest here covers a high ridge, some

[1] The sky was overcast.

three hundred feet above the open plain. Down in the plain, parallel to this ridge and at its base, runs the high road from Clermont to Varennes, with a row of farms and wide fields between it and the edge of the wood. Had Drouet gone anywhere but along the ridge he would have had to cross some twenty streams, to climb and fall over as many ravines (*all of clay*), to flank a dozen clay ponds and marshes, and with all this there was no continuous path. He could not have done it in two hours, let alone one. He was compelled to follow the ridge. It so happens that there runs all along the ridge a green ride called "the High Ride." It is a Gaulish track of great antiquity, known to the peasantry as "the Roman Way." It does not come down as far as Clermont, it leaves the forest at the farm and huts of Lochères. To this farm Drouet must have made his way by the lanes and gates of Jacques and Haute Prise — once at Lochères, a hard gallop along the High Ride brought him in six or seven miles to the Crossed Stone (called also the Dead Girl); here another green ride crosses the main ride of the ridge. He took this cross ride to the right hand: it leads down and out of the forest; one comes out of the wood a mile or so from Varennes with the town right below one and what was then a lane (now it is a county road) through the open valley fields. Just before entering the town a detour (by where the tile-works are now) would get him into the Rue de Mont Blainville, and so to the Bridge: a detour serving the double purpose of avoiding possible troops at the entry to the town and of getting ahead of any carriage coming in from Clermont. He cannot but have taken this detour, have noted the waggon by the bridge as he passed it (he later used it to block the bridge) and then have come up the main street from the river.

APPENDIX C

THE ORDER TO CEASE FIRE

THE order to cease fire, which forms the frontispiece of this book, and which is the last executive document of the French monarchy, has been misunderstood by not a few critics, and its value thereby lessened.

It is, as I shall presently show, authentic, and therefore of the highest possible interest to every student of history. The traveller will find it to-day in the central glass case of the square Revolutionary Room in the Carnavalet Museum. The body of the writing is not in the hand of Louis himself, but the signature is undoubtedly his. The lines were scribbled in haste by some one attendant upon the King, signed by him, and sent to the palace.

Now no event of such importance and so recent has been more variously described by eye-witnesses than the fall of the palace in 1792; and the particular incident of the order to cease fire suffers, like every other detail of those famous hours, from a plethora, and therefore a conflict, of evidence.

It may be remarked in passing, and by way of digression, that such difficulty cannot but attach to any episode of hard fighting, on account of the mental condition which that exercise produces. There is exactly the same trouble, for instance, in determining with exactitude the all-important moment of the evening in which the Guard failed at Waterloo.

We may confidently say, however, that two separate messages were sent to the palace. The first was a verbal message to cease fire, which reached Hervillé, who was directing the whole operation. Hervillé, as we know, refused to obey, having the action well in hand, and being yet confident of success. Either after the southern end of the Tuileries had been forced by the populace (who, as we know now, turned the flank of the defence by fighting their way through from the Long Gallery), or while that capital incident was in progress, Durler, a captain of the Swiss Guards, commanding no more than a company, but probably the company which had the best chance of retreating, asked for orders. It is difficult to believe that he would have done so unless the position was already desperate. The order which reached him was a repetition of the former one, but it was written, not verbal, and it is this second written order the facsimile of which forms the frontispiece to this volume. Durler did not see it written. He had gone in person to learn what he should do, but he was back again with his men before the note was handed to him. He was a perfectly honest and trustworthy man and his testimony remains. It is evident from this testimony that, by the time the note came, all was over.

As to the pedigree of the document: —

Durler rose to the rank of general before his death. He naturally regarded this piece of historic writing as among the most precious of his possessions, and left it to his family who were resident in Lucerne. Chateaubriand, visiting Lucerne on the 15th of May, 1832, saw it in that town. From General Durler's daughter and heiress it descended to his grandchildren, Schimacher by name, and was in the early eighties the property of M. Felix Schimacher of Lucerne, whose agent in Paris was a banker, Mr. de Trooz.

M. Cousin, the curator of the Municipal Museum of Paris (the Carnavalet), hearing of it, approached Mr. de Trooz, and offered a large sum on behalf of the city. The offer was accepted. The pedigree of the document was drawn up by M. Dagobert Schimacher, lawyer in Lucerne, and the whole despatched to Paris, where the purchase was completed on the 27th of July, 1886, and the document deposited in the Museum, where it now lies.

APPENDIX D

ON THE LOGE OF THE "LOGOTACHYGRAPHE"

THE Manège was pulled down after the consular decree of year XI., which originated the Rue de Rivoli; the historical reconstruction of its arrangements on the 10th of August, 1792, is the more difficult from the fact that the only accurate plan of it which has come down to us[1] dates from a period *earlier* than December, 1791, in which month (on the 27th) the order was given to change nearly the whole of its dispositions. The box of the *Logographe* can be fixed in this plan (though not in the new place it occupied after the 5th of January, 1792).[2]

We know[3] that it was near the President's Chair, and this was on the south side of the Manège, in the middle. It was in this box that the Queen had appeared when her husband had accepted the Constitution on the return from Varennes; and it was in this box that the Royal Family were supposed, until lately, to have stayed in the three days after the fall of the palace.

There were many such grated boxes for reporters up and down the Hall: the proximity of the *Logographes* to the Chair being due to the desire for accurate verbatim reports to be recorded from the best acoustic position of the Hall.

But our establishment of the *Logographe's* box is of

[1] In the *Histoire des Edifices*, &c., by Paris.

[2] The work was finished by the 26th of January, 1702.

[3] By the 7th clause of the order cited.

little value to the history of the 10th of August, because, though a confusion was till recently made between the two, the box in which the Royal Family were put was that of the *Logotachygraphe*, a journal not yet published, but in preparation, and one which had already obtained leave to have its reporting place in the Hall. Its exact situation we cannot determine, but it was certainly not far from the Chair on the south wall, and presumably in the eastern half of it.

APPENDIX E

UPON THE "LAST PORTRAIT OF THE QUEEN" BY KUCHARSKI

THREE "last" portraits of Marie Antoinette, each very similar to the two others, though not replicas, are known to exist: each is ascribed to the painter Kucharski, who appears for a moment at the Queen's trial, and who is known to have painted her at Court.

These portraits are, one in Arenberg Gallery at Brussels, another in the Carnavalet, and the third in the new Revolutionary Room on the third floor at Versailles. This last is the one which is reproduced here, because M. de Nolhac, by far the best authority, has assured me of its authenticity. On the other hand, it must be mentioned that the Belgian one was vouched for by Auguste d'Arenberg[1] who bought it in 1805, and who quotes the testimony of the painter[2] himself, who was then alive.

[1] See "Notes sur quelques Portraits de la Galerie d'Arenberg," in the *Annales de l'Academie Royale d'Archeologie de Belgique*, 4th series, vol. x., 1897.

[2] On this painter there exists a monograph by Mycielski (Paris, 1894), and an article published in the December number, 1905, of the *Revue d'Art, Ancien et Moderne*.

He appears to have affirmed that he saw the Queen in the Temple when he was on guard, took the sketch noting the details of dress, &c., and completing the work at home.

APPENDIX F

ON THE AUTHENTICITY OF THE QUEEN'S LAST LETTER

THE few doubts that some have put forward against the authenticity of this famous document will unless history abandons its modern vices, increase with time, for it is a document exactly suited to the type of minute, internal, literal, and documentary criticism by which tradition is, to-day, commonly assailed. It will be pointed out that the psychology of this letter differs altogether from that of the mass of Marie Antoinette's little scribbled notes, and equally from her serious political drafts and despatches. Critics will very probably be found to dispute the possibility of such a woman at such a time producing such a document. The style fits ill with what she was in Court just before it purports to have been written, and also with what she was on her way to the scaffold just after. Most important of all, perhaps, the sentences are composed in a manner quite different from that of any other letter of hers we possess; they have a rhythm and a composition in them: the very opening words are in a manner wholly more exalted and more rhetorical than ever was her own.

It will be further and especially pointed out that the moment when it was discovered was the very moment for forgery, and this point is of such importance to the discussion that I must elaborate it.

By nightfall of June 18th, 1815, the experiment of founding democracy in Europe was imagined to be at an end:

Napoleon was definitely defeated. On the 7th of July the first forces of the Allies entered Paris, and on the 20th of November was signed the second Treaty of Paris, whereby the reinstatement of the old régime in France was accomplished at a price to the nation of 700,000,000 francs and all of its conquests. All the power of a highly centralised Government was now in the hands of Louis XVIII., and it was in the highest degree profitable to prove oneself a friend to what had but a few months before seemed a lost cause. Document after document appeared professing a special knowledge of the woes of the Royal Family, petition after petition was presented in which the petitioners (nearly always in the same conventional and hagiographical style) spoke of the Royal "martyrs" in the Temple and in the Conciergerie.

In the light of such a character attaching to this particular moment, note the following sequence of dates in connection with the production of the document we are discussing.

Not two months after the signing of the Treaty of Paris the French Chamber voted the Law of Amnesty. The seventh clause of this Act banished the regicides who had sat in the Convention. Among these was a certain Courtois, a man now over seventy years of age, who had bought a large country house and estate near the frontier. Note, further, that Courtois had started as a small bootmaker and was one of the very few politicians of the Revolution who had followed our modern practice of making money out of politics. His honesty, therefore, was doubtful: a thing which we cannot say of the enthusiasts of the time. Of *those* we can say that their imaginations or their passions may warp their evidence, but in the case of Courtois we know that he was a professional politician of the modern type, and would do a dishonest thing for money.

Now this Courtois had been one of a Commission named by the Convention to examine Robespierre's papers after the fall of Robespierre on the 28th of July, 1794. He was what the French call the Reporter of the Commission — that is, the director of it — and it was called the "Courtois Commission." The Commission published their report of what they had found in Robespierre's house. It was a report two volumes in length for which Courtois was responsible, and of which he was practically the author.

This minute and voluminous report *made no mention of the Queen's letter*. Not a word is heard of it during all those twenty-two years until the aforesaid Bill of Amnesty is before the French Parliament of the Restoration and the regicides, including old Courtois, passing his last days on his comfortable estate, are to suffer exile. Then for the first time the Queen's letter appears. On the 25th of January, 1816, Courtois writes to a prominent lawyer, an acquaintance of his wife's, a Royalist, and in touch with the Court, telling him that he had kept back ten pieces among the mass of things found in Robespierre's house, three of them trinkets, a lock of hair, etc., one or two letters of no importance — and the capital point of all, this letter of Marie Antoinette's to her sister-in-law. He offers to exchange these against a special amnesty to himself, or at least of a year's delay before he is exiled, in order, presumably, to allow him to realise his fortune.

This is not all: the letter was not written until Courtois' wife was dead; and it was written on the very day of her death and the moment after it — the moment, that is, after the death of the only person who would presumably know — if he allowed anyone to know — whether he had or had not carefully concealed these documents for so many years.

The Government of Louis XVIII. offered money for the letter, and, having so lulled the suspicions of Courtois, sent one of its officials without warning into his house and seized his effects. Some days afterwards the letter (which no one had yet seen or heard of) is produced by Royal order and shown to Madame d'Angoulême (who is said to have fainted when she saw it), and ordered to be read from every pulpit during Mass on the 16th of October of every year; a vast edition of it is brought out in facsimile and distributed broadcast, and the letter itself is enshrined among the public exhibits at the Archives.

A lengthy analysis of the sort just concluded is necessary to make the reader understand how and why a strong attack upon the authenticity of the letter will sooner or later certainly be made. I owe it to my readers to say why the apparently strong presumption against this letter does not in my opinion hold.

First let me recapitulate what is to be said against it:

(1) There is no contemporary trace of it.[1]

(2) It appears at a moment when forged documents of that sort were of the highest value both to a despotic Government and to the vendors or producers of them.

(3) That moment is no less than *twenty-two years* posterior to the supposed writing of the letter, and, during all those twenty-two years, of the many who should have seen it, of the *three* public men (all enemies) through whose hands it must have passed, no one has heard of its existence nor mentioned it in a private correspondence, nor

[1] The woman Bault, who was wardress of the Conciergerie, says that her husband told her of such a letter, but her evidence is given after Louis XVIII. had published it, and for all those twenty-two years she had said nothing about it. Moreover she talked of its discovery with the usual clap-trap phrases of "The Omnipotence of Heaven showing its ineffable goodness by restoring us this monument in its most admirable way, &c." And *the only contemporary account*, while it does mention the lock of hair which the Queen desired given to a friend, says nothing of the letter.

apparently so much as spoken of it in a conversation to a friend.

(4) It is heard of from a man who would have every interest in forging it and who is known to have been very unscrupulous in political dealings for money.

(5) He makes his offer on the very day when the last witness there could be against him dies.

(6) The document, when it does appear, appears without any pedigree, or chain of witnesses to vouch for it, nor even any tradition. It is vouched for only by the people who had most interest in creating such a relic and is forced upon the public with every apparatus at the command of a despotic Government.

(7) Most important of all, the letter is written in a high and affecting style wholly different from all that we know of Marie Antoinette's writing, and quite inconsistent with her demeanour at the moment, consonant only with the sanctity which it was at that moment desired to give to the Royal Family.

Nevertheless I believe the document to be without the slightest doubt authentic, and I will give my reasons for this certitude:—

(1) To forge a letter of Marie Antoinette's is peculiarly difficult. There have been many such attempts. They have been discovered with an ease familiar to all students of her life.

This difficulty lies in the great irregularity of her method of writing, coupled with the exact persistence of certain types of letter. She never in her life could write a line straight across a page. She never made two "d's" exactly the same, and yet you never can mistake one of her "d's." She never crossed a "t" quite in the same manner twice, and yet you can always tell her way of crossing it. The absence of capitals after a full stop is a minor point but a considerable one. She always brought the lower loop of the "b" up to the up stroke, so that it looks like an "f"; she always separated her "l's" from the succeeding letter.

Let the reader compare the document of which I am speaking, reproduced in facsimile opposite page 526, and her letter of the 3rd of September, 1791, to Joseph II. (opposite page 400), and he will see what I mean. The first is reproduced on a four-fifths scale, the second in facsimile, but the points I make can easily be followed upon them. Note the first "d" in the first line of the letter written in prison, the second "d" and the third "d" all in the same line. Next look down to the seventh line and note the "d" in "tendre," and see how the first three "d's" though irregular are of the same type, and how the fourth, though much less hooked, is obviously written by the same hand. Look down two lines lower to the "d" in "plaidoyer"; it has a complete hook and is quite different from the other letters, and three lines lower, in the word "deux," the hook has a sharp angle apparent nowhere else on the page. Now if you turn to the "d's" in her letter to her brother of the 3rd of September, 1791, you will find exactly the same characteristics. Not one "d" like another, yet all obviously from the same hand; the "d" in the second line with a full hook to it, the two "d's" in the twelfth line much vaguer.

So with the "t's," they are crossed in every kind of way with a short straight line, a long curved one, a little jab followed by a straight, now with a slope downward, now with a slope upward, but all evidently from the same hand, and their very variety makes it impossible for them to be a forgery. The "l's" written separately from the letter following each, are obvious everywhere, so is that irregularity of line of which I have spoken. Let the reader look at the third line of the letter of the 3rd of September, 1791 (opposite page 400), and at the seventh line of the letter written in prison, and ask himself whether it would have been possible to copy such native irregularity.

The identity of handwriting is apparent even from these two documents. It is absolutely convincing to any one who has seen much of her penmanship.

(2) To the faults in grammar and in spelling I should pay little attention — those things are easily copied; but it is worth remarking that on the third line of the letter written in prison she spells the infinitive of "montrer" without the final "r" as though it were a participle, while in the letter written to her brother in 1791 she makes no such error. She puts an "e" in "Jouis," and so forth. All these discrepancies are a proof of the authenticity of the letter. She spelt at random, and her grammar was at random, though she got a little more accurate as she grew older. It would, on the contrary, be an argument *against* the authenticity of the letter if particular mistakes, discovered in a particular document of hers, were repeated in this last letter from the Conciergerie.

(3) The letter was immediately exposed to public view; the paper was grown yellow, the writing was apparently old, the ink in places faded, the creases deep and worn. Now all these accidental features could no doubt be reproduced by a modern forger with the advantage of modern methods, modern mechanical appliances, modern chemical science and photography. They could not have been achieved by a forger of 1816.

It seems to me, therefore, a document absolutely unassailable. The arguments against it are of the same sort which modern scepticism perpetually brings against every form of historical evidence that does not fit in with some favourite modern theory. I must believe the evidence of my senses, and I am compelled to admit that a woman, every expression of whose soul was different from this, and whose whole demeanour before and after writing the letter betrayed a mental condition quite inconsistent with the writing of it, was granted for perhaps an hour (in spite of a full day's fast, the fear of imminent death and the breakdown of her health and of all her power), an exaltation sufficient to produce this wonderful piece of prose, and a steadfast control of language and a discovery of language miraculously exceptional to her character and experience.

No other conclusion is possible to a student unless, like any Don, he prefers a sceptical hypothesis to the testimony of his eyes and the judgment of his common sense.